The Impact of Irish-Ireland on Young Poland, 1890–1919

The Impact of Irish-Ireland on Young Poland, 1890–1919

John A. Merchant

East European Monographs, Boulder
Distributed by Columbia University Press, New York
2008

EAST EUROPEAN MONOGRAPHS, NO. DCCXXIV

Copyright 2008 by John A. Merchant
ISBN: 978-0-88033-623-9
Library of Congress Control Number: 2008938728

Printed in the United States of America

CONTENTS

INTRODUCTION 1

CHAPTER ONE: MELODIES DISSONANT & HARMONIOUS—
Establishing the Polish-Irish Relationship, 1800–1849 9
  I. Loss and Exile, 1790–1890 10
  II. Polish-Irish Melodies: Thomas Moore and the Polish Salon 21
  III. The Enduring Charm of Home: Re-Writing Moore in Exile 30
  IV. Moore and the November Uprising: The Vernacular of Emigration 37
  V. Beyond 1830: Moore and the Poetry of Oppression 49

CHAPTER TWO: THE POLISH-IRISH FAMILY—
The Literature of Exile, 1850–1890 57
  I. The Daughter of Erin: Exclusivity in the Polish National Family .. 58
  II. Poland and Ireland: In Progress, Salvation 67
  III. The Veteran's Wife: The Polish National Family Redux.......... 73

CHAPTER THREE: MODELING VITALITY—
Young Poland, New Art, & Europe, 1890–1918 81
  I. Young Poland and the Zest for Life 81
  II. Looking Out, Looking In: Young Poland and the West 85
  III. The Artistic Identity of Young Poland:
       Cosmopolitanism and Essentialism 97

Chapter Four: Between Art and the Nation—
Young Poland and Irish-Ireland, 1989–1908 105
  I. Artistic Essentialism: The Polish Debut of W. B. Yeats 105
  II. The Case for Poetic Drama:
      The Countess Cathleen & Miriam's *Chimera*.................. 117

v

III. The Art of Collective Feeling: Kasprowicz and Yeats 124
  IV. The Pairing of Genius:
     Synge & Wyspiański in Pawlikowski's Theater 143

CHAPTER FIVE: MODELING THE IRISH THEATRE—
Art in the shadow of War, 1919–1918 161
  I. Poles of the Western World: Irish-Ireland and Polish Essentialism 161
  II. Toward a National Theater: Synge's *Playboy* & the Polish Theater. 189
  III. Returning to Bohemia: Pawlikowski and *The Well of the Saints* . . . 204
  IV. New Beginnings: Irish Drama in the Polish War Theater 210

CONCLUSION:—
The Legacy of the Polish-Irish Connection 225

Notes. 231
Bibliography 273

INTRODUCTION

> Barely do we pull back the edge of the veil from the temple of the Irish nation when we stand amazed by the poetic wonders produced in the collective soul of that nation spiritually akin to Poles.[1]
>
> —Jerzy Płoński (1898)

> Entirely parallel to the political rise of Erin... the powerful work of spiritual growth advances forward of that double of our nation, those "Poles of the Western World."[2]
>
> —Adolf Nowaczyński (1918)

It is a commonplace in critical discussions of Polish literature to characterize Poland's continued existence under the system of partitions in the nineteenth century exclusively in cultural terms. In large part a reflection of the dominant influence of Polish Romanticism on the Polish national imagination, framing Poland's survival as a nation in terms of an idea fails to address fully a fundamental reality of the Polish experience after the final partition in 1795. Despite being divided internally and prevented from establishing any measure of cultural or political autonomy, Poles as individuals did not cease to identify themselves as Polish. While the form this sense of self-identification took in art and literature varied greatly, the unwavering certainty of this internalized national being remained constant. The problem facing Poland as a nation in the nineteenth century, therefore, was not cultural survival so much as it was resolving an ongoing internal debate over how best to unlock the latent power contained within this identity.

As the nineteenth century came to a close, Poles in the partitioned lands of Poland were confronted with numerous centennial events reminding them that they were entering into their second century as a politically and culturally subjugated nation. For the young Polish intellectuals coming of age in the early 1890s, the primary stumbling block was not that of conceiving the Polish nation as an "imagined community," but rather it was finding a way of

The Impact of Irish-Ireland on Young Poland, 1890–1919

tapping into what they considered to be the neglected yet deeply meaningful sense of national identity. Far from taking the form of an exclusionist or strictly nationalist movement, *Młoda Polska* (Young Poland), as it came to be known, emerged in the years 1890–1918 as a unique cultural movement in which Polish intellectuals attempted to combine native forms of expression with the ideas of European modernism to create work that was at once artistically innovative and inherently Polish. Characterized varyingly as neo-romanticism, modernism, and a conflux of other competing "isms," the contradictory pull of these two forces within Young Poland has made it difficult for Polish literary scholars to characterize it simply.[3] As an examination of the impact of a parallel movement, Irish-Ireland, on Polish culture during the years 1890–1918, this study focuses on Young Poland's maturation in terms of the competing streams of essentialism and cosmopolitanism. These two principles developed in tandem and separately according to the aims of Polish intellectuals hoping to restore a sense of vitality to the Polish nation at its innermost core. As such, Young Poland's outward and inward tendencies worked to define it as a cultural movement fundamentally concerned with the problem of artistic expression of identity.

Young Poland from its inception was a cultural movement predicated on complete openness to cultural impulses from abroad. Polish writers and artists traveled abroad in large numbers to study and gather new ideas, Polish periodicals printed columns reviewing the developments in the foreign literary press or theater, and Polish journals regularly featured numerous translations of works by non-Polish writers. This did not constitute something new in Polish culture, but rather there was an intentionality of purpose to the importation of foreign cultural impulses that distinguished Young Poland from other periods of Polish literature. While art and literature from the major French and German metropoles had an understandably strong presence as centers of European modernism, Polish intellectuals increasingly turned their attention farther afield to lesser known cultures in Europe, Asia, and North America as Young Poland developed. The writers and critics of Young Poland as a generation connected Polish readers to world culture to an extent uncommon in Polish history. With the aim of introducing these new impulses into Poland, Polish intellectuals during this period became in many cases prolific translators in multiple languages.[4] "In the sphere of the Polish experience," Franciszek Ziejka has observed, "readers and writers were connected to the masterpieces of European and world literature. [Young Poland's translators] answered the dramatic question circulating at the time of the form our culture should take. Thanks to them, Polish literature entered into a direct dialog with European literature."[5] Focused as it was on restoring a sense of vitality to what was perceived as a flagging nation, Young

Introduction

Poland was by nature Janus-faced, with one face pointed outward toward the world and the other directed inward. Young Poland, therefore, as a movement was, to paraphrase the title of Jan Cavanaugh's study of early modern Polish painting, looking out to look in.[6]

Of all the different cultural impulses that helped to shape Young Poland's perception of itself, Irish-Ireland represents one of the most intriguing and overlooked. Similarly to Young Poland, Irish-Ireland was a cultural movement whose energy and creative vitality grew out of a deep-seated concern with the conception of identity. Central to this debate was the liminal position of the Anglo-Irish minority, which Irish nationalists considered an element of English hegemony but that felt itself to be part of the Irish cultural nation. While figures such as D. P. Moran and Arthur Griffith sought to cast Ireland's cultural revival exclusively in terms of the opposition of Irish and English culture, prominent figures within Irish-Ireland, such as William Butler Yeats, John Millington Synge, and George Moore, among many others, attempted to create forms of artistic expression that were at once intrinsically Irish and thoroughly modern. With the establishment of the Abbey Theatre in 1904, these young Irish intellectuals succeeded not only in creating an authentically Irish style of drama in the English language, but they also firmly established the place of the Irish theater squarely within the broader stream of the modern European theater.

The extent to which Young Poland and Irish-Ireland at the turn of the twentieth century were equally engaged in this process of revitalizing identity by drawing on new sources from without and within the national culture not only points to the unique inner workings of these two individual movements, but it also helps to explain the ties that bound them together. Because of the largely unidirectional nature of the Polish-Irish relationship, Polish intellectuals in the areas of criticism, poetry, and theater played a pivotal role by acting as intercultural agents, to borrow the language of Naoki Sakai, between Young Poland and Irish-Ireland.[7] While useful, Sakai's notion of the translator functions as a heterolingual intermediary, negotiating and shaping the exchange of ideas between different cultural and linguistic communities does not go far enough in characterizing Young Poland's relationship to Irish-Ireland.[8] At once open to new impulses and concerned with matters of identity, the Polish-Irish dialogue for Young Poland took the form of a mediated, self-directed discourse. For the Polish intellectuals who wrote about and translated the work of Irish-Ireland, the goal was not, as Goethe suggested, to transport their contemporaries into the Irish context, but rather Polish intellectuals translated and transposed Irish literature into Polish as a way of addressing their own needs and worldviews.[9] Sakai has more successfully characterized this process as a "schema of cofiguration," in which translation operates as "a means by which a national community represents itself to itself."[10] In this way, literature originally informed by and aimed at answering the internal cultural needs of Irish-Ireland, reemerged anew as part of Young Poland's ongoing struggle to be both modern and national.

What makes an analysis of the Polish reception of Irish literature intriguing, however, is the extent to which the individuals negotiating the exchange between Ireland and Poland identified with what was transpiring in Ireland. The reason Polish intellectuals were interested in Irish-Ireland was the result of the fact that they recognized elements of themselves in it. Adam Zamoyski has observed that the true value of comparing the historical experience of Poland and Ireland did not simply lie in their similarity, but in their "parallels of predicament and similarities of reaction."[11] The intellectuals of Young Poland found Irish-Ireland appealing, because they recognized their Irish counterparts to be using art as a similar means of breaking free from the stasis of "becoming," to borrow a term of Gilles Deleuze and Felix Guattari, and embracing national "being" in the fullest sense. Unlike the literature of the French symbolists or the German naturalists, the literature of Irish-Ireland, also known as the Irish Literary Revival, was rooted in variety of cultural agendas all aimed at establishing a distinct, meaningful sense of self in the here and now.[12] Irish-Ireland's intense focus on the question of identity pointed to the fact that Irish intellectuals, regardless of their political inclinations, were striving to find cultural authenticity in clear opposition to English imperial culture. The challenge was not simply not to be English, but rather to be emphatically Irish. The tension and vitality that grew out of this internal cultural debate was evidence of the degree to which Irish intellectuals were involved in the process of defining Ireland as a nation. Because of this, the art produced by Irish-Irelanders did not register with Young Poland on the same level as other foreign cultural impulses, but as the work of individuals facing challenges and engaging in cultural projects similar to their own.

In light of this self-identification, Polish intellectuals by means of critical analysis, performance, and translation formed an imagined community or perhaps more accurately described, a community of the imagination with Irish-Ireland. It is important to point out that all of the individuals writing about, performing, and transposing Irish literature for Polish audiences were also actively involved in shaping Young Poland. In most cases, they were writers themselves, while in others they were literary critics or political activists contributing to the revitalization of Polish life. This was one of the striking features of Young Poland's apprehension of foreign literatures. The Polish intellectuals importing new art and literature from abroad were the same individuals who were creating it. Given the delicate balance between the principles of essentialism and cosmopolitanism, it was impossible

Introduction

for the intellectuals of Young Poland to look abroad and to create their own work without participating in the larger debate over the proper orientation of Poland's cultural outlook. From the beginning, therefore, the nature of Young Poland's relationship to external cultural impulses was inseparable from the persistent question of the artistic identity of the Polish nation.

Due to the debate over the nature of art and its relationship to the nation, Irish literature functioned variously in the context of Young Poland depending on who was involved. Each writer rendering Irish literature into Polish or commenting on developments in Ireland had both an artistic and a cultural agenda within Young Poland. The intentions of Jerzy Płoński, a foreign correspondent in London for the journal *Życie* (Life), writing about Yeats in 1898 were quite different both in tone and purpose from those of Adolf Nowaczyński, who published a series of articles on Irish-Ireland a decade later. The selective nature of Polish intellectuals' interest in Irish culture, furthermore, not only meant that Poles received a limited notion of Irish culture, but also that this understanding was shaped fundamentally by the underlying needs and often idiosyncratic tastes of the those introducing it. Although a number of Polish critics, such as Nowaczyński and Marya Rakowska, exhibited not inconsiderable knowledge about Irish history and culture, Young Poland's tendency towards a lyrical, often exalted rhetorical style of expression often made it difficult to separate fact from fiction. For the most part, though, Polish critics were less concerned with accuracy than they were with tapping into the essence of things. In the case of Stanisław Lack, who translated Yeats's "The Heart of Spring" in 1902, critical inquiry was not a tool to comment upon art, but rather it was an art form in and of itself.

Whether it was in terms of style or subject matter, Irish-Ireland succeeded in maintaining a consistent relevance by speaking to the desire of Young Poland's artists and writers for new and invigorating approaches to art. The timing and route by which Irish literature entered Poland, however, played a crucial role in shaping its reception by Young Poland. Yeats's poetic drama *The Countess Cathleen* assumed a different significance when it appeared in the journal *Chimera*, in a translation by the poet Jan Kasprowicz, in 1904 than it did as a performed work on the stage of *Teatr Rozmaitości* (The Variety Theater) a decade later during the early months of World War I in 1914. With a range of topics that included the theory of art, poetics, folk art, poetic drama, and theater reform, the reception of the literature and drama of Irish-Ireland sheds valuable light onto the personal and collective motives of Polish artists on a variety of levels and at important points in the development of Young Poland. In this way, along with the evolution of Young Poland it is also possible to trace the changing Polish perception of Ireland and the place of Irish culture in the partitioned lands of Poland.

The Impact of Irish-Ireland on Young Poland, 1890–1919

Given the visibility and unmistakably symbolic significance of the theater for both Young Poland and Irish-Ireland, by far the most dynamic points of contact between the two movements took place by means of the stage. In drama more than in any other artistic medium the challenge of producing work that was both innovative and distinctly national was felt strongly. The Abbey Theatre's success in establishing itself in Ireland and abroad as the national theater of Ireland, albeit far from smooth, presented those active in the Polish theater with a source of artistic inspiration and a ready cultural model to follow. The inability of Young Poland to establish a stable, recognizable national theater brought the success of the nascent Irish theater into sharper relief. Unlike the Irish theater, which was concentrated in Dublin, the theater in Poland was divided and hampered by geopolitical constraints, which resulted in the theater developing unevenly and under different conditions in each of the Polish partitions. Young Poland's reception of Irish drama, therefore, varied greatly according to when and where it was produced in respect to the broader evolution of the Polish theater. Stage productions of Synge under the direction of Tadeusz Pawlikowski in Lwów and Kraków in Austrian Galicia differed from those under Arnold Szyfman in Warsaw in the Russian partition both in terms of local conditions and artistic sensibility. Because the importation of Irish drama involved the twin processes of translation and performance, Young Poland's reception of Irish drama was further complicated by a number of simultaneous and often conflicting layers of interpretation and emphasis.

The theater also proved to be the ideal crucible in which Polish intellectuals could combine the opposing strains of cosmopolitanism and essentialism. For some, such as Pawlikowski and Szyfman, the goal was to link the Polish theater to the wider European movement of theatrical reform, while for Nowaczyński and others the underlying significance of the theater was its ability to mobilize the nation by presenting it with a truer vision of itself. As rising stars of the modern European theater, Yeats and Synge satisfied the desire of many active in the Polish theater for innovative approaches to drama and stagecraft. At the same time, the ability of the Irish playwrights to fashion a distinctly Irish theater and to contribute to Ireland's cultural and national revival by means of the stage was an undeniable attraction to those within Young Poland who were actively trying to accomplish the same feat in the Polish theater. The importation of Irish drama into the Polish theater, however, proved to be challenging on a number of levels, as Polish audiences, critics, and theater companies sought to find an analogue for this uniquely Irish form of drama within the prevailing tendencies of Polish drama in respect to style, taste, and experience. Appearing at various times on the stages of all the major theaters of the day in the partitioned lands

Introduction

of Poland, Irish drama made a small yet undeniably significant contribution to the gradual stabilization and maturation of the Polish theater, a process which would not truly come to an end until Poland regained independence in 1918. In summary, the reception of Irish-Ireland in Poland grew out of and was shaped by Polish needs at the turn of the twentieth century. Driven by a desire to be both Polish and modern, the vitality of Young Poland stemmed from the ongoing cultural debate over the question of the nature of the relationship between the nation, identity, and art. Perceiving Polish culture to be in a state of stasis, the intellectuals of Young Poland were attracted to Irish-Ireland in their search for fresh ideas to revitalize national life. With its vigorous striving for both cultural renewal and artistic innovation, Irish-Ireland offered Young Poland a vibrant, contemporaneous example of a movement in which cosmopolitan and essentialist tendencies were present in equal force. Nowaczyński's characterization of the Irish as "Poles of the Western World" in 1918 is particularly revealing, for it speaks to the extent to which Young Poland's perception of Irish-Ireland grew out its own aims and sense of self rather than provide a true representation of Irish conditions. This study, therefore, reveals as much about the deep-rooted motivations and stages of development of Young Poland as a cultural movement as it does of the reception of the literature, drama, and cultural politics of Irish-Ireland in the lands of partitioned Poland in the years 1890–1918.

CHAPTER ONE

MELODIES DISSONANT & HARMONIOUS:

ESTABLISHING THE POLISH-IRISH RELATIONSHIP, 1800-1849

THE ROOTS OF THE POLISH-IRISH CONNECTION, AS THEY MANIFESTED themselves during the Young Poland period, lie in the experience of the nineteenth century. As a result of the successive partitions of Poland at the close of the eighteenth century, in the years 1772–1795, successive generations of Poles were faced both with a profound sense of loss and the moral imperative to reverse the status quo. Powerless to undo Poland's political erasure, however, Polish intellectuals sought to preserve through culture what could not be maintained by military or political means. Divided though it was into the Austrian, Prussian, and Russian partitions, Poles retained a sense of national unity through their common linguistic and cultural heritage. Following a series of attempts at physical resistance in the Napoleonic campaigns of 1806–1813, the prospect of a political solution to the Polish question seemed less and less likely. With the collapse of the November Uprising of 1830, the necessity of cultural self-preservation reached crisis levels, as Poles by the thousands were forced to leave the Russian partition, or Congress Kingdom, for an uncertain life in the foreign capitals in Europe. Cut off from the past and with little hope for the future, Polish émigré writers sought ways to come to terms with their situation. The Irish poet Thomas Moore (1779–1852), whose *Irish Melodies* and *Lalla Rookh* combined nostalgia for Ireland's gloried past and bittersweet sentimentalism for personal ruin, presented the generation of Polish Romantics with a model for coping with the twin challenges of national loss and nomadic exile. Moore would not only provide Polish writers with a common vernacular, he also came to represent in the minds of the Poles a champion of all downtrodden nations. Translated to varying degrees by Polish writers of all rank, Moore's

The Impact of Irish-Ireland on Young Poland, 1890–1919

poetry helped bring into focus the Polish experience in the nineteenth century. In doing so, it formed the basis of the Polish-Irish connection.

I. LOSS AND EXILE, 1790-1890

The one constant and unifying trait of the Polish experience in the nineteenth century was the problem of loss. Whether it was the conservative republicanism of Polish political and cultural leaders in the years immediately after the final partition of Poland in 1795, the exalted Romantic messianism of the exiled poets Adam Mickiewicz (1798–1855) and Juliusz Słowacki (1809–1849) in the 1830s and 1840s, or the progressive socio-cultural ideology of the Warsaw positivists in the 1870s and 1880s, a profound sense of loss resulting from the partitioning of Poland informed Polish life over the course of the century. The underlying conundrum facing Poles in the years 1790–1890 was reconciling the imprinted sense of Polishness, or "jestestwo" (being), in the words of the Romantic critic Maurycy Mochnacki (1803–1834), that they felt with the immutable political reality facing them. As the inheritors of social, cultural, and political traditions that had developed over the hundreds of years of Poland's existence as a sovereign power, Poles in the nineteenth century found themselves to be a nation without a state. Divided politically and geographically with the imposition of the Austrian, Prussian, and Russian partitions, the primary challenge facing Poles during this period was countering the very real threat of erosion to this common sense of Polishness. Confronted with the predicament of loss at the close of the eighteenth century, the Polish experience in the century that followed was one of ceaseless reaction.[1]

Polish efforts to address the crisis of loss in the period directly following the final partition of Poland, 1795–1815, took two separate but distinctly institutional forms. There was a determined element in Polish society, which continued to look for a military solution to Poland's plight. Inspired by Napoleon and Revolutionary France, already by 1797 a Polish legion formed in Italy under the leadership of General Henryk Dąbrowski to fight for France and, eventually, for the liberation of Poland. Polish hopes for freedom with the help of the French did come to pass, with Napoleon's two Eastern campaigns during the years 1806–1813 temporarily restoring a measure of Polish autonomy in the form of the Duchy of Warsaw (1807). The prospect of a free, independent Poland with Napoleon's march eastward on Russia in 1812 inspired Poles to enlist in the imperial army, swelling the French ranks by 100,000 troops. The Polish dream of independence, however, quickly dematerialized with the retreat of the French

Chapter 1: Melodies Dissonant & Harmonious

a year later, and the earlier feeling of loss intensified following the Congress of Vienna in 1815, when Russian control in Poland tightened.

While the valiant effort of the Polish legionnaires carried on the republican legacy of a portion of the *szlachta* (nobility), it did not represent the sole response of the political and intellectual elite to Poland's partition. The Polish reaction to the trauma of the partitions took a secondary, cultural, form as well. In addition to constituting a political crisis, the loss of Polish autonomy for many leading figures in Polish society represented a dangerous threat to Poland's integrity as a cultural nation. Many of the same individuals who had been involved in the concentrated efforts to reform Polish society at the close of the eighteenth century, which culminated in the May 3rd Constitution of 1791, turned their attention to the preservation of Polish culture following the final partition. The formation of the Towarzystwo Przyjaciół Nauk (The Society of the Friends of Learning, 1800–1832), which was led at various times by Stanisław Staszic (1755–1826), an influential Enlightenment thinker and political reformer, and Julian Ursyn Niemcewicz (1758–1841), also a writer and politician, was representative of this conscious effort to preserve Polish culture by sponsoring research in the areas of history, language, and literature. Treating history and culture as proof of Poland's existence as a nation, Staszic and the other members of the Society supported a variety of scholarly projects aimed at preserving its cultural past. Most notable among these was Samuel Bogumił Linde's *Słownik języka polskiego* (Dictionary of the Polish Language, 1807–1814), which was the first comprehensive dictionary of the Polish language. Situated in Warsaw, the former seat of Polish royal power, the leaders of the Society had ambitions of centralizing projects of cultural preservation for all the partitioned lands of Poland.[2] This was an indication of the extent to which the Society and other institutional attempts at cultural preservation were reflections of the ethos of the old Rzeczpospolita (Republic).

It was significant that Polish efforts to preserve Polish culture were not confined to the intellectual elite of the former capital. Influenced by progressive Western ideas on education, Prince Adam Czartoryski (1770–1861) attempted to reform the Polish educational system as the superintendent of education in the Vilnius region of the Russian partition. Czartoryski's plan was calculated primarily to support Polish culture, but his efforts had a political element to them as well. Faced with the threat of Napoleon, Czartoryski hoped that his modernizing policies would make Poland a model state and win the support of Tsar Alexander I for its cause. While this plan had little effect on the course of subsequent events, Czartoryski's attempts to strengthen and to preserve Polish culture in the Russian partition would prove to be much more important in the years to come, for it

11

was at the University of Vilnius and the famous Lycée in Krzemieniec that Polish Romanticism first took root in the early 1820s. Despite the intentions of Staszic, Niemcewicz, and the other Society members to administer the documentation and conservation of Polish culture and history from centrally located institutions in Warsaw, the drive to maintain a living sense of Polish cultural identity would be a youth movement located largely in the Lithuanian and Ukrainian territories. Mickiewicz, the father of Polish Romanticism, attended the University of Vilnius, while Słowacki, who was also a student in Vilnius, Antoni Malczewski (1793–1826), Józef Bohdan Zaleski (1802–1886), and others would form what came to be known as the "Ukrainian School" of Polish Romanticism. With the rise of the Romantics, it would be in terms of the intangible essence, or spirit, of Polish culture and not the vestiges of the moribund Republic that Poles would address the persistent problem of national loss.

The opposition between Warsaw and the outlying provinces came to be emblematic of the philosophical divide that emerged between the Classicists, as they were known, and the Polish Romantics. It was not a difference of patriotism, for both sides were concerned with the problem of maintaining Polish cultural identity in the absence of a free and independent Poland. There were, in fact, Romantic elements in much of the Classical literature being created prior to 1820. Niemcewicz's novels and his *Śpiewy historyczne* (Historical Songs, 1816), a collection of poems chronicling significant figures throughout Polish history, was indicative of the deep interest of Polish writers in the history of their nation in the years following the final partition. For the generation shaped by the values of the Enlightenment, however, the treatment of historical themes in Polish literature remained subordinate to the established rules of Classical literature, which favored form and rationality over individual expression and emotion. Allowed a measure of autonomy by the Russian authorities in the cultural life of the Congress Kingdom, including Polish schools and universities, a Polish army, and Sejm (Diet), the educated elite viewed themselves as the arbiters of Polish cultural illumination. The tendency, therefore, among Polish writers was not to confront the deep sense of national loss felt by Poles, but rather to shape the recollection of the past according to the taste and style of the educated classes in Warsaw.

On the other hand, influenced by the ideals of German and English Romanticism, and inspired by the image of Napoleon as Poland's providential man, Polish Romanticism emerged in the 1820s as a movement with a starkly different view of both the nation and of Polish history. Figures such as Mochnacki and Kazimierz Brodziński (1791–1835) began to argue for the ability of literature to express the uniqueness of the Polish nation. This constituted a shift away from the political nationalism of the Enlightenment generation, with

Chapter 1: Melodies Dissonant & Harmonious

its emphasis on the collective institutions and the historical fact of the nation, or Republic, to a subjective understanding of the nation as a cultural ideal.[3] The Polish Romantics developed a cult of history, for it was in history that they felt the distinctiveness of the Polish nation could be found. "The historical life of a people," Mochnacki asserted in his 1830 work *O literaturze polskiej w wieku XIX* (On Polish Literature in the 19th Century),"is, in my opinion, nothing other than the continual, unbroken process of recalling oneself, from the beginning... through all intervening times. It is the apprehension of feeling oneself in the full expanse of native being."[4] The danger of ignoring or forgetting history, Mochnacki's argument suggested further, was for the nation to lose its sense of being. In order to survive as a nation, therefore, it was not necessary to have a state, but it was crucial to be actively involved in this process of self-realization.

Polish Romanticism in many ways evolved as the art of memory, because it was through the imaginative recollection of the past that one could actively represent the spirit (duch) of the nation as an ideal. The shift in the 1820s away from official history and the received tastes the educated classes in Warsaw to the living color and hidden mystery of the Polish people in the wilds of the Ukrainian steppes and the small villages of Polish-Lithuania was indicative of the Polish Romantics' desire to relocate the individuality of the Polish nation. For the Romantics, Poland did not survive the tragic losses of the eighteenth century through institutions and societies, but rather in the legends and stories of its people. The notion of communal poetry (poezja gminna), which Mickiewicz discussed in the foreword to his 1822 collection *Poezja* (Poetry), was indicative of the emerging Romantics' response to the problem of uncovering the historical uniqueness of the nation. Mickiewicz linked the vitality of a society to its level of creative freedom and social harmony. In looking back through history, Mickiewicz took the ancient Greeks as his ideal, for they exhibited the perfect balance of originality, imagination, and creative freedom. "As poets," Mickiewicz explained, "the Greeks in their greatest period of art always sang for the populace; their songs were a store of feelings, beliefs, national keepsakes, decorated with invention and pleasant release; and so they had a strong influence on the survival, strengthening, and of course, the formation of the national character."[5] It was when poets and the people became separated that nations experienced trouble and ceased to develop their own culture. By remaining closely tied to the people, poets not only ensured the continued vitality of the nation, but they also prevented it from losing its distinctiveness by imitating another culture.

Although Mickiewicz based his ideal on the ancient Greeks, he believed the roots of Romantic poetry to be in the Middle Ages. Combining the elements of knightly valor, Christianity, and a living folk culture, this period in the history of the Polish nation figured as the perfect corollary to Romantic literature. As a transposition of the Middle Ages into the present, Mickiewicz's determination to infuse his poetry with a folk sensibility meant that certain formal changes were needed. "In the Middle Ages," Mickiewicz explained, "tales and songs circulated among people. Their character had to be more or less uniform, suitable to the entire genre; subjects taken from knightly history, embellished with fabrications; feelings for the fair sex in expressions of affection or cheerful jibes; natural speech and simple verses suitable for singing."[6] Ballads and romances, which was also the title of Mickiewicz's first collection of poems, were in Mickiewicz's estimation the most widespread forms of communal poetry in medieval times. These forms not only retained their closeness to the people, but they also exhibited the qualities of simplicity, drama, and mystery that characterized Romantic poetry. In light of this foreword, it was evident why Polish critics perceived Mickiewicz's landmark poem "Romantyczność" (The Romantic), written in 1821 and published a year later, to be a programmatic statement of the new Romantic literature. The poem describes a young village girl's encounter with her former, dead lover and the difference of opinion between the believing villagers and a skeptical, learned old man regarding the reality of the spiritual encounter.

> Martwe znasz prawdy, nieznane dla ludu,
> Widzisz świat w proszku, w każdej gwiazd iskierce;
> Nie znasz prawd żywych, nie obaczysz cudu!
> Miej serce i patrzaj w serce![7]

> You know the dead truths, unknown to the people,
> You see the world in minutiae, in the light of every star;
> You do not know the living truths, you do not perceive miracles!
> Have a heart and look in your heart!

Romantic poetry was not to have the cold formality of a Classical exercise, but rather the inherent vitality of the language, legends, and stories of its people. Poland's history as an ancient nation came to life through poetry, which tapped into the collective folk memory. It was in this cultural history, moreover, that the seeds for Poland's future lay.

The fascination of the Polish Romantics with history grew increasingly complex in the 1820s. Mickiewicz published two long poems, *Grażyna, a Lithuanian Tale* (1823) and *Konrad Wallenrod* (1828), both of which were situated in the distant history of Polish Lithuania in the Middle Ages. Malczewski's epic poem *Maria* (1825) similarly took place in the vast, untamed wilds of the Ukrainian

Chapter 1: Melodies Dissonant & Harmonious

Steppes in the seventeenth and eighteenth centuries. In situating their tales long before the tragedy of the partitions, Mickiewicz and Malczewski's goal was not to memorialize Poland's gloried past or to escape the reality of the present, but rather to reveal the living presence of history in the life of the nation. In doing so, they fulfilled Mochnacki's vision of literature as the self-realization of Poland's historical being. Mickiewicz's *Grażyna*, which told the story of Grażyna, the wife of a Lithuanian Prince named Litafor, who dons her husband's armor to fight the Teutonic Knights, with whom the latter has made a pact to fight the Grand Duke of Lithuania, was not a representation of authentic history but the poetic expression of the innate heroism and patriotic feeling of the Polish nation. For Mickiewicz during this early period, the power of history lay not in fact, but in its power to inspire. *Konrad Wallenrod* told the tale of Konrad, a pagan Lithuanian who rises to the position of Grand Master of the Teutonic Knights and decides to lead an intentionally disastrous campaign following the sudden recollection of his native identity. History, therefore, was not a question of verity, but of imaginative power. The point was not to intone the dead letter of the past, but to prefigure the future. In this regard, the past held clues to Poland's historical mission as a cultural nation. Although history shaped the poetic imagination of the Polish Romantics, their primary focus was the future.

The response of the Polish Romantics to the problem of loss and history took a sharp turn following the November Uprising of 1830. Having begun largely as a youth movement among Polish officers inspired by heroic ideals of Mickiewicz and Polish Romanticism, what began as a local outbreak grew into a full-fledged national uprising with Russian intransigence to immediate offers of mediation by more conservative Polish leaders. Despite a well-trained military and considerable foreign sympathy, the Polish revolutionary army was outmatched. In addition to the large number of Poles deported to Siberia, some 10,000 Poles, known as the Great Emigration, left Poland for an uncertain future in Western Europe. While this solely affected the Russian partition of Poland, the failure of the November Uprising and the psychic weight of the Great Emigration, which comprised of Poland's political and cultural elite, made a tremendous impact on the Polish national imagination. For the next thirty years, the driving force behind Polish cultural life would reside abroad. The problem of loss, therefore, now combined with the strange reality of exile. Shaped by the position and nature of émigré life, the revelation of Poland's historical mission, in the minds of the Polish Romantics, assumed greater import.

In his article "Exodus," Benedict Anderson considers the experience of exile to be a particularly powerful "nationalizing moment," because it is precisely at the moment when people are removed from their hum-drum realities that they

The Impact of Irish-Ireland on Young Poland, 1890–1919

are truly confronted with the question of identity. "Exile," Anderson maintains, quoting John Dalberg-Acton, "is the nursery of nationality."[8] Although the loss of Polish sovereignty at the end of the eighteenth century did not involve the forced expulsion of large numbers of people or the settlement of foreign plantations, it is arguable that the feeling of loss resulting from the successive partitions in the years 1772–1795 carried with it a feeling that Polish life from the outset of the nineteenth century represented a form of internal exile.[9] Allowed to reside and to participate to varying degrees in the administrative and cultural institutions of their respective partitions, Poles quickly became aware that their insistent Polishness made them at best tolerated non-citizens and at worst enemies of the state. Poland's true "nationalizing moment," however, took place following the collapse of the November Uprising, when the core of Polish society found itself forcefully removed from everyday reality and thrust into a state of itinerant exile.[10] Removed entirely from the geographic territory of the Polish Republic, the conception of Poland as a political nation associated with clearly defined borders gave way to the Romantic ideal of the Polish nation as a spiritual entity.

In viewing the nation as a divine creation instead of the fruit of human labor, the Polish Romantics gave the fate of the Polish nation a distinctly moral dimension.[11] The Polish Romantics' emphasis on historicism and heroism in the 1820s changed following the November Uprising into an understanding of Poland's historical mission as that of the universal savior of the world. Polish suffering, made most evident by the exodus of thousands of Poles from the Congress Kingdom, formed the basis of the ideology of Polish Romantic messianism. Poland, like Christ, suffered needlessly for the redemption of all mankind. This religious interpretation of the Polish situation found greatest expression in Mickiewicz's *Księgi narodu polskiego i pielgrzymstwa polskiego* (The Books of the Polish Nation and Polish Pilgrimmage), published in Paris in 1832. Written in a simple, Biblical style and aimed at giving a moral lift to the Polish émigré community in Paris, particularly to exiled Polish soldiers, Mickiewicz conceived of Poland's place in history as part of the cycle of crisis and redemption that had characterized human experience since the beginning of time. Mickiewicz's historiography directly linked the Polish experience to the general course of human history, emphasized by the subtitle to *The Books of the Polish Nation* that read "from the beginning of the world to the suffering of the Polish nation."[12] Mickiewicz understood the history of human experience in religious terms, viewing it as a constant desire to return to the original state of freedom and faith that existed at the beginning of time. "At the beginning," Mickiewicz explained, "there was faith in one God, and there was freedom on the earth."[13] The low points in history occurred when humanity strayed from

Chapter 1: Melodies Dissonant & Harmonious

these twin virtues of faith and freedom. Mickiewicz associated tyranny and godlessness with empire, pointing out the crises in human history as taking place successively with the Romans, the rise of absolute monarchies, and the empire building of the late eighteenth and early nineteenth centuries. In *Dziady IV* (Forefather's Eve, 1832) Mickiewicz had already established the Polish conflict with Russia as a battle between good and evil, with devils and angels battling for the souls of Polish prisoners. In Mickiewicz's view, however, Poland's role in history was not to suffer passively, but to redeem the world through its torment. "And just as the resurrection of Christ," Mickiewicz maintained, "brought to an end the entire bloody sacrifice, so, too, will the resurrection of the Polish nation end the Christian war."[14]

As a chosen nation, the Poles in Mickiewicz's mind had a special role to play in history. In the second book, *The Books of the Polish Pilgrimage*, Mickiewicz made explicit the connection between the tragedy of Polish experience and the redemptive role the Polish nation had to play in the post-1830 era. Mickiewicz was careful in his choice of words, insisting that Poles were neither outcasts nor exiles, but rather pilgrims entrusted with a mission. "For the moment," Mickiewicz explained, "the Pole is called a pilgrim, who has taken a pledge of wandering to the Holy Land, the Fatherland of the free, vowing to wander until he finds it."[15] The Polish nation, for Mickiewicz, no longer corresponded to a geographical area, but rather manifested itself as a moral stance to the world. It was not enough for Poland to suffer like Christ; it also had to actively work for the redemption of humanity. "Christ said," Mickiewicz pointed out, "Whosoever shall go with me, let him leave his father and mother and risk his soul. The Polish pilgrim replies: Whosoever desires Freedom, let him leave his country and risk his life."[16] Exile, therefore, indicated both a moral and a political condition. Dedicated as it was to his fellow "bracia-wiara-żołnierze" (brethren-faith-soldiers), Mickiewicz hoped with the *Books of the Polish Nation and Polish Pilgrimage* both to give a moral lift to the Polish émigré community in Paris and to attach a sense of activism, if not purpose, to the painful experience of exile.[17] As the universal defenders of freedom, Mickiewicz encouraged his compatriots to emulate the chivalric valor of Christian knights and the pious fearlessness of the ancient Apostles. As such, emigration did not represent the defeat of the Polish desire for freedom, but rather it was a sign of Poland's mission to extend this struggle to the rest of the world.

The position of exile left the Polish émigré community with few realistic options to address the now multiple layers of loss that impacted their lives. There were political groups within the Polish emigration, which proposed differing solutions to the Polish situation. Conservatives, commonly known as the

"Hôtel Lambert" group for the Parisian residence of their leader, Prince Adam Czartoryski, maintained a constant diplomatic campaign with governments across Europe in the hope of garnering international support for the Polish cause. On the left, radical groups such as the Democratic Society promoted ideas of agrarian democracy and social revolution both abroad and in Poland. For the majority of the Poles in the capital cities of France, England, and Germany, however, Poland remained little more than an abstraction. Where Mickiewicz largely abandoned poetry for a life of political activism following the publication of *Master Thaddeus* in 1834, Słowacki and Zygmunt Krasiński (1812–1859) in the 1840s turned to mysticism. Long visionary poems, such as "Król-Duch" (King-Spirit, 1847) by Słowacki and "Przedświt" (Predawn, 1843) by Krasiński, reinforced the conception of the Polish nation's destiny as an active spiritual force in the history of the world. For Słowacki, the history of the Polish nation was that of the various incarnations of the Spirit, a ceaselessly revolutionary force. Much in the same way the Spirit, working through powerful individuals, shaped the Polish nation, Poland as the Christ of Europe would likewise redeem its fellow nations in the future through the relentless process of creative self-evolution. Much more conservative by nature, Krasiński viewed Poland's innocent, Christ-like suffering as a sign of its mission to save the world from revolutionary upheaval. Concerned primarily with the rising prospect of social revolution in the years prior to the Spring of Nations in 1848, Krasiński stressed unity among all Poles, both the gentry and the peasantry, as Poland's predestined deed to save the world from bloodshed and turmoil.

Although there were some efforts to force real change within Poland, such as Reverend Piotr Ściegienny's (1801–1890) revolutionary agrarian movement in Lublin, the focus of Polish political and intellectual life in the 1840s and 1850s remained abroad. Many Poles, most notably Mickiewicz, participated in political struggles throughout the European continent, taking part in liberation movements in Italy and Hungary in 1848, and Turkey in 1855. Inspired by the motto "for our freedom and yours," the hopes of these Poles rested on the belief that by contributing to the national struggles of others, widespread social upheaval would take place throughout Europe and Poland would be liberated. Thrust among the struggling peoples of Europe as itinerant exiles, it became clear that Poles could expect little from either foreign governments or revolutionaries. The opportunities, however, presented by the Spring of Nations and the Crimean War passed with little impact on the Polish cause. By 1855, Poland's three great poets, Mickiewicz, Słowacki, and Krasiński, were dead. With the death of Czartoryski in 1861, moreover, the Polish emigration lost its most widely recognized political figure. For the Polish émigré community, with

Chapter 1: Melodies Dissonant & Harmonious

the deaths of its chief visionaries and its leading diplomat exile lost much of its creative energy and political potential.

With the generation of the Great Emigration having lost its leadership position, the focus of Polish intellectual life ceased to remain exclusively located abroad. A slight relaxation in Russian control following the death of Tsar Nicholas I in 1855 allowed for a modicum of liberalization in the Congress Kingdom. For the long-oppressed Poles in the Russian partition, this limited freedom was cause for a sharp increase in patriotic feeling. Despite concessions from Margrave Alexander Wielopolski (1803–1877), the head of the Civil Administration, which offered Poles new constitutional and educational freedoms, tensions in the Congress Kingdom soon grew out of hand. The January Uprising of 1863, which erupted over the imposition of mandatory conscription, spread into a nationwide guerilla war that united the radical and conservative elements of Polish society. Although the uprising was not the grand Romantic gesture of youth of the November Uprising, the January Uprising was the result of a strong moral revolution in Polish society. Having been held under strict Russian control for over thirty years, Poles wanted some control over their own affairs.

While the uprising succeeded in forcing the hand of the Tsar to emancipate the peasantry in 1864, as part of the escalating struggle between the opposing sides over the loyalties of the people, it was a disaster for Polish society. With the elimination of the last vestiges of the rebellion in the fall of 1864, Poles again faced severe policies of oppression as they had in the 1830s. The Russian authorities, however, went a step further in their response to the January Uprising, eliminating the Congress Kingdom and reorganizing it as a thoroughly Russian province. In addition to rescinding Wielopolski's liberalizing moves, large numbers of Poles once more were sent into exile and in the succeeding years new measures designed to Russify Polish life came into effect. The tragedy of the January Uprising for many Poles was that a doomed rebellion, fueled by Romantic ideals, had once again decimated an entire generation of Poles and destroyed any progress that had been made.

As early as the 1840s and 1850s, the late Romantic poet Cyprian Kamil Norwid (1821–1883) had criticized the idealized conceptions of Polish Romantic messianism, countering them with a more clear-eyed view of the Polish nation. Norwid's critique of Romantic nationalism prefigured the shift that would take place in Polish society following the defeat of the January Uprising. In drawing a distinction between Poland as a society and Poland as a nation, Norwid stressed the need for Poles to turn away from the reckless idealism of messianic self-sacrifice prevalent in the emigration and to embrace a more practical, constructive approach to cultural life in Poland. In terms of heroism, Norwid admitted, Poland was a great nation, but in regard to the work that made up daily life they were sorely lacking as a society. "We are no society," Norwid declared in an 1862 letter, "We are a great national banner. Perhaps they will hang me one day for these truths... but even if today I had the rope around my neck, I would utter hoarsely that Poland is the last society on earth and the first nation on the planet."[18] While it would be incorrect to label Norwid a Positivist writer, in his poetry and letters he did suggest to his contemporaries the need for Poles to turn their attention back toward Poland and the real work of progressing as a civilized nation. Norwid's poetic masterpiece, "Promethidion" (1851), which translates as the offspring of Prometheus, did not suggest the Byronic rebelliousness of Mickiewicz's messianic nationalism, but rather the creativity and regenerative power of honest labor.

Norwid's distinction between society and nation are useful benchmarks in tracing the changes that took place following the defeat of the January Uprising. Although Poles did not abandon patriotic attachment, they addressed the problems of loss and exile, which fundamentally shaped Polish Romantic literature, by focusing on improving the existing conditions in Poland in the present day. For Warsaw Positivists, such as Eliza Orzeszkowa and Bolesław Prus, Polish society was in dire need of transformation. Influenced by the philosophy of August Comte and Herbert Spencer, Polish Positivists viewed the persistent problems of loss and exile to be the direct result of Polish sins. Whether it was the stubborn recklessness of the Polish gentry at the close of the eighteenth century or the self-destructive messianism of the Polish Romantics, Polish society had suffered greatly as a result. A cult of science replaced the Romantic fascination with history, and ideas of social progress gained currency over individual heroism and mystical conviction. Having suffered thirty years of repression following the November Uprising, the events of 1863 drove home the fruitlessness of Romantic nationalism. The thorough integration of the Congress Kingdom, renamed "Vistula Land," into the Russian Empire presented Poles with newfound opportunities, and so the heroes of the Polish Positivists were individuals who emulated the ideals of progress in the areas of business, farming, and education.[19] Emphasis was no longer on Poland's mythical past or its shining future, but rather on improving life in Poland in the here and now. To be a true, patriotic Pole was to contribute to the country's moral, economic, and social regeneration. Particularly telling in this regard is Orzeszkowa's chastisement of Joseph Conrad for his choice not to write in Polish. For Orzeszkowa, the loss of a literary genius of Conrad's order, whose father was deeply involved in the activities of the January Uprising, was symbolic of the damage that the ideals of Romanticism had inflicted upon Poland.

Positivism in Poland did not represent a permanent turn away from the legacy of Polish Romanticism. As Beth Holmgren points out in her penetrating study of literary capitalism in Russia and the Kingdom of Poland during this period, Prus's novel *Lalka* (The Doll, 1890) contained a complicated analysis of capitalism and the traditions of Romantic nationalism.[20] Orzeszkowa similarly touched on legacy of Poland's Romantic past in *Nad Niemnem* (On the Niemen, 1888), having the heroine, Justyna, an impoverished member of the gentry, marry a poor villager, Jan, whose family keeps alive the memories of Poland's heroic past. In both cases, however, Polish society appeared in a state of significant disintegration, led most notably by a derelict and irresponsible aristocracy. By clinging to antiquated notions of entitlement and idealism, Polish Positivists portrayed this portion of Polish society, a potentially powerful source of innovation and change, as an impediment to economic and social progress in Poland. Heroic action for the Positivists no longer took the form of the Romantic *sortie* or the mystical self-annihilation, but rather in gestures that improved Polish society collectively. In order for Poles to escape the deadly cycle of loss and exile, they would have to find new heroes imbued with the values of progress, enlightenment, and collective action.

Threatened with further cultural erasure in the Congress Kingdom, or Vistula Land, the reaction of the Warsaw Positivists following the January Uprising represented, to borrow Norwid's distinction, a selection of society over the Polish nation. The failure, however, of capitalism and the ideology of progress to improve Polish life, made evident by the labor strife of the 1880s, exposed the limitations of Positivism. Combined with the aggressive policies of *Kulturkampf* in the Prussian partition, which also struck at the vestiges of Polish cultural identity in the areas of education and religion, the social unrest of the late 1880s moved many Poles to consider essential questions of cultural and national identity. Faced with the ominous specter of cultural and political erasure, Poles began the 1890s with the keen awareness that the problem of loss had to be addressed in a substantial way, or Poles could forever be exiles in their own country. Shaped by the collectivizing values of Positivism, the new generation of *fin de siècle* Polish writers and artists sought to elevate Polish society by turning their attention once again to expressing Poland's cultural national identity.

II. POLISH-IRISH MELODIES: THOMAS MOORE AND THE POLISH SALON

Much has been written about the influence of Byron on Polish Romanticism, particularly in regard to the form it took in the 1820s. A number of works, including Malczewski's *Maria*, Słowacki's *Kordian*, and even portions of

The Impact of Irish-Ireland on Young Poland, 1890–1919

Mickiewicz's *Forefather's Eve*, revealed traces of Byron's reckless heroism. Similar recognition has been given to Sir Walter Scott, whose historical novels proved to be important models for such works as Niemcewicz's *Jan z Tęczyna* (Jan from Tęczyn, 1825) and Mickiewicz's *Master Thaddeus* (1834). Little scholarly attention has been paid to the Polish reception of Thomas Moore (1779–1852), who ranked with Byron and Scott in terms of international celebrity in the nineteenth century. By any measure, Moore was a literary celebrity. Moore's reputation stemmed largely from his *Irish Melodies* (1807–1834), which totaled ten volumes, and his popular Romantic tale, *Lalla Rookh* (1817), which by 1841 numbered forty-one editions.[21] In his poetry Moore, who left Ireland at the age of twenty never to return, captured the Irish experience following the Act of Union in 1800. Although Irish autonomy had long since been curtailed, the legal absorption of Ireland into England by means of the Union for many in Ireland, Protestant and Catholic alike, signaled the end of an era. Infused with the indistinct language of personal loss and national remembrance, Moore's poetry in many respects reflected the transition from the dying Gaelic order of Irish society to its new Anglo-Irish identity. In doing so, he not only captured his compatriots' feelings of nostalgia and memory, but he also helped shape the English perception of the Irish historical experience in the guise of sweet poetry of personal experience. Moore, who was closely aligned with Whig political circles and who circulated in the elite circles of English society singing his *Melodies* in drawing rooms along with musical accompaniment, was less threatening than the ever-present specter of social upheaval within the Irish populace. Moore succeeded in preserving a sense of Irishness in both Ireland and England at a time when official governmental policy was to centralize English rule. The elements of memory, melody, and personal loss combined to create a poetic style perfectly suited to the spread of Romanticism in England and the European continent in the 1820s and 1830s.

Given his wide international reputation, it was not unexpected that Moore would attract a following in Poland. The early appeal of Byron and Scott among the Polish Romantics spurred a broader interest in English literature. The Irish historian Eoin MacWhite claimed that quantitatively Moore was less translated into Polish in comparison to other Slavic countries, partially because of the ready access to published French translations. "[T]his deficiency in quantity," MacWhite admitted, "is more than compensated for by the high literary qualities and the important national standing of his translators and of the Polish literary figures who expressed interest in and admiration for his work."[22] While few of Moore's translators attempted to render extensive amounts of his work into Polish, MacWhite was not entirely accurate in capturing the broad and

Chapter 1: Melodies Dissonant & Harmonious

lasting appeal of Moore's poetry among Poles in the nineteenth century. Of the major Polish Romantic poets, Mickiewicz, Niemcewicz and Słowacki translated one or more of Moore's *Melodies* into Polish, while Krasiński knew his work well and lofted a project of assisting with an edition of Polish *Melodies*. The list of minor writers who translated Moore was significantly longer, including Antoni Edward Odyniec, Józef Korzeniowski, and Krystyn Ostrowski to name but a few. Moore's poetry, particularly after the November Uprising of 1830, was not simply fashionable among Poles, it rose to the level of a common vernacular to express the trauma of national loss and exile.

Moore was not just appreciated from afar. On the contrary, a number of Polish émigrés met or corresponded with the Irish poet, who lived in England, while in exile following the November Uprising. Stanisław Egbert Koźmian, who met the Irish poet during his extensive travels in England, Ireland, and Scotland in the 1830s and 1840s, claimed that Moore had no equal among English writers for Poles.[23] "Among the young poets," Koźmian maintained, "there was not one who did not translate or imitate Moore before the November Uprising, even though not many of them knew his work in the original."[24] The strong attraction Polish writers felt toward Moore was in some respects surprising, because the Irish poet did not express an overt interest in Polish affairs. Although Moore was sympathetic to the Polish cause, going so far as to become a member of Thomas Campbell and Lord Dudley Stuart's Literary Association of the Friends of Poland, he never dedicated a poem specifically to Poland or the Polish cause. The extent of attention Moore gave to the Polish cause in his poetry was the long, rambling poem *Fables for the Holy Alliance* (1823), in which he made several allusions to the treatment of Poland by the tripartite forces of Austria, Russia, and Prussia. Moore was not alone in this regard, as there was a limited response from other Irish writers to the plight of Poland. James Clarence Mangan and Aubrey de Vere both touched on the Polish experience, but only indirectly. Mangan's "Siberia" portrayed the harsh natural reality of exile, while de Vere's "Irish Colonization: 1848" likened English indifference to the tragedy of the Famine to its lack of action versus Polish partition.

> Thy shield of old torn Poland twice and thrice
> Invoked: thy help as vainly as Ireland asks[.][25]

Moore's appeal among Poles did not stem from his being an outspoken champion of the Polish cause, but rather it grew out of his poetry that paired the sweetness of personal loss with the power of national memory. This was in line with Moore's own ambivalent relationship to Ireland and Irish politics. He was respectful of Daniel O'Connell and his achievements, but he disdained his methods. His journal entries portray a man acutely aware of his standing among his countrymen but concerned with his legacy as Ireland's national poet. Moore, however, was always at his best when working with the indistinct language of memory and Romantic sorrow. Works such as *Memoirs of Captain Rock* (1824), in which Moore dabbled in sectarian politics, were capable of raising a stir, but they were much less successful, both in artistic and financial terms, than his *Melodies*. As a national poet of international celebrity, Poles attached to Moore a role in and significance to the Polish cause of which the Irish poet was not immediately aware. The spread of Moore's influence and popularity among the Polish *literati* says as much about Moore as it does about the changing needs of the Polish audience. While Byron remained influential among Polish Romantics in the 1820s, his rebellious, nonconformist vision of the world became less and less attractive as Polish poets matured and developed their own styles. Byron's heroic recklessness could not express the feelings of loss, memory, and suffering that characterized the Polish collective experience and Moore's poetry exuded. Moore's strength as a poet was his ability to write simultaneously on the planes of the personal and the political, the emotional and the historical, and the particular and the nebulous. Masked in sweet, vague language bordering on sentimentality, Moore's *Irish Melodies* (1808–1834) had the flexibility of appealing to both the powerful and the oppressed. On the surface, Moore's *Melodies* were inoffensive poems of personal nostalgia for a lost love or of an émigré's wistful thoughts of home. Mixing together elements of memory, Irish topography and national mythology, and traditional Irish folk songs, Moore's poetry was also capable of expressing the Irish experience of national loss in the nineteenth century. This blend of the individual and the collective experience appealed to young Polish Romantics looking for new forms of expression, but who at the same time were mindful of their recent unhappy national history. The ability of Moore's poetry to operate on these two planes made it easier for the new generation of Polish poets looking to act as heterolingual agents, appropriating Moore's deceptively powerful poetry to give voice to the Polish national experience.

Many Poles would have been introduced to Moore in the context of the salon, most likely first read aloud amongst fashionable society in the form of French translations. This soon changed, as young Polish Romantics became interested in English literature and began to translate Moore from the original. This fit with the spread of Moore's popularity in England and Ireland, as his *Melodies* were recited if not sung with musical accompaniment. In his journals, Moore chronicled a long career of performing his *Melodies* for the elite of English society. While the context of the literary salon suggests a setting based on fashion and

Chapter 1: Melodies Dissonant & Harmonious

social convention, for post-partition Poland it took on a surprisingly powerful national significance. Poles in the Congress Kingdom were allowed a degree of autonomy in the 1820s, but after the debacle of the Decembrist Uprising in 1825, the Russian authorities strictly curtailed public life for Poles. Held in the homes of the aristocracy or gentry, the Polish literary salon was both a social gathering and a private sphere, albeit temporary, of Polish interaction.

The most famous in this regard was undoubtedly that of Salomea Bécu, Słowacki's mother, first in Vilnius and after 1827 in Krzemieniec, Volhynia. Słowacki grew up in a highly intellectual environment. His father was an instructor at the famous lycee in Krzemieniec and later a professor of literature at the University of Vilnius, and his stepfather was a professor of medicine also at the University of Vilnius, It was Madame Bécu, however, a highly literate woman passionate about French literature, whose salon brought together the young literary talents of the day, including Mickiewicz and Antoni Edward Odyniec (1804–1885). Part social gathering, part poetic training ground, Madame Bécu's salon helped, most likely via French translations, to introduce this young generation to the leading Romantic writers of the day. For Moore, this was the ideal setting for a Polish audience to encounter his poetry. Recited aloud or perhaps even sung to the accompaniment of a piano, Moore's poetry was particularly well suited to the self-involved sentimentalism of the Romantic salon. As the poet of "national airs," moreover, he also represented to the young, aspiring Polish Romantics a model to be studied and emulated. The importance of salons such as the one hosted by Madame Bécu grew dramatically in importance in light of subsequent events. By 1823, Mickiewicz and a secret literary circle of students in Vilnius, known as the Philomaths, had been deported to Russia. Following the November Uprising, Słowacki and many of his contemporaries would leave Poland never to return. This private Polish space, a domestic haven for culture and society, would be left behind for a life of exile. Even so, the Polish salon would remain a portable vehicle for the maintenance and sustenance of Polish culture and social interaction.

It was most likely in his mother's literary salon that a young Słowacki first encountered Moore's poetry. His mother's salon functioned as a poetic tutorial of sorts for the young poet, exposing him to the most fashionable literary talents of the day, such as Moore, Alphonse de Lamartine, and Byron. Although they were not published until 1832, by which time Słowacki had settled in Paris, Słowacki's translations of four of Moore's *Melodies* date back to this earlier, more formative period in the young Polish poet's career. Marian Bizan and Paweł Hertz dated Słowacki's experiments with Moore's *Melodies* to the years 1825–1827, when he was a university student in Vilnius.[26] Słowacki more than likely used a

French version of the *Melodies* for his translations, because he did not even begin learning English until 1828.²⁷ Zbigniew Sudolski claimed that Słowacki's source was Louise Swanton Belloc's *Les Amours des Anges et les Mélodies irlandaises de Thomas Moore* (1823), to which Madame Bécu had been introduced by Odyniec.²⁸ Bizan and Hertz, however, suggested that the situation might well have been reversed. "Glancing over [a melody] entitled '*La vallée de voeux*,'" Madame Bécu recalled in a letter to Odyniec in 1826, "reminded me that you once intended to write about Belvedere. If you plan to write, then read this *Melody*, because I like it very much."²⁹ Regardless of the source, it is clear that Słowacki experienced the Irish poet's melodies in the environs of his mother's salon.

Of Słowacki's four *Melodie*, two of the poems, "*Pożegnanie*" and "*Melodia Moora*," were straightforward translations of Moore's "Farewell! But whenever you welcome the hour" and "Oh, think not my spirits are always as light," while "*Melodia 1*" was a loose rendition of "As a beam o'er the face of the water may glow" and "*Melodia 2*" was a Ukrainian love melody of Słowacki's own invention patterned after Moore. It is significant that the figure in the poems Słowacki chose to translate, a melancholy young man, was sitting amongst friends at a social gathering. Terrance Brown has suggested that poems such as this were designed to suit the specific sensibilities of the salon. "They suggest," Brown explained, "how the joys of sociable good fellowship… are passing joys, are an alleviation of the customary lot."³⁰ In "*Melodia 1*," which Słowacki more freely adapted from the original, the imagery in his Polish version further intensified this feeling of transience.

> Oh! this thought in the midst of enjoyment will stay,
> Like a dead leafless branch in the summer's bright ray;
> The beams of the warm sun play round it in vain,
> It may smile in his light, but it blooms not again.³¹

> Po nim przyszłość już pomnik zasłania grobowy,
> A szczęścia [on] nie dozna, tak jak czuł za młodu.
> Jego radość jak słońce, które w dzień zimowy
> Rozjaśni mgliste niebo, lecz nie stopi lodu.³²

Słowacki's insertion of words such as "pomnik" (grave) and "grobowy" (gravelike), gave his translation an even more melancholic feel than Moore's original. In doing so, he intensified Moore's reference to the lifeless branch, which Słowacki compared to the passing rays of the sun over an icy landscape. Life, like the branch, is warmed with moments of camaraderie and happiness, but they do

Chapter 1: Melodies Dissonant & Harmonious

not remain long enough to melt away the frozen exterior of personal sorrow. The masterful employment of memory was one of the primary elements that attracted the Polish Romantics to Moore's poetry. Although the internal suffering of the lyrical subject keeps him apart from the warm circle of his comrades, memory has the ability to prevent the lingering embers of camaraderie from dying out. In "Farewell!" (*Pożegnanie*), the lyrical subject's separation from the revels of his companions creates a strong feeling of melancholy. Fellowship represents a respite from memory, because the spirits that seem to be "free from a pang," or the "heart-beaming smile of to-night," represent life in actual time. While the "revels," "joys," and "wiles" of gatherings with friends are precious, they are fleeting and only acquire weight and substance through recollection. Memory and feeling can protect against the vicissitudes of life in ways that logic and reason cannot.

> Long, long be my heart with such memories filled!
> Like the vase, in which roses have once been distilled –
> You may break, you may shatter, the vase if you will,
> But the scent of the roses will hang round it still.[33]

> Długo me serce, szczęścia chowając pamiątki,
> Podobne będzie czarze napełnionej różą,
> Którą chociaż rozbiją, choć do szczętu zburzą,
> Zapach róży rozbite zachowają szczątki.[34]

Responding perhaps to the physicality of Moore's imagery, Słowacki used "pąmiątki" (souvenir) in place of "memories," thereby enhancing the metaphor of the heart as a repository of recollection. Damage to the heart, as Moore's verses suggested, could cause both physical and emotional pain.

The conventions of the salon are more apparent when considering that Słowacki was at most seventeen when he translated Moore. If viewed in this light, Moore's appeal for Słowacki as a translator grew out of his desire as a young poet to refine his skills. Słowacki's *Melodie* represented a form of poetic training by translation or more accurately, by imitation. As a young poet Słowacki was actively involved in experimenting with the styles of foreign poets, such as Moore and Lamartine. Stefan Treugutt maintained that Słowacki's four adaptations of Moore's poetry reveal a great deal about the pace with which he was changing as a poet, ridding himself of "a pseudo-classical stylization."[35] This notion of Słowacki approaching Moore's poetry from the perspective of a rapidly maturing poet is supported by the kind of poems he chose to translate from the extensive series of *Irish Melodies*. If he had desired, Słowacki could have selected from poems such as "Go where glory awaits thee," "Tho' the last glimpse of Erin with sorrow I see," or "Before the Battle," which were replete with heroic, patriotic imagery. Treugutt emphasized that Moore's international celebrity had as much to do with these overtly Irish melodies as it did with his sentimental love poems. "The *Irish Melodies*," Treugutt explained, "captured the hearts of readers above all with notes of the honest patriotic suffering of his people."[36] Having nine editions of the *Melodies* from which to choose, Słowacki's overlooked this aspect of Moore's poetry, preferring to translate his more vague and sentimental poems.

Juliusz Kleiner pointed out that Słowacki's interest in Moore at this time also stemmed from his experimentation with the Romantic sentimentalism of Lamartine.[37] Drawn to this melancholy poetry, Słowacki chose to translate poems by Moore that were also heavy with mood. In each verse there is a divide between the happy exterior of the poet and an inward reality of misery and suffering. In "Oh! think not my spirits are always as light!" the lyrical subject explains this hidden pain to an uncomprehending friend.

> Oh! think not my spirits are always as light,
> And as free from a pang, as they seem to you now[38]

> Ach nie myśl, że mą duszę, zawsze tak wesolą,
> Nigdy ponura smutków chmura nie okryje[39]

What stands out from both "*Pożegnanie*" and "*Melodia Moora*" is the stark contrast between public equanimity and private sorrow. The fact that Słowacki chose not to translate the poems with overt references to Irish history did not make them any less relevant to the Polish experience. With some of *Irish Melodies* overtly addressing events in Irish history and others dealing strictly with personal matters, Moore made it easy for the contemporary reader to connect the historical, or political, and the personal. "The messages of the *Melodies*," Brown argued, "were the poignancy of loss, the charm of ruination, of buildings, a people's youth, and the poetic appeal of the buried life."[40] Memory and loss were indistinguishable in Moore's poetry. "Sorrow for Ireland," Brown explained further, "is indistinguishable from sorrow for oneself, so send round the bowl and be happy awhile."[41]

Słowacki translated these verses by Moore several years before the November Uprising and subsequent Great Emigration, but suffering and separation was nothing new to Poland. After all, the final partition of Poland had taken place about thirty years earlier, and Polish hopes of salvation in the person of Napoleon had expired about a decade before. Much closer to home, a crackdown by the

Chapter 1: Melodies Dissonant & Harmonious

Tsarist authorities on youth movements resulted in several high school and university students in Vilnius, including Mickiewicz and his fellow Philomaths, being deported to Russia in 1823. Intimately involved in the cultural life of Vilnius because of his stepfather's university ties and his mother's literary salon, such a shocking turn of events must have made an impact on a young man of such poetic and melancholic sensibilities. Słowacki, however, had experienced some personal tragedy in his life, when his closest friend, Ludwik Spicnagel, committed suicide in 1827. Although it would be several years before Słowacki would experience the hurt of emigration, Moore introduced the young poet to a mode of expression that enabled him to treat historical and national themes on the plane of the spirit.

It would be many years before Słowacki would transform the lessons learned from Moore into a philosophy of universal history. Before then, he would turn his attention to Byron and Shakespeare to continue developing his talent as a poet. In choosing to translate poems by Moore that phrased history in terms of personal experience, Słowacki received an early lesson in the power of poetry to elevate the experience of the nation to the level of the universal. He would transform the national memory into a philosophy of universal history in *Król-Duch* (King Spirit, 1847), envisaging the nation as the product of the successive work of enlightened individuals over time. As such, he reconceived memory as the actions of creative and heroic individuals in the collective past of the nation.

Słowacki's encounter with Moore in the context of the salon set the pattern for Moore's reception in Poland prior to the November Uprising. Given the international acclaim of his oriental romance, *Lalla Rookh*, it is not surprising that this was the first work by Moore to appear in print in Polish.[42] Published in prose form by Wanda Malecka in 1826 under the title *Lalla Rukh, Xiężniczka mongolska* (Lalla Rookh, the Mongolian Queen), Moore's work was essentially a commercial venture aimed at appeasing the growing appetite for Romantic literature. Malecka, who was of noble birth and highly educated, was the publisher of journals aimed primarily at women.[43] Her decision to publish Moore came at the initiative of Bruno Kiciński, the editor of *Tygodnik Polski i zagraniczny* (The Polish and Foreign Weekly), who recruited Malecka to take part in a series of new works published under the title *Biblioteka romansów, powieści, podróży, biografii, poematów* (The Library of Romances, Novels, Travels, Biographies, Poems). In addition to Moore's *Lalla Rookh*, in 1826 Malecka also translated Sir Walter Scott's *The Lord of the Isles*. She followed these works with translations of works by Marie Sophie Cottin in 1827 and Byron in 1828.

In choosing to translate Moore's work into prose instead of verse, Malecka seemed to be targeting the burgeoning Polish market for historical romances. As a means of meeting this demand, it was more than likely that Kiciński recruited Malecka for her history of successfully publishing for literary-minded women. Moore's ability to mask potentially troublesome political motifs in vague sentiment and the oriental trappings of the Far East also made *Lalla Rookh* an appealing choice for a publisher in the increasingly draconian climate of the Congress Kingdom. In this regard, *Lalla Rookh* was in keeping with the changing nature of Polish literature, as Mickiewicz with *Grażyna* and Malczewski with *Maria* couched tales of resistance and heroism either in the distant past or in exotic locales. Not surprisingly, *The Fire Worshippers*, the portion of Moore's poetic tale describing the struggle of the Ghebers against the invading Muslims, would become a favorite among Polish translators for its tale of heroic resistance and its Romantic orientalism.[44] Published four years before the outbreak of the November Uprising, Malecka's translation was part and parcel of the initial spread of Romanticism, especially in its Byronic phase, in Poland. Where Byron would largely fall by the wayside following the tragic events of 1830, Moore's popularity among Poles would continue to develop and deepen in the successive decades as Poles by the thousands confronted life in exile.

III. THE ENDURING CHARM OF HOME: RE-WRITING MOORE IN EXILE

One of the most impressive measures of Moore's influence on nineteenth century literature was his ability to penetrate some of the more distant reaches of the earth. This was precisely where Mickiewicz found himself when he translated Moore's "The Meeting of the Waters." Henryk Zbierski dated Mickiewicz's translation to the period of his trip to the Crimea in 1825 following his forced exile to Russia two years earlier.[45] MacWhite was correct in asserting that the majority of the Polish translations of Moore's work took place outside of Poland following the November Uprising.[46] The experience of exile, however, was not limited to the Great Emigration of 1831, nor was it confined to Western Europe. For Mickiewicz and Józef Korzeniowski (1797–1863), exile came early and it took place in the far eastern reaches of the Russian Empire. In their translations of Moore, they did not write with the collective mentality of the Great Emigration, Mickiewicz's nation of pilgrims, but rather from the point of view of the solitary exile. To be sure, Mickiewicz and Korzeniowski were far from being the only Poles banished to the Crimea or to Siberia, but their approaches to Moore were shaped by the personal experience of loneliness and separation of the political deportee.

Chapter 1: Melodies Dissonant & Harmonious

Despite being deported early in his literary career, by 1825 Mickiewicz was already a poet of considerable reputation, both within Poland and in Russia. Considering his physical and cultural isolation from his homeland, it was a seemingly unusual choice for him to translate Moore's "The Meeting of the Waters." Unlike Słowacki's choice of poems, this poem contains an overtly Irish reference to the picturesque "Vale of Avoca," a scenic river valley situated in County Wicklow. Mickiewicz, however, disposed of this problem in his translation, by removing the Irish poet's references to "Sweet vale of Avoca!," thereby excising its inherent Irishness altogether. In contrast to the changes the poet made on linguistic grounds, Zbierski maintained that in this instance Mickiewicz's removal of the Irish site of the poem revealed the conscious intentions of the author.[47] "Moore," Zbierski pointed out, "immortalized the river. For Mickiewicz, it was just a geographic name, which said little to him, or the Polish reader."[48] Removing the Irish reference allowed Mickiewicz to deterritorialize, "delocalize" using Zbierski's terminology, the poem in order to elevate the central thrust of the poem to a more universal plane. Possible insight into Mickiewicz's choices as a translator can be found in the poems he was writing at the time, which came to be known as the *Sonety krymskie* (Crimean Sonnets, 1826). Amounting to a diary of the poet's internal experience, as Miłosz viewed it, Mickiewicz projected his feelings onto the vast, exotic landscape of the Crimean Peninsula.[49] This was in many respects what Moore doing in "The Meeting of the Waters." Mickiewicz's deterritorialization of Moore's poem was a further instance of the Polish poet's endeavor at the time to map his own soul.

The experience of traveling to Odessa and Crimea naturally lent Mickiewicz's translation of "The Meeting of the Waters" a distinct coloring. Banished to the far reaches of Russia, Mickiewicz had to negotiate between Moore's recollections of Ireland, his revelatory travels in the Crimea, and his own memories of home. By translating a poem about an unfamiliar spot in Ireland, Mickiewicz was able to give voice to his own predicament. This was possible, in large part, because of Moore's unique evocation of place. Included in the first volume of his *Irish Melodies* (1808), "The Meeting of the Waters" expressed Moore's longing for his native land. In a footnote to the melody, Moore acknowledged visiting the Vale of Avoca a year prior to publishing the poem, which further strengthened the personal resonance of the location.

> There is not in the wide world a valley so sweet,
> As that vale in whose bosom the bright waters meet;
> Oh! the last rays of feeling and life must depart,
> Ere the bloom of that valley shall fade from my heart.

> Yet it was not that Nature had shed o'er the scene
> Her purest crystal and brightest of green;
> 'Twas not her soft magic of streamlet or hill,
> Oh! no - it was something more exquisite still.
>
> 'Twas that friends, the beloved of my bosom, were near,
> Who made every dear scene of enchantment more dear,
> And who felt how the best charms of Nature improve,
> When we see them reflected from looks that we love.
>
> Sweet vale of Avoca! how calm could I rest
> In thy bosom of shade, with the friends I love best,
> Where the storms that we feel in this cold world should cease,
> And our hearts, like thy waters, be mingled in peace.[50]

Although the melody celebrates the beauty of the Avoca Valley, Moore's focus was not the actual geographic location of the setting but the emotional, intangible ways a person relates to place. Once again the pull of memory is strong here. The Irish poet had been living outside his native land for nearly a decade by this time, returning periodically to Ireland when time and money allowed. As an émigré poet, therefore, in "The Meeting of the Waters" Moore described the emotional cost of being permanently separated from friends and family. While he praised the beauty of the valley, it was the memory of time spent there with loved ones that made it such a beautiful place in his mind.

By leaving out the overt Irish reference, Mickiewicz was able to bridge the gap between the original poem and his own version. Understood in another way, oscillating between the roles of poet, exile, and Pole, Mickiewicz succeeded in relaying Moore's feelings of nostalgia and loss as an Irish poet living in England into the context of the Polish experience. In a very subtle manner, Mickiewicz in this stanza comingled passing references both to Ireland and his native land.

> Nie dlatego o tobie tak wspominać miło,
> Że cię szmaragd odziewa i kryształ oblewa,
> Że masz żywe strumienie, urodziwe drzewa:
> Ach! w tobie coś droższego, coś milszego było![51]
>
> It was not for you that one remembers so fondly,
> That emerald adorns you and crystal washes you,
> That you have living streams, beautiful trees:
> Oh! in you there was something dearer, lovlier!

Chapter 1: Melodies Dissonant & Harmonious

His use of the word "szmaragd" (emerald) in place of "bright green" would have produced an association with Ireland, the "szmaragdowa wyspa" (the Emerald Isle). In contrast to this, the replacement of "hill" with "urodziwe drzewa" (beautiful trees) would have been an image closer to the great forests of Mickiewicz's native Lithuania than with the rolling Irish river valley. In this way, Mickiewicz's alteration of Moore's poem revealed his deep, personal identification with the poem's central message. Writing in the Crimea, exiled far from friends and family in Lithuania, Poland's national poet was homesick.

Understood on this level, Mickiewicz created a poem in Polish that was both true to the original and to itself. Mickiewicz and Moore converged in their renditions of "The Meeting of the Waters" as two mature poets living and writing in exile. The meeting of the waters of the rivers Avon and Avoca provided Moore with a concrete place around which to construct his poem, but it also gave him a metaphor for the life-restoring powers of friendship. The removal of the Irish reference in Mickiewicz's translation did little to reduce the emotional power of the poem. On the contrary, as Zbierski contended, Mickiewicz essentially exchanged one invocation for another.[52]

> Daj Boże, abym wrócił w to miłe ustronie
> I obok mych przyjaciół spoczął na twym łonie,
> Kiedy przeminą wszystkie życia niepogody
> I zmieszają się serca, jako twoje wody![53]

> Grant Lord that I return to that lovely spot
> And next to friends rest in its bosom,
> When all of life's adventures should cease
> And mingle our hearts like your waters.

Mickiewicz's version, however, seemed to carry within it an extra emotional charge, transforming the apostrophe in Moore's original into a near prayer in the Polish version. The emotional difference between the two poems, if any, may be attributable to the fact that Moore lived a life of voluntary exile, returning when time and resources allowed, while Mickiewicz had been transported to Russia for political reasons with no prospect of return.

Despite his avowal in an 1828 letter to Odyniec that "Moore dies in translation," Mickiewicz clearly experienced something personal and meaningful in rendering Moore's poem into Polish.[54] In removing the reference to Avoca, he avoided the deadliness of literal translation and succeeded in capturing the spirit of Moore's poem in Polish. The central theme, moreover, of "The Meeting of the Waters" had a deeper, more meaningful significance for his future direction as a writer. "The topic," Zofia Szmydtowa maintained, "was close to Mickiewicz, close to him were the lyrical motifs: recollection, longing, and the dream of meeting again with friends in a place bound with their presence."[55] Mickiewicz's most famous work, *Pan Tadeusz* (Master Thaddeus), was an epic poem heavy with nostalgia for his native Lithuania and the Old Polish Commonwealth. Roman Koropeckyj has argued that *Master Thaddeus* represented a form of social drama about the Polish social collective's experience of crisis and revitalization following the November Uprising of 1830.[56]

> Litwo! Ojczyzno moja! ty jesteś jak zdrowia;
> Ile cię trzeba cenić, ten tylko się dowie,
> Kto cię stracił. Dziś piękność twą w całej ozdobie
> Widzę i opisuję, bo tęsknie po tobie.
>
> O, Lithuania, my country, thou
> Art like good health; I never knew till now
> How precious, till I lost thee. Now I see
> Thy beauty whole, because I yearn for thee.[57]

Whereas "The Meeting of the Waters" expressed Mickiewicz's longing for his native home on a personal level, *Master Thaddeus* was written to universalize the nostalgia of the entire Polish nation, cut adrift with the Great Emigration. Alone in Crimea and far-removed from his compatriots, Mickiewicz was left to traverse the common waters of memory with Moore.

While most of Moore's translators formed part of the mass exodus from Poland to the West, Józef Korzeniowski (1797–1863) suffered the fate of Mickiewicz and other Poles who were transported by the authorities to Russia. A talented writer in his own right, his translation of Moore's "In the Morning of Life," published in *Pamiętnik sceny warszawskiej* (An Album of the Warsaw Stage) in 1838 under the title "Melodya z Moora," (A Melody from Moore) represented Korzeniowski's coming to terms with his situation. Already at the tender age of twenty-three a part of the Warsaw literary world, where he tutored a young Zygmunt Krasiński and met Franciszek Morawski, in 1823 he became a professor at the prestigious Krzemieniecki Lycée, which was the focal point of the "Ukrainian School" of young Romantic Polish poets, such as Słowacki and Malczewski. Although located far from the drama unfolding in Warsaw with the outbreak of the November Uprising, Korzeniowski and the Lycée were soon drawn into the conflict. Suspected of fomenting pro-revolutionary feeling among his students, Korzeniowski was arrested in 1830. Released but not allowed to resume his teaching duties, the situation came to a head in the fall of 1833, when the academy was officially closed. Korzeniowski was then ordered to relocate to Kiev, where he received a teaching position at the newly founded Saint Vladimir University, established by the Tsar in 1834. Living under difficult circumstances, in the spring of 1838 he was accused of contacting a conspiratorial youth organization and transported to Kharkov (Kharkiv), a city in northeast Ukraine. In Kharkov, Korzeniowski was made the governor of the general gymnasium and the inspector of schools. Korzeniowski's moves to schools situated further and further in the East suggest that the Russian authorities valued his talents as a literary man and educator, but suspected his political views as a patriotic Pole.

Despite proving to be a popular and successful educator, Korzeniowski never accepted his fate as anything less than forced exile. The presence of a Polish community made his personal situation more tolerable, but it did not erase the desire to return with his family to his native Poland. Korzeniowski eventually succeeded in achieving his goal, but not until eight years had passed. As with Mickiewicz, Korzeniowski's sole translation of Moore took place following his deportation into the depths of Russia. In typical fashion, Moore stood the standard concepts of human emotion on their head, suggesting that true pleasure could only be experienced in times of sorrow.

> In the morning of life, when its cares are unknown,
> And its pleasures in all their new lustre begin,
> When we live in a bright-beaming world of our own,
> And the light that surrounds us is all from within;
> Oh, 'tis not, believe me, in that happy time
> We can love, as in hours of less transport we may: –
> Of our smiles, of our hopes, 'tis the gay sunny prime,
> But affection is truest when these fade away.
>
> When we see the first glory of youth pass us by,
> Like a leaf on the stream that will never return;
> When our cup, which had sparkled with pleasure so high,
> First tastes of the other, the dark flowing urn;
> Then, then is the moment affection holds sway
> With a depth and a tenderness joy never knew;
> Love, nursed among pleasures is faithless as they,
> But the Love born of Sorrow, like Sorrow, is true.

In climes full of sunshine, though splendid the flowers,
Their sighs have no freshness, their odor no worth;
'Tis the cloud and the mist of our own Isle of showers
That call the full spirit of fragrancy forth.
So it is not mid splendor, prosperity, mirth,
That the depth of Love's generous spirit appears; –
To the sunshine of smiles it may first owe its birth,
But the soul of its sweetness is drawn out by tears.[58]

As had been the case with Mickiewicz, Korzeniowski's experience of deportation added another level of meaning to Moore's sentimental poem. For Korzeniowski this was not a poem of nostalgia for his youth, but rather his translation directly addressed the mixture of misery and intense love of home that accompanied his life as an exile. The raw beauty of Crimea inspired Mickiewicz, but his thoughts in the *Crimean Sonnets* were often of home. Similarly for Korzeniowski, the positions of authority and responsibility he held in both Kiev and Kharkov were no consolation for the pull of his native Poland.

W krainie pysznej – słońca, choć dni tak iskrzące,
A przecież pierś jej kwiatów zwiędły zapach roni
Nasza mgła, nasze niebo chmurne i płaczące,
Wlewa w czyste ich łono, cała pełność woni.
Tak i czucie namiętne błyśnie śród radości,
I chociaż często uśmiech daje byt miłości,
Cała dusza jej szczęścia, w łzach tylko zamknięta.[59]

In grand climes – despite days of sparkling sunshine,
Yet faded is the odor the flowers shed
Our fog, our stormy and mournful sky,
Fills its bosom, emits its full scent.
And so passionate feeling shines amid happiness,
And though love often brings laughter,
Happiness in all its soul is only found in tears.

Replete with feelings of nostalgia for home and wonder at the intangible power of memory, Moore in "In the Morning of Life" captured the essential state of being of the émigré. Life abroad, however pleasant or hospitable is transitory in comparison to the enduring, evocative power of the homeland. Given his refusal to accept his fate and his desire to return with his family to Poland, Korzeniowski's choice of *Melodies* to translate was fitting.

As it was for Mickiewicz, the difficult experience of exile coincided with enormous growth as a writer. Two years after his published translation of Moore appeared, Korzeniowski wrote *Karpaccy górale* (The Carpathian Mountaineers), a play detailing the story of a Ukrainian man who avoids being drafted into the Austrian army and who becomes a bandit. Full of the color and folk imagination of the Carpathian shepherds, this work marked a change in Korzeniowski's writing, as it examined the lives of real people in terms of their social and ethnographic conditions. Closer in spirit to *Robin Hood* and other popular folk legends of local heroes, *The Carpathian Mountaineers* was nonetheless similar in theme to another work by Moore, *Memoirs of Captain Rock* (1824). While Korzeniowski's contribution to Polish literature would primarily be remembered for his social novels, *The Carpathian Mountaineers* would become part of the Polish dramatic repertoire that would be revived with the emergence of the Young Poland generation.

IV. MOORE AND THE NOVEMBER UPRISING: THE VERNACULAR OF EMIGRATION

It was following the 1830 Uprising that translations of Moore into Polish began to accumulate in earnest. Regardless of his ambiguous relationship with his own country, Poles often held Moore up as a decidedly national poet. For an entire generation of Poles cut off from their homeland and subsisting on the aeriform invocations of national memory, Moore's poetry provided a means of coping with the twin problems of loss and displacement. As a poet with close ties to English high society, Moore for obvious reasons could not, or chose not, to write overtly "nationalistic" poems. Leith Davis has maintained that Moore's skill lay in "reformulating the basis of Irish nationalism into a more abstract 'spirit of the nation'... based on general national characteristics." What resulted was the sentimentalizing of the nation, which rendered Ireland an "emotional ideal."[60] His masterful use of mood and feeling in his poetry made it adaptable to the needs of any number of struggling nationalities. Long since forced to consider their country in cultural terms, the exigencies of the Great Emigration made this quality of Moore's poetry particularly attractive to Poles after 1830. As indicated by the translations of deportees such as Mickiewicz and Korzeniowski, Moore's work contained within it the language of the émigré. Faced with an indefinite life of voluntary exile, or pilgrimage in the language of Mickiewicz, the Poles of the Great Emigration adopted Moore as a common vernacular of the Polish experience.

The events of the November Uprising also thrust many Poles out into the world for the first time. It was during this period that Polish émigrés also began to make the journey to England and Ireland, where they sought support for the Polish national cause. Comprising the political and intellectual elite of Poland, these émigrés carried with them the belief that they embodied the living spirit of the Polish nation. Upon receiving little official interest from England, these Polish emissaries turned to Moore and Irish political leaders such as O'Connell as sympathetic advocates for the plight of Poland. Moore was no longer a writer to be passively read and translated, but rather a potential political ally worth making the pilgrimage to meet. Considered by many Poles to be the poet of the oppressed, earlier approaches to Moore via the salon or literary self-reflection gave way to the necessity of intercultural negotiation.

Moore's power as a mediator between beleaguered Poland and world public opinion took a variety of forms. In some cases, as with Zygmunt Krasiński, Moore's influence was felt indirectly. Although Krasiński did not translate Moore into Polish or correspond with him, he nonetheless displayed a thorough familiarity with the Irish poet's work. Krasiński, who was a prolific letter and journal writer, routinely interspersed his letters to his father and friends with references to Moore's poetry. As an expatriate Romantic poet with an abiding interest in English literature, Krasiński's attraction to the Irish poet was natural. It was, however, in the context of his lengthy correspondence with his English friend Henry Reeve that Krasiński made an appeal for the Polish cause through the special agency of Moore.

Living in a perpetual state of voluntary emigration, Krasiński exhibited the same relationship to memory that was so prevalent in Moore's *Melodies*. In a letter to his father from Geneva in February 1830, Krasiński seemed overwhelmed with the melancholy of separation and memory. "Everything," Krasiński reflected, "seems boundlessly sad in this life. Everything is endlessly tangled, the past flies away so quickly that memories barely suffice in recalling it, other than in grammar there is no present on this earth, and every instant the future changes into the past."[61] As if on cue, Krasiński's next thought involved Moore. "I sit now by a roaring fire," Krasiński explained, "with two candles on the table, with Moore and Byron."[62] Krasiński naturally wanted to assure his father that he was making productive use of his time abroad. His interest in subjects such as mineralogy, a subject his father suggested he study, was noticeably outdistanced by his desire to become well-rounded literary man. This led the young Polish poet to learn the English language, which in turn brought him closer to English poetry and to

Chapter 1: Melodies Dissonant & Harmonious

Moore in particular. "I am making progress in the English language," Krasiński informed his father in the same letter, "I am constantly reading Byron, Moore, Washington Irving, Southey, Campbell."[63] As was the case for most of his contemporaries, Krasiński considered Moore to be compulsory reading.

In the correspondence of Krasiński and Henry Reeve, who was a literary critic and ambitioned becoming a writer, Moore's usefulness as a common vernacular, to be quoted and exchanged whenever a point needed to be made, was apparent. Writing to Reeve from Rome in December 1830, Krasiński quoted Moore's "The Meeting of the Waters" in reference to an observation Reeve had made regarding Krasiński's travels to Rome.

> Yet it was not that nature had she o'er the scene
> Her purest of crystal and her brightest of green;
> [...]
> T'was that friends, the beloved of my bosom, were
> Near, etc., etc.[64]

As Krasiński and Reeve were both well read literary men, it was not surprising that their correspondence was littered with allusions to and quotes from a wide array of writers. In many respects, Krasiński developed as a writer through his extensive correspondence. His letters to Reeve were illuminating, because the two men exchanged a great deal of commentary on the craft of writing. In some cases, as those above, it took the form of poetic citations, while in others the two friends exchanged advice on their various projects.

It was in the context of the latter that Krasiński suggested that his friend try his hand at writing a collection of *Polish Melodies* in English on the lines of Moore. Writing to his friend in French from Rome in 1830, Krasiński hoped that a project of this sort would promote the Polish cause among English reading audiences.

> Si vous voulez, mon cher, vous mettre a écrire des Polish Melodies, écrivez-moi, je vous en prie, ce que vous voudriez savoir sur le caractere national, sur l'histoire, vous doutes et vos soupcons, as Tristram Shandy says, et je me ferai le plus grand plaisir de vous écrire tout cela, pour que les chants que vous consacrerez a une malheureuse et grande nation soient dignes de vous et portent le caractere national.[65]

> If you would like, my dear, to put in writing some Polish Melodies, write me, I beg of you, what you would like to know of the national character, of the history, your doubts and your suspicions, *as Tristram Shandy says*, and it will give me the greatest pleasure to write you all about it, for the songs that you would consecrate would make a great nation proud of you and would carry a national character.

The Impact of Irish-Ireland on Young Poland, 1890–1919

Although nothing seems to have come out of this proposal, the fact that he would offer to help his English friend to capture the Polish national character for a collection of *Polish Melodies* reveals a great deal about Krasiński's respect for the persuasive power of Moore's poetry. Krasiński clearly understood the role that Moore's *Irish Melodies* played in garnering English sympathy for and in sustaining the cause of Ireland. Unable to write such verses in English and recognizing that Poland's fate resided in gaining foreign support, Krasiński clearly hoped that Reeve would be to Poland what Moore was to Ireland. A selection of melodies on Polish history and culture would have targeted the sympathies of English reading audiences. Coming as it did during the November Uprising, Krasiński's proposal held considerable political urgency. By searching for a way in which to translate the success of Moore's *Melodies* into a political and cultural tool that would benefit his afflicted homeland, Krasiński attempted to negotiate a way for the voice of the Polish nation to be heard during a time of crisis. Indirectly, therefore, Moore represented a potential intermediary between oppressed Poland and the free world.

Krasiński was not alone in perceiving Moore's *Irish Melodies* as a valuable model for preserving the Polish national cause. Soon after leaving Poland in the Great Emigration, another Polish writer, Karol Forster, attempted in 1834 to translate Niemcewicz's *Śpiewy historyczne* (Historical Songs, 1816) into French, complete with illustrations and historical commentary, as a propaganda tool for Poland. Forster, a former civil servant in Warsaw during the brief period of Russian liberalization, was familiar with Moore's work, having translated Moore's classical work *The Epicurean* in 1829. The choice of Niemcewicz's *Historical Songs* was telling. Loosely modeled on Moore's *Irish Melodies*, it dealt with various aspects of Polish history dating back to the formation of the Polish nation. Although Niemcewicz's verses were unknown outside of Poland, Forster was clearly taking the international success of Moore's *Irish Melodies* as a model to be emulated. As a mediator between Ireland and England, Moore succeeded in rearticulating powerful national feeling in the sweet, diffuse poetic language of mood and feeling. It seemed that by translating *Historical Songs* into French that Forster hoped for a similar reaction to his own country's plight.

Not all Poles of the Great Emigration viewed Moore in political terms. Odyniec, who together with Mickiewicz had frequent Madame Bécu's literary salon in the early 1820s, took to translating Moore as a means of financial support, becoming the Irish poet's most prolific Polish translator. Moore's fame and popularity among Poles were the two motivating factors behind the close attention Odyniec paid to the Irish poet. Although he began his literary career as a poet while still a student at the University of Vilnius, he soon adopted the role of the translator as a matter of expedience. Odyniec worked as a translator to assuage the acute financial difficulties he experienced when the Russian authorities sequestered his estate in 1830, thrusting him into a life of exile. Maria Dernałowicz maintained that Odyniec's translations "represent the best portion of Odyniec's literary work."[66] In Polish literature, therefore, Odyniec was less valuable as a poet in his own right than as a purveyor of the world's great Romantic writers into Polish.

Odyniec published a translation of Moore's *The Fire Worshippers* in his first set of his *Tłumaczenia* (Translations) in the years 1838–41. These three volumes also included translations of Byron's *Mazeppa*, and Scott's poem *The Lady of the Lake*. This collection followed the 1835 publication of *Poezja* (Poetry) in Paris, which featured Mickiewicz's version of Byron's oriental poem *The Giaour* and Odyniec's translation of Byron's *The Corsair*. A year later Odyniec announced the publication of the next three volumes of his translations, which included Moore's *Paradise and the Peri* and works by Scott, Schiller, and Pushkin. The fact that Mickiewicz would allow Odyniec to publish his version of Byron's *Giaour*, which the latter had corrected, together with Odyniec's translation of *The Corsair* indicates the extent to which Mickiewicz valued his friend's abilities as a translator. Mickiewicz mentioned his publishing venture with Odyniec in a letter in 1833 to Ignacy Domeyko, a mutual friend from Vilnius. "Maybe at present they will be less praised," Mickiewicz asserted, "but later they will always be valued."[67] Mickiewicz, who was directly addressing the Polish emigration in his own work at the time, understood the value of Odyniec's translations to the thousands of Poles scattered throughout Europe. He had deliberately written his *The Books of the Polish Nation and the Polish Pilgrimage* in simple, straightforward language so that it was easily comprehensible to the entire Polish émigré community. Much in the same way that *The Books of the Polish Nation* and *Master Thaddeus* were conceived to soothe aching Polish hearts, Mickiewicz knew that Moore's poetry spoke to the same feelings of pain and *anomie*. Again, it was the ability of Moore's poetry to function as a common language for the Polish emigration that gave Odyniec's translations their inherent worth.

Although financial considerations dictated Odyniec's choices as a translator, they thrust him into the world of Romantic literature.[68] While Moore's commercial appeal helped sustain him financially, Odyniec would eventually adopt a much more personal connection to his Irish counterpart. In a letter to Julian Korsak, his brother-in-law, dated August 28, 1829 from Weimar, an early stop in his peregrinations around Europe, Odyniec reflected on the contemporary literary world of which Moore was a part.

> I see as if it were an azure arch spread out over the entire earth. The West, still burning with the living fire and glow of the already setting Sun - that is Byron. The East radiating with dawn – that is Adam. The Moon full and at the zenith of its road – that is Goethe. A threesome of Stars – suns of the first order – are Chateaubriand and Walter Scott for Europe, and for America Cooper. The Pleiades of sunny planets – are Manzoni, Moore, Béranger, Lamartine, Tieck, Tegner and our Ursyn. The vaporous-flaming meteor – is Victor Hugo. The Northern Star – Pushkin. The rest of the aforementioned stars and starlets, which either group together in a constellation, or like a meteor flash, fall, and die.[69]

As had Krasiński, throughout his correspondence Odyniec routinely employed Moore's words to recollect memorable scenes or experiences. In doing so, he displayed a similar tendency among his compatriots to treat Moore's poetry as a means of expressing the pain they felt from the twin experiences of national loss and exile. The personal affinity he felt for Moore, however, seemed also to register on a level that was distinctly personal. While he did not place himself in the galaxy of literary stars, in his memoirs Odyniec could not help but identify with the Irish poet. In a letter to Korsak in late December 1829, Odyniec likened himself to Moore, who had joined Byron in celebrating the publication of *Childe Harold* in London.

> Accompanying him then inseparably the author of *Lalla Rookh* could play my role here today glass for glass, as if he had not also earned a right to the ovations and regard of the world. For me the lack of these rights replaces the lack of pretension to them, and so bravely and without scruples I rush everywhere with Adam to dinners, evenings and receptions (because they do not have balls here in Advent), to which I would not be invited without him.[70]

While he clearly valued Moore as a poet, it is telling that Odyniec would identify the lack of respect the Irish poet received to his own relationship with Mickiewicz.

In the celestial ordering of the literary universe, Mickiewicz and Byron were the rising and setting suns. It would seem from his letter to Korsak that he considered himself to be a poetic talent of similar rank, or orbit, as Moore. Odyniec and Moore, both émigrés from downtrodden nations, were forced to support themselves with their pens and could only circle in the shadow of such greatness. Unlike Moore, Odyniec as a translator was not an original talent deserving of accolades, but rather through his work he reflected the light of the great celestial bodies of Romantic poetry for the benefit of his countrymen.

Chapter 1: Melodies Dissonant & Harmonious

Having been given a glimpse of the otherworldliness of literary fame through Mickiewicz, Odyniec seemed to understand that his role was to mirror the brightness of poetic genius so that Poland and the Polish people would remain connected to the broader European cultural universe. Odyniec's contribution as a translator continued to be felt in his native country long after their original publication. Reissued in 1874 and then again posthumously in 1897, Odyniec's translations introduced successive generations to the key works of the Great English Romantics. Mickiewicz's prediction that Odyniec's translations would continue to be valued proved accurate with respect to Young Poland, whose rediscovery of the Polish Romantics was paralleled by a similar reconsideration of the major English Romantic writers, such as Moore, Percy Bysshe Shelley, Samuel Coleridge, and John Keats.[71]

The depth of Polish identification with Moore was most apparent in the actual interactions between émigré Poles and the Irish poet in England in the 1830s and 1840s. Niemcewicz, who spent two years in England with Prince Adam Czartoryski seeking English assistance for Poland as an unofficial representative of the Polish revolutionary government, was the first and notable Polish writer to have met Moore during this period. Unlike the majority of Moore's Polish translators, Niemcewicz (1758–1841) was significantly older and had personally experienced each stage of independent Poland's precipitous decline. He made his debut in public life as a deputy to the Four Year Sejm, or Diet, (1788–1792) by vigorously supporting the cause of reform within the Old Polish Commonwealth. Niemcewicz's speeches to the Sejm were full of pathos for the Polish nation. "It was precisely then, during the Great Sejm," Bolecki explained, "the Niemcewicz conception of the nation crystallized."[72] After spending eight years, from 1796–1804, in the United States, where he had married and settled down, Niemcewicz returned to Poland, where he concentrated his efforts on cultural affairs. The central thrust of Niemcewicz's activity during the 1820s was to preserve the twin beacons of Polish cultural and national identity.[73] Niemcewicz was particularly active as a writer during this period, publishing *Śpiewy historyczne* (Historical Songs, 1816), which helped to foster a popular, patriotic memory among the Polish population in the Congress Kingdom and *Jan z Tęczyna* (Jan of Tęczyn, 1824), the first Polish historical novel. Like many of his class, Niemcewicz was an opponent of the November Uprising. When it became clear, however, the entire nation was in arms, he helped form an interim government in revolutionary Poland supporting the conservative political camp of Prince Czartoryski. Selected for his considerable experience abroad and his knowledge of the English language, Niemcewicz was sent on a diplomatic mission to England to gain support for the Uprising in July of 1831. He left

Poland for good at the age of seventy-two, accompanying Prince Czartoryski on his diplomatic journey to England.

This experience alone set Niemcewicz apart from his fellow translators. When Niemcewicz met Moore in 1832, he did so as an envoy of the Polish nation. Niemcewicz's encounters with Moore reveal the extent to which Irish and Polish interests had converged after 1830. Hopes of enlisting British military support for the Polish uprising had been quickly discouraged. "Discussions with the Foreign Minister of England, Lord Palmerston," Bolecki explained, "as well as with the Prime Minister of the British government, Lord Grey, ended in fiasco."[74] Not recognizing the Polish revolutionary government, or Niemcewicz as its emissary, there was little hope of gaining official English support for the Polish cause. "There remained," Bolecki maintained, echoing Adam Zamoyski's observation of the Polish historical experience, "only private action."[75] Niemcewicz circulated among the elite circles of liberal Whig politicians and aristocrats, as well as among the sympathetic "radical" political circles, in which the Irish, led by Daniel O'Connell, featured prominently, with the hope that they could be persuaded to call for English political and financial support for the Polish cause.[76] This brought him into contact with Moore, who had close personal ties to Lord John Russell and Lord Lansdowne. Niemcewicz's experience as a politician and statesman, his fluent command of both English and French, and his access to aristocratic political and social arenas, made him a natural candidate for the role of intercultural negotiator. His meeting with Moore, however, would be one of two national poets in the communal non-place of exile.

Niemcewicz's dual position as émigré and envoy placed him into a curious relationship with Moore, who had built his literary career while residing in England the greater part of his adult life. Because of his connections to Whig leaders and to the drawing rooms of England's social elite, Moore crossed Niemcewicz's path as a matter of course. Consistent with the pattern he had established in his earlier travels, moreover, Niemcewicz's continual appetite for learning ensured that the Polish statesman did not take the meeting for granted. "Besides his private political activity and great social activeness," Bolecki has maintained, "he led an unusually intensive cultural life."[77] In his meticulously kept *Pamiętniki* (Journals), Niemcewicz provided some insight into how he viewed Moore's poetry and how he felt Ireland related to Poland. During the same trip to the English countryside in which he met Moore, he acknowledged after reading Moore's *Melodies* that "there are many similarities between the situation of Ireland and our country, though I would gladly exchange our present position for Ireland's lack of freedom."[78] The evident irony in Niemcewicz's observation stemmed from the fact that Poland's dissolution transpired through intrigue and violence, scattering the Polish nation

Chapter 1: Melodies Dissonant & Harmonious

to the winds, whereas Ireland's incorporation into England took place through peaceful political means. Niemcewicz, furthermore, was intelligent enough to recognize the ability of Moore and O'Connell to participate respectively in the English cultural and political dialogue on a level that was unheard of in the Congress Kingdom of Poland.

Niemcewicz's introduction to Moore took place at a social luncheon, at which both he and Moore were guests, in an English country house not far from the Irish poet's home in Sloperton Cottage in Wiltshire.[79] Niemcewicz met the Irishman again at another luncheon some days later, the patrons of which had also invited Moore as a guest. With the shrewd eye of an experienced observer, Niemcewicz captured an insightful image of Moore in his journals. "The famous poet's stature," Niemcewicz observed upon their first meeting that "is truly diminutive... [He is] not altogether handsome, but his face and eyes splashed with flashes of gaiety."[80] Sitting at lunch with Moore, he noted his comical wit, which he guessed Moore had "probably improvised."[81] Having heard that Niemcewicz had translated his *Melodies* into Polish, Moore asked him for a copy. After lunch, Moore entertained the gathering by singing some of his *Melodies*. Here Niemcewicz's earlier wry observations of the amusing Irishman vanished, commenting that Moore's melodies were "full of sad sweetness" and that "those national notes have something particular about them."[82] Possibly recalling his *Historical Songs*, which had engendered so much patriotic feeling in his homeland, Niemcewicz reflected that there are no "melodies for me at any rate like national songs, especially when you sing about the misfortune of your homeland."[83] Although Niemcewicz obliged Moore's request for a translation, he noted in his journals that his gift to Moore was not "without conditions," for he had "asked him reciprocally to write a verse about my poor homeland."[84] By engaging Moore in this way, Niemcewicz laid bare the extent to which he considered Poland to be the primary subject of the translational relationship between the two national poets.

The life of the itinerant patriot, even one entrusted with a solemn mission and comfortable in the world of powerful men, could not have been an easy one. It was possible that Niemcewicz recognized in Moore a reflection of his own life and the sacrifices he had to make because of the sad fate that had befallen his country. As poets and national representatives, both men were entrusted with the task of interpreting their country's respective experience to foreign audiences. Niemcewicz recorded in his journals that he translated several of Moore's *Irish Melodies* upon the occasion of meeting the Irish poet at his home in England. The only extant translation is that of the melody "Remember thee!," which appeared in the seventh series of Moore's *Irish Melodies* (1818). His rendering of the poem, which he presented to Moore as a memento of his appreciation, revealed a vernacular between these two national poets. In regard to the format of this translation, it is important to recognize that Niemcewicz meant his rendering to appear together with Moore's original. He made as much clear in the journals of his travels, recalling "[I] gave Moore today my translation of one Melody ("Remember, etc."), under each line of English putting the Polish verse as he wished,"[85]

> Remember thee! yes, while there's life in this heart,
> *Nie zapomnę cię, Polsko, póki tylko żyję,*
> It shall never forget thee, all lorn as thou art;
> *Póki w tych skrzepłych piersiach zwiędłe serce bije.*
> More dear in thy sorrow, thy gloom, and thy showers,
> *Przez twój ucisk, łzy, nędze, okropne przygody,*
> Than the rest of the world in their sunniest hours.
> *Droższaś mi, niż kwitnące w potędze narody.*
>
> Wert thou all that I wish thee, – great, glorious, and free –
> *Gdybyś była, w jakim cię widzieć pragnę stanie,*
> First flower of the earth, and first gem of the sea, –
> *Kwiatem narodów, pierwszą perłą w oceanie,*
> I might hail thee with prouder, with happier brow,
> *Z większą pychą odemnie byłabyś widzianą,*
> But, oh!, could I love thee more deeply than now?
> *Leczbyś nie mogła nigdy więcej być kochaną.*
>
> No, thy chains as they rankle, thy blood as it runs,
> *Brzęk ciężkich kajdan twoich, krew coś hojnie lała,*
> But make thee more painfully dear to thy sons –
> *Miłość ku tobie wiernych synów twych zwiększała,*
> Whose hearts, like the young of the desert-bird's nest,
> *Jak gdy Feniks pisklętom swoim pierś otwiera –*
> Drink love in each life-drop that flows from thy breast![86]
> *W każdej krwi kropli Polak nowych sił nabiera.*[87]

Just as the nation featured prominently in Niemcewicz's own writing, he inserted it where Moore continued to use the personal invocation.

Upon examination of Niemcewicz's translation of "Remember thee!," several interesting points are immediately striking. In the initial line of his translation, which read literally "I will never forget you, Poland, as long as I live," Niemcewicz

Chapter 1: Melodies Dissonant & Harmonious

added a specific reference to Poland. Instead of simply rewording Moore in Polish, Niemcewicz transformed what in the original was a vague ode to an unspecified homeland, ostensibly Ireland, into a direct lyric poem addressed to Poland. This was quite a different than what Mickiewicz had done with "The Meeting of the Waters." Moore, not speaking Polish and having very rarely written about Poland in his poetry, as a reader could not have been expected to recognize such a foreign element in the translation. In his journals, however, Niemcewicz recalled that Moore had specifically requested that he transcribe his translation in interlinear fashion. There was a side to Moore's personality, evident in his journals, which clearly appreciated such tangible evidence of his popularity or influence among foreigners.[88] The result, regardless of Moore's intentions, was a poetic document of Niemcewicz's mission in England and his experience as a fellow poet-émigré. In juxtaposition to the English text, moreover, not only did Poland become part of the poem, but certain other elements unique to Niemcewicz's reading did as well.

> Wert thou all that I wish thee, – great, glorious, and free –
> *Gdybyś była, w jakim cię widzieć pragnę stanie,*
> First flower of the earth, and first gem of the sea, –[89]
> *Kwiatem narodów, pierwszą perłą w oceanie,*[90]

Clearly absent, though, and almost surprisingly so, was the lyrical voice's "wish" for the addressee, "great, glorious and free." By leaving these words out, Niemcewicz strengthened the final line, emphasizing Poland's return as a nation among nations. In the third and final stanza, however, Niemcewicz once again inserted Poland into the poem, creating a balance of sorts with the first stanza in his translation.

> Whose hearts, like the young of the desert-bird's nest,
> *Jak gdy Feniks pisklętom swoim pierś otwiera –*
> Drink love in each life-drop that flows from thy breast![91]
> *W każdej krwi kropli Polak nowych sił nabiera.*[92]

Where Moore used elaborate poetic imagery to describe filial devotion to the Irish nation, Niemcewicz extended the metaphor of the phoenix to the more explicit notion of blood expiation by Poland's sons. Niemcewicz transmuted the innocuous phrase "life-drop" as "krwi kropli" (drops of blood), "hearts" as "Polak," and "love" as "sił" (strength). In spite of his conservative political ties, Niemcewicz seemed still to be swayed by the exalted mood of the November Uprising.

By laying the Polish underneath the English, perhaps somewhat pedagogically for Moore's benefit, the two verses march in tandem to the same beat. Niemcewicz's translation was a faithful one, but it was also possible to read the end result as two distinct poems. When the immediate tension with the original is removed, the translation can be seen solely as its own creation.[93] The inherent obliqueness of Moore's poem allowed Niemcewicz to actualize it as he thought appropriate. As a result, he replaced vague or natural images laden with mood, such as rain and sunshine, in Polish with images of ominous political suffering like oppression, tears, and poverty. Like many of his poems, "Remember thee!" is about ideal love for one's country. Moore's poem, therefore, allowed considerable room for Niemcewicz to create his own Polish version without altering its meaning in any essential way. As a patriot determined to bring aid to his struggling nation and an exiled poet who had written national melodies of his own, it seems clear that Niemcewicz had given his Irish counterpart a personal and calculated poem.

It is also important to note that Niemcewicz, in the first stanza, employed a lyrical "I," while Moore's poem remains neutral and disembodied until the second stanza. "Remember thee!" in effect became "Nie *zapomnę cię, Polsko*" (I will not forget you, Poland). Niemcewicz transformed what originally was a command or invocation to an unknown heart to remember, into a personal declaration not to forget. In his role as poet and representative of Poland's political interests, therefore, Niemcewicz seemed to apply particular weight to this "I". While it may appear that Niemcewicz was taking liberties, Moore's writing actually invites this kind of activity on the part of the reader. The disarming power of Moore's poetry rested in its ability to use mood to evoke an association with a particular event or situation in the readers' minds. Niemcewicz's reading of Moore was not a false one. Rather, his gift to Moore all the more clearly revealed the multiple roles of envoy, poet, and exiled Pole he invoked as a translator. If translation, as Sakai suggests, is the means by which a nation represents itself to itself, then Niemcewicz's tacit audience, Poland, remained an invisible partner in this exchange. Coming from one national poet to another, Niemcewicz's underlying intention was to negotiate the empathetic gap between Ireland and his distant homeland.

Niemcewicz, unlike his fellow Polish translators, had the rare privilege of visiting Moore at his home at Sloperton Cottage. After visiting so many grand houses, he seemed almost relieved to be in a modest cottage with a garden. Niemcewicz first met Moore's wife, Bessy, who though appeared "pale and a little withered, must have been very beautiful when young."[94] He then met Moore's two sons, when "finally out came the little rhymster." Niemcewicz

Chapter 1: Melodies Dissonant & Harmonious

again remarked on Moore's diminutive size, noting that everything in his host's house was on a small scale. Moore, he determined, had been expecting him, for upon entering his tiny studio Niemcewicz observed Bayle's *Dictionary* open to a reference to Father Sawicki, a Pole who had been in Moscow. Most notably as a translator of Moore's poetry, Niemcewicz also observed the chair and writing desk at which the poet did his writing. Reflecting on his visit to Moore's cottage later, however, it was the image of Moore as a family man that struck Niemcewicz rather than Moore the great poet. "Moore and his wife," Niemcewicz concluded, "appeared content with country life. If I could be as happy as he, let it be God's will."[95] Throughout his meetings with Moore, Niemcewicz seemed to be torn between the personal and the political. Whatever he may have seen of himself in the Irish poet, his own fate would resemble the pathos of Moore's poetry more than it would the Irishman's domestic contentment. It was on this score that the experience of the two national poets experience diverged sharply. Both were émigré writers, but Moore lived in England by choice and in time would receive a government pension. Niemcewicz, in contrast, had no choice but to make his way around Europe as the emasculated envoy of a country that no longer existed and to which he could not return.

V. BEYOND 1830: MOORE AND THE POETRY OF OPPRESSION

The nature of Niemcewicz's encounters with Moore as a form of poetic negotiation between Poland and Ireland initiated a pattern that would be repeated by other Polish émigré writers. As a world-renowned poet, Moore attracted considerable unsolicited correspondence and visits from foreign admirers of his poetry. It is not surprising that Moore noted in his journals a steady stream of references to Poles in the 1830s and 1840s. Following Niemcewicz was Krystyn Józef Ostrowski (1811–1882), a minor poet representative of the class of fiercely patriotic young Poles who had fought in the November Uprising and subsequently had to flee to the West, where they continued to struggle for democratic causes of all kinds. Published In 1836 by *La Librairie Polonaise* under the title *Nuits d'exil, Les Amours des Anges, Grajina* (Nights of Exile, Loves of the Angels, Grażyna), Ostrowski's translation was addressed to the massive community of new Polish émigrés centered in Paris. Replete with Polish patriotic and cultural symbols, the title page included a crowned eagle, military banners, a harp and tablets featuring the names of Poland's storied cultural and political figures. Further underscoring the patriotic flavor of the publication, Ostrowski was identified as an "*officier d'artillerie*," who included the simple dedication, "*A ses Compagnons d'exil et A ses Frères d'armes*" (To his Companions in exile and To his Brothers in arms).[96] Published just a few years after his arrival in Paris, *Nights of Exile* seemed to be part of Ostrowski's intention of winning French public support for the Polish cause. Ostrowski was also clearly aware of his Polish audience, a group all too familiar with the experience of exile, as he paired his translation of Moore together with Mickiewicz's heroic tale, *Grażyna*. Publishing Moore and Mickiewicz side-by-side, Ostrowski made the tacit link between Poland and Ireland explicit. Despite its aim of popular appeal, however, *Nights of Exile* and the volume that followed it a year later *Semaine d'exil* (A Week of Exile), did not prove to be as successful as Ostrowski had hoped.

The work, which also included Ostrowski's own original poetry, was pairing of two opposites. Whereas *The Loves of the Angels* is a long poem on the decay of ideal love, *Grażyna* is a heroic tale of ideal love, or sacrifice, for one's country. By pairing Moore's text about spiritual love with Mickiewicz's tale of patriotic love, Ostrowski seemed to be making a point about the role of poetry in the life of the nation. In his "*Allocution*" dedicated "*A Thomas Moore*," Ostrowski played with the theme of Moore's poem, comparing the Irish poet, as the poet of all oppressed nations, to the angels who gave up their immortality to experience human love.

> *Barde nationale des peuples qu'on immole,*
> *Quel est donc le pouvoir de ta sainte parole?*
> *D'ou te vient la splendour de ce front etoile,*
> *O Moore! n'es-tu pas un archange exile?*[97]

> National bard of immolated peoples
> What then is the need for your holy speech?
> Whence comes your splendor abreast this star,
> Oh Moore! are you not exiled Archangel?

In his panegyric of Moore, Ostrowski explicitly linked the Irish poet to the Polish cause, stressing the inspiration and succor that the Polish national cause received from his poetry.

> *L'aigle blanche apportait sous un ciel plus serein*
> *Les chants mélodieux de la harpe d'Érin,*
> *Et souvent a ma voix l'écho de la Vistule*
> *Redisait les soupirs du moderne Tibulle.*[98]

Chapter 1: Melodies Dissonant & Harmonious

> The white eagle bore under cloudless sky
> The melodious songs of Erin's harp,
> And often in my voice the echo of the Vistula
> Repeated the sighs of the modern Tibullus.

Like Tibullus, the Roman poet who dreamed of an ideal life, Moore through his poetry at once disarmed the powerful and gave hope to the weak. In this way, Moore seemed to occupy a dual role as both a model for the oppressed Poles and an anodyne for Polish national suffering.

While Ostrowski recognized the part Moore had to play in raising Irish national awareness with the disarming sweetness of his poetry, he could not forget the fact that Poland was still suffering in the wake of the November Uprising.

> *Mais la belle Pologne et ses fils expirants,*
> *Sanglante, se débats sous la main des tyrans,*
> *Ses destins sont toujours plus obscurs et plus mornes,*
> *Et comme nos amours, nos regrets sont sans bornes.*[99]

> But beautiful Poland and her dying sons,
> Bloody, struggles under the hand of tyrants,
> Whose fates are always more obscure and dismal,
> And like our loves, our regrets are without limit.

Speaking more directly to Moore's *Loves of the Angels*, Ostrowski illustrated how the Irish poet could both protect against the pain of exile and preserve the national memory. In doing so, moreover, Ostrowski also revealed a great deal about the appeal of Moore's poetry to his Polish reading audience.

> *Venez, entourez-moi des images du ciel,*
> *Reprenez vos discours, que votre voix cherie*
> *Me parle de passe, d'enfance, de patrie,*
> *De vos ailes de flamme entourez son cerceuil,*
> *Et voilez a mes yeux sa blessure et son deuil.*[100]

> Come, surround me with images of heaven,
> Resume your discourse so that your dear voice
> Speaks to me of the past, of childhood, of Patria,
> Surround her coffin with your flaming wings,
> And shield from my eyes her injury and mourning.

Unlike the translations done by his countrymen, Słowacki, Mickiewicz and Niemcewicz, Ostrowski did not choose to translate any of Moore's verses that described visions of loss or memories of an irrecoverable past. Instead, he chose Moore's last long poem, which was a more philosophical tale on the relation of love to the soul. For Ostrowski, and other fervent romantics like him, Moore's poetry was both solace and inspiration.

In addition to translating Moore's *Loves of the Angels* into French, Ostrowski corresponded with the Irish poet from Paris. In a journal entry dated October 9, 1836, Moore acknowledged having received a copy of Ostrowski's translation. "He gives me a title of which I am not a little flattered," Moore admitted, "calling me the 'National Poet of all oppressed countries."[101] Moore recognized Ostrowski's hyperbolic Romantic tendencies, which Zygmunt Krasiński had remarked upon some six years earlier in 1830. "The Castellan Ostrowski and his family were here for a few days," he reported in a letter to his father, "[His son, Krystyn,] is a very good boy, but still one of the many of the many among our young people, who changing into Romantics laugh at Homer, shout about Byron, but have never read him and who are ready to fight a duel with anyone who says that Moore is a bad poet, or that this or that person is not a great man, is not *pater patriae*."[102] Although he was pleased by Ostrowski's characterization, Moore found the praise somewhat amusing. "But he also makes a Fallen Angel of me," Moore reflected, "addressing my Bardship thus, in what he calls an Allocution... His appealing to myself for the confirmation of this suspicion of his is not a little comical."[103] When viewed in light of Moore's assessment, it is easier to grasp the purpose of Ostrowski's translation.

In what is perhaps the strongest illustration of Moore's familiarity with and interest in Poland, he responded to a spontaneous ovation from his countrymen while at the theatre during his last visit to Ireland in 1838, humbly acknowledging the influence of his poetry in other countries.

> I am unworthy of this reception... as humble interpreter of those deep, passionate feelings – those proud and melancholy aspirations – which breathe throughout our undying songs – as the humble medium through which that voice of song and sorrow has been heard on other shores, awakening sympathy of every people by whom the same songs, the same yearnings for freedom are felt... Striking is the fact that on the banks of the Vistula the Irish Melodies have been translated into a Polish sense, and are adapted by that wronged and gallant people as expressive of their own disastrous fate [cheers].[104]

Moore, it appeared, had begun to accept the title attributed to him by Ostrowski. Not only was he aware that he was read and translated by Poles, scattered though

Chapter 1: Melodies Dissonant & Harmonious

they were throughout Europe, but he had also come to understand the closeness of experience between Ireland and Poland. The random exchanges Moore had with Polish refugee writers clearly registered with the Irish poet, because more than once in his journals he recalled the facts and emotions they had expressed to him. Although he had deflected Ostrowski's designation of him as the poet of all oppressed nations with humor, Moore seemed to be deeply flattered by the title.

Although not entrusted with the same diplomatic responsibility as Niemcewicz, of all the Polish refugees Stanisław Egbert Koźmian had probably the most extensive contact with Moore and Ireland. Koźmian, like Niemcewicz, also visited Ireland, where he met O'Connell while he was imprisoned in Richmond Gaol in 1844. Raised by his uncle, Kajetan Koźmian, who was, among other things, a poet of the classical school and a senator-castellan in Warsaw, Koźmian demonstrated a taste for poetry at an early age. Having made the acquaintance of the poets Zygmunt Krasiński and Konstanty Gaszyński while a student before 1830 he was writing by then his own poetry. That same year he published a Polish translation of Moore's *Paradise and the Peri* in Warsaw's *Pamiętnik umiejętności moralnych i literatury* (The Journal of Moral Knowledge and Literature). Like many of his generation, Koźmian was enveloped by the events of the November Uprising, serving in the Honor Guard to General Chłopicki. Taken prisoner briefly in 1831, Koźmian upon his release crossed the border to Prussia and began nearly two decades of continual migration. Koźmian made the acquaintance of General Zamoyski in Belgium, where he was in charge of directing the activities of the conservative political faction grouped around Prince Czartoryski, the so-called Hotel Lambert group, in the Belgian Army. Perhaps as a result of Zamoyski's patronage, Koźmian then visited England at the beginning of 1833. Niemcewicz noted a visit in that year from the young Polish émigré in his journal, during which he asked for references to Birmingham. It would be in that city Koźmian first encountered O'Connell, a meeting he would recall nearly thirty years later in the journal of his travels, *Anglia i Polska* (England and Poland, 1862).

Koźmian's first meeting with Moore in 1840 apparently reinforced that emotional commitment Moore had made to Poland two years earlier in his impromptu Dublin address. In his journals Moore gave the credit for his introduction to the young Polish émigré to Lord Dudley Stuart, the co-founder of the Literary Association of the Friends of Poland, for whom Koźmian served as secretary regarding Polish matters. "Lord Villiers Stuart," Moore recalled, "mentioned to me a young Pole who has translated parts of Lalla Rookh & who is very anxious to meet me."[105] It was Moore, however, and not Koźmian who in the end made the arrangements to meet six days later on August 5. "Accordingly

53

he came at the appointed time," Moore observed of his admirer, "a gentlemanlike & intelligent young fellow & speaking English remarkably well. [He] was one of those students who began the revolution, and has translated a number of my things."[106] Koźmian not only told Moore of his translators, but he also assured the poet of his popularity among Poles in and out of Poland. While Moore's sympathy for the Polish cause had been evident early on with his participation in the Literary Association of the Friends of Poland in 1823, further encounters with Polish émigrés such as Koźmian and Krasiński deepened the lasting impression made on Moore's mind.

Upon meeting Koźmian again four years later in 1844, Moore again learned of the on-going oppression and censorship in the Russian partition of Poland. In addition to forming personal links between Moore and his Polish counterparts, such visits also deepened his appreciation of Polish history and culture. Recalling in his journal along with Koźmian's visit that he had also received an Irish translation of his *Melodies* by the Archbishop of Tuam, Moore expressed his preference for those just given him by the young Pole. "The translations into Polish," Moore explained, "were more precious because they were snatched from the fire in the last rout and flight of the Poles from their persecutors."[107] Remarkable as this statement was, Moore had little affinity for Celtic Ireland, and the drama surrounding Koźmian's translations suited Moore's Romantic sensibility and poetic ego much better. The translations that Koźmian had mentioned to Moore were certainly his 1830 translation of *Paradise and the Peri*. Koźmian, like Ostrowski, also felt that the poem reflected Moore's talent as a poet of the sublime. "[*Paradise and the Peri*]" Koźmian explained in a footnote to his translation, "is the most beautiful passage from the poem *Lalla Rookh*. If its beauty were taken together with the *Loves of the Angels*, it would earn Moore the name of the poet of heaven, as Byron is of hell, and Scott of earth."[108] Koźmian may have been playing on the Irish poet's sentimentality when he told him of the daring rescue of his verses from destruction. Moore, however, already understood the Polish message, and his recollection may have been the result of the Irish poet romanticizing the plight of Poland.

Koźmian reflected years later on the Poles' intense interest in Moore, both prior to and following the November Uprising, in a chapter on Moore in *England and Poland*. "He did not dedicate a single verse to Poland," Koźmian admitted, "but everything with which he moved Ireland, whether praising her beauty or her history, or mourning her later misfortune, was as if it befit our fate, as if he was speaking directly to us."[109] It was precisely this feeling of equipollence and solidarity that drew Koźmian and his compatriots to Moore. In an interesting observation, Koźmian declared that no other English poet compared to Moore

Chapter 1: Melodies Dissonant & Harmonious

in terms of popularity in Poland. "About Milton," Koźmian maintained, "we have forgotten. The taste for Pope departed together with the supremacy of the Classical school, Shakespeare we have only now begun to learn. Byron had a greater impact, but on a smaller number of readers."[110] Moore's appeal cut across generational lines, speaking to the fundamental wound that all Poles felt as a partitioned nation. "Everyone," Koźmian explained, "with equal affection reads Moore, young and old, Classicists and Romantics, men and women, and even children are entertained by pictures from *Lalla Rookh* as if with tales from *A Thousand and One Nights*."[111] There were so many translations and imitations of Moore prior to and following the November Uprising that Koźmian felt at times as if Moore was, in fact, a Polish poet. "He spoke," Koźmian asserted, "and he will continue to speak, to the Polish soul with two of the most engaging attributes: the radiance of eastern imagination and longing for an oppressed country." To him, Moore was not just a poet of exceptional talent, but he was also a poet with a unique relationship to the Polish nation. "*Lalla Rookh*," Koźmian insisted, "will continue to charm future generations like the present one, with its poetic tendency toward fables, folk tales, legends. While *The Irish Melodies* will never cease to be a genuine and noble expression of the most enduring of feelings and the most stubborn of hopes, which the most ancient misfortune of Ireland and the dazzling martyrdom of Poland radiate."[112]

Moore was not without his critics in Poland. Koźmian, Krasiński, and Słowacki, among others, all expressed frustration at various times with the superficial quality of some of Moore's writing. Much of this criticism, however, was directed at Moore's later writing or in the case of Krasiński, took the form of admonitions to his friend Henry Reeve of the danger the Irish poet's immense popularity posed to a young writer's developing identity. Moore's esteem among Poles was not limited to the years immediately preceding or following the November Uprising. On the contrary, Moore continued to be translated in Poland in the later nineteenth and twentieth centuries. Given the ease with which the generation of Poles associated with the Great Emigration identified with Moore, it was not surprising that writers of Young Poland would also take an interest in the Irish poet. Jan Kasprowicz, who became the first to translate the poetry of William Butler Yeats into Polish, would include Moore in his 1907 anthology of English poetry, *Poeci angielscy* (English poets). Although the crisis of 1830 by this time had faded, Kasprowicz and the other intellectuals of Young Poland remained bound to Ireland by the same dynamic of predicament and reaction. As the poet of oppressed peoples, Moore formed a connection between Poland and Ireland that would survive until both countries regained their independence.

CHAPTER TWO

THE POLISH-IRISH FAMILY:

THE LITERATURE OF EXILE, 1850-1890

THE RELATIONSHIP FORMED BETWEEN POLAND AND IRELAND IN THE aftermath of the November Uprising, which caused the Poles to adopt Thomas Moore as a poet of their own, was difficult to sustain as Polish revolutionary hopes were repeatedly dashed in the decades that followed. While poets such as Mickiewicz and Słowacki continued to invoke the messianic language of self-sacrifice for the national cause, it became increasingly clear when the "Spring of Peoples" in 1848 passed without changing Poland's situation that partition and exile had become a permanent state of being for the Polish nation. Whether it was the costs associated with the loss of human life or the emotional toll that came with persistent rebellion, the idealism of Polish Romantic nationalism proved difficult to sustain as Poland entered its second half-century of political limbo. With the waning of the generation known as the Great Emigration, the focus of Polish cultural life gradually began to shift home to the partitioned lands of Poland. A widening rift emerged within Polish society in regard to the Polish national imagination and the optimum political strategy for making the country whole again. As had been the case with Moore after the November Uprising, the Polish-Irish connection once again can be viewed as a litmus test for the changing needs of Polish society. The sharp decline of works of genius relating to Poland and Ireland in the years 1850–1890 coincided with the fall from ascendancy of the ideals of Polish Romantic nationalism, which were formed in exile, and the rise of a pragmatic, internally focused strategy of righting the socio-economic and political woes of the partitioned lands of Poland.

The Impact of Irish-Ireland on Young Poland, 1890–1919

1. THE DAUGHTER OF ERIN: EXCLUSIVITY IN THE POLISH NATIONAL FAMILY

The shared vernacular of national loss and suffering that had been evident in the Polish attraction to the poetry of Moore suggested a kinship of experience between the Poles and the Irish. Mickiewicz expressed the bond between Poland and Ireland in explicit terms when he paired the two countries together in *The Books of the Polish Nation and the Polish Pilgrimage*, published in Paris just a year after the collapse of the November Uprising. Mickiewicz's vision of Poland's historical mission was not limited to his country alone. On the contrary, he understood Poland to be among a number of true Christian nations that would carry out the work of redeeming mankind. Ireland and Poland, in Mickiewicz's conception, emerged as brethren bound by a common spiritual mission.

> Otóż Kościół chrześcijański był owym ojcem,
> A dziećmi starszymi byli Francuzi i Anglicy,
> i Niemcy; a pieniądzem dobry byt i sława
> światowa, a lichwiarz był diabłem; a młodszymi
> braćmi Polacy i Irlandczycy, i Belgowie, i inne
> narody wierzące.

> And so the Christian Church was the father,
> and the French and English and Germans were
> the older children: but with money came prosperity and world
> fame, and the usurer was the devil; while the younger
> brothers were the Poles and the Irish, and the Belgians,
> and other believing nations.[1]

Poland and Ireland could find common cause as two members of an idealized brotherhood of nations, which were governed by the universal principles of faith and freedom. As much as Mickiewicz and his fellow Romantics believed Poland's cause to be linked to the struggles of other peoples, Poland's mission to suffer alone as "the Christ of nations" was a barrier that precluded the Irish gaining admission into the Polish national family.

The apparent contradiction, which allowed Mickiewicz and his countrymen to fight for universal freedom, on the one hand, and to conceive the nation in exclusivist terms, on the other, supports Benedict Anderson observations regarding the occurrence of family terminology in the language used to portray the nation.[2] Whether conceived as a motherland or as brothers in arms,

Chapter 2: The Polish-Irish Family

"nationalism often speaks of the nation as if it were a family writ large."[3] The basic relationship of the national family, however, tends to exclude marital unions, because the idea of the nation by definition must be pure and innocent. While the nationalist devotion to the nation is often portrayed as that of children to a mother, the relationship among compatriots by extension is that of brothers and sisters. "The mother (motherland)," Anderson has pointed out, "who makes claims on the lives of young males is the woman who gave them all birth and whom they all have in common: she is also, in a direct sense, the woman they can not/must not have, even think of having, sexually."[4] The same taboos associated with the construct of the family extend to the nation, imposing a similar order of purity on its offspring, or compatriots. "We are all aware," Anderson has suggested, "of the pronominal predilections of nationalism, which likes to speak in a celibate language of 'you, brothers and sisters,' whose selfless solidarity, whose innocence, depends on a deep, unstated incest taboo."[5] Familial ties also bind the living to the generations that preceded them, the dead, and to those that will come after they have left the national stage, the unborn. Although the different generations come and go over time, their common devotion to the nation as an omnipresent guardian unites them as a family.

The various ties that define the nation as a family, albeit useful, tend to become problematic when it is a question of including a group of people viewed as residing outside of the national family either by blood or cultural identity. Since the conception of the nation has to be pure, Anderson argues, celibacy is mandatory and mixed marriages are categorically ruled out.[6] As a relationship established by choice, marriage poses a threat to the established notions of tradition, inheritance, and genetic continuity that inform the national family. In the highly developed strain of messianism in Polish Romantic nationalism, Anderson's celibate vocabulary of the national family was supremely evident. At its height, during the Great Emigration when thousands of former Polish soldiers who had taken part in the November Uprising found themselves abroad, the Romantic heroic ideal was that of the solitary revolutionary-cum-dreamer.[7] For the generation of exiled Poles fighting for their downtrodden nation in Italy, Hungary, and Turkey, the solemn commitment to the ideal of the Polish nation ruled out any thoughts of domesticity. This conception of the Polish national family corresponds with Mickiewicz's notion of the Polish émigré as a pilgrim, a kind of spiritual freedom fighter, which he laid out in *The Books of the Polish Nation and the Polish Pilgrimage*. While Poland and Ireland's sibling relationship derived from the revolutionary messianic ideal, as conceived by Mickiewicz and the other Polish Romantics, was prominent in the 1830s and 1840s, the idea of the nation as a family unit was not entirely absent. Mickiewicz's national epos, *Master Thaddeus* (1834), ends with a highly symbolic marriage uniting two rival Polish gentry families. Mickiewicz was careful to situate the marriage at an auspicious moment in the history of the Polish nation, during Napoleon's eastward march on Russia. Koropeckyj has described *Master Thaddeus* as a dramatization of crisis and revitalization, in which Mickiewicz drew upon an idealized vision of Poland's buried past to project an ideal, collective hope for the future.⁸ For the generation of the Great Emigration, a union such as the one between Thaddeus and Sophia, albeit attractive, was only viable as a nostalgic vision of the past, not as an achievable ambition. Morally bound to fight for God and country, these self-sacrificing sons and daughters abandoned thoughts of home and family until they fulfilled their duty to *Matka Polska* (Mother Poland).

The Polish national struggled gained a sense of urgency in the 1850s, as the 1830 generation entered its third decade abroad and leading cultural figures such as Chopin, Słowacki, and Mickiewicz began to pass away. Tomasz August Olizarowski's (1811–1879) play *Dziewice Erynu* (The Daughter of Erin), which was published in Paris in 1857, at first glance seemed to contradict Anderson's assertion of the nation as a pure, idealized family. Olizarowski, who was a participant in the November Uprising and a minor Romantic figure, organized his drama around the prospective marriage between an exiled Polish soldier, Artur Zawisza, and the daughter of an aristocratic Irish Catholic family living in London, Lora O'Ruark.⁹ While Olizarowski's decision to situate a Polish-Irish marriage within the framework of emigration was an interesting commentary on the perceived affinity of Poland and Ireland in the nineteenth century, the prospect of a bilateral national family in *The Daughter of Erin* was merely illusory. By the conclusion of the play, the author not only reaffirmed the essential purity of the Polish nation, but he also elevated the gesture of patriotic devotion to a vision of messianic self-sacrifice. Aside from the choice of Ireland as the partner in this international union, what made Olizarowski's play such an interesting example of the Polish Romantic ideal of the national family was the extent to which it portrayed the filial devotion of Poland's soldiers as a moral force in the world. Published two years after the death of Mickiewicz, in 1855, the timing of *The Daughter of Erin* was significant, for it represented a belated attempt to inject some of the youthful energy of individualism and self-sacrifice typical of the Byronic Polish poetry of the 1820s into what were in actuality the waning years of the Polish Romantic ideal.

Opening in London, the plot of *The Daughter of Erin* centers around the love affair between Artur, an exiled Polish soldier, and Lora, the daughter of Lord O'Ruark, the Prince of Breffni. A conflict quickly develops when a Russian officer, Kurin, also falls in love with Lora and conspires to win her for himself. Lured back to Warsaw from London by Kurin to take part in a doomed uprising, Artur

Chapter 2: The Polish-Irish Family

is quickly arrested by the authorities in the draconian political climate of Warsaw. Lora and her family follow in pursuit of Artur with the hope of using their social status to save him, but they, too, are arrested under suspicion of encouraging the people of Warsaw to revolt. The O'Ruarks appeal for Artur's life only to discover that they are too late. Kurin, experiencing a change of heart because of Artur's selfless act of national devotion, leads a group of idealistic young Russian officers in committing suicide to restore their honor and to purify the Russian national soul. Lora accepts Artur's self-sacrifice as a spiritual act, and looks forward to their reunion in heaven. The final scene finds the O'Ruarks back in Ireland, but with Lora dressed in a nun's habit and Lord O'Ruark quoting at length from the Gospels. With its motifs of extreme individualism and national expiation through death, in *The Daughter of Erin* Olizarowski was clearly harkening back to plays such as *Forefather's Eve* and *Kordian*, which were written in an earlier, more overtly heroic phase in Polish Romanticism. Published in the late-1850s, though, Olizarowski's patriotic drama was a bit of an anachronism in terms of its timing and more than a little wishful in respect to its vision.

The names of the main protagonists, Lora O'Ruark and Artur Zawisza, would have immediately struck Polish readers from the outset as being laden with nationalist symbolism. The former was a loose approximation of Moore's popular Oriental love story, *Lalla Rookh*, which was very popular in Poland, while the latter would have had even stronger resonance for Poles in the person of Artur Zawisza (1808–1833), a student in Warsaw who had taken an extremely active role in the November Uprising and in the attempts to extend the fighting following its collapse.[10] Zawisza was part of an inner circle of determined revolutionaries who were arrested and executed in 1833 following an attempt to reignite the revolution in the Russian partition of Poland.[11] The name "*Zawisza*," furthermore, would have also reminded many Poles of *Zawisza Czarny z Garbowa* (Zawisza the Black of Garbów), a famous knight from the Battle of Grunwald in 1410 against the Teutonic Knights, who died in 1428 during one of the numerous battles between the Poles and the Turks. Zawisza became the subject of works by Krasiński, who immortalized him in his ballad "Zawisza" in 1830, and Słowacki, who wrote a metaphysical drama about him a little over a decade later.[12] As an indication of the name's revolutionary pedigree, the National Committee of the Polish Emigration also used "Zawisza the Black" as a *nom de plume* in an open letter to the Belgian Minister of War, published in the émigré paper "*Pielgrzym Polski*" (The Polish Pilgrimage) in Paris in 1833, in an effort to expose Wojciech Chrzanowski as a traitor to the Polish cause and thereby make him unfit for a position in the Belgian army.[13] In its various associations, the name "Artur Zawisza" carried with it the idea of extreme devotion to the nation, to the point of self-sacrifice. As a former participant in the November Uprising and a life-long Polish patriot, Olizarowski was not only keenly aware of the symbolic value of his choice of character names, but it suggested a deliberate attempt to return to the revolutionary poetry of the 1820s and 1830s.

Featuring as it did the prospective marital union of a Polish émigré soldier and an Irish aristocrat, Olizarowski's drama on the surface ran counter to the idea of the national family as something that was either pure or exclusive. In reality, however, Olizarowski employed the plot device of marriage between Artur and Lora as a means of reinforcing the idea of the national family as that of pure, filial devotion. The O'Ruarks want to include Artur as their son and to make him a member of their family, but personal happiness is precisely what Artur cannot have as a committed Polish patriot.

ARTUR
Mniemasz że przestanę
Być Arturem Zawiszą? że mnie obowiązki
Nowe odejmą dawnym? że porywam związki,
Które mnie z tobą, z wami i Ojczyzną łączą?
Nie bracie! Zawiszowie w ten sposób nie kończą.
Polegaj na mem słowie. – [14]

ARTUR
Do you think that I would cease to be
Artur Zawisza? That for me new obligations
Would replace the old? That I would break the bonds,
That tie me to you, to us and to the Fatherland?
No brother! Zawiszas do not end that way!
Count on my words. –

The O'Ruarks wish for Artur to marry their daughter, but as a proud Irish family they admire his sense of patriotic zeal and commiserate with Poland as one of an extended family of oppressed nations. Although Artur is a homeless émigré without prospects, as a loyal Pole and an ardent Catholic, he appears as Lora's equal, if not her moral superior. The Russians in the play, in contrast, are not framed using the language of the family, but rather of empire. Notions of family for the Russian characters have no place in their single-minded desire for hegemony.

AMBASSADOR
Czy wiesz czego chce Rossja?

Chapter 2: The Polish-Irish Family

KURIN
Chc być panią świata.

AMBASSADOR
Tak, panią, nie kochanką, nie ofiarą [.][15]

AMBASSADOR
Do you know what Russia wants?

KURIN
To be ruler of the world.

AMBASSADOR
Yes, ruler, not mistress, not victim [.]

When the Russian Ambassador vouches for Kurin's noble lineage to enhance his standing with the O'Ruarks, he does so by lying. The absence of a moral center renders the Russians little more than barbarians in the eyes of Artur and the O'Ruarks.

The central problem of *The Daughter of Erin* is the tragedy of the potential marriage and the impossibility of the Polish-Irish family. The same traits that make Artur an attractive match for Lora also work to prevent their relationship from developing further. Artur loves Lora, but domestic happiness is not an option for a dutiful, patriotic Pole as long as Poland is not free.

ARTUR
I ja pomnę, że jestem naszej biednej synem;
I ja wobec jej nieszczęść nie śmiem być szczęśliwym;
I ja być nie przestałem synem jej prawdziwym.
Pierwej byłem jej synem jak kochankiem Lory.[16]

ARTUR
And I remember that I am the son of our poor country;
And I do not dare be happy in light of her misfortune;
And I have not ceased to be her true son.
I was her son before I was Lora's lover.

Despite wishing that Artur would marry their daughter, the O'Ruarks nevertheless understand that his primary bond as a son is to the Polish national family.

O'RUARK
Jest w samym Bogu prawo, że nie krew jedynie
Stanowi pokrewieństwo: weź w naszej rodzinie
Miejsce syna i brata; przed wszelakim światem,
Po sercu i po duchu, bądź synem, bądź bratem!
Synem moim, a bratem jedynaczki mojej.
Pójdź i nazwij ją siostrą! Niechaj się uzbroi
Tem słowem przeciw słowom: kochanki i żony.[17]

O'RUARK
It is God's own law, that blood not only
Represents kinship: take in our family
The place of son and brother; before the entire world
In heart and in spirit, be a son, be a brother!
Be my son, and a brother to my only daughter.
Go and call her sister! Defend yourself
With this word against the words: lover and wife.

Bound by a shared feeling of pure, patriotic love, the relationship between Lora and Artur represents a sublimation of desire, becoming with the latter's death a spiritual marriage.

LORA
O mój miły Arturze! mężu duszy mojej,
Mężu serca mojego! dusze mojej duszy,
Serce serca mojego![18]

LORA
Oh my dear Artur! Husband of my soul,
Husband of my heart! soul of my soul,
Heart of my heart!

Instead of becoming a wife in the earthly sense, Lora eventually becomes a bride of Christ both literally, as a nun in an Irish convent, and figuratively, as the spiritual counterpart to Artur, the patriotic pilgrim and messianic son of the Polish national family.

Sharing the same moral values of faith and fatherland, over the course of the play Artur and the O'Ruarks are the embodiment of Mickiewicz's vision of a Polish-Irish spiritual brotherhood. Poland and Ireland share an affinity as

Chapter 2: The Polish-Irish Family

faithful, Catholic nations, by whose example the morally corrupt, imperial order will collapse and die away.

> O'RUARK
> Albionie! korsarzu, faktorze narodów!
> [...]
> Ty jedno tylko słowo *Interes* rozumiesz:
> Dla Interesu wszystko poświęcisz i stłumisz.[19]
>
> O'RUARK
> Albion! The pirate, factotum of nations!
> [...]
> You understand only one word *Business*:
> For business you sacrifice and suppress everything.

The O'Ruarks, having witnessed a transformation of the moral order of Russian-ruled Poland with the conversion of Kurin, return home with the conviction that Ireland, too, would reform England by virtue of its example. Bound by crisis but divided by their respective national missions, the Poles and the Irish for Olizarowski can only unite as independent and distinct national families. As a veteran of the November Uprising, Olizarowski understood the common struggle for national sovereignty that bound Poland and Ireland, but as an advanced nationalist and committed patriot he knew there was clearly no place for a mixed marriage in the presence of "Mother Poland," to whom self-sacrifice and complete filial devotion was vital. Rather than put forward a rival vision of the Polish national family as a union of displaced persons, *The Daughter of Erin* highlighted its inherent purity.

Just as Ostrowski's collection of patriotic poetry, *Night of Exile*, Olizarowski's play was aimed at the Polish émigré community in Paris. The purpose of *The Daughter of Erin* was not revitalization, but rather a reinforcing of the Mickiewiczean ideal of complete and utter devotion to the national cause. As both a dedicated patriot and a poet, Olizarowski clearly did not want his compatriots to forget their obligations to their beleaguered homeland. Following the destructive *jacquerie* in Austrian Galicia in 1846 and the disappointment of the Spring of Peoples in 1848, the Polish revolutionary movement was at a crossroads. More pertinent to *The Daughter of Erin*, the death of Poland's soldier-poet, Mickiewicz, and the failure of the Crimean War (1854–1856) to bring about any change in Poland's situation threatened to douse Polish revolutionary fervor for good. Tsar Alexander II's assurance of reforms and concessions in the aftermath of the conflict represented a measure of progress, but the hopes for striking a major blow against Russia never materialized and passed with little effect in the Congress Kingdom.

As an ardent patriot, Olizarowski was keenly sensitive to this blow to Polish national morale. Born the son of a legionnaire in Dąbrowski's Polish Legion, Olizarowski had spent the previous two decades working tirelessly as a poet and polemicist in various cities throughout Europe and Poland in support of the Polish national cause. By 1857, however, Olizarowski was alone in Paris with little means of material or emotional support, having been deported from the Prussian partition of Poland in 1852 on suspicion of conspiracy. In this regard, *The Daughter of Erin* can be read as a deliberate attempt on Olizarowski's part to regain a portion of what had been lost by keeping alive the flames of patriotic feeling among his fellow émigrés in Paris. The choice of Ireland as the Poland's revolutionary partner in *The Daughter of Erin* was an interesting one, but Olizarowski, who had spent the years 1836–1845 in London lobbying for English support of the Polish cause, had been witness to vitality of the Irish national movement under the leadership of Daniel O'Connell and the emergence of Young Ireland. As Julian Niemcewicz had learned as part of the Polish diplomatic mission to garner English support following the November Uprising, the Irish had a great deal in common with the Poles but little in terms of practical support to offer.

For Poles, therefore, the underlying message of *The Daughter of Erin* was that regardless of developments taking place elsewhere in Europe they were on their own. In his draconian portrayals of Warsaw under Russian rule in *The Daughter of Erin*, Olizarowski tried to return to the Mickiewiczean imagery of *Forefather's Eve* and the collective experience of the Great Emigration. Lacking the visionary genius of Mickiewicz, Słowacki, and Krasiński, Olizarowski did little more than rise above patriotic stock formula. The true value of *The Daughter of Erin*, however, was not its contribution to Polish letters, but rather the degree to which it captured a singular moment in the Polish experience of the nineteenth century. *The Daughter of Erin*, furthermore, revealed less about the Polish-Irish relationship than it did about the determined Olizarowski's effort to preserve the sense of belonging and purity of devotion to the Polish nation that had been laid down in *Forefathers' Eve* and *The Books of the Polish Nation and the Polish Pilgrimage*. When Polish national hopes were once again revived with the loosening of restrictions in the Congress Kingdom in the 1860s, it was not altogether surprising that Olizarowski returned to Poland to lend his pen to the cause. The failure of the January Uprising of 1863 not only sent Olizarowski back into exile, where he eventually died in St. Casimir's in Paris, the same refuge that

Chapter 2: The Polish-Irish Family

housed Cyprian Kamil Norwid, it marked the end of the revolutionary hopes of the Great Emigration and the waning influence of Polish Romantic nationalism.

II. POLAND AND IRELAND: IN PROGRESS, SALVATION

The devastating failure of the January Uprising of 1863 and the repressive measures of the Russian authorities that followed it effectively brought to an end three decades of Polish revolutionary activity and with it the unchallenged ideology of the Polish national family, such as that depicted in *The Daughter of Erin*. A new generation weary of the extremism of Polish Romantic messianism began to look for an alternate means by which to better the lives of their beleaguered countrymen. For many of the Polish families that lost their homes, livelihoods, and loved ones to the decades-old national struggle, the prospect of making real social and economic change in the partitioned lands of Poland without loss of life or forced deportation was an attractive alternative to the reckless and self-destructive behavior of the previous generation. Influenced by the positivism of Auguste Comte and the utilitarianism of John Stuart Mill and Herbert Spencer, a new generation of Poles began to push for the improvement of the quality of life in the partitioned lands of Poland by practical means, such as education, industry, and social reform. In the place of the recurring cycle of uprising, repression, and exile, Polish Positivists argued for realizing political aims by working pragmatically within the existing political framework. Where the Romantics stressed idealism and the heroic gesture of the individual, the Positivists opted for reason and collective action. Whether it was the increased industrialization of the Polish economy or the emancipation of the peasantry, this new generation of Poles perceived practical change to be the antidote to Poland's status as a country weakened by decades of fruitless and destructive resistance.

As Beth Holgrem has pointed out in her study of Polish print capitalism in the Russian partition, literary representations of Poland and of the Polish question also underwent considerable change during the Positivist period. "The sociopolitical context of a post-1863 Russian Poland," Holgren explains, "fundamentally redefined what could be heroic and who could be a hero, and writers obligingly produced the new scripts."[20] In the place of idealized visions of the past or unrealistic dreams of national martyrdom, Positivist writers offered rational measures of building a functioning society in the Polish territories. Realistic images of merchants, teachers, and farmers actively living and working in the partitioned lands replaced the essentialized portraits of the Polish nation that dominated in Polish Romantic literature. It was in many respects a return to the political discourse surrounding the partitions of Poland at the close of the eighteenth century, when Polish society was divided between a camp advocating the cause of revolution, led by Tadeusz Kościuszko, and a camp demanding constitutional reform, with Stanisław August Poniatowski, the last king of Poland, as its leading member.²¹ Polish Positivists argued against the revolutionary nihilism of the previous generation employing examples of industrious individuals selflessly working toward the betterment of Polish society as a whole. The reorientation in political means that took place following the January Uprising constituted a rejection of Romanticism's "rule of the spirit," embodied most conspicuously by its three leading poets or "wieszcze" (seers), in favor of a cult of progress aimed at rebuilding Poland organically as a strong and viable society. "If the Insurrectionists were the high-priests of the nation's Soul," Norman Davies has suggested, "the Conciliators were the guardians of its Body."²² In ceasing to view the nation in essentialist terms, Polish Positivists instead employed the language of constructive work and positive socio-economic development in the hope of bettering Poland's position in the world.

It was in keeping with the turn away from thoughts of rebellion following the January Uprising that there was no place in Positivist literature for idealized conceptions of the Polish-Irish relationship, such as that depicted by Olizarowski in *The Daughter of Erin*. This was because the idea of the nation as a family had also undergone revision, as the selfless filial devotion of Polish Romantic nationalism lost favor to the progressive values of self-improvement, domesticity, and industry of Positivism. With science and other measures of progress gaining authority over the moral imperatives of the previous generation, as Henryk Markiewicz has pointed out, literature not only had to change but it also had to justify its existence.²³ The didactic nature of Positivist literature meant that all representations of Poland, much less the Polish-Irish relationship, had to offer something to advance and to better the lives of the Polish people in the present day. In contrast to the impossibility of the potential family in *The Daughter of Erin*, in mature Positivist works such as Bolesław Prus's *Lalka* (The Doll, 1890), Eliza Orzeszkowa's *Nad Niemnem* (On the Banks of the Niemen, 1888), and Henryk Sienkiewicz's *Rodzina Połanieckich* (The Połaniecki Family, 1895) the motifs of marriage and family provided the structure for in depth analyses of Polish society transformed by the rise of a new, bourgeois class. While Olizarowski had organized his drama around Artur's decision to forego domestic happiness in his selfless devotion to Mother Poland, Prus in *The Doll* associated the downfall of the novel's main character, a rising Polish entrepreneur named Stanisław Wokulski, with his romantic obsession with Izabela Ȯęcka, the pretty

Chapter 2: The Polish-Irish Family

but vapid daughter of an impoverished aristocratic family. In *On the Banks of the Niemen*, Orzeszkowa utilized the marriage between the son of a farming family and the daughter of a noble family in a remote part of provincial Poland as the basis for a revitalization tale that involved the removal of social barriers, reverence for a common heritage, and the practice of honest labor. In addition to making the act of marriage the centerpiece of *The Połaniecki Family*, Sienkiewicz subordinated it to the ability of the protagonist to repurchase the family estate as a result of his entrepreneurial success. For Polish Positivists, therefore, the family, with all of its practical associations with gradual progress and peaceful domesticity, displaced the nation as the central focus of patriotic zeal.

The absence of literary representations of the Polish-Irish relationship during the Positivist period, dating from *The Daughter of Erin* in 1857 to the publication of Edmund Naganowski's short story *Żona weterana* (The Wife of the Veteran) in 1890, revealed less about Polish interest in Ireland than it did about the changing needs and attitudes of Poles. Polish writers after 1863 did not approach literature as a source of inspiration or moral support for the nation, but rather they subordinated artistic expression to the need for viable economic and social models that could contribute to the immediate and tangible improvement of Polish life in pragmatic terms. As such, Polish Positivists, inspired by the utilitarianism of Mill and Spencer, were more likely to find their ideal in the increasing political and industrial power of Victorian England rather than in the dreamy melancholy and buried sorrow of Moore's Ireland. In the final analysis, Ireland simply did not factor into the Positivist imagination.

Weakened by a similar combination of poverty, social unrest, and economic stagnation, Ireland did not immediately present itself to reform-minded Poles as an attractive example for Poland to emulate. The reevaluation of the Polish-Irish connection during the Positivist period was understandable given the fact that the image of Ireland Poles had come to know through the *Irish Melodies* was itself in the midst of changing as well. The deaths of Ireland's political giant, Daniel O'Connell, and a number of its leading writers, most notably Thomas Davis, James Clarence Mangan, and Moore, signaled the end of a uniquely fruitful era of Irish cultural nationalism, in both its political and its literary dimensions, by the middle of the nineteenth century.[24] The devastation of the Famine further punctuated this break, leaving a permanent mark on the Irish national psyche, but it was also cause for greater focus on the socio-economic conditions in Ireland. As a result of English reforms instituted under Gladstone in the late 1860s and early 1870s, Ireland experienced positive change in a number of areas, including political participation, religious observance, and land ownership. With the rise of new figures such as Sir Isaac Butt and Charles Stewart Parnell, who sought to redress Irish grievances by means of parliamentary action, a delicate *rapprochement* emerged between Ireland and England. The failure of Fenianism either to dictate or to halt this process of political engagement mirrored the extent to which the advocates of revolutionary nationalism had been marginalized in Polish political thinking. In the shadow of enlightened English rule, therefore, a new image of Ireland emerged during the Positivist period of what could be achieved through open and productive work in lieu of conspiracy and revolution.

The extent to which the treatment of the Polish-Irish relationship had changed following the January Uprising was evident in the utter lack of literary interpretations of the Polish-Irish connection. The fact that the only serious treatment of the subject was a pamphlet by Ignacy Domagalski, a Polish priest, entitled *Irlandia i Polska* (Ireland and Poland), published in Kraków in 1876, indicated the degree to which the essentializing ideology of the Polish Romanticism had given way to the Positivist reassessment of the nation in socio-economic and political terms. Coming as it did from a priest, moreover, indicated the degree to which the pragmatic politics of Positivism had penetrated the Polish national imagination. Although the characteristics of Positivism ran counter to the fundamental doctrines of the Catholic Church, in *Ireland and Poland* Domagalski's argument reflected elements of political pragmatism and social reform that was consistent with its core philosophy. Despite their apparent conflict, there was a degree of overlap between Polish Positivists and the Polish Catholic Church in terms of their mutual opposition to Polish revolutionary nationalism and strong support for the politics of conciliation.

Domagalski described for his readers how the Irish in the nineteenth century, led by O'Connell and the bishops of the Catholic Church in Ireland, had chosen the path of peaceful, incremental change over conspiracy and rebellion. With his condemnation of Polish revolutionary activity, especially among the clergy, and his defense of the politics of conciliation, Domagalski in *Ireland and Poland* reflected the conservative stance of the so-called Kraków "Historical School," commonly known as *Teka Stańczyka* (Stańczyk's Briefcase). Rather than present the Polish-Irish relationship in the familial terms of the nation, Domagalski pointed to Ireland as a practical and a spiritually justifiable example of how to cope with Poland's plight as an oppressed nation. While Domagalski agreed with Mickiewicz's characterization of the Polish-Irish relationship as a kinship born in common suffering, he argued the real and lasting basis of the Polish-Irish connection resided rather in their common faith in God and a total acceptance of the doctrines of the Catholic Church.[25] Whereas Poland's identity as a Catholic nation represented a revolutionary

Chapter 2: The Polish-Irish Family

position to Mickiewicz, Domagalski's ultramontane position suggested that the Poles had betrayed their heritage and had strayed from their allotted path as a nation. "Catholic Ireland," Domagalski explained to his readers, echoing the words of Christ, "calls to Catholic Poland – Follow me!"[26] The Poles had a lot to learn from the Irish, because in choosing the moral authority of the Catholic Church over the path of violent resistance the Irish had begun to reap the benefits of fair treatment and political redress from the English. "Ireland today," Domagalski maintained, "can already view the luminous dawn of a better future destiny... Thus, it is not a useless thing to inquire what lesson Ireland's experience and successful results can give us."[27] In a reversal, therefore, of Mickiewicz's messianic vision of Poland's historical mission in *The Books of the Polish Nation and Polish Pilgrimage*, Domagalski suggested to his compatriots that Ireland had a redemptive role to play for Poland by serving as an example of what could be gained through constructive and peaceful means. It was clear that for Domagalski there was no place for expiatory acts of self-sacrifice, such as what Olizarowski conceived in *The Daughter of Erin*.

As a priest, Domagalski reserved his strongest criticism for the Polish clergy, which participated in large numbers in Polish secret societies and suffered greatly as a result. Pointing to figures such as Reverend Piotr Ściegienny, Domagalski underscored the failure of the Polish Catholic Church to condemn revolutionary activity and to lead by example.[28] In particular, the success of O'Connell's constitutional Catholic Association in incorporating the Irish clergy, in addition to attracting large portions of the Irish populace, represented a fundamental difference between the of political responses of the Poles and the Irish for a good portion of the nineteenth century. "We Poles," Domagalski complained, "were not loyal to the Tsar, and that is why we did not get our institutions back."[29] The determination of the Irish clergy, under the leadership of Cardinal Paul Cullen, actively and as a group to condemn secret societies such as the Fenians in the aftermath of the Famine represented a continued commitment to the path of constitutional reform as the best means for redressing Irish grievances. In contrast, Polish priests tolerated and in many cases took active roles in leading clandestine revolutionary organizations. Domagalski attributed the failure of Aleksander Wielopolski, who was the head of the Civil Administration for the Congress Kingdom at the time of the January Uprising, to implement his measures of social reform in large part to a lack of support on the part of the Polish Church.[30] The crux of Domagalski's argument was that while the Irish enjoyed increased civic and religious freedom as a result of working within the system, the Poles suffered yet further repression from the Russian authorities for their fruitless commitment to conspiracy.

The Impact of Irish-Ireland on Young Poland, 1890–1919

In *Ireland and Poland*, Domagalski was openly critical of the Poles in the Russian partition. As a priest residing in Kraków, he had little to say about the Polish response in the Austrian and Prussian partitions of Poland. While Domagalski acknowledged that conditions were markedly better in Galicia, his concentration on the aftermath of the January Uprising in the Congress Kingdom obscured the diverse challenges Poles faced in each partition. This was especially true for the Polish Church, which enjoyed greater freedom in Galicia under Austro-Hungarian rule than it did under either Prussian or Russian control.[31] Faced with the policies of *Kulturkampf*, which were designed to erode aspects of Polish culture in the Prussian territory, the Polish Church out of necessity adopted a defensive if not combative position and became a force for cultural solidarity for Poles.[32] The situation in the Russian partition was also dire, but it differed in the sense that the Polish Church had to struggle to maintain a presence in the face of church closures, the deportation of priests, and Russian oversight of Episcopal appointments. Rather than undermine Domagalski's position, these discrepancies only served to reinforce his central argument. In writing from the point of view of conciliation, Domagalski was urging his compatriots throughout the partitioned lands of Poland to adopt the tenets of non-violence and constructive work, which were proving to be successful for the Irish.[33]

As damning an indictment of the Polish revolutionary cause as *Ireland and Poland* was, it was not representative of Polish society as a whole, nor did it speak for all the parts of the Polish Church. Domagalski's brochure represented an attempt to reinterpret the Polish-Irish connection in terms of the conservative politics of Austrian Galicia. While Domagalski's supporters echoed his condemnation of revolutionary activity and pointed out the efforts of prominent members of the Polish aristocracy to seek freedom through peaceful and legal means, his critics dismissed his arguments as either unrealistic or outright damaging to Polish interests.[34] The criticism leveled at Domagalski, which accused him at best of presenting a false comparison and at worst of acting as a Russian agent, underscored the difficulty of applying solutions to the Polish question uniformly across the partitions. For Domagalski's detractors, the possibility of a figure such as O'Connell emerging to lead the Poles through a similar mixture of moral pressure and political organization was not only improbable under Russian rule, but it seemed certain to provoke renewed deportations and violent repression from the authorities. In language reminiscent of *The Daughter of Erin*, Domagalski was also criticized for his condemnation of revolution on religious grounds when Polish Catholics, including many priests, were willing to suffer for the cause of the nation and religion. In the critique of ultramontanism in *Ireland and Poland*, there were also echoes of the conflict that existed in Ireland between physical force nationalists and the leaders of the Irish Catholic Church. Part and parcel of this criticism was the conviction that Poles were not only justified in ignoring Rome's denunciation of revolutionary activity, but also that in their resistance they were preserving Poland's national heritage as the defenders of Christianity against the allure of the politics of conciliation and the forces of godless tyranny.

The renewed concern for the practical well being of Poland as a political and a social entity that emerged in Positivism constituted a fundamental change in the way in which Poles thought about their relationship to the nation. In place of the intangible, essentializing ties of national kinship espoused by the Romantics, the Positivists attempted to frame the Polish question in terms of socio-economic development and political pragmatism. In the last analysis, the transition from Romanticism to Positivism resulted in the reconceptualization of the nation as a product of the body rather than that of the spirit. It was in keeping with this transformation that Ireland's affinity with Poland could only be represented as a constructive political or social model, not as a suffering and martyred nation. As a sign of this, the Polish national imagination was no longer subject to the spiritual authority of the Great Emigration, but rather was rooted in the practical work of Poles living in the lands of partitioned Poland toward self-betterment. Figures such as Domagalski played on a key aspect of Poles' cultural identity, their faith, as a way of persuading them from a reckless submission to the demands of Mother Poland. In this way, during the period of Positivism, "society" replaced "family" as the term used to describe the connection between the Polish people and the land in which they lived.

III. THE VETERAN'S WIFE: THE POLISH NATIONAL FAMILY REDUX

As the first generation of Poles since the January Uprising came of age in the 1880s and 1890s, concern for the disorder caused by the 1863 uprising gave way to disillusionment with the Positivist politics of conciliation and pragmatism. With the failure of the Positivists' policies of organic reform to remove or negate the diverse pressures on Polish cultural identity, young Polish intellectuals were increasingly drawn again to reconsider their fellow Poles as an essentialized national family.

The wane of Positivism altered fundamentally the way in which Poles perceived Ireland and the Irish. Although the Irish under the leadership of Charles Stewart Parnell were making great strides toward achieving the kind of political progress long desired by Polish Positivists for Poland, the new generation of Poles refused to view the Irish strictly in these terms. Whether it was in the House of Commons or in the congested districts of the West of Ireland, the Irish in the 1880s began to express a determination to assume control over their own affairs. Rephrased in the lyrical language of the literature emerging in Poland in the wake of Positivism, Ireland was alive at its core, while Poland remained stifled and dormant under foreign military and bureaucratic occupation.

Disheartened by the failure of the scientific certainty of Positivism to restore national health and pride, it was not surprising that Ireland would also begin to be transformed in the Polish imagination. Edmund Naganowski's short story *Żona weterana* (The Wife of the Veteran), published in Lwów in 1890, the same year as *The Doll*, differed from *The Daughter of Erin* in a number of intriguing ways. What made Naganowski's story compelling was the extent to which the details of his life intermingled with the action of the story. Of all the Poles to write about, travel to, or imagine Ireland in the nineteenth century, Naganowski was by far the closest to being an Irish cultural insider. Born into a wealthy aristocratic family that had its estate confiscated by the Russian authorities, Naganowski (1853–1915) left Poland as a young man, ultimately ending up in Ireland sometime about 1878. Having received a Master's degree in English from University College, Dublin in 1884, he taught for two years in Waterford, before moving to London where he found a position at the British Museum.[35] Naganowski built his career as a writer and journalist by regularly publishing works that drew on his experience in Ireland and England. Aside from *The Wife of the Veteran*, he published two novels in Polish, *Hessy O'Grady* in 1885 and *Anglia wszechmożna* (England All-powerful) in 1891, as well as innumerable articles for a variety of Polish newspapers. As a journalist, Naganowski became a regular contributor of information about Irish history and culture to Poland at the close of the nineteenth century.[36]

In contrast to Positivism's focus on the internal conditions of the Polish partitions, Naganowski made the cultural netherworld of exile once again the backdrop for a literary representation of Polish-Irish kinship. Whereas Olizarowski situated his drama in the experience of the Great Emigration, *The Veteran's Wife* took place in contemporary London. The plot of Naganowski's story features a Polish-Irish couple comprised of Marcin Rzutkowski, a veteran of the Hungarian Campaigns of 1848–49, and his wife, Bessy, née O'Halloroughmore, who is of Irish extraction. Trapped in the daily grind of urban London, Marcin makes the daily journey from his wife's boarding house to his factory job and back with the masses of other workers in London. Under the strict control of his wife, Marcin's life consists largely of this daily commute to work and his

Chapter 2: The Polish-Irish Family

many domestic responsibilities. Surreptitiously involved in a Polish émigré social club, Marcin is persuaded to give an address at the organization's annual Christmas dinner. Well aware that his wife would not agree to him attending such a frivolous event, Marcin devises a ruse to leave the house and to attend the dinner. Upon learning that she has been duped, Bessy puts on her finest gown and makes her way to the Polish hall, determined to catch her husband in his act of disobedience. Instead, Bessy is so surprised and moved by the patriotic fervor of her husband's speech that she apologizes for her past treatment of him and vows to attend all Polish functions with him in the future.

Naganowski's invigorating, inclusive depiction of the Polish nation in *The Wife of the Veteran* represented a subtle, yet sharp departure from the tragic, exclusionary vision found in *The Daughter of Erin*. As the story of a successful Polish-Irish national family, *The Wife of the Veteran* at first glance appears to contradict Anderson's central claim that heterogeneous conceptions were impermissible in the national family. In her analysis of Polish émigré drama after World War II, Halina Filipowicz has argued how the construct of the family, as the embodiment of the home, has been used in Polish drama to sublimate nationalist ideology. "National ideologies," Filipowicz asserts, "often depend on essentializing equivalences between gender/sexuality and nationhood."[37] In particular, Filipowicz has not only pointed out the usefulness of the language of the family as a traditional mask for the conservative view of the Polish nation, but she has also illustrated its usefulness as a powerful means of extending and preserving Polish distinctiveness in the context of exile. "The world," Filipowicz explains, "is the treacherous domain of the pursuit of power and material gain. Typically, it is the domain of the male. The home, presided over by the woman, represents the sanctuary of the 'true' self... This phantasmic female is the unyielding and faithful guardian of the home and its traditions and hence of national self-identification."[38] Relocated to Paris or London, the émigré Polish home, through the traditional roles of the family, both preserves Polish difference and negates all foreign or alien elements. In the wake of repeated failures to overthrow foreign occupation by force, many Poles, predominately soldiers, living in exile in the 1860s and 1870s began to look upon exile as something permanent. Unable or unwilling to return home, Mickiewicz's vision of the Polish condition as a national pilgrimage came into conflict with the sober reality of an unending life in emigration. Faced with this realization, therefore, an understanding of the Polish nation as an inclusive yet protective family offered comfort in the face of the uncertainty of exile. For the émigré, the motif of the family ensured the continuity of the Polish nation abroad while also guarding against the forces of assimilation.

Naganowski in many respects dramatized in *The Wife of the Veteran* what may have been the fate of Artur and Lora had they succeeded in marrying in *The Daughter of Erin*. The drudgery of Marcin's life, comprised of the repetitiveness of work and the dull routine of marriage, was due to the substitution of the vital bonds of the national family with the Victorian ideals of propriety and bourgeois domesticity.

> Uroczyste święto Bożego Narodzenia zeszło p. Marcinowi, jak mu schodziły wszystkie niedziele – na obsługiwaniu żony w kuchni, na lepszym niż zazwyczaj posilaniu ciała i na spoczynku w fotelu *enface* żoninego. Nie wiem, czy gdzie drugie takie małżeństwo – to wiem, że p. Marcin nie wiedział zgoła, o czemby mógł z żoną rozmawiać, nie wywołując sprzeczki.[39]

> The festive holiday of Christmas passed for Marcin as all Sundays did for him – in helping his wife in the kitchen, in better than average victuals for the body and in a nap in the easy chair *enface* his wife's. I don't know if there is another such marriage – I only know that Marcin did not have the slightest idea what he and his wife could talk about without provoking a fight.

Caught in a society in which time and social relations were rigidly ordered, there is no space in *The Wife of the Veteran* for emotion or romantic attachment between Marcin and Bessy. The feelings of *anomie* and misery may have reflected Naganowski's own experience of living in a mixed marriage and trying to make ends meet in London. Naganowski's decision to identify Bessy with Ireland, even though she had no real ties to Irish culture, underscored the extent to which he was casting the Polish-Irish relationship exclusively in essentialist terms. What mattered in the context of Victorian England was propriety and social standing, and this is what Bessy initially valued in her husband.

> Lecz najdumniejszą była mistress *Dżetkauke* ze swego męża! Jemu osobiście, *in propria persona*, uczucia tego nigdy wprawdzie nie okazywała [...] *Ja* przynajmniej mogę dziękować Bogu, że *mój* mąż jest dżentelmanem! Nie znam ani jednego mężczyzny z tak dżentelmańskim wychowaniem![40]

> Mistress *Jetkauski* was proudest of her husband! To him personally, *in propria persona*, she never truly expressed this [...] *I* can at least thank God that *my* husband is a gentleman! I know of no other man with such gentlemanly behavior!

Their home was neither Polish nor Irish, but rather the facade of an English one, devoid of feelings of identity.

The rigid nature of Marcin and Bessy's marriage runs counter to their natural or national inclinations. Despite having lived in England some thirty-five years,

Chapter 2: The Polish-Irish Family

Marcin remains a Polish patriot at heart. Bessy, too, is a proud Irishwoman, though she was born in England and has never been to Ireland. In their mutual love of oratory, however, both characters reveal glimpses of their in-born identities. While Bessy's fondness for declaiming poetry bores Marcin, it is less the recitation than the formality of the Victorian drawing room that makes him feel this way. Marcin's own willingness to give the Christmas address at the Polish Club stems from his suppressed feelings of patriotism.

> Marcin Rzutkowski czuł się mowcą z urodzenia, z Bożego daru, z gimnazjalnego wykształcenia w Płocku, gdzie skończył cztery klasy – i wreszcie z powołania do stanu duchownego, któremu tylko Ojczyzny nie był w stanie poświęcić!⁴¹

> Marcin Rzutkowski felt himself to be a speaker from birth, as a gift from God, from his high school training in Płock, where he finished the fourth class – and finally from the calling to the spiritual state, he was unable to give his life only to the Fatherland!

Marcin's speech, for which he has been chosen because of Marcin's knowledge of English, functions as a release of his innermost feelings. Reflecting on his own difficult marital situation, but unaware that his wife is in attendance until the very end, Marcin's address is a form of negotiation between the Polish exiles and their foreign-born wives.

> Kto wie, najmilsi, czy nie odmłodniałyby serca nasze, gdybyśmy w drogich, choc rodem obcych żonach naszych zdołali rozniecić święte płomienie miłości naszej polskiej ojczyzny… Czyby wam nie przybyło życia, mężkiej siły, odwagi i nadziei, gdyby istoty, umiłowane przez nas na wygnaniu, zjednoczyły się z nami silnie i potężnie pod wspólnem sztandarem i dzieląc chleb nasz codzienny przy domowem ognisku, dzieliły z nami wszystką serdeczność dla biednej naszej Matki Polski!⁴²

> Who knows, my dears, whether our hearts would not grow younger, if we were able to kindle the flame of love for our Polish fatherland in our dear but foreign wives… Would there not be more life, manly strength, courage and hope, if you the being, beloved by us in exile, united strongly and powerfully with us under a common standard and sharing our daily bread before the hearth, shared with us with all sincerity for our poor Mother Poland!

Without the support of his wife, Naganowski portrays Marcin and his marriage as being incomplete. Oblivious to this patriotic side of her husband, Bessy at last sees him as a true Pole and a complete man. Whereas in *The Daughter of Erin* the prospect of a Polish-Irish family was impossible in light of the exclusive nature of the Polish national family, Naganowski suggested in *The Wife of the Veteran* that patriotic attachment was enough to overcome the boundaries imposed by identity.

Naganowski underscored the potential interchangeability of the Polish and Irish national families with the character Brygita Shanagan, a Polish widow who was married to an Irishman from the same county as Bessy's family. Despite having no stronger ties than this, Bessy and Brygita view one another in terms of family ties.

> Ten jeden fakt upoważniał żonę polaka i wdowę po irlandczyku do przyznania sobie wzajemnego powinowactwa. Marcinowa była więc "*ciocią* Rzutkowską" – a Brygita "siostrzenicą Shanagan". Niechże się spotka irlandczyk z antypodów z ziomkiem Irlandji... z pewnością odkryją obaj niewątpliwe między sobą pokrewieństwo.[43]

> This single fact enabled the wife of the Pole and the widow of the Irishman to the conferment of mutual kinship. Bessy, therefore, was "*Aunt* Rzutkowska" – and Brygita "niece Shanagan". Supposing an Irishman from the opposite end of the earth met a countryman from Ireland... they would both undoubtedly discover they were related.

Brygita, whose husband was an active member of "the United Irish Brotherhood," is a curious example of the hybrid Polish-Irish family. Left with nine children to support, Mrs. Shanagan is aided by funds from both Polish and Irish patriotic organizations. Brygita, the daughter of a veteran of the November Uprising, speaks Polish poorly, but all of her children have adopted the "mother tongue." With the death of her husband, however, Brygita maintains a nominal presence on the margins of Polish and Irish national life. As a widow, Brygita's feelings of national identity have become weakened to empty ritual. The selfless devotion, therefore, of *The Daughter of Erin* gives way in *The Wife of the Veteran* to the vital Polish-Irish marital bond. Where Brygita leaves the celebration at the Polish Club to go home to her children, Marcin and Bessy partake in the festivities until the early hours of the morning. In this regard, Naganowski reinterpreted the family as an open, evolving form of cultural self-preservation against the loneliness and hardship of émigré life in London.

Taking place as it does in the hall of the Polish Club, Naganowski created a separate, protected space within Victorian England for this renewed international family. Based on Marcin and Bessy's addresses to the crowd, this was not their refuge alone. On the contrary, in her speech Bessy appeals to all the wives of Polish émigré soldiers to gather together in support of their husbands. There was a Dickensian element to Naganowski's construction of the ending

Chapter 2: The Polish-Irish Family

to *The Wife of the Veteran*, with Bessy undergoing a Christmas Day conversion. Where she had been controlling and unresponsive before, following Marcin's patriotic self-revelation Bessy promises her husband complete freedom and more importantly, her full involvement in his Polish activities.

> Martin! [...] ja byłam bardzo głupia i niedobra dla ciebie... ale czemużeś tak się ukrywał przedemną? Ja myślałam często, że ty już nic nie wart na świecie, boś zapomniał swojej dawniej chwały i nie dbasz ani o Polskę ani o Węgry, ani o Irlandję! Wszystko to moja wina! [...] Teraz wszystko będzie inaczej! Dam ci dwa razy tyle pieniędzy na tydzień, możesz tu przychodzić otwarcie, razem tu będziemy przybywać na wielkie zabawy...[44]
>
> Martin! [...] I was very stupid and unkind to you... but why did you hide yourself from me? I often thought that you were worth nothing in the world because you had forgotten your former glory and no longer cared for Poland or Hungary or Ireland! It is all my fault! [...] Now everything will be different! I will give you twice as much money per week, you may come here openly, and we will come here together for grand events...

Upon discovering Marcin's concealed national devotion, Bessy not only recognizes her husband as a complete individual for the first time, but she also awakens her own dormant Irish patriotism. Bessy's Irishness, however, is not a conflict or rival attachment, but rather the natural well of patriotic feeling within her as an Irishwoman ironically helps to transform her into the keeper of the Polish home. Having never truly known Ireland, Bessy in effect has no real identity, and as such she is able to adopt the Polish national family as the emotional equivalent of her own. Bessy's Irish identity, therefore, gives way before Marcin's patriotic gesture, and she at last fully becomes Mrs. Rzutkowska, a Polish wife. Although Naganowski presented an inter-national union in *The Wife of the Veteran*, in the end the revitalized marriage of Marcin and Bessy reflects the emotionalism and purity of intention of the national family "writ large." Within the free space of the Polish Club, therefore, the Polish national family fully comes into being as the union between two émigrés making a home in the heart of the dominant English culture.

In light of Filipowicz's analysis of Polish émigré drama, Naganowski's story was remarkable for the absence of a Polish woman in the home to reinforce traditional norms.[45] At the conclusion of the story, however, Bessy emerges as the ideal "Polish" wife. Where she had insisted on Marcin's punctuality at home and separation from Polish émigré life before, with her conversion she abandons Victorianism and devotes herself to supporting his full participation as a member of the Polish emigration. In her analysis of a post-World War II émigré drama entitled *The Encounter*, Filipowicz uses language to describe a character that could be applied to Bessy. "It is tempting," Filipowicz observes, "to conclude that she fits the Victorian ideal of the domestic angel. In fact, she fits the Polish ideal of the patriotic mother, who does not shirk from her obligation to the cause of Poland's freedom."[46] In this regard, Bessy upholds the ideological structure of the national family, as conceived by Anderson and Filipowicz, and thereby the assures the essential Polish identity of the Rzutkowski's home, by assuming her position as its guardian.

In his condemnation of the stifling rigidity of Victorian England, Naganowski in *The Wife of the Veteran* created by extension a damning critique of the ideology of Positivism in partitioned Poland. The pressures of work, thrift, and social acceptability that combine to crush Marcin emotionally at the outset of the story give way to the raw emotion of the Rzutkowski's dramatic reconciliation at its conclusion. Appearing as it did during the decline of Positivism in Poland, *The Wife of the Veteran* foreshadowed the emergence of Young Poland, which as a cultural movement began once again to imagine the Polish nation in essentialized terms. The Irish for Naganowski clearly represented an equal partner for Poles at the turn of the century in regard to the multiple levels of loss, including physical displacement, exile, and loneliness. It was precisely this desire for essence and the rejection of the Positivist belief in progress and reason that defined Young Poland as it emerged in full force in the 1890s.

In the years 1890–1918, the driving force behind the national imagination no longer resided in the experience of the Polish emigration, as young writers and artists began to return to Poland after spending a number of years in Paris, Munich, or London. Although the Polish national predicament remained unresolved, Young Poland had a dramatically different reaction to it than previous generations. The place of Ireland underwent a similar revision in the Polish mentality. In addition to challenging the Positivism's pragmatic understanding of the nation, the intellectuals returning to the partitioned lands of Poland ceased to view the Irish exclusively as brothers or brothers-in-arms. Rather, in their Irish-Ireland counterparts the emerging artists and writers of Young Poland started to perceive a similar combination of vitality and self-assertiveness, which complemented their profound desire for the renewal of Polish cultural-national identity. Young Poland, therefore, imported the poetry, drama, and cultural activism of Irish-Ireland as a way of striking a balance between the often-opposing forces of cosmopolitanism and essentialism.

CHAPTER THREE

MODELING VITALITY:

YOUNG POLAND, NEW ART, & EUROPE, 1890-1918

In the first issue of the Kraków journal *Życie* (Life) in January 1900, the final year of its short-lived existence, the editorial staff made known its ambitious plans for the coming year. "Young Polish literature," *Life's* editors maintained, "is currently in stasis. The great creations sleep in isolation, in solitude, the strong talents mature, and to clear paths for them, to fight with the antipathy for all that is young, strong, sincere and disinterested – this is the task of *'Life'*."[1] In this declaration, the editorial staff for *Life* expressed Young Poland's fundamental reason for being as a movement, which was to counteract the perceived stagnation of Polish cultural life. From its inception in the early 1890s until its end in 1918, the importation of a wide variety of artistic impulses from abroad played a crucial role in this project of cultural renewal. Due to the multiplicity of interests among Polish intellectuals and the geopolitical fragmentation of Poland, Young Poland did not crystallize behind a single impulse or idea, but instead it countered the perceived vegetation of Polish cultural life with an ever-changing, protean vitality. Translation functioned as a critical tool in this endeavor, because it was by rendering a wide range of foreign works from all periods into Polish that the writers and artists of Young Poland interjected new energy and ideas into the cultural life of Poland.

I. YOUNG POLAND AND THE ZEST FOR LIFE

Young Poland was a multi-faceted movement, which produced a tangled synthesis of approaches and styles. At its heart, it constituted a fundamental change in worldview from the Positivist generation that preceded it. While the lines of demarcation between the two periods were fluid, the period 1890–1918

The Impact of Irish-Ireland on Young Poland, 1890–1919

represented a wholesale transformation in the way Poles viewed the role that art and the artist played in society. Young Poland consisted primarily of those Polish intellectuals coming of age following the failed January Uprising of 1863, with the majority being born in the 1890s or just after the turn of the century. In his literary history, *Polska literatura współczesna* (Modern Polish Literature), Antoni Potocki observed that the early 1890s not only witnessed the thirtieth anniversary of the January Uprising, but also the centennial of numerous significant events in the history of the Polish nation, including the ill-fated May 3rd Constitution of 1791 and the final two partitions of Poland, in 1792 and 1795.[2] For the younger generation weary of the Positivist ideology, which subordinated the literary imagination to the social and material needs of the country and emphasized cooperation within the existing political system, anniversaries such as these aroused a great deal of national feeling. "There were not, of course, revolts," Potocki explained, "but there was a rising of all the till-then latent social strengths under the common sign of the rebirth of society."[3]

Faced with these reminders of Poland's devastated past and its ongoing effacement, young Polish intellectuals considered the Positivist ideology of the previous generation to be a key contributor to Poland's cultural paralysis. As one of the early figures of Young Poland, Zenon "Miriam" Przesmycki (1861–1944), a literary critic and publisher, protested against the subordination of art to a utilitarian purpose, such as social ideology or commercial enterprise. "I wrote," Miriam reminded the readers of *Świat* (The World) pointedly in 1891, "that literature as art for us today is in ruins and I do not withdraw that word."[4] Poland's troubles increasingly began to be understood by the Young Poland generation, both in cultural and social terms, as problems of the Polish psyche. On all levels, therefore, Poland during this period experienced a kind of cultural and national reckoning. "We stand as a society," Potocki maintained, "[–] we have surmounted not only external pressure... but what is more important – we are overcoming internal paralysis, we are learning again – to live."[5] Taking their cue from the early modernists in the West, young Polish intellectuals in the late 1880s and early 1890s began to seek out new forms of artistic expression. Whether it was naturalism, impressionism, decadentism, or symbolism, Polish writers and artists began to move away from the pragmatism and realistic aesthetics of Positivism, turning instead their focus inward with an emphasis on more personal, individualized self-expression. By the time Potocki was writing his literary history, in the years 1911–1912, Young Poland was already firmly established, having witnessed the emergence of major talents in all aspects of art, literature, music, and the theater.[6]

Chapter 3: Modeling Vitality

Young Poland had not yet materialized at the beginning of the 1890s, when a distinct air of pessimism and depression prevailed over Polish cultural life. This, too, masked the general reaction to the ideological, collectivizing nature of Positivist aesthetics. The feelings of discontent in the early 1890s grew out of the general feeling of cultural malaise that had spread over *fin-de-siècle* Europe. Influenced early on by French decadentism and the philosophy of Schopenauer, this melancholy side of Young Poland presaged the resurgence in cultural life that would take place full force by the end of the decade. Potocki characterized this fundamental transition in Polish society as a shift from a "kult zbiorowości" (cult of the collective) to a "kult jednostki" (cult of the individual). The "we" of the Positivist generation, in which the intelligentsia occupied a programmatic leadership position, was replaced by the "I" of the individual artist in the 1890s. Taking hold with the poetry of Kazimierz Przerwa Tetmajer in the early 1890s, and later spreading to prose fiction and criticism, in such figures as Stefan Żeromski and Stanisław Przybyszewski, the expressive power of the individual rapidly gained primacy during the Young Poland period.

Rather than coalesce into a collective ideology or a homogenous style, with these changes the cultural life of the nation grew to include a wide range of competing perspectives. Diversity, in this regard, was a sign of vitality and renewed cultural life. "There is no longer one intelligentsia for all society," Potocki insisted, "but there are as many intelligentsias as there are groups and interests in society intersecting – this is the new slogan of progress."[7] The rise of the autonomous artist for many of the intellectuals of Young Poland period was suggestive of the hopeful return of an independent Poland. The determination of Poles not only to live, but to develop as a modern nation ultimately stemmed from the shift toward greater individual reflection and self-expression on all levels of society. Part of the trouble with attempting to apply an overarching label to Young Poland is that its inherent diversity resisted it. "Modernism," the literary critic Ignacy Matuszewski pointed out in his celebrated work *Słowacki i nowa sztuka* (Słowacki and New Art), "precisely because it rested on the border of subjectivism was not able, and did not want, to create a uniform aesthetic trend, but disintegrated into several, multicolored streams that stem from that same psychic source, yet which flow in different directions."[8] Although the individualization of artistic expression naturally precluded the adoption of an overarching aesthetic for Young Poland, the change in mentality was unmistakable. "The human ego," Matuszewski explained, "appeared to modernists not as a uniform whole, but as an entire range of states, psychic 'moods,' that everyone can share with the rest and treat autonomously."[9]

The Impact of Irish-Ireland on Young Poland, 1890–1919

This change toward a more individualized, subjective relationship to art extended to every realm of cultural life. It was not simply a matter of poetry acquiring increased prestige or of a certain style of expression suddenly gaining currency, but rather of a complete reorientation of thinking in regard to the nature of art and literature. In his 1891 article entitled "*Harmonie i Dysonanse*" (Harmonies and Dissonances), Miriam put forward a kind of creative manifesto for the emerging Young Poland generation. If Polish intellectuals wanted to produce real art, then the nature and place of art in society had to be viewed differently.

> If I say that literature is art, I want it to mean, on the one hand, that it has its own goal and is not in the least a tool exclusively for promoting this or that idea or tendency, whether it be national or moral or scientific. On the other hand – that it has the appropriate means, both internal and purely technical, leading to the realization of that goal, the consciousness of which is indispensably necessary to the literary artist, or that it is to say that – like in other art forms (painting, sculpture, music, etc.) – [it has] the same passion, impetus, intuition, talent, divine grace, without a systematic literature of an appropriate school whose scope and means are lacking.[10]

Influenced by Materlinck and the French symbolists, Miriam considered the essence of art to reside in its ability to reflect the inner life of the artist and reality. For Miriam the fundamental nature of art laid not in sentimental feeling, but in imagination itself. Relying on inner visions, artists developed new forms of art that, in turn, would lead society in new directions. "One of the qualities of genius," Miriam pointed out, "is the creation of new things, the opening of new, unknown roads, the embodiment and revelation of the unconsciously sprouting buds of the future."[11] As the experience of the nineteenth century made unmistakably clear, Poles could not escape national paralysis by means of force or practical work. Where Poles had succeeded in the century following partition, however, was in the realm of art. Whether it was Mickiewicz or Prus, the individual genius of Poland's creative artists had represented the most effective means of maintaining its cultural distinctiveness in the nineteenth century. For Young Poland, therefore, the challenge of revitalizing the nation was not a question of taking action or imposing an ideology, but rather of tapping into the innate creativity and imaginative freedom of its individual artists.

Faced with the unalterable reality of living in a partitioned nation, the intellectuals of Young Poland seized on the notion of artistic freedom as a means of reviving Polish cultural life. Whereas Positivist theories of organic work and practical politics were thought to have contributed to Poland's cultural stasis, the youthful, Dionysian energy of the new lyricism of Polish literature worked to renew the nation by drawing upon the essence of the nation. "It was," Potocki determined, "something akin to learning to move again after a long illness. When the world plays with and intoxicates the senses, as every new feeling in withering control is a new reason for returning to life!"[12] Though it would be problematic to refer to Young Poland in a strict sense as a nationalist movement, it would be equally difficult to deny the impact this youthful "ferment," to use Potocki's characterization, had on reviving a strong sense of Polish cultural and national identity. Art, after all, possesses the ability to transcend physical reality, and Polish intellectuals scattered in Warsaw, Kraków, Lwów, and Poznań found common cause in the pursuit of art. The penetration of poetry into all areas of Polish cultural life was not a shift in taste from one generation to another, but rather an opening up to new forms of expression that took the inner world of Polish artists into account. "This connection of speech according to internal rhymes," Potocki pointed out, "is nothing other than the mature expression of creative individuality in an increasingly living organism."[13] The primacy of poetry was important not merely for the fact that it showed Poland was still alive, but also for the energy with which it expressed itself. "We see," Potocki explained, "that poetry with its own rhymes combines those same factors of creative energy and individual creativity into a powerful essence, which the entire nation today wants to bring together in achieving full existence."[14] Faced with a century of political effacement as a partitioned country, the emergence of this new, unique lyrical voice was both powerful and liberating. This "liberating of the spirit before the liberation of the body" through art, Potocki stressed, was "the only right attained in the midst of lawlessness."[15]

II. LOOKING OUT, LOOKING IN: YOUNG POLAND AND THE WEST

While the liberation of the artist was not an exclusively Polish phenomenon, it was nonetheless a motivating factor behind Young Poland's openness to foreign art and literature. In the earliest stages of its development, Young Poland turned its attention abroad both as a means of escaping the ideological constraints binding Polish literature, as well as a way of refreshing Polish cultural life with new, freer aesthetic ideas. Based in large part on the practical philosophy of August Le Comte, Herbert Spencer, and John Stuart Mill, Poles during the Positivist era had never been cut off from the flow of ideas across the European continent. Young Poland, therefore, did not represent a radical reorientation toward the outside world, but rather it marked a noticeable intensification. Writing for the

The Impact of Irish-Ireland on Young Poland, 1890-1919

Warsaw incarnation of *Life* in the late 1880s, Miriam was already pointing to Europe as a source of potential renewal for Poland. "It is a straightforward thing," Miriam explained in 1887 in "Nasze zamiary" (Our Goals), "that above all we will make allowances in our familiar writing. For the refreshing, however, and the all around growth of aesthetic taste, for the widening of literary horizons, for the strengthening and... subtlety of feelings of beauty – wider than before we open the window to Europe, where of late so many new ideas, literary trends completely unknown to us have emerged."[16] Maria Podraza-Kwiatkowska has argued that Miriam was not an original literary thinker in this early transitional period, but that he relied on others outside of Poland with the conscious goal of connecting Poland with the wider European culture.[17] Originality would come in time, but Miriam's primary goal was the wholesale elevation of Polish culture. Openness to trends in Western art remained a vital means of achieving that end. It would take time, furthermore, for Young Poland to form its own identity, and the importation of foreign impulses allowed a much-needed influx of new ideas during this necessary period of maturation.

Desiring to uncover new and exotic forms of artistic expression, but at the same time wanting to express themselves uniquely as Poles, the intellectuals of Young Poland cultivated a double perspective concerning foreign cultural impulses. Europe was appealing, because that was where new ideas concerning art could be found. As a cultural movement concerned with questions of identity, however, Young Poland was also at work in expressing a sense of its cultural and national distinctiveness. As a result, it developed a dualistic outlook that allowed it to refresh itself at once from the outside and from the inside. While the modernist aesthetics of Young Poland would seem to rule out the presence of national elements, the reality was quite the opposite. The artists of Young Poland heeded the critics' calls for pure art and eternal truths, but they could not help rendering them in a Polish sense. "It is possible only here to proclaim," Ziejka has argued, "that [Young] Poland is involved in the same spiritual conflict that is developing in the drama of all young Europe – they just color it differently – they express it from a different – native – point of view."[18] In her recent study of Polish modernist art, Jan Cavanaugh has argued that Polish modernist painters, although they integrated trends in European painting into their work, such as impressionism and symbolism, went a step further and put their own, uniquely Polish stamp on their art.[19] "The paradoxical nature of Polish modernism," Cavanaugh explained, "is precisely what gave the period its vitality and definition. The confluence of contradictory aims – on the one hand, to resuscitate a hundred-year-old national tradition and, on the other, to keep pace with the onrush of international currents – gave a distinctive character to

Chapter 3: Modeling Vitality

the art of the era."[20] Polish painters, therefore, such as Jacek Malczewski and Ferdynand Ruszczyc, could be considered symbolists or impressionists in the broader European sense, but the subject matter and imagery in their work made it unmistakably Polish. The same double viewpoint existed in Polish literature, as the tension between modernist formal elements and national subject matter in literary works such as Wyspiański's *Wesele* (The Wedding) and Władysław Reymont's *Chłopi* (The Peasants), lent them added energy and imaginative power. It was not enough simply to be modern. For Young Poland, the goal was to be modern and Polish.

The dissemination of ideas from the East and West into Poland undoubtedly owed a great deal to the Polish literary press. Perhaps the key difference between the generation coming of age at the close of the nineteenth century and their predecessors was the speed with which information was spread. The expansion of the print media, often much maligned by intellectuals of Young Poland, played a part in the propagation of ideas and art forms from abroad. High-quality literary journals, such as *Life* (1897–1900) and *Chimera* (1901–1907), which did much to shape the character of Young Poland, routinely employed foreign correspondents on their staff. Polish intellectuals living or traveling abroad, such as Jerzy Płoński and Nekanda Trepka for *Life* in London, reported on new foreign authors and reviewed significant exhibitions or theatrical performances. Polish journals during this period also regularly featured sections that recounted the latest developments in the foreign press or listed the publication of literary or critical works of note. In his regular column in *Life*, "Przegląd przeglądów" (The Review of Reviews), Stanisław Lack used the pretext of reviewing the foreign press as a means of putting forth the overriding aesthetic position of the journal's editorial staff. As many of these journalists were in a position to introduce their compatriots to an entirely new artist or writer, Polish journals acquired a cultural currency as agents of artistic innovation in Poland. Often short-lived, these high-minded literary journals succeeded in creating a space for the dissemination of new art and literature, both from Poland and abroad. Polish intellectuals were not only in tune with developments taking place outside of Poland, but they also were able to follow Young Poland's parallel development in real time.

There was also a practical aspect to Young Poland's fascination with the outside world that fueled artistic innovation. As a result of improvements in general education, not only did the reading population grow, but so did the number of people traveling abroad to supplement their education. The partitioning of Poland ironically worked to facilitated this process of cultural renewal from within and without, as Vienna, Berlin, and St. Petersburg represented the most immediate cultural outlets available to intellectuals in the Austrian, Prussian, and Russian territories. Instead of cutting off Polish cultural contact with the outside world, this internal division made dealings within these foreign cultural circles more a matter of course.[21] Much in the same way that Poles in the early nineteenth century suddenly found themselves to be a nation without a country, at the century's close Polish intellectuals in the tripartite lands of Poland awoke to the realization that they were multinationals. In the absence of a legitimate and sovereign Poland, they could take comfort and refuge in the idea of Europe.

According to the Polish literary scholar Franciszek Ziejka, the number of young Poles studying and traveling abroad during the Young Poland period increased dramatically.[22] Paris was the prime destination for the majority of Poles, due in part to its historical identification as the center of Polish émigré life and to its prominence in bohemian art circles. Polish students, however, could be found at scholarly institutions throughout the European continent. Ziejka has also stressed the fact that travel abroad was common, if not *de rigueur* for young Polish intellectuals.[23] In this way, experience abroad was a mixture of self-education, sightseeing, and cultural reconnaissance. On another level, in the minds of Polish intellectuals contact with foreign cultures worked to underscore Poland's rightful position among the cultured nations of the world. While they could feel at one with European culture walking among the ruins of Rome, the art galleries of Paris, or the parks of London, the one thing they could not do was to forget that they were Poles.[24] This was not the inspired moral pilgrimage of Mickiewicz or the enduring exile of Naganowski, but the willing intellectual journey of Polish artists in search of what was true and lasting in art. Ziejka has suggested that the model of two competing cultures, European versus Polish, failed to explain Young Poland's position to Europe. "In their work," Ziejka has observed, referring to the writers Stanisław Wyspiański and Tadeusz Miciński, "the national is visibly raised to the universal. There is no difference between Polish and European. That which is Polish is at the same time European."[25] What Ziejka failed to add, however, was that Young Poland could not help but do this. Because of Young Poland's abiding interest in giving expression to its Polishness, the pure, universal aspects of art were bound to give way to national elements. It was this tension between two such divergent forces that contributed to Young Poland's inherent vitality.

Travel in Europe and beyond was especially common among Polish artists and writers. The experiences of these Polish intellectuals abroad had an immeasurable impact on the future direction of Polish culture, as they used their knowledge and contacts to introduce new ideas into Poland. After resigning from his editorial position at the Warsaw based *Life* in 1888, Miriam traveled throughout Europe, with longer stays in Vienna and Paris, where he made contacts with the key figures of new artistic trends and made the acquaintance of creative artists such as Maeterlinck. Miriam relayed the new ideas he encountered back to Poland in the articles he published in journals like *Świat* (The World) and *Kraj* (Country). In a more dramatic way, the return of Stanisław Przybyszewski to Kraków in 1898 created a true sensation among Polish intellectuals, electrifying the bohemian atmosphere of the new generation of artists in Kraków. Przybyszewski had made a name for himself among modernist circles in Berlin, where as a writer and editor in the heart of Young Germany he had established personal contacts with leading German, Scandinavian, and Czech artists and writers. Widely considered to be the genius of Young Poland, Wyspiański's travels abroad, first throughout Europe for seven months in 1891 and again for an extended stay in Paris in 1892, had the quality of an artistic apprenticeship. "It was an 'artistic' journey in the full sense of the word," Ziejka has explained, quoting Wyspiański, "having the goal of giving [him] the imagination of general creativity and civilization in art."[26] Whether it was his tour of gothic cathedrals in France, attending performances of Wagner's *Ring* cycle in Germany, or visiting ancient ruins in Italy, Wyspiański absorbed what was most essential and later transformed it into art in the form of his plays, stage designs, and graphic design. "Wyspiański never appeared in the role of the globetrotter," Ziejka has maintained, "noting surface impressions and remarks. He attempted delve himself into, to discover the secrets of the masterpieces of architecture and art uncovered along the road itself – to enrich himself."[27] Wyspiański transformed the sum of his experiences abroad into the energy of artistic expression, blending elements of the art, music, poetry, and drama he encountered abroad with Polish history, folklore, and mythology to form an artistic palette that was truly, to use the term of the Polish theater director Ludwik Schiller, "monumental."

Europe in the minds of the intellectuals of Young Poland offered the potential of new life or nourishment to the perceived weakened cultural life of the Polish nation. Far from being limited to the major capitals, Polish artists and writers made their way to countries as diverse as Japan, Greece, and the United States.[28] While brief and frequent trips abroad were common, translations of foreign literature became a standard vehicle by which this much-needed sustenance found its way into Poland. Polish journals and literary gazettes of all aesthetic and ideological orientations consistently featured translations of poetry, prose, and criticism from abroad. In this regard, Young Poland's translators augmented physical travel outside of Poland by means of their literary journeys. This foreign exploration was not limited to printed literature, as advances in technology allowed for high-quality reproductions of artwork by foreign artists as well.[29] Podraza-Kwiatkowska has suggested that Young Poland's appreciation of foreign cultures was fundamentally shaped by its tendency toward the synchronicity of ideas. "Time and space," she explained, "surrendered to such a muddied formulation that in consequence it would lead in the future to the exposition of the values of cultural simultaneity and syncretism."[30] It was not that the intellectuals of Young Poland were endeavoring to become European, as Ziejka's argument implies, as much as they were trying to be fully human. Rendering modern foreign literature into Polish brought the world closer through a journey of the imagination, while at the same time contributed to the enrichment of Polish letters by challenging its powers of expression.

The ultimate success of this endeavor rested on the extent to which Young Poland's translators rendered literature from all times and places into meaningful and artful Polish. In his history of Polish literature, Potocki cited Edward Porębowicz, a professor of Romance Languages in Lwów and a translator of an impressive range of European folk songs, as just such a translator. "Thanks to him," Potocki proclaimed, "today we can commune in magnificence with the kingly spirit of the poetry of the world."[31] In addition to folk songs, Porębowicz, who published many of his translations in *Chimera*, answered Miriam's challenge of elevating Polish culture by translating masters of European literature, such as Dante, Byron, and Calderon, as well as folk songs from countries as diverse as Ireland, Portugal, and Norway. "It is clear," Potocki observed, "that the eternal glow of the original shines on the work of this most excellent translator. One should truly praise Porębowicz that he learned to capture this glow in the crystal depths of his soul and redirect it in one great beam of light on the young, emerging world of Polish lyric poetry."[32] For a figure such as Porębowicz, the end goal of translation was not mere cosmopolitanism, but rather it was capturing the essence of the work that mattered most. Young Poland's natural inclination towards syncretism made it possible to transcend national traditions and time periods, so that a journal such as *Chimera* could print translations of ancient English or Scottish ballads alongside the modernist prose of Wacław Berent or the symbolist poetry of Charles Baudelaire.

The act of translation for Young Poland had a dual function. Translations of literature from a wide range of cultures and eras complemented Young Poland's natural tendency toward unity in art. On the other hand, artful translation, such as that by Porębowicz, also had the effect of introducing new poetic forms into Polish poetry. Potocki referred to two such intermediaries, Miriam and the poet Antoni Lange, as "those talents - the essential reflectors of Western changes, brightening the often cellar-like murk of the basement of Polish prison life. Between the two, Lange and Miriam could complete the chapter of the foreign influence on the literature of Young Poland, taking each in turn as if to familiarize

Chapter 3: Modeling Vitality

the poetic fledglings in the native nest with ever fresher nourishment."[33] The sheer volume of the new literature introduced to Polish reading audiences was less important for Young Poland than the quality of translations. This explains why Potocki favored a translator such as Lange over Miriam, because where the latter approached European culture systematically, armed with a ready philosophical and aesthetic plan, Lange as a poet "had the ability to exchange form for form."[34] While ideas had their place, it was the ability to put the Polish experience into words that concerned the creative minds of Young Poland.

Although a great number of highly prolific translators emerged during this period, Lange was prototypical of Young Poland's intellectual-wanderer due to his wide-ranging translation interests.[35] "It would require wide brackets," Potocki explained, "to enumerate all the foreign worlds through which he wandered, beginning with the era of the French 'symbolists' and 'decadents,' and ending with the irreplaceable Upanishads, the ancient Hebraic texts, and ancient Greek literature."[36] The exotic and unfamiliar cultures were of intense interest to Young Poland, but what mattered most was the ability of the translator to render the works of foreign writers as artfully as possible into the Polish language. The combined effect, therefore, was a form of cultural absorption, adding vigor to moribund Poland while at the same time preserving its uniqueness. The exotic did not interest Young Poland simply for the sake of being unusual, but rather for what it could do to meet deeply held Polish needs. The primary drive behind translation was inside out and not the other way around.

What was most remarkable about Young Poland's approach to translation was the central role played by its leading writers. Lange in this regard was not an isolated case. Albeit with varying success, the poet Jan Kasprowicz likewise translated literature from a wide range of periods and cultures, including English, German, Greek, and Dutch. Other writers, such as Tadeusz Boy-Żeleński (1874–1941), concentrated on artfully translating extensively from one or two languages.[37] The act of translation was not limited to literature, as leading intellectuals rendered works by the leading critics and philosophers of the day into Polish as well. In addition to translating works by Poe and Yeats, Lack translated works by Kierkegaard and Walter Pater into Polish. Translations of the critical writings of the leading contemporary thinkers, such Nietzsche, played as equally important a role as literary renditions. In light of the spread of new aesthetic ideas, innovative philosophical treatises on the creative power of the individual were of equal interest to Young Poland as new poetic styles or forms of narration.

It was common practice for literary journals to feature renditions of foreign works by Young Poland's leading writers alongside original Polish-language material. One of the earliest and most influential in this regard was Kraków-based *Life*. The publication of translations of foreign works, both fictional and critical, was an integral part of its artistic mission. In its prospectus for the year 1900, the editorial staff of *Life* went to pains to emphasize its contribution toward the regeneration of Polish cultural life through foreign art and literature. "Today," the editorial staff maintained, "'*Life*' has emerged from its '*Sturm und Drang*' [...] period. Today it finds itself on the road onto which it will calmly and surely progress – and that group of people, which have gathered around '*Life*' begin to believe that through good will and authentically patriotic desire Polish society wants to support [...] the wish for Polish literature to rise to the level of all-European art, so that next to foreign publications, in which previously we have acquired information regarding what is happening in the West or East, we could with pride place the Polish journal: *Life*."[38] The point was not to imitate Western models, but rather to elevate Polish art and literature to the level to which it equaled it. As evidence of this, alongside the Polish writers *Life*'s editorial staff intended to publish in 1900, it listed the planned translations of writers from, among others, France, Norway, Russia, Ireland, Germany, and the Czech lands.[39]

Miriam's sumptuously designed *Chimera* (1901–1907) was one of the few Polish journals to exceed *Life* in this regard. In addition to such diverse writers as Cyprian Kamil Norwid, Samuel Coleridge, Bolesław Leśmian, Ralph Waldo Emerson, Otokar Brzezina, and Tadeusz Miciński, Miriam, as editor, included reproductions of works of art by foreign and Polish artists, including Albrecht Dürer, Franciszek Siedlecki, Hokusai Katsushika, Edward Okuń, and Edward Burne-Jones. In his prospectus for the new journal, published in 1901, Miriam voiced his desire that *Chimera* act as both a champion and defender of high-minded art in Poland. In this regard, Miriam, too, viewed the place of foreign art in *Chimera* in terms of a mission to rescue Polish cultural life from further degradation. "Everything," Miriam lamented, "most often associated with the name 'ideal,' today is a hollow sound, which long ago lost all kinship with its mother, Idea."[40] As an advocate of symbolist art, it was understandable that Miriam bemoaned what he perceived to be an increasing level of materialism in Poland. His keenness, however, to introduce his countrymen to foreign works of art had its limits, as he considered the tendency in Polish society to take a superficial approach to foreign cultural trends to be equally dangerous. "To be a guard," Miriam declared, "to be a sincere, holy, and passionate temple for art issuing from the absolute abode, that is what *Chimera* desires."[41] Taking an approach similar to *Life*, to which he was invited to contribute toward the end of its run, Miriam intended to publish works by the leading Polish and foreign artists, both past and present, in *Chimera*. "Next to our capital creators of the present day," Miriam explained, "the bronzed voices of the forgotten masters of times gone by will be heard; subsequently will pass through the treasures of foreign peoples, whose most treasured works are unknown to us. The appearance of all these treasures will undoubtedly stimulate new, future talents."[42] The drive behind the importation of foreign art and literature was Young Poland's desire for a cultural renaissance, but the means by which this was achieved was to be multi-pronged. While *Chimera* and *Life* were the most committed among the journals of Young Poland to reproducing fine art and literature from abroad, they were far from alone in this practice.[43]

Because of Young Poland's innate tendency toward syncretism, it was not constrained by the same rigid cultural nationalism that distinguished other contemporaneous movements, such as its counterpart Irish-Ireland. On the contrary, the ability of Young Poland to blend together works from a variety of genres, time periods, and nationalities, brought Poland closer to the outside world and freed Polish culture to develop in a number of different directions simultaneously. In journals such as *Life* and *Chimera*, textual translation figured as the primary means by which Polish intellectuals introduced Young Poland to new artistic forms and cultural norms. Just as Polish artists could not limit their work to purely universal elements in pursuit of modern art forms, the translators of Young Poland also operated according to their own Polish sensibilities. Young Poland's translators acted as intercultural agents, bridging the gap between foreign literary forms and the Polish reading audience. For Young Poland, there was no question for Young Poland's translators as to whether a given work was translatable or not.[44] Informed by a syncretic view of art and culture, the intellectuals of Young Poland turned their attention to works of Shakespeare or Rimbaud, Whitman or Kierkegaard, with equal ease. It was ironically Young Poland's acceptance of the impenetrability of human experience and the unity of art, which simplified their tasks as translators. While it was possible for figures such as Lange or Kasprowicz to wander through an array of foreign literatures, they could not do so without relinquishing their identities as Polish poets. Textual translation for Young Poland, therefore, reflected Polish needs and attitudes as much if not more than it did Polish interest in foreign cultures. The physical translation, appearing in one of Young Poland's many journals or in book form, was not just a palimpsest in this regard, but rather it was symbolic of literature's power as the living, revitalizing word. The intellectuals of Young Poland felt that if Poland was to regain its cultural health as a vibrant, independent nation it needed to be an active and connected participant in world culture.

The importation of new artistic impulses from abroad was not limited to high-minded literary journals such as *Life* or *Chimera*. Although the initial impetus for Young Poland as a cultural movement came from the literary world, it expressed itself with equal vigor in the areas of art, music, and drama. The theater posed a slightly different problem for Polish playwrights and directors than did straightforward literary translation. The act of importing new plays and dramatic techniques involved a literary component in the question of repertoire, but it also encompassed new concepts of acting, directing, and stage design. Because drama takes place in a physical environment, the act of performance poses quite different problems for the translator of a play intended for the stage than does a literary work meant for publication. Involving a number of disparate talents, including the director, the actors, the stage designers, and the textual translator, theater added several more layers of complication to the ordinary challenge of literary translation. For Young Poland, the construction of new, modern theaters in Kraków (1893), Lwów (1900), and Warsaw (1913) represented the transformation of the Polish theater in physical and technical terms. It is not insignificant that the last of these theaters to be constructed was Arnold Szyfman's *Teatr Polski* (The Polish Theater). Szyfman's theater was the first truly modern, independent theater to take hold in Warsaw, and was influential in preparing the way for the establishment of a national theater in independent Poland. Above all, the performative aspect of theater places it in a distinct category of translation. Along with the importation of foreign works of drama come new theories of stage design, directing, and acting. With the rise to prominence of the theater during the Young Poland period, the translation of dramatic works for the stage formed a quintessential part of the effort to renew the Polish dramatic repertoire and to modernize the Polish theater.

With the emergence of Tadeusz Pawlikowski in 1893, when he was made director of the newly built Civic Theater in Kraków, Young Poland experienced the same kind of vibrant change in the theater that it did in literature. While Pawlikowski did not translate foreign works into Polish himself, he was nonetheless equally innovative in introducing new forms of performance. In changing the traditional approach to directing, Pawlikowski and the directors succeeding him triggered a chain reaction that resulted in the overall modernization of the Polish theater. New styles of directing required an entirely different repertoire of plays. Without such material in the Polish repertoire at the outset of this period, Pawlikowski drew upon the importation of dramas from outside Poland or older, previously unperformed plays to meet the initial demand. Pawlikowski not only commissioned translations of new, foreign works, but he also paid for his actors or fellow directors to attend theatrical performances abroad with the hope of finding new material to debut in Poland. In time, Pawlikowski's solicitation of original Polish plays would bring to the stage a new generation of playwrights, including Wyspiański, Gabriela Zapolska (1857–1921), Lucjan Rydel (1870–

Chapter 3: Modeling Vitality

1918), and Jan August Kisielewski (1876–1918). Under Pawlikowski, the initial stages of the modern Polish theater began to take shape.

The development of a new dramatic repertoire and style of direction also entailed change in the field of acting. Faced with the new demands of naturalistic, symbolic, and psychological drama, Polish actors had to abandon traditional acting techniques in favor of an ensemble approach to performance that took into consideration more expressive forms of dramatic expression. Changes in the artistry of modern drama likewise demanded innovation in regard to questions of infrastructure and technology. New lighting techniques and rotating stages were two of the changes needed to create the proper atmosphere to bring modern theater to life. The artistic approach to stage design also gained in importance under Pawlikowski, attracting artists such as Karol Frycz (1877–1963) and Franciszek Siedlecki (1867–1934) to the theater. In his careful attention to developments taking place in the theaters in the West, Pawlikowski ensured that the Young Poland theater remained closely connected to the changes taking place in the broader European movement of theatrical reform. Layered in this way, performance on the stage developed in parallel to the general practice of literary importation already taking place in the Young Poland period.

As much as it was influenced by the introduction of new literary and dramatic forms, Young Poland was equally engaged in the practice of cultural translation. Much in the same way that Polish intellectuals looked abroad for new writers or artists to reinvigorate cultural life in Poland, Polish critics turned their attention to developments taking place in the international arena as a means of finding ways to meet the cultural, social, and politics needs of the Polish nation. Ranging from Miriam's analysis of the revitalizing power of the Belgian symbolists or the social importance of the Parisian art theaters, on the one hand, to the socially engaged articles of Wilhelm Feldman, the editor of *Krytyka* (The Critique), on the other, Young Poland maintained an abiding interest in the cultural and political developments taking place outside of Poland. While the notoriety of the modernist, art for art's sake adherents within Young Poland endowed it with the reputation as a socially and politically detached bohemian art movement, its level of engagement in developments abroad revealed quite a different story. Polish critics, such as Adolf Nowaczyński and Wilhelm Feldman, analyzed the cultural developments taking place in the West and East with the hope of influencing the direction of social, political, and cultural life in Poland.

The political reality facing Poles in the Austrian, Russian, and Prussian partitions distinguished projects of cultural translation from either the textual or the performative forms. The problems of censorship and political sensitivity meant that the arts in Young Poland were not immune to geopolitical matters, but the concern of cultural criticism with the existing reality and potential future of Poland endowed it with an additional degree of sensitivity. To this end, cultural translation involved different levels of negotiation, with the critic oscillating between the foreign example, the national community, and the dominant political reality. If viewed in terms of Sakai's characterization of the nation as an active subject, it is clear that Young Poland's cultural critics, such as Nowaczyński, were as involved in representing the Polish nation as their fellow writers, artists, and performers.[45] Where the latter operated in terms of creative invention, the former dealt with the language of analysis. Just as it was remarkable that the literary translators of Young Poland were the very same people producing its literature, talented Polish writers took an active part in the practice of cultural translation. In addition to being talented creative writers in their own right, figures such as Nowaczyński, Boy-Żeleński, and Stanisław Brzozowski (1878–1911) were also formidable critics in their own right. The involvement of creative individuals in the parallel processes of creation and translation was an indication of the extent to which they represented two sides of the same coin. The overlapping qualities of translation in its various forms revealed Young Poland as a movement dedicated to the larger project of cultural and national revitalization.

The prevalence of translation in its various forms during the Young Poland period was indicative of deep need for vitality in Polish culture that brought it into being as a movement. Regardless of their status as the inhabitants of a long divided, oppressed nation, Polish intellectuals viewed themselves as equal participants in the predominant European culture. Limited, if not entirely disenfranchised politically, members of the Polish intelligentsia viewed the emanations of innovation and change scattered throughout the European continent at the close of the nineteenth century as evidence of cultural potency, if not viability. Even if considered in the broader sphere of Polish politics, openness to and the importation of ideas from the outside world were commonplace. One of the chief architects of Polish conservative nationalism, Roman Dmowski, was known for advocating an ideology of cultural self-sufficiency. Dmowski's brand of integral nationalism, however, was not immune to foreign influence, as over time he came to view Japan as a model for Poland to emulate.[46] Polish socialists were similarly bound by ideology, but figures such as Bolesław Limanowski and Stanisław Mendelson adapted their internationalist politics to create a unique form of Polish socialism informed by the Polish need for social equality and national liberation. The same double perspective that informed Young Poland, therefore, shaped the need to look abroad for solutions to Poland's pressing social and political woes.

Chapter 3: Modeling Vitality

Young Poland's relationship to the outside world via translation represented a contemporary response to the initial tragedy that befell the Polish nation at the close of the eighteenth century. The double challenge of preventing the erosion of the national identity and of ensuring the continued vitality of the living culture was the story of the Polish experience in the nineteenth century. As the inheritors of this twofold problem, it was logical that Young Poland came to be referred by some as Neo-romanticism. Elements of lyricism, folk coloring, and historicism were characteristic of both movements, and the openness of the Romantics to Europe was similar to that of Young Poland. Understanding Young Poland as a reformulation of Romanticism, however, would be a misconception. The Positivists, too, inherited the crisis of the eighteenth century. Eschewing the intense individualism and revolutionary fervor of the Romantics, their response was to focus on strengthening Polish society through the implementation of rational social and political policies. In its desire to revitalize and elevate Polish culture from within, Young Poland also exhibited elements of neo-Positivism in its response to the century-old Polish question. Faced with the ongoing reality of partition within Poland and a perceived sense of cultural stagnation, Young Poland steered clear of extreme expressions of ideology and social policy. The underlying beauty of art for this new generation of artists was that it made natural self-expression possible, while avoiding at the same time the common pitfalls of experienced by past generations of Poles.

III. THE ARTISTIC IDENTITY OF YOUNG POLAND: COSMOPOLITANISM AND ESSENTIALISM

The question of Young Poland's openness toward foreign cultural influence and Polish national identity was not without controversy. The modernist aesthetics of the art for art's sake movement alarmed many conservative Polish critics, who feared the weakening or contamination of Polish culture from foreign elements. Tensions peaked with a series of polemics between two conservative commentators, Stanisław Szczepanowski and Marian Zdziechowski, and a young contributor to *Life*, Artur Górski. In addition to framing the discussion over Poland's proper relationship *vis à vis* Europe, the debate signaled Young Poland's coming of age as a movement. Appearing in *Life* in April of 1898, the placement and timing of Górski's article "Młoda Polska" (Young Poland) came to be viewed as a manifesto of the artistic sensibilities of the new generation of artists. This placed Yeats's introduction into Poland, which had taken place two months earlier, in a curious relationship with Young Poland's bold self-assertion.

Young Poland's first exposure to Yeats, therefore, took place in the same climate of debate surrounding Poland's relationship to new art and to the Europe.

In an article published in the conservative nationalist organ, *Słowo Polskie* (The Polish Word), in 1898 entitled "*Dezynfekcja Prądów Europejskich*" (The Disinfection of European Trends), Szczepanowski, referring primarily to French literature, expressed outrage at the negative influence recent trends European literature had had on Polish cultural life. "In recent years," Szczepanowski complained, "*guano* has become its exclusive product. For several years it presents itself as one great stinking pile of manure, where among a variety of phosphorescence and miasma it forms the quintessence of putridity: *guano*."[47] Szczepanowski's objection to the new, modern literary trends was not so much a moral one as it was aesthetic and, more importantly, nationalistic. In terms of aesthetics, he disdained the adherents of all the new *isms* in literature and art – decadentism, parnassism, impressionism and so forth – because, in his mind, they valued novelty over artistic merit. "What is most strange," Szczepanowski maintained, "is the pretension as if these authors are bringing in something new. This novelty exists only for the ignorant."[48] It was not the case that Szczepanowski wanted to cut Poland completely off from contact with Europe. On the contrary, he acknowledged the inevitability of contact with the outside world and its necessity to keep the nation strong. The problem, for him, was that he felt Poland had been weakened under the influence of unhealthy literary fashions imported from abroad. "All European trends," Szczepanowski maintained, "sooner or later make their way to us. It must be this way and it is good that it is."[49] He perceived each culture, however, as containing both positive and negative elements, which could either be a source of strength or weakness for the civilization receiving it. "Thus, the fatal necessity," Szczepanowski cautioned, "that the nation, which does not learn to assimilate itself to those civilizing strengths, dies from civilizing disease. Those, therefore, who stand guard over national tradition should carry out, so to speak, a moral quarantine to disinfect European trends, so that only those healthy elements reach us and are of use, not of ruin."[50] The challenge, in his view, was for Poland to take advantage as much as possible of what foreign cultures had to offer, but without relinquishing its cultural autonomy. As the arbiter of Polish cultural life, Szczepanowski wanted to reign in the individualism of Young Poland by subordinating it to the prevailing ideology of the national tradition. In doing so, Szczepanowski could not have taken a position further removed from the new, Young Poland generation.

The main target of Szczepanowski's vitriol was the young, bohemian generation, which he considered to be entirely under the influence of the "art for art's sake" trend in European art circles. Szczepanowski warned that what was considered to be progressive in art in actuality was contributing the moral decline of the nation and, at bottom, was unpatriotic. "The Greeks," Szczepanowski asserted wryly, "did not look for beauty when the Persians threatened and they defended the independence of their homeland. But as long as the heroic mood lasted, all the unwitting offspring of their spirit donned the undying garment of beauty. Seek heroism and perfection, and you will have beauty and fortune."[51] The young generation's preoccupation with aesthetics and new literary trends meant that they had their priorities wrong. In a position reflecting his background as a businessman and a politician in Galicia, Szczepanowski praised the heroic spirit of the Romantics, while stressing the need to rebuild the nation. "In the combined strength of individuals," Szczepanowski concluded, "lies the strength of the nation. [...] Every emissary of demoralization is hellish."[52] The intellectuals of Young Poland, ironically, could not have agreed more with the conservative critic. The source of this demoralization, and where to find the appropriate antidote, was where the two sides parted ways.

Zdziechowski, a literary critic, joined Szczepanowski in his criticism of the young generation's seemingly blind acquiescence to foreign literary trends that same year, expressing his views in a talk later published as *"Płazy a ptaki"* (Reptiles and Birds). While acknowledging that Szczepanowski had exaggerated his fears somewhat, Zdziechowski pointed out that the issue at hand was actually a continuation of a very old debate. "The battle between Szczepanowski and *"Life"*," Zdziechowski explained, "is not an argument between aesthetes and politicians, but is an expression of a very old debate between two worldviews on beauty and art – and in this case I stand firmly on Szczepanowski's side."[53] In a reflection of his strong Catholic values, Zdziechowski did not object to importation of foreign artistic and literary forms *per se*, but rather he was troubled by the lack of moral substance in the new aesthetic trends. He felt the young generation's inordinate concern with content and form, in pursuit of artistic truth, to be lacking the crucial element of the artist's soul. "In the work of an artist," Zdziechowski maintained, "we look for, though often fail to find, the soul of the artist, because life is the search for the soul, so that we may be able to love and honor it."[54] He believed that the young generation of writers and artists, taking their cue from European modernism, had made the mistake of pursuing art forms that opted for the cult of sensuality devoid of any divine presence. Expressions of the "naked soul" of the artist, far from being spiritually or aesthetically true, in his view, were deeply troubling and ultimately harmful. "Therefore," Zdziechowski argued, "virtue, heroism, fatherland, faith – in a word, perfection, the moral ideal above all, and after that artistic beauty as a reward for work on the realization of the ideal moral – this is the slogan of those who hold the position of the author's article about disinfection in the relation of art to life: good plus beauty."⁵⁵ For Zdziechowski, art that merely expressed the artist's internal feelings or personal vision constituted the weakest form of dilettantism. All was not lost, however, as he pointed to other leading European cultural figures, such as John Ruskin and Leo Tolstoi, who managed to balance artistic beauty with a strong moral conviction. "Today young Poland noisily proclaims itself," Zdziechowski concluded optimistically, "we do not know what it will bear, but despite all the unsettling signs, we do not have cause as of yet to lose hope."⁵⁶

The most notable response from the young generation of new artists and writers to these articles came from Górski. Published serially under the pseudonym "Quasimodo" in *Life* in 1898, Górski's article, "*Młoda Polska*" (Young Poland), came to be perceived as a manifesto for the emerging aesthetics of the young generation, which afterward adopted "Young Poland" as an all-encompassing term for its diverse artistic interests. Reacting against the programmatic tone of Szczepanowski's and Zdziechowski's articles, Górski defended the artistic freedom of Young Poland. "Let programs create people who want to act," Górski asserted, "we do not have that in mind at all. On the contrary, we write precisely in order not to act. Literature is our maiden."⁵⁷ Górski took exception to the insinuation that the younger generation was somehow less patriotic because of its interest in new artistic ideas. Turning the tables on his opponents, he argued that the younger generation's willingness to plumb the depths of their souls was of more service to the nation than the older generation's cautious conservatism. "Here in Galicia," Górski complained, "talent and love of art gives one the right to nothing, neither to bread or life, nor to social respect; it only gives one the right to one thing, insult. We drowned because we swam to the depths, in a storm, at night, looking for pearls and coral at the bottom of the sea for our Homeland – you did not even manage to leave the shore."⁵⁸

At the heart of the matter was the older generation's objection to the notion of artistic freedom. Rather than be considered as attempts by Polish artists to seek universal truths, the conservative figures within Polish society condemned Young Poland out of hand as dilettantes, blindly aping trendy fashions in Western art and contributing nothing to the Polish national cause. It was precisely on this point, however, that Górski struck his hardest blow at his opponents. "You ask, where is our 'heroic deed?" Górski declared, "And with what right do you pose us this question? [...] Are you not the representatives of that generation, which published *Stańczyk's Briefcase* and the theory of triloyalism? Was it not you who looked on indifferently as we were raised in schools with no patriotism?! [sic] with even no feelings of national individuality? We learned general history from German... handbooks, wrapped in German spirit and worldview, national

Chapter 3: Modeling Vitality

history was treated *per non est*, and all demonstrations most severely forbidden."[59] Whether it was a university protest, an expression of national feeling by workers and peasants, or the artistic expression of a young poet, Górski castigated the older generation for its shortsightedness. Blind conservatism such as this, in Górski's view, squandered Poland's most vital asset, the talent of its youth. By crippling the future of the nation in this way, there was little hope and little need for Polish autonomy in the years to come.

In opposition to the conservative protectionism of the older generation, Górski asserted the necessity of artistic freedom. While stressing his love for the Polish nation, he argued that the partitions of Poland had cut the nation off from its own past and altered its natural relationship to the outer world. The tradition, therefore, heralded by the older generation was only that of post-partition Poland, which did not take into consideration Poland's deep cultural and historical roots. "We declare," Górski insisted, "that we do not measure the value of beliefs by a specification and for each principle we offer full respect, if it is based on a sincere foundation – it is a different matter, when certain emotional or intellectual theories erect a Chinese wall and a low ceiling."[60] Young Poland's openness to foreign cultures grew out of its desire to return the country to its rightful position as a healthy nation among nations. "And understood thus," Górski explained, referring to the experience of the nineteenth century, "'tradition' and 'national spirit' break us – and we shatter ourselves with her from a young age. Other factors combine to create the modern Polish soul – we want to give that expression in art, though it is in opposition to the older generation. If there is harmony between the artist and society that is when masterpieces appear, about which the entire nation can be enthusiastic with one common mind and heroic feeling."[61] The contention of critics such as Szczepanowski and Zdziechowski that art be subservient to an ideological position, whether it was nationalist or socialist, meant that they and not the young generation were the true decadents. By putting up a wall to outside ideas and resisting individuality of expression, they were demoralizing the cultural atmosphere in Poland and ensuring that it would continue to disintegrate internally. "We are living in a time of great bankruptcy of ideas," Górski pointed out, "which not long ago stirred the mind, proclaimed the spring of peoples, and inspired poets.[62]" The generation that comprised Young Poland, by joining in the prevailing trend toward individualism in Europe, sought to liberate Poland in both heart and mind. "New artistic and literary trends have emerged," Górski maintained, "not uniform, nor taken from one source, but possessing something in common, that they were all in opposition to the objective method and materialistic understanding of the human soul."[63]

Górski was less troubled by accusations of Young Poland's immorality, but he did object to claims that the new forms of artistic expression they adopted were unpatriotic. "We love everything that is native," Górski stressed, "we believe in the great future of our nation, and our strongest desire is to be the basis of praise of our Fatherland, which we will serve to the last beat of our hearts."[64] Besides feeling slighted for not receiving the respect he felt the talents of his generation deserved, Górski also bristled at the thought that Young Poland was responsible for importing harmful Western ideas into Polish cultural life. "In this foundation of our native culture," Górski declared, "we stand unmoved, like a tree is rooted in the soil – and if we give our careful attention to the West, we do so as other nations do: we take from their literature that which could have some use for us, but what is harmful and foreign to us, we discard like a used lemon.[65] Far from advocating a position of pure aestheticism, Górski concluded by stressing the maintenance of Poland's national identity. "And that is precisely why," Górski explained, "we insist that our art be Polish, Polish through and through – because if it loses its nativeness, it loses its strength, value and its reason for being."[66] In support of this position, Górski singled out Poland's national poet, Adam Mickiewicz, who succeeded in raising Polish poetry to a level on par with European literature but who did so through an intensely held individualism. Expressing what was true and internal, for Young Poland artists and writers, was to be authentically Polish.

While Górski's response to Young Poland's conservative critics represented a remarkable assertion of both its openness to foreign cultural impulses and its deeply held Polishness, the most extreme expression of the modernist aesthetics of the nascent cultural movement would come a year later with the publication of Przybyszewski's "Confiteor" in *Life* in 1899. In the article, Przybyszewski, the journal's editor, sent a clear message to Young Poland's detractors that it would not accept any limitations to its artistic freedom. Where Górski called for artistic freedom as a way to bolster the life of the nation, Przybyszewski argued for the complete separation of art and society. "Art," Przybyszewski insisted, "has no goal, it is a goal in and of itself, it is an absolute, because it is a reflection of the absolute – the soul. And because it is an absolute, it cannot be used in any score, it cannot be in service of any idea, it is the mistress, the genesis, from which all life arose."[67] Art that had a tendency of any kind, whether it be the conservative patriotism of Szczepanowski or the moral concerns of Zdziechowski, ceased to be art in the true sense. For Przybyszewski, art was a metaphysical experience, with the artist plumbing his soul to express the eternal, unchanging truths of human existence. The artist, therefore, could not be beholden to political ideologies or social philosophies, but rather functioned as a priest with art as the highest religion.

Chapter 3: Modeling Vitality

Przybyszewski's extreme defense of the autonomy of art resembled much more closely the kind of amoral, unpatriotic decadent art feared by Szczepanowski and Zdziechowski. Przybyszewski's insistence on the absolute independence of the artist did make the relationship between art and the nation a problematic one. "The artist," Przybyszewski maintained, "is neither a servant nor a director, he belongs neither to the nation nor to the world, he serves no idea nor any society."[68] As the editor of *Life*, however, Przybyszewski was involved in the elevation of Polish art and literature. Despite his position of extreme aestheticism, Przybyszewski could not entirely rule out the place of art in the life of the nation. Art in its truest, purest form was autonomous, but it was not entirely antithetical to the nation for the latter, too, had its origins in the unchanging eternity of human existence. "The nation," Przybyszewski allowed, "is a portion of eternity, and the roots of the artist are embedded in it, from it, from the native soil the artist draws his most vital strength."[69] Young Poland, therefore, drew from the vital, unchanging soul of the Polish nation in order to create pure, Polish art.

In this way, a journal such as *Life*, which published the finest art and literature from Poland and abroad, found a way to be modern while showcasing Poland's distinctive contribution to world culture. It also inspired Polish artists to seek new ways to tap into their true, Polish strengths by printing the finest in Polish and foreign literature and art.[70] As a result, Przybyszewski and the other contributors to *Life*, and by association Young Poland as a whole, could be viewed as making a valuable contribution to the revitalization of Polish cultural life.

> Our ideal, editorial effort will be to offer only those works, which fertilize either the thought or the new form of the youngest generation of artists, to raise the journal to such a level so that no one will need to reach to another publication for information of a purely artistic nature. And in order to accomplish this, we have linked to our editorial staff the greatest critical strengths from abroad, so that our publication does not provide information, as often happens in Polish periodicals, from the tenth hand of people poorly or superficially conversant with individual literatures, but information originating from people, who have followed the entire literature for years and live in it.[71]

Bound by the universal nature of art, the relationship between Poland and the outside world was, from the perspective of Przybyszewski and Young Poland, an integral one. Openness to impulses from the West and East enhanced not detracted from Polish culture, because it inspired Polish artists and writers to seek new ways of expressing what was authentic about the Polish nation. The closing of Life in 1900 meant the loss of one of the most dynamic forces in the

The Impact of Irish-Ireland on Young Poland, 1890–1919

Polish literature of the day, but not before it played a critical role helping to establish Young Poland as an open and vibrant cultural movement.

As Young Poland continued to develop in the early twentieth century, the challenge of reconciling the desire to create art that was both modern and Polish only intensified. The polemics over the place of foreign art in the 1890s revealed the tension between the principles of cosmopolitanism and essentialism to be one of the defining characteristics of Young Poland. Shaped by the particular needs of Polish intellectuals working in the areas of criticism, poetry, or the theater, the critical reception of foreign cultural impulses within Young Poland took place along a continuum between these two principles. As one of the only cultural institutions under Polish control, albeit constrained by censorship, the theater surfaced as an especially important area in which Young Poland struggled to reconcile questions of artistry of identity.

With the introduction of William Butler Yeats in Jerzy Płoński's article in *Life* in 1898, Irish-Ireland emerged early on as a cultural movement developing along a similar trajectory and facing the analogous problem of balancing art and identity as Young Poland. Far from being the isolated observations of a foreign correspondent in London, the light Płoński shed on the new Irish poet was only the beginning of what would prove to be a consistent and sincere interest on the part of Young Poland in on the cultural developments taking place in Ireland. The nature of Irish-Ireland's impact on Young Poland would continue to develop as both movements matured and succeeded in establishing their respective identities. Over the course of the next twenty years, Irish-Ireland's ability to meet the changing needs of Young Poland established it position as a largely unheralded, but vital contributor to the ongoing processes of cultural and national revival that took place prior to the achievement of independence in 1919.

CHAPTER FOUR

BETWEEN ART AND THE NATION:

YOUNG POLAND AND IRISH-IRELAND, 1989-1908

In her study of the reception of Yeats in Poland, Jolanta Dudek maintains that Polish intellectuals expressed interest in Irish-Ireland precisely because it harmonized with the prevailing cultural predilections of Young Poland.[1] Dudek's observation hints at the manifold commonalities that existed between Young Poland and Irish-Ireland, such as a renewed interest in folk culture and mythology, a deepening lyricism, and an intense debate over questions of modernity and cultural-national identity. What she fails to describe, however, is the extent to which Polish intellectuals appropriated Irish-Ireland as a means of bolstering their own creative work at what was a crucial stage in Young Poland's development. Whether it took the form of translations of Yeats by Stanisław Lack and Jan Kasprowicz or stage productions of John Millington Synge by Tadeusz Pawlikowski, the vibrancy and increasing cultural currency of Irish Ireland made it attractive to Polish writers and artists as a means of enhancing and reinforcing modernist art in Poland.

I. ARTISTIC ESSENTIALISM: THE POLISH DEBUT OF W. B. YEATS

In February 1898, Polish readers were introduced for the first time to William Butler Yeats in the regular column of one of *Life*'s English foreign correspondents, Jerzy Płoński, entitled "Z nad Tamizy" (From the Thames). Płoński's article was proof positive that the editorial staff at *Life* were serious about publishing only informed, first-hand accounts of the latest developments in European arts and letters. In the first installment of the article, Płoński brought the young Irish poet to the attention of his Polish reading audience as one of the brightest new talents to appear on the "English" literary scene.² By the end of his article, however, it was clear that Płoński not only considered Yeats to be emerging as a distinctly Irish presence within English literature, but also that he shared a deep affinity with Young Poland in his determination to balance essentialism and cosmopolitanism in the pursuit of art.

Albeit a little-known foreign correspondent for *Life*, Płoński embodied Young Poland's preoccupation with seeking out exotic new sources of art and literature. In his article, Płoński represented England and English literature as being something rather new to Polish readers. This was reflective of the comparatively weak presence of English literature in Poland at the close of the nineteenth century. While it is true that over the previous quarter of the century English literature, both the Romantics, particularly Shelley, and the Pre-Raphaelites, such as Ruskin and Browning, attracted increasing attention from Polish intellectuals, on the whole it was not as well known in Poland as its continental rivals. Given Yeats's own ambiguous position at the time in English and Irish literature, oscillating as he was back and forth between the literary circles of London and Dublin, it was not surprising that Płoński framed the Irish poet's initial introduction in light of literary developments then taking place in England. Yeats, along with Thomas Hardy and a number of other lesser-known writers, was part of an efflorescence of new English literary talent. "In all areas," Płoński explained, referring to English literature, "pulsates that blood and beat of life, appearing not only in the intensification of production, but mainly in the clear effort of nearly all writers to bring to literature something of their own, something in a sense above all new."³ Płoński believed the diversity of approaches in English literature were a fresh change, in comparison to French literature, in which all innovation suffocated under the crowds of imitators and new movements calcified into cliques and schools. In Płoński's estimation, Yeats clearly had something to offer not only English literature, but also to Polish reading audiences. "[Yeats's]volume of fantastic stories or poetic prose," Płoński maintained, "under the title 'Secret Rose' [sic] afford me the opportunity to present readers of *Life* this great poet."⁴ Although Irish literature was decidedly more exotic than either English or French literature, by introducing Yeats in *Life*, a journal at the creative center of Young Poland, Płoński ensured that it established a presence in Poland at a crucially formative and dynamic period in Young Poland's development.

In the second installment of "From the Thames," it was clear that Płoński's interest in Yeats derived particularly from the Irish poet's ability to tap into the myths and legends of Ireland as a symbolist writer. "Here at once," Płoński pointed out, "the general outline of his [Yeats's] authorial physiognomy emerges:

Chapter 4: Between Art and the Nation

transcendentalism... If he does not always soar out of the earthly sphere, he always resides in an enchanted palace of fable, legend, and myth."[5] Many of the writers of Young Poland, Wyspiański chief among them, were also drawn to the essentializing power of folk tales and ancient myths. In Yeats's poetry, Płoński seemed to have found this perfect balance of individual genius and national mythology. "I do not know," he mused, "if any other nation preserved and produced such an innumerable treasure of myths, or if any other poet could equal Yeats's flights of fantasy. Barely do we pull back the edge of the veil from the temple of the Irish nation, than we stand amazed by the poetic wonders produced in the collective soul of that nation spiritually akin to Poles."[6] In his presentation of Yeats, Płoński touched on one of the central dilemmas of Young Poland. At the same time that young, cosmopolitan Poles were looking abroad for new ideas to revitalize Polish art, they were also engaged in plumbing the depths of their collective cultural and historical identity.

In pointing out the prevalence of folk culture, in the form of local fables, legends and myth, Płoński touched upon an important aspect of Yeats's poetry for Young Poland. Yeats's recognition of the value of the folk imagination put him directly in line with the prevailing preferences of Young Poland at the time. Płoński's real purpose, however, was not to expound upon Irish folklore, but rather to explain to his readers how Yeats utilized the Irish folk imagination to create poetry that was both culturally authentic and universally symbolic.[7] In this way Płoński revealed a great deal about the fundamental artistic identity of Young Poland. "The fervent faith of the Celtic people," he explained, "did not uproot the deep feelings of natural beauty and so all these poetic creations exist in spirit harmoniously with the sacred. Wells, fields, thickets, lonely trees have their own histories, the exuberant but naive imagination of the people colors everything, seeks wonders in everything that impacts it strongly and involves mystery."[8] Płoński could have used the same language to describe the emotionalized visions of the Tatra Mountains in Jan Kasprowicz's poetry collection *Krzak dzikiej róży* (The Wild Rose Bush), or the otherworldly landscape of Kraków in Wyspiański's play *Legenda I* (The Legend). In three years' time, moreover, Wyspiański would feature the *chochoł* (a capsheaf), among a number of other fantastic phantoms, as a major character in his dramatic masterpiece, *Wesele* (The Wedding). For many Poles, Płoński's presentation of Yeats as a visionary would also have evoked memories of Mickiewicz's Parisian lectures, in which he referred to the Poles' in-born gift of second sight, and more recently, of the symbolist aesthetics advocated by influential critics, such as Miriam and Przybyszewski.

For those Poles looking abroad to Paris or Berlin for new artistic impulses, Yeats's ability, as the most prominent Irish Ireland literary figure, to create a unique form of poetry that was both modern and Irish was evidence of the creative potential for Young Poland. "The Irishman," Płoński explained, paraphrasing Yeats, "preserved in less perfect form the visionary gift, which disappeared in more rapidly and happily developing nations."[9] As an artist submerged in this supernatural realm, Yeats's relationship to the Irish folk imagination was of special interest to Płoński and the intellectuals of Young Poland. "Yeats possesses this gift to the highest degree," Płoński maintained, "everything that concerns the true Irish intellect, not excluding cosmic strains, finds perfect expression in his writing. It would be difficult to tell which he is more: Irishman or artist."[10] In this observation, Płoński was approaching the truth about Yeats's present and future development as a poet, as the challenge of trying to unite the Irishman and artist grew increasingly difficult with the rise of vocal Irish nationalist groups.

Young Poland faced a similar challenge of striking a balance between the often-conflicting forces of essentialism and cosmopolitanism. Although it was originally conceived to be a purely artistic movement, Young Poland quickly grew in complexity as Polish writers and artists insisted upon their contribution to the revitalization of Polish culture. "We demand our art to be Polish," Górski insisted in 'Young Poland,' "through and through Polish – because if it loses its native character, it thus loses its strength, value and reason for being."[11] Płoński recognized in Yeats a similar attempt to reconcile these divergent forces. Yeats maintained a visible presence at national events such as anniversary of Robert Emmet's death, but as a poet he expressed his Irishness on a deeper, more symbolic cultural plane. Young Poland as a movement was less interested in the political demonstrations of Irish-Ireland nationalists than it was in Yeats's ability as a poet and playwright to articulate the vitality of Ireland's cultural identity in a modern, poetic medium.

Płoński's analysis of Yeats as a poet addressed many of the challenges that faced the young intellectuals of Young Poland. The primary difficulty evident in Yeats's own situation was that of producing beautiful poetry, devoid of material or ideological tendencies, while at the same time attempting to find a uniquely Irish form of self-expression. "Having absorbed himself in the national mythology and received her spirit," Płoński emphasized, "[Yeats] repudiated almost everything that is not tied to Erin. That world of magic for him is a totally real world, because it is – ideal. It exists, because in his view all things exist only as a matter of immortal imagination and present themselves appropriately to mood, which is also immortal."[12] Yeats, therefore, was instinctively attractive to Young Poland as a writer whose Irish identity was inseparable from his vocation as a poet. In this regard, Yeats represented precisely the type of poet Miriam had envisioned in his landmark articles in the early 1890s. By refusing to

Chapter 4: Between Art and the Nation

separate the transcendental and the ethnographic in his poetry, Yeats retained the ability to access the internal and external facets of his identity. It was clear from Płoński's analysis of Yeats that he viewed the Irish poet to be both an innovator and a kindred spirit. "The world is grateful to the poet for revealing himself," Płoński concluded, "and although it resides so terribly far from our trivial intellectual sphere that foreign and frightened we enter the land of the poet – he has managed to speak to and to enchant readers."[13] Indicating his awareness of the kind of criticism conservative figures such as Szczepanowski and Zdziechowski had been leveling at Young Poland, Płoński pointed out that Yeats was neither a modernist dilettante, nor an obscure, unreadable symbolist poet. On the contrary, he rightly predicted that Yeats would produce an Irish literary masterpiece sometime in the near future.

Płoński's critique of Yeats, with its equal emphasis on the latter's identity as both a symbolist and an Irish writer, revealed the extent to which Yeats was in harmony with the goal of a new, symbolist art that began in the early 1890s with Miriam and was then further reinforced by Przybyszewski and others at the turn of the century. Consistent with the general character of Young Poland as a cultural movement, Polish symbolism was a syncretic approach, which posited that art should contain something eternal and that the visible world was merely an illusion, or symbol, of this hidden truth.[14] "Every being," Miriam explained in his 1891 article on Maeterlinck, "every object, every occurrence has in it a hidden, uniquely true meaning, which always leads us to infinity."[15] Because of this dualistic conception of existence, which demanded of the artist an intellectual and a transcendental consciousness, art had to deal with the essence of things and, as such, had at its core an eternal, unchanging quality. "Art," Przybyszewski maintained in 'Confiteor'"is the reflection of the life of the soul in all its emanations, independent of that which is good or bad, ugly or beautiful."[16] Symbolism appealed to Young Poland artists, because it allowed the possibility of pure, idealized forms of creative expression, while still satisfying their inherent need for cultural essentialism. In stark contrast to their Positivist predecessors, for Young Poland symbolism made it possible to be both artistically pure and authentically Polish. Fables and legends were a particularly useful means of satisfying both of these desires, because they represented a synthesis of history and myth, or humanity's external and internal sides. This is precisely what Ignacy Matuszewski pointed out in his critical analysis of Słowacki's poetic masterpiece, *Król Duch* (King Spirit).[17] In this way, artists through the act of creation could not only penetrate the depths of the Absolute, but through legends and myths they could also experience the "pierwiastek metafizyczny" (metaphysical element) of the nation.[18] Płoński's description of Yeats, therefore, immediately placed the Irish poet alongside Słowacki, Maeterlinck, and the French Symbolists in the context of Young Poland's ongoing discourse over the aesthetics of symbolism, or new art. "Great art, vital art, undying art," Miriam insisted, "was and always will be symbolic."[19] The challenge for Young Poland, as Yeats had so successfully met for Irish-Ireland, was to create art that was not only symbolic, but authentically Polish as well.

Despite Płoński's high praise of Yeats, his article did not immediately result in the publication of any of the Irish poet's work in *Life*. Plans, however, had been in preparation for publishing Yeats's "Rosa Alchemica," as well as works by a number of other English writers, including Wilde and Swinburne, but they were left unrealized when the Kraków journal ceased publication in 1900.[20] When the first translation of a work by Yeats appeared in another Kraków journal, *Nowe Słowo* (The New Word), in 1902, it was no accident that it came from a writer who had played a key role on the editorial staff of *Life* from its inception, Stanisław Lack (1876–1909). Lack had been one of the chief promoters of the aesthetics of new art on the editorial staff of *Life*, developing a dense style of criticism interwoven with elements of impressionism and symbolism. Well traveled and multilingual, as a critic and translator for *Life*, Lack played an active role in defending the aesthetics of extreme literary modernism in Poland.[21] Following the collapse of *Life* in 1900, Lack traveled extensively abroad, spending time in France, Italy, and the United States. Returning to Kraków in 1902 to write for *The New Word*, a progressive journal aimed first and foremost at addressing women's social issues, Lack continued the work of *Life* in a column entitled "Literatura zagraniczna" (Foreign Literature). Because of its primary designation as a social journal, *The New Word* did not have the same cachet as *Life*, nor did it share its heightened aesthetic focus. Lack would eventually gain greater influence over its artistic orientation in 1903, when he became the journal's literary director. His translation of Yeats's story "The Heart of Spring" early on in his term at *The New Word* not only suggests a degree of continuity of interest in the Irish poet, but it also illustrates the critical approach Lack was developing and would soon apply to Wyspiański with great effect.

Generally associated with the Art for Art's sake movement in Poland, Lack stood apart as both a critic and a translator within Young Poland. His influence on Young Poland is difficult to measure, in part because of his premature death in 1909, stemming from a chronic lung ailment. By the late 1890s he had moved away from the subjective approach to art of his contemporaries and toward an understanding of it as a reflection of the "eternal presence" (*wieczna obecność*) of nature, prefiguring aspects of the work of the French philosopher Henri Bergson. The opaqueness of Lack's critical work, however, was intentional, for

Chapter 4: Between Art and the Nation

Lack understood the role of the critic to be much like that of the artist. For him, the purpose of criticism was not to explain or to inform, but rather to unveil fundamental, unchanging truths. "New criticism," he asserted in his landmark series, 'The Review of Reviews,' "is symbolic, solely, and as a result it becomes a work of art, as well as a symbol."[22] The result, as Wojciech Głowala has argued in his foreword to Lack's writings, was a style of literary criticism that was an art form in and of itself, but at the cost of comprehensibility.[23] "The artist," Lack maintained, "similarly to religion (art is religion), connects the individuality of man to his eternal type, which he calls God, Nature; either way, the name is indifferent. In this way, the individuality of the artist becomes an instant, a moment, which under the hand of a second artist [the critic] rises to the meaning of a symbol."[24] Lack drew upon the vocabulary of symbolism, but in doing so he created a critical language that was entirely his own.

It is because of Lack's complex style that "The Heart of Spring" proved to be such an illuminating work for him to have chosen as a translator. Yeats's story describes the preparations of an elderly mystic for death after a long life of contemplation. Afraid for his master but more frightened by his contact with the supernatural world, the young servant asks the old man what will become of him. The mystic explains that in order to understand the meaning of human existence, he devoted his life to study of its secrets by communing with nature and interacting with the fairies and spirits of the land. Informed by one of the fairies that the moment of transformation was near, the old man instructs the young adept to prepare his hut, the ruins of a small monastery destroyed by the Queen's men, with an array of green branches and flowers. Following his master's orders unthinkingly, the young servant returns at dawn the following morning to find his master dead amidst the symbolic adornments. Unable to recognize the traces of pollen from the flowers on the old man's chest or the fulsome song of a thrush alighting from a nearby bush as signs of his master's transcendence, the servant sadly concludes that his master had been foolish to abandon his simple life of religious contemplation. On one level, "The Heart of Spring" functioned as a metaphor for Yeats's conception of the fate artist in society, but on a deeper, more significant level the story touched upon the power of art to reveal the perpetual, universal truths of human existence.

Norman Jeffares has suggested that *The Secret Rose* for Yeats constituted above all a conscious attempt to distance himself from popular literature by establishing an aristocratic literature in Ireland.[25] "[*The Secret Rose*] is at any rate," Yeats concluded, in a letter to John O'Leary in May of 1897, "an honest attempt towards that aristocratic esoteric Irish literature, which has been my chief ambition. We have a literature for the people but nothing yet for the few."[26]

The Impact of Irish-Ireland on Young Poland, 1890–1919

As if to underscore this point, Yeats prefaced *The Secret Rose* with a quote from the play *Axel*, by Villiers de L'Isle Adam, which read, "As for living, our servants will do that for us."²⁷ In "The Heart of Spring," the old man's young servant unthinkingly carries out his duties, ignorant of the "Song of the Immortal Powers," to which his master dedicated his energies to understanding.

> 'It were better for him,' said the lad, 'to have said his prayers and kissed his beads!' He looked at the threadbare blue velvet, and saw it was covered with the pollen of the flowers, and while he was looking at it a thrush, who had alighted among the boughs that were piled against the window, began to sing.²⁸

> – Byłoż lepiej – rzekł chłopiec – odmawiać pacierze i koronki, [...] Spojrzał na wyszarzały niebieski płaszcz aksamity i widział, że pokryty był pyłkiem kwiatów, a kiedy tak nań patrzył, drozd, który był wyfrunął z pośród gałęzi nagromadzonych pod oknem, zaczął śpiewać.²⁹

The inability of the old man's servant to comprehend his act of transcendence for Yeats mirrored the failure of popular society to appreciate non-literal conceptions of human existence and by extension, to value art that flew in the face of mundane reality.³⁰ It was the lonely fate of the artist to be consumed by the pursuit of art, which Yeats symbolized through the death and spiritual rebirth of the old master. The old man, who embodied Yeats's idea of the artistic elite, recognized in his charge a fundamental blindness to the transcendence of his spiritual passage, taking it almost as a sad fact of human existence. "'You are afraid,'" the mystic declares to his servant, "and his eyes shone with a momentary anger."³¹ The aged mystic alone, after years of contemplation and consultation with the fairy spirits, is able at last to penetrate the illusion of the physical world but he knows that this secret knowledge will inevitably be lost with him.

> I have sought through all my life to find the secret of life. I was not happy in my youth, for I knew it would pass; and I was not happy in my manhood, for I knew that age was coming; and so I gave myself, in youth and manhood and age, to the search for the Great Secret. I longed for a life whose abundance would fill centuries, I scorned the life of fourscore winters. I would be – no, I *will* be! – like the ancient gods of the land.³²

> Przez całe życie szukałem rozwiązania zagadki życia. Nie byłem szczęśliwy w młodości, albowiem wiedziałem, że młodość przeminie; i nie byłem szczęśliwy w wieku męskim, albowiem wiedziałem, że starość nadejdzie; tak więc w młodości, w wieku męskim i w starości oddawałem się poszukiwaniom za wielką Zagadką. Pragnąłem życia, którego pełnią miała sobą stulecia objąć całe, wzgardziłem życiem, które zaledwie ośmdziesiąt miało zim. Chciałem być – nie chcę być – jako Starożytni Bogowie naszej ziemi.³³

Chapter 4: Between Art and the Nation

The desire of the old man to comprehend the inner world of human life reflected the function Yeats felt artists should ideally play in national life, which in an 1898 article entitled "The Autumn of the Body" he likened to priesthood. "The arts are, I believe," Yeats contended, "about to take upon their shoulders the burdens that have fallen from the shoulders of the priests, and to lead us back upon the journey by filling our thoughts with the essences of things, and not with things."[34] It was on this score that Yeats and Lack converged as visionaries seeking to invest art with essential meaning.

As was the case with Yeats, Lack did not care whether his criticism was broadly accessible to the public. Instead, he emphasized the progressive role played by the artistic elite, which did not respond to the dictates of society but brought about change by virtue of their unique creative vision.[35] This is why Yeats's story is so instructive in terms of Lack's work as a thinker and critic, which in many respects represented a continuation of the polemics surrounding symbolist art in the 1890s. The chasm of misunderstanding that existed between Yeats's mystic and his servant underscored the important yet solitary role Lack attributed to the progressive force of genius in the world. "A thought," Lack explained, "thrown out by the genius creates an impression in the sensibilities of people and from there it issues forth as a reality."[36] What had begun as a vision of artistic genius in a given work of art in time came to belong to a previously unknowing collective. "Every idea," Lack stressed, "has its own material that has existed for ages and from which it must realize itself [...] People overcome with the idea are people of destiny."[37] For Lack, Wyspiański was such an individual in Poland, for by shaping the eternal stuff of life with his intellect he created a distinct symbolic vision that would eventually be embraced by his compatriots as an inherently Polish form of creative expression. Appearing at a time when Wyspiański's genius was accepted but not fully understood, Lack's translation of "The Heart of Spring" can be read as an early example of how Young Poland perceived the work of Yeats and his Irish-Ireland counterparts as a means of understanding itself. Lack did not return to Yeats again as a critic or translator, but the significance of the contribution of "The Heart of Spring" to Lack's understanding of art and his later approach to Wyspiański cannot be overstated.

It was not simply a case of Yeats's story operating simultaneously on the planes of the transcendental and the literal that made it relevant to Lack as a critic. On the contrary, the visionary poetics Yeats began to develop at the end of the 1890s was a perfect complement to Lack's concept of eternal presence. With the publication of *The Secret Rose* in 1897, Yeats transformed the local and the personal ethnography of earlier work such as *The Celtic Twilight*, published in 1893, into a mystical exploration of the role of the artist in society. "It may be," Yeats maintained in 'The Celtic Element in Literature' in 1897, "that the arts are founded on the life beyond the world, and that they must cry in the ears of penury until the world has been consumed and become a vision."[38] In *The Celtic Twilight* (1893), Yeats had drawn upon the folk tales and myths of the Irish countryside with the conscious aim of creating a uniquely Irish literature in English. Although replete with references to the supernatural, Yeats rooted this intial collection of stories more deeply in the landscape and folklore of the Sligo of his youth. With stories such as "The Heart of Spring," however, Yeats made the turn from what Gregory Castle has termed "fair equivalents" in *The Celtic Twilight* to the pursuit of "divine substances" in *The Secret Rose*.[39] Whereas in the former Yeats attempted to combine ethnographic faithfulness with a distinct aesthetic, in the latter he began to stress visionary aspects over anthropological and cultural authenticity.

There is no evidence to suggest that Lack was interested in spiritualism or the occult, as Yeats famously was, but the mystical imagery and the transcendental worldview of the stories in *The Secret Rose* lent themselves well to Lack's dense, artful criticism. In spite of its Irish veneer, in the "The Heart of Spring" Lack clearly encountered Yeats revealing his hand as the mystic visionary instead of the folk revivalist. Put in the parlance of Lack's criticism, Yeats's work was rooted in a vision of the "eternal presence" of existence, or the Absolute, rather than in a literal interpretation of the surface reality of everyday life. Critical approaches that viewed art in terms of the individuality of the artist, the form of the work, or a specific ideology, in Lack's view, ignored its most basic characteristic. "Art," Lack further explained in a 1908 article for *Krytyka* (The Critique) entitled 'Dwa zasadnicze motywy muzyki Wyspiańskiego' (Two Fundamental Motifs of the Music of Wyspiański), "is able to reach to the past and to the future, for in reaching there in spite of everything we do not go beyond the limits of eternal presence."[40] Lack in his thinking was close to Miriam, who understood art as a window into eternal essence of life, and not the product of a form, school of thought, or political ideology.[41] In Lack's tautological perception of the world, however, all things were complete in and of themselves, as if they had always existed ready made. History, too, for Lack was a falsehood, for there was nothing new in the world, just repeated emanations of primordial ideas such as love and hate. "Life is absurd," Lack explained in his 1902 analysis of *The Wedding*, "A walking dream cannot end (in this lies the power of a work of art)."[42] Devised by Yeats expressly to serve Irish cultural goals, the universality of the Irish poet's vision of the elderly mystic's transcendence was an ideal subject for Lack. "In the soul," Lack observed in 1897 in "Przegląd przeglądów" (The Review of Reviews), his regular column for *Life*, "there is no room for egoism, because it is there that the pain of life seethes, the entire

Chapter 4: Between Art and the Nation

bloody tempest of life is concentrated in one point, which becomes the universe."[43] The importance of "The Heart of Spring" rested in the fact that it provided Lack with a modern day parable by which he could make clear his complex theory of art as a symbol of the unseen yet timeless unalterability of human existence.

By creating an Irish folk literature rooted in such a visionary conception of the world, Yeats was also consciously attempting to universalize Irish history by depicting it as a spiritual rather than a historical or political struggle. R. F. Foster maintains that for all its mysticism and occult imagery, at its heart *The Secret Rose* dealt with the figure of the artist. "Art," Foster explains of Yeats during this period, "is seen as spiritual transmutation, achieved through visions with a strong application of Celtist top-dressing."[44] In this way, Yeats was able to accomplish a number of things. With characters such as Michael Robartes and Red Hanrahan, he drew on the Irish bardic tradition to create what amounted to a mythology of self.[45] Rooted as it was in Yeats's interest in symbolic art and the occult, the universalization of the Irish experience also enabled him to fashion a modern Irish cultural identity that was at once inclusive and non-sectarian. As a result, he was able to create a modern, vital Anglo-Irish literature unsullied by political faction or ethnic identity. The fact that Yeats would continue over the years to revise and to reconfigure the stories from *The Secret Rose*, *Rosa Alchemica*, and *Stories of Red Hanrahan*, was indicative of the lasting relevance these stories would have to his evolving identity as an Anglo-Irish poet.

Yeats's use of Irish folklore and the occult to create self-mythologizing visions was an attractive literary model for Lack, especially in regard to his budding interest in the work of Wyspiański. Given its timing, Lack's translation of "The Heart of Spring" read as a particularly incisive representation of the approach he would take in analyzing the work of Wyspiański, whose popularity within Young Poland far outstripped his comprehensibility at the time. "The work of [Wyspiański]," Wojciech Głowala has suggested, "does not function only as one of many examples of his writing, but rather as the source of its laws and its greatest realization... At times we have our doubts whether the laws of Lack's critical world were not created specially for use on Wyspiański."[46] Lack certainly had no such relationship with Yeats, but his translation of the "The Heart of Spring," which appeared in the issue of *The New Word* preceding his first critique of Wyspiański, did offer a vision of the artist as the archetype of creative self-realization. In the place of Yeats's dying mystic or Michael Robartes, therefore, Lack pointed to characters in Wyspiański's *The Wedding* or *Bolesław Śmiały* (Boleslas the Brave). For Lack, meaning could not be found in the superficial costumery of reality, but through legends artists could instill the unchangeability of nature into human history. It was the artist who gave this timeless essence recognizable shape and by whose artistry created something meaningful. "The conflict between [King Boleslas the Brave] and [Saint Stanislas]," Lack pointed out, referring to Wyspiański's play *Boleslas the Brave*, "is eternal, and it will always exist."[47] These two characters, unaware aware of their situations and incapable of altering their behavior, represented the creative realization of the laws of eternal presence. "This drama," Lack explained, "must transpire as it took place, it does not lie in the power of anyone to place it on a different course, for the deed is embedded in the being of Boleslas the Brave."[48] In Lack's understanding, the actions of the King are unalterable just as it is impossible to change the nature of existence. "Wyspiański's drama," Lack emphasized, "is not... a transposition of the past into this epoch, but rather it has always existed, then and now. Wyspiański, the consciousness of his intellect, uncovers it. The method changes according to the time and the conditions, to the color of the sky and the earth, but The Spirit is constant and it always finds its own way."[49] It was the ability of creative geniuses of the rank of Yeats and Wyspiański to give these eternal stories, or ideas, artistic shape that made them such pivotal forces in the life of the nation.

The gap of understanding between the dying mystic and his servant in Yeats's story also serves as a commentary on Lack's position within Young Poland. The reason Lack's criticism proved to be incomprehensible to so many within Young Poland was because it dealt above all with the presentation of ideas.[50] Much in the same way that Yeats's mystical character was a rejection of Philistinism in favor of the Irish poet's vision of esoteric art, Lack utilized a tautological approach with which he strove to unveil art rather than to explain it. While Yeats wore the alternating hats of artist and critic, Lack conceived the relationship between the two roles to be interrelated, if not symbiotic. "[The critic]," Lack explained, "creates a synthesis of the 'discussed' artist and connects him to eternity, and above all to his eternal type."[51] Lack as a critic remained vague and indefinable for Young Poland because of his attempt to reveal what he perceived to be the unchanging truth or "eternal presence" of a given literary work by utilizing closed, indistinct language consistent with its inner logic. In choosing, as it were, to write about literature from the inside out, Lack suffered the fate of Yeats's dying mystic, whose effort at transcendence was interpreted by his literal-minded servant as inexplicable foolishness. With his evolution as a critic cut short by illness, Lack remained a nebulous presence within Young Poland. While Lack was not alone as a critic in reaching and striving for something new, which was difficult to define, his determination to utilize his complex theoretical conceptions as a full partner of art kept him apart from his contemporaries. Although his ideas remained opaque, through his writings and translations Lack revealed himself to be a critic who was intent upon bettering Young Poland's understanding of itself.

Chapter 4: Between Art and the Nation

This would become increasingly apparent in the years following the publication of Lack's translation of "The Heart of Spring," with the works of Wyspiański taking the place of those of Yeats.

II. THE CASE FOR POETIC DRAMA: *THE COUNTESS CATHLEEN* & *MIRIAM'S CHIMERA*

Given the image of Yeats generated by Płoński's critique and Lack's translation as a poet attempting to balance symbolic vision with native expression, it was fitting that a translation of Yeats's play, *The Countess Cathleen*, by the Young Poland poet, Jan Kasprowicz, would appear in Miriam's journal *Chimera* in 1904. As the publisher and the editor of *Chimera*, Miriam was in a position to introduce the type of elevated, symbolic art he had been advocating in his writing for over a decade. "To be such a guard [of art]," Miriam explained in the prospectus for *Chimera* in 1901, "to be a genuine temple, a divine and passionate cult of art flowing from its absolute abode – that is what *Chimera* wants."[52] Dating back to the early 1890s, Miriam had deplored the fact that art had been left by the wayside in favor of materialism, journalism and popular entertainment. In his capacity as a critic and a publisher, Miriam wanted to foster in Poland a genuine openness to the autonomous world of art. For Miriam, such art recognized no borders nor was it limited by time. While he did not use Lack's terminology, Miriam in *Chimera* clearly strove to publish art for which purity and timelessness of eternity were defining characterisrsics. "Next to the capital creators of our day," he explained further, "the bronzed voices of forgotten masters of bygone days come back to life; in turn the treasures of foreign peoples draw nearer, whose dearest gems are largely unknown to us. The display, therefore, of all these treasures undoubtedly will awaken new, future talents."[53] By publishing Kasprowicz's translation of *The Countess Cathleen* in *Chimera* Miriam not only ensured that Yeats would continue to be read in Poland in terms of symbolist aesthetics, but with it he also hoped to stimulate the creative imagination of Young Poland.

As a self-proclaimed "temple of art," there was an ideological, if not political element to *Chimera*, which evolved out of Miriam's view of art as a battleground on which the well being of the Polish nation was at stake. For Miriam, the theater was an especially telling indicator of cultural health, because of its ability to influence public taste. In an article entitled "Nadsceny i kabarety artystyczne" (Side Stages and Artistic Cabarets), which appeared in *Chimera* in 1901, Miriam framed his position in terms of what he perceived to be the alarming prevalence of popular culture in Warsaw. "Art is not entertainment," Miriam insisted, "nor is it a way of satisfying the meager tastes after a good meal of sentimentality, or also the taste for crude, thoughtless jokes and the allusions of rumor-mongering pamphlets."[54] Real art, he felt, was disinterested and removed from the coarse realities of daily life. Miriam's stance on the state of art was particularly evident in his bitter opposition to traveling German cabaret and circus troupes, whose light entertainment had managed to capture the imagination of theatergoing audiences in Warsaw. The only way that the theater could aspire to its calling would be for it to abandon frivolous amusement in favor of a dramatic form of expression that was disinterested and timeless. Pointing to the *Théâtre d'Art* and the *Théâtre Libre* in Paris, Miriam argued that artistic theater did not have to remain an abstract idea, but that it also had the potential to broaden and enlighten society intellectually. It was not simply a question of exchanging German popular entertainment for French intellectual theater. Miriam pointed to the drama staged in these Parisian theaters, which was disinterested in terms of ideology and nationality, because it did not deaden the imagination, but rather challenged the intellect and aspired to a deeper truth.

Miriam complained of Warsaw's lack of culture and its failure, felt most acutely in the theater, to fulfill its proper role as a vital influence on Poland's overall creative development in an article entitled "Reforma teatrów" (Reform of the Theaters, 1901). Despite being regarded as a champion of esoteric art, removed from the realities of the world, Miriam had a keen appreciation for the fundamental role that the theater could play in society. "The theater," he stressed, "everywhere, and here in particular – more broadly than the other fine arts occupied a place in social life and its influence reaches places that even pure music, published literature and the fine arts cannot reach."[55] Miriam, perhaps with a sense of self-recognition, condemned the casualness with which the Polish press glibly referred to the theater as a "temple of art," but did little to give life to the title. As a result, there emerged a divergence between the theater of the masses and the theater of the elect and cultured elite. "Those small *Théâtres d'Art*," Miriam maintained, "arising thanks to the divine, disinterested sacrifices of true artists and admirers, attempt to enrich the repertoire with all the masterpieces they can, not hesitating in the face of the most subtle things, not concerning themselves with accessibility and staging."[56] While popular entertainment was capable of making the crowd laugh or cry, it could not make it dream or feel deeply. Challenged by fashionable social outings or vaudeville variety shows, real artistic theater had become a rarity. Miriam cited the work of Maeterlinck, Alfred Jarry and Aurélien-Marie Lugné-Poe as examples of true, symbolic drama that contained "elements of eternity and infinity."[57] To avoid falling into the trap of popular theater, Miriam advocated first and foremost the expansion of the dramatic repertoire. His only demands were the talent of the author and the value of the drama as a work of art. He ideally envisioned a theater under the control of a literary-aesthete, someone with the appropriate taste and artistic vision to present transcendental drama of this kind. Miriam could have been describing the Irish Literary Theatre, with Yeats as its guiding force, as an example of just such a theater. With its juxtaposition of damnable materialism and spiritual self-sacrifice, *The Countess Cathleen* answered Miriam's call for poetic drama as an antidote to the dispiriting influence of popular culture in the theater.

With his emphasis on Irish mythology and unconventional dramatic forms, the theater Yeats would bring to maturation with the Abbey harmonized well with the style of reformed, poetic theater Miriam was promoting in *Chimera*. The Irish poet's attempt to represent what was essential about Irish identity without consideration of its marketability also answered to the call Miriam was making in Poland for an artistic theater. "The Irish upper classes put everything into a money measure," Yeats complained in an article in 1901 in *Samhain*, "When any one among them begins to write or paint they ask him, 'How much money have you made?' 'Will it pay?'... The poor Irish clerk or shopboy, who writes verses or articles in his brief leisure, writes for the glory of God and of his country."[58] By creating a theater dedicated to staging anti-commerical drama, Yeats and the Irish-Ireland theater avoided the trap of falling victim to popular tastes. For Yeats, a theater of this sort was not only more creative it was also inherently more Irish. Much in the same way that Miriam loathed the influence of German vaudevillian troupes, Yeats wanted the Irish theater to remain free of the strong pull of English culture. "Literature," Yeats insisted in a 1903 article in *Samhain*, "must take the responsibility of its power, and keep all its freedom."[59] Adopting a tone that would have certainly pleased Miriam, Yeats worried less about pleasing the tastes of the audience than he did about the mission of the Irish theater. "I would sooner our theatre failed," Yeats declared, "through the indifference or hostility of our audiences than gained an immense popularity by any loss of freedom."[60] For both Miriam and Yeats, the only way the artist could help elevate the nation was through the pursuit of art free from ideology. As the polemics surrounding the emergence of Young Poland in the 1890s had made readily apparent, the concept of the autonomy of art was a highly political position in and of itself.[61] The attempt by the intellectuals of Young Poland and Irish-Ireland to rectify the internal tension between the principles of essentialism and cosmopolitanism revealed the ideological power of art as a tool of cultural and national realization. In an essay in 1904 entitled "The Dramatic Movement" published in *Samhain*, the same year *The Countess Cathleen* appeared in *Chimera*, Yeats echoed much of what Miriam had been writing for years regarding the regenerative power of art. "Literature," Yeats concluded, "is not journalism because it can turn the imagination to whatever is essential and unchanging in life."[62] The theater, too, had to change if it was to be able to stage esoteric dramas such as those envisioned by Yeats in Ireland and Wyspiański in Poland.

In his plea for poetic drama, Miriam reflected the broader struggle for theatrical reform that had been taking place in Europe and was beginning to receive attention in Poland. Influenced by the ideas of symbolism, the previous, veristic approach to the stage was no longer adequate. If true art was inherently symbolic, its realization on stage presented new and serious challenges for all involved in the theater. Miriam recognized in writings on Maeterlinck that symbolism entailed a fundamental shift in European drama away from traditionally realistic or naturalistic forms and toward a form of poetic theater. "The Belgian poet," Miriam insisted, "acting totally consciously perceives the two sides of human existence, the limited and unlimited, the intellectual and transcendental, and he wants to emphasize both in the characters in his dramas."[63] In order to represent the intellectual and the transcendental sides of humanity on the stage, new theatrical forms were needed.[64] In turn, these innovative approaches to acting and stage design required an entirely new kind of play. "That reform," Miriam maintained, "ushers in – on the one hand – new content, new factors, new elements into drama and demands of them new appropriate and adequate forms."[65] As an advocate of poetic drama, therefore, Miriam was able to contribute to the advancement of the theatrical reform movement in Poland without any direct involvement in the theater.

As the editor of *Chimera*, Miriam helped make *The Countess Cathleen* comprehensible by promoting a similar type of poetic drama through the publication of critical articles on the theater and plays by foreign and Polish dramatists. In *Wanda*, by the late Romantic poet Cyprian Norwid, Miriam discovered a Polish model for the kind of purely poetic drama he had long admired in the work of Maeterlinck and Villiers de L'isle Adam.[66] Part mystery play and part national myth, *Wanda* was based on the Polish legend of Princess Wanda, who committed suicide by leaping into the Vistula River to avoid marrying the German Prince, Rytyger. While Polish intellectuals had no difficulty in looking abroad to Wagner, Hauptmann, Sudermann, Maeterlinck, and Strindberg for innovative ideas for the theater, there was a growing desire among Young Poland's writers at the turn of the century to find uniquely Polish theatrical forms and sources.[67] This is precisely what drew the attention of Wyspiański to the national legends of Wanda, Krak, and Bolesław the Brave. As both a national legend and an otherworldly drama, *Wanda* served as a uniquely Polish example of the kind of poetic drama Yeats was creating in the Irish theater.

Chapter 4: Between Art and the Nation

The re-discovery of Norwid's *Wanda* was an important event for Young Poland first and foremost because it represented a new kind of drama. In spite of the drama involving Rytyger and Wanda, the focus of Norwid's play was not action nor character development, but rather the creation of a complete, symbolic vision of the nation. As such, *Wanda* was a proto-modernist play in its construction, which made it ideal for publication in *Chimera*.[68] Because of these same qualities, it would be several years before Miriam brought Norwid's play again to light, where it read almost as a contemporary work next to *The Countess Cathleen*. The scholar Alina Witkowska has explained that the apparent modernity of Norwid's play was due to the fact that it was an atypical Romantic drama. "Already in Norwid's earlier work," Witkowska maintained, "characters begin to appear that one could call quiet heroes... They are somehow immersed in the matter of reality, doing little or are in hiding, but their figures embody the Christian moral values accepted by the author as the spiritual good of human history."[69] In similar fashion to her Irish counterpart, Wanda voluntarily sacrifices herself in a selfless gesture to save her people, the peasantry, who unknowingly faced a threat when Rytyger, the invading German prince, chooses Wanda to be his queen. The real predicament facing Wanda, however, was not that of rejecting Rytyger and his army, but of making the transition from a pagan to a Christian identity in Poland. The tension between the pagan and Christian elements comes to climax in the play's final scene, when a burial mound rises spontaneously out of the earth and Wanda, no longer appearing as a pagan goddess, recreates Christ's victory over death by her own sacrifice.

> WANDA
> Dobrzy ludzie!... widziałam cień ogromny Boga,
> Przechodzący po polach jak szeroka droga,
> A to był tylko ręki jednej cień – ta ręka
> Jakby przebitą była, bo słońce padało
> Przez wnętrze dłoni, na wskroś, jak przez wypaść sęka.
> Ja stałam – i patrzyłam w to rozdarte ciało,
> Jak ptak z ciemności w jasną poglądа szczelinę,
> I dano mi jest widzieć – to...
> *Bierze gromnicę zapaloną z rąk Piasta i wchodzi na*
> *stos – potem, ciszej, kończy*
>   ... że dla was zginę...[70]
>
> Good people!... I saw the shadow of a great God,
> Passing through the fields like a wide road,

> And that was just the shadow of one hand – that hand
> Was as if pierced, because the sun passed
> Through the palm, completely, as if through a knothole.
> I stood – and stared at that torn flesh,
> Like a bird in darkness spies a bright crevice,
> And I was given to foresee...
> *She takes a burning torch from the hand of Piast and steps
> on to the pyre – then, quieter, finishes*
> ... that I die for you...

Her message is symbolically extended throughout Poland when, desiring to extinguish Wanda's burning pyre, the people call for all the water in the Vistula River. Rytyger, true to his barbarian destiny, regroups his army and speeds off to sack Rome. By sacrificing her life, Wanda redeems the Polish nation and establishes its Christian identity at the dawn of its formation.[71]

Attacked as he had been for his apparent asocial aestheticism, Miriam revealed with *Wanda* the potent political role symbolic art could play in the evolving cultural life of the nation. In *Wanda*, and later *The Countess Cathleen*, the noble, aristocratic figure central to the play was not a realistic or a naturalistic representation taken from real life, but an abstract symbol of a unique aesthetic, moral and metaphysical purity. Despite the conscious religious imagery in *The Countess Cathleen*, the peasants, the Countess, the devils, and the setting enabled Yeats to reach back to the mythical pre-dawn of Ireland's Celtic origins and to universalize it as a battle between good and evil. Norman Jeffares in his biography of Yeats maintained that the Irish poet at the turn of the twentieth century was looking for ways to fuse paganism and Christianity in his works.[72] In an article entitled "First Principles," published in the journal *Samhain* in 1904, Yeats reflected upon the value of *The Countess Cathleen* as an antidote to the shallowness of propaganda and political gain. "'It is the soul of one that loves Ireland,'" Yeats recalled, while writing *The Countess Cathleen*, "plunging into unrest, seeming to lose itself, to bargain itself away to the very wickedness of the world, to surrender what is eternal for what is temporary.'"[73] For Yeats, *The Countess Cathleen* was not an attempt to idealize the past, but a conscious effort to transcend it in the hope of creating a non-secular, visionary Irish art. Yeats's clash with Irish cultural nationalists, which began with this play, grew out of the latter's fear of an art that was ambiguously universal and non-Catholic.

Miriam did not face the same heightened sensitivity regarding the past as did Yeats, but his open disavowal of all ideology in art placed him at odds with many in Young Poland on both the left and the right. Sławińska has claimed that

Chapter 4: Between Art and the Nation

Wanda represented Miriam's contribution to the on-going debate within Young Poland as how best to represent the ongoing national tragedy of partition.[74] Franciszek Ziejka, moreover, has maintained that the publication of *Wanda* in *Chimera* helped to establish it as an important theme for Young Poland.[75] With its blend of ancient folk legend, national history, and religiosity, *Wanda* revealed an entirely new stock of creative possibilities for Polish writers. Miriam was not the first among his contemporaries to gravitate to the Wanda legend. The Wanda tale had already gained some currency with Wyspiański's 1898 play *Legenda I* (The Legend I).[76] In his version, though, Wyspiański focused the action of the drama on the impending death of the legendary founder of Kraków, King Krak, who in Polish mythology was Wanda's father. In doing so, Wyspiański heightened the dramatic tension surrounding Wanda, which had originally been the working title of his play, and the subsequent threat to Polish sovereignty posed by the invading German army. Sławińska has characterized Wyspiański's dramatic style as a blend of neo-Romantic, symbolic, and peasant elements, which combined together to reveal the collective purpose of the Polish nation.[77] Wyspiański, however, desacralized the Wanda's self-sacrifice by making her the daughter of a river queen. In peopling his play with water sprites, nymphs and water elves, Wyspiański created a mythological underwater kingdom in the Vistula River.[78] Wyspiański's creatures may have been borrowed from Western or non-Slavic folklore, but in situating these citizens of the "other Kraków" in the Vistula River he created a mythology of his native city.[79] Although both Norwid and Wyspiański drew inspiration for their dramas from the Wanda burial mound situated on the outskirts of Kraków, in *The Legend* Wyspiański localized the action in a way that Norwid did not. In using social imagery that was decidedly unworldly, Wyspiański, in contrast to Norwid, created non-secular, artistic vision of the collective Polish nation that was powerful because it was larger than life.

The fact that Wyspiański published his second version of the Wanda tale, *The Legend II*, in 1904, the same year Kasprowicz's translation of *The Countess Cathleen* appeared in *Chimera*, revealed the extent to which Yeats's work as a poet and a dramatist remained in step with Young Poland's ongoing development. The difficulty the Polish theater faced in actually realizing Wyspiański's mythical drama on the stage, however, was evident in Tadeusz Pawlikowski's to wait until 1905 to produce *The Legend I* in Lwów. Despite the difficulty of realizing such visionary drama on stage, Yeats's "nationalist play" nevertheless had considerable currency in the contemporary Polish theater. Kasprowicz's translation of *The Countess Cathleen* did not face the obstacles encountered by Wyspiański's *The Legend*, for Miriam presented it, as he had *Wanda*, as a poetic drama, rather than as a play meant to be realized on the stage.[80] As such, Yeats's play stood first and foremost as a distinct literary work of art, or a symbolic vision of a deeper truth, which would have to wait for a new type of theater before it could appear in the theater. For Young Poland, it would be a decade before a Polish director made an attempt to stage *The Countess Cathleen*. Folowing the outbreak of World War I, Yeats's sublime drama would find new appeal for Poles both as a model of innovative, poetic drama and as a means of escape from the bleakness of wartime Warsaw. In 1923, after Poland had regained its independence, Miriam again turned his attention to Yeats, but this time it would be as a translator of Yeats's *Stories of Red Hanrahan*.[81]

III. THE ART OF COLLECTIVE FEELING: KASPROWICZ AND YEATS

Given the significant part that peasant themes played in his poetry and his penchant for translating English poetry, it was not surprising that the translator of *The Countess Cathleen* was the poet Jan Kasprowicz (1860–1926). Though deeply rooted in the poetic mode, Kasprowicz's symbolist play *Bunt Napierskiego* (The Revolt of Napierski) had been successfully staged in Kraków in 1899, which was the last year of Pawlikowski's term as the director of the Civic Theater before relocating to Lwów. With its combination of folk imagery and religious symbolism, Yeats's folk drama was a useful vehicle for Kasprowicz's further development as a poet. In the Countess's symbolic self-sacrifice for the salvation of the collective soul of the Irish people, the Polish poet's aesthetic, social, and moral concerns all found equal fulfillment. The social plight of the Irish people, suffering in the midst of a famine, struck a real chord in Kasprowicz's identity as a writer, while the stark vision of an earthly battle between good and evil resembled Kasprowicz's poetry at the time. *The Countess Cathleen* in some respects was a return to themes that had figured prominently in Kasprowicz's earlier collection of poems, *Z chałupy* (From the Cottage, 1887). The Irish peasants in Yeats's play faced the same burdens of poverty, hunger, cold, and temptation, as the peasants in Kasprowicz's poetry. Despite its idealized setting, *The Countess Cathleen* depicted the same process of decay in the traditional social order of the countryside that Kasprowicz lamented in his poetry. As such, Yeats's play complemented the persistent strain of social humanitarianism that had been basic to Kasprowicz's poetry and prose since his youth.

The articles Kasprowicz published during his early years as a social radical displayed his awareness of the historical condition of the Irish peasantry, but by

Chapter 4: Between Art and the Nation

the time his translation appeared in *Chimera* he was less concerned with socio-economic realities than he was with metaphysical questions. The fact that Yeats's drama was not a realistic portrayal, culminating as it did with Heaven's direct intervention to redeem the Countess's soul, suited both Kasprowicz's social and aesthetic sensibilities. This was possible, as the Yeatsian scholar David R. Clark has carefully explained in *Yeats and the Theatre of Desolate Reality*, because Yeats matched the contrast between spiritual and material elements to the struggle between good and evil. "Universal spiritual values," Clark maintained, "are represented by the Christian God and spirits, who are at home everywhere. They struggle with universal material values, represented by Satan and his demons, who, wherever they may go, are foreign exploiters. The plague-smitten land, the starving peasants, and the enslaved gods of ancient Ireland represent the Irish land and people as individual targets of temptation by material values."[82] The Countess's fruitful orchards and lush pastures, where her shepherd tends innocent sheep, is an earthly paradise, a Garden of Eden free from evil and misfortune. Yeats's decision to recast an Irish national catastrophe, the Great Famine, in moral terms satisfied Kasprowicz's identity as a modern poet who had transformed his strong social conscience for the Polish people into a metaphysical vision.

The timing of his translation of Yeats was significant, for Kasprowicz was in the process of making a subtle shift in his poetry. Lipski has specified the years 1898–1905 as an important period of creative transition for Kasprowicz, when the Polish poet began to abandon symbolism for expressionism.[83] Kasprowicz began to distance himself from the unchanging serenity of symbolism in the two cycles of poems that comprised *Hymny* (1898–1901), *Ginącemu światu* (To the Perishing World) and *Salve Regina*.[84] In their place, Kasprowicz developed a poetic voice that was much more dynamic and dissonant in tone. Where Lack and Miriam had been advocates of the literature of essence, far removed from the psychology of the author, Kasprowicz's visionary poetry was filtered through and shaped by his consciousness. Although he did not cease to write about the Polish peasantry, it became much more difficult to distinguish his folk themes from his expressionistic style as his poetry grew more complex. With a poetic mode that was almost Biblical, Kasprowicz fused Polish folk culture into the tone and language of his poetry. As a result, Kasprowicz's aesthetic sensibility influenced the manner with which Yeats's work would be received in Poland.

Much more than an arbitrary distinction, expressionism and symbolism represented two very different creative modes, each evolving from distinct artistic traditions. Evolving as it did at the turn of the century, Kasprowicz's poetry at this stage could be qualified as a form of proto-expressionism. In the Polish context, the roots of expressionism were German, dating from the "*Sturm und Drang*" period in late 18th century German literature and then further elaborated by the Polish Romantics. In many ways, the genealogical links between Polish Romanticism and expressionism, as it took form in the work of Kasprowicz, were more natural than with symbolism. The defining features of Polish expressionism were subjectivity, the extreme inner emotions of the artist, active social and ethical engagement, and an intense dynamism. As Maria Podraza-Kwiatkowska has pointed out, Miriam disdained expressionist art, because it did not reflect the objective, eternal essence of symbolism, but rather it was a destabilized literary form, thoroughly shaped by individual consciousness, ambiguity, and pessimism.[85] Unlike symbolist or even impressionist art and literature, in expressionist poetry the inner emotion or psyche of the artist fundamentally shaped the form and tone of expression. Edvard Munch, who thanks to Przybyszewski gained currency for Young Poland in the late 1890s, and his Polish admirers, Konrad Krzyżanowski and Wojciech Weiss, were particularly good examples of the expressionist technique in painting, which "expressed psychological states in visual form."[86] Aside from Kasprowicz, there were a number of prominent Young Poland writers in whose work expressionism was also especially evident, including Przybyszewski, Tadeusz Miciński, Wacław Berent, and Władysław Reymont.[87] As a poet, Kasprowicz did not seek the sublime detachment of Yeats or Miriam, but rather in his poetry he attempted to filter the raw experience of human existence through the filter of his own emotions.

Kasprowicz's poetry in *Hymns* sheds light on his attraction to *The Countess Cathleen* and his transition in becoming an expressionist poet. Comprised of eight long poems in all, *To the Perishing World* represented a lyrical protest against the painful nature of human existence, while *Salve Regina* suggested the possibility of God's redeeming love. Kasprowicz did not approach these metaphysical questions in abstract terms, but rather he revealed them as an expression of his own tormented inner feelings. In *Hymns*, moreover, Kasprowicz replaced the perfectly static symbolist vision of beauty with a stark, black and white view of the world. While retaining the element of dualism present in symbolism, in *Hymns* it was difficult to differentiate between humanity, nature, and the divine order of the world. As a result, Kasprowicz portrayed human experience as a constant battle between good and evil, and faced with innumerable trials and torments his lyrical subject struggled with the concept of a God who was alternatingly vengeful and indifferent. In these poems, he was no longer dealing with an objectified Polish peasantry, but with a subjectivized image of the Polish nation. Kasprowicz did not try to separate himself from the Polish experience, but rather he internalized it and expressed it through his own tortured feelings.

Although Kasprowicz avoided overtly national themes in these poems, his use of the peasant dialect and the traditional prayers and songs made them

Chapter 4: Between Art and the Nation

unreservedly Polish in form. Kasprowicz's ability to blend his modernist aesthetics with his social and ethical convictions resulted in a poetic style that was truly innovative in the poetry of Young Poland. In *Hymns*, he did not portray the world as an objective reality, but rather identified himself with the Polish people through the communal experience of prayer and spiritual suffering. By associating himself with the plight of the Polish people in a world of good and evil, Kasprowicz disassociated himself in *Hymns* from the balanced, intellectual harmony of symbolist poetry. Through his subjective style, he placed himself, and the faith of the Polish people, at the center of a world in which good and evil were real, dynamic forces that affected their lives.

The misery of the peasantry in *The Countess Cathleen* is not the result of blind social forces, but the direct result of intervention of forces from the spiritual world. The demonic merchants in *The Countess Cathleen* make it clear that the terrible famine at the root of the peasants' suffering is not the work of God, but of Satan.

> FIRST MERCHANT
> The famine is hale and hearty; it is mine
> And my great master's; it shall no wise cease
> Until our purpose end...[88]

> PIERWSZY KUPIEC
> Zdrów on i czerstwy, nasz i on naszego
> Przemocarnego władcy! nie ustąpi,
> Dopókąd swego nie dobieży celu.[89]

Yeats's starving peasants find themselves in a position of having to choose between a life of strenuous, unrewarded faith and the effortless convenience of sin.

> SHEMUS
> God, and the Mother of God, have dropped asleep,
> For they are weary of the prayers and candles;
> But Satan pours the famine from his bag,
> And I am mindful to go pray to him
> To cover all this table with red gold.
> Teig will you dare me to do it?[90]

> SZEMUS
> Pan Bóg się zdrzemnął razem z Matką Boską,
> Pomęczyły ich modły i gromnice;

A za to szatan z dzieży swej głód sieje –
Myślęgo prosić, aby stół ten okrył
Czerwonem złotem. Chcesz, abym to zrobił,
Teig!⁹¹

In spite of Shemus's vulnerability, the devils deliberately attempt to impair his awareness of the presence of evil in the world by enticing him to burn the sacred quicken wood and by plying him with a numbing wine.⁹²

SECOND MERCHANT
Wine that can hush asleep the petty war
Of good and evil, and awake instead
A scented flame flickering above that peace
The bird of prey knows well in his deep heart.⁹³

DRUGI KUPIEC
Wino, co umie uśpić drobną walkę
Pomiędzy dobrem a złem, budząc w zamian
Aromatyczny żar, co strzela w górę,
Jako ów spokój, który na dnie serca
Zna ptak drapieżny.⁹⁴

As in *Hymns*, it was not simply the moral failings of a few individuals that was at stake in Yeats's play, but the moral foundation of an entire nation, and by extension the world. At the conclusion of Act I in the 1899 version of the play, the merchants, who are forced to reveal their true intentions by Maire, Shemus's pious wife, describe a catastrophic vision of the outcome of the impending battle between the forces of Heaven and Hell.

THE SECOND MERCHANT
My master will break up the sun and moon
And quench the stars in the ancestral night
And overturn the throne of God and the angels.⁹⁵

DRUGI KUPIEC
Tak pan mój słońce zdruzgoce i księżyc,
I gwiazdy zgasi w swej odwiecznej nocy,
I tron wywróci Boga i aniołów.⁹⁶

Chapter 4: Between Art and the Nation

In a speech at the close of Act II, the Countess chastises her servants for despairing at the demons' success in stealing the peasants' souls and looting her gold. In explaining her rationale, the Countess recounts a vision reminiscent of the active, spiritual universe that defined Kasprowicz's expressionist poetry.

CATHLEEN
Old man, old man, He never closed a door
Unless one opened. I am desolate,
For a most sad resolve wakes in my heart:
But always I have faith. Old men and women
Be silent; He does not forsake the world,
But stands before it modelling in the clay
And moulding there His image. Age by age
The clay wars with His fingers and pleads hard
For its old, heavy, dull, and shapeless ease;
At times it crumbles and a nation falls,
Now moves awry and demon hordes are born.[97]

KSIĘŻNICZKA KASIA
Stary człowieku, nigdy On nie zawarł
Bramy, jeżeli nie otworzył drugiej.
Jestem w rozpaczy, bo budzi się we mnie
Plan wielce smutny: ale ja mam wiarę ——
Przestańcie płakać, starzy moi ludzie —
Nie zapomina On świata, lecz ciągle
Lepi go w glinie, lepi na swój obraz
I podobieństwo. Wieki za wiekami
Glina buntuje się przeciwko Jego
Palcom, bój ciągły tocząc o swój stary,
Ciężki, ponury i bezkształtny spokój...
Czasem się skręci i skurczy, i wówczas
Lud jakiś pada – dziś się wykręciła
W stronę przeciwną i powstały hufce
Duchów piekielnych.[98]

Yeats's stark, black and white portrayal of the peasant world, in which good and evil is actively present, suited the change that was taking place in Kasprowicz's writing at this time. Much like *Hymns*, the world Yeats portrayed in *The Countess*

Cathleen is an on-going battle between good and evil, with humanity weak and helpless in between. The intervention of divine forces in the historical world of men, Lipski has emphasized, was one of key characteristics of expressionism.[99] The arrival of the two devils disguised as wandering merchants to prey on the souls of the starving Irish peasants mirrored the Manichaeistic tension that pervaded much of *The Perishing World*. Faced with perpetual hunger and uncertainty, Kasprowicz posited, perhaps it was appropriate to turn to Satan, since an absent and seemingly uncaring God allowed humanity to suffer.

> Szatanie!
> Ty kościotrupa chwyciłeś pod ramię
> I nad wysokość jego ostrej kosy
> Wzrosłeś w niebosy –
> A grom nie pada!
> Z nieukojoną żałobą
> Klękam przed Tobą!
> Zlituj się, zlituj nad ziemią,
> Gdzie ból i rozpacz drzemią,
> Gdzie ból i rozpacz dzwonem się rozlega
> I w strasznej pieśni brzmi...
> Szatanie![100]

> Satan!
> You grasped the skeleton by the arm
> And above the reach of his sharp scythe
> Extended yourself to heaven –
> And a thunderclap does not fall!
> With inconsolable mourning
> I kneel before you!
> Have mercy, mercy on the earth,
> Where pain and despair slumber,
> Where pain and despair peal with a bell
> And resound in a horrible song...
> Satan!

Yeats's vision of God closely resembled the all-powerful, Old Testament God pervading *Hymns*. For Kasprowicz, humanity was part of the divine matter with which God created the universe. Created imperfect, it was humanity, not God, which was ignorant of its true place in this natural order.

Chapter 4: Between Art and the Nation

O pełen kary
I przebaczenia pełny!
Chociaż Ci nasze te grzechy utrudnią
Stanąć nad nimi z powieką zamkniętą,
Niech Twoja litość stokroć większą będzie
Niżeli wszystek nasz grzech![101]

Oh full of retribution
And forgiveness replete!
Though our sins hinder you
You stand above them with closed eyes,
May your mercy be a hundredfold greater
Than all our sins!

The overriding force in the wild, unforgiving universe for both Yeats and Kasprowicz is God's selfless, forgiving love.

Yeats did not intend to write a Catholic drama when he created *The Countess Cathleen*, but Yeats's play nonetheless resonated with *Hymns* in its vision of the world as a spiritual struggle. In regard to the religious and aesthetic structure of the play, the version that Kasprowicz chose to translate was significant, because this three-act form intensified the tragedy of the Countess's death and transformed the struggle for the Countess's soul into an epic battle between God and the Devil.[102] Richard Ellman in *Yeats: The Man and the Masks* has pointed out that Yeats's play was originally given the subtitle *A Miracle Play*, with his intention being to write a series of such plays. It would seem to matter little that Yeats's intention, as Ellman explained it, was not necessarily to produce Christian plays in the medieval tradition, but to reveal the invisible world.[103] Given his well-documented involvement with the theosophy movement at the time, his attraction to symbolist literature, and his abiding interest in Irish legends and mythology, *The Countess Cathleen* encapsulated Yeats's attempt to create a distinctly Irish form of esoteric art.

According to Lipski, the medieval passion and mystery plays were the first to present Kasprowicz with an expressionist form for his poetry.[104] Golgotha, in particular, had long since been a theme in Kasprowicz's poetry, dating back to his earliest modernist poem, "Chrystus" (Christ). In *Hymns* this motif was strongest in "Moja pieśń wieczorna" (My Evening Song), in which the image of a blood red sun setting over the fields of Poland created an apocalyptic vision of the collective Polish people. Yeats's play, in the form that Kasprowicz encountered it, was a modernist passion play. Taking the place of Christ, the Countess Cathleen redeems a sinful people with her sacrifice and ascends into heaven following a battle between the armies of good and evil. For Kasprowicz, there was no sense of exalted detachment or universal symbolism, but rather the mystery of Christ's suffering was relived through the daily experience of the Polish people. With its motif of the messianic redemption of the Polish peasantry, Kasprowicz had explored similar ground in *The Revolt of Napierski*. The fact that he returned to this motif in 1903, when he began writing *Marchołt gruby a sprośny* (Marchołt the Fat and Bawdy), a morality tale featuring a sixteenth century literary figure, gave some indication of the currency this theme had with Kasprowicz at the time he was translating Yeats's play.[105]

The form of the mystery play provided both poets with a ready dramatic form that was flexible enough to support tales of national mythology and to retain the universal purity of modernist symbolist drama. In Yeats's play, however, a conflict exists between the Countess's commitment to God and her attachment to her people. Her dilemma, according to Clark, is to choose between serving God or the Irish people. "She chooses to serve her people," Clark maintains, "We learn, however, that to serve her people is to serve her God."[106] Keeping in mind the strength of the cult of Mary in rural Poland, a reality that was instinctive to Kasprowicz, the Countess's gesture of self-sacrifice in the Polish context read as a form of identity politics. For Kasprowicz, as a Pole, the central motif of national redemption at the hands of a divine intermediary in *The Countess Cathleen* had clear associations. The legends of Grażyna and Wanda were already deeply embedded in Polish literature, and the figure of the Black Madonna of Częstochowa was ever present in Polish national mythology. These archetypes, if not the Virgin Mary herself, were close to Kasprowicz's artistic and religious sensibilities. Because of Kasprowicz's reputation as a poet with a strong social vision and a close association with the plight of the Polish peasantry, it was not surprising that he may have obscured Yeats's non-secular visionary aesthetics. In this regard, *The Countess Cathleen* was not so much a story of universal struggle as it was an allegory of the Polish nation in Irish garb.

In his biography of Yeats, Foster has cited another nationalist reading of *The Countess Cathleen*'s religious content. "Though Yeats would eventually classify it as an anti-politics play," Foster has emphasized, "his demon soul-merchants must, to a contemporary audience, have looked like Protestant proselytizers or English oppressors; and Famine Ireland was, to any reader of John Mitchel, an inescapably political *mise-en-scène*."[107] While folk culture and peasant themes were equally popular with Kasprowicz and Yeats, the difference between the two poets was that the former brought to his writing the first-hand experience of life in the peasant world and the latter did not. In early his early work, such

Chapter 4: Between Art and the Nation

as *The Celtic Twilight*, Yeats made a concerted effort to link himself to the people and folklore of the Irish countryside, but as a member of the Protestant ascendancy he remained apart from the culture of the Irish countryside and a target for Irish nationalist criticism. It was Kasprowicz's ability, having risen from a peasant background to becoming a modernist poet, which made him such an intriguing interpreter of the peasant experience as a translator of Yeats. Based on his early writings as a social radical, Kasprowicz's awareness of this particularly Irish reading of the play would have been acute.[108] If viewed in light of his roots in the Polish countryside and the agrarian radicalism of his youth, it would not have been difficult for Kasprowicz to adapt Yeats's motif to the context of the Prussian partition of Poland. Instead of English proselytizers or oppressors, in Kasprowicz's countryside the demons would be German colonizers and Satan would be Bismarck.[109] Despite the change in context, the outcome, the spiritual corruption of the peasantry and the destruction of the traditional socio-ethical order, was the same.

By the time that Kasprowicz translated *The Countess Cathleen*, he was living in Lwów, the capital of Austrian Galicia, where under the relatively benign rule of the Catholic Hapsburg dynasty he could escape the extreme acculturation policies he had experienced in the Prussian partition. While Kasprowicz's personal situation may have changed for the better since the mid-1880s, foreign cultural hegemony was a still more volatile issue than ever in the Prussian and Russian-controlled partitions of Poland.[110] This endowed Yeats's poetic drama with a contemporary relevance for Polish readers.[111] The cultural parallels between Poland and Ireland evoked by *The Countess Cathleen* would remain a ready subtext for the Polish readers when in 1907 and 1912 Kasprowicz's translation reappeared in print, and in 1914 when it was again emphasized in the Polish theatrical debut of Yeats's play in Warsaw.[112] In Poland, as in Ireland, this secondary reading retained its potency as long as independence remained a question.

Despite the pertinence of this nationalist reading, neither writer could be limited by it because of the mutual desire to penetrate intellectually the universal mystery of life. Kasprowicz, like many of his Young Poland contemporaries, carried out his metaphysical inquiry by means of a synthesis of European and Eastern religious and philosophical thought. As a result, he could appreciate Yeats's symbolic drama for what it truly was. While the religious motif provided the play with its dramatic structure and expressionistic intensity, *The Countess Cathleen* was also a metaphysical investigation of the mystery of existence. After the climax, when the bedraggled army of angels defeat the demons of hell, Aleel, the poet, makes a declaration that seemed reminiscent of the roles that Yeats and Kasprowicz attempted to play as the poetic representatives of their collective peoples.

ALEEL
Look no more on the half-closed gates of Hell,
But speak to me, whose mind is smitten of God
That it may be no more with mortal things;
And tell of her who lies here.[113]

ALEEL
Przestańcie patrzeć na te wpół otwarte
Wierzeje piekieł, mówcie raczej do mnie,
Którego serce tak przejęte Bogiem,
Że już o ziemskich nie chce myśleć sprawach –
Mówcie mi o tej, która tutaj leży.[114]

As a poet, Aleel is not only capable of perceiving the invisible world, narrating as he does the culminating battle, but he also intervenes and forces the angels to reveal the mystery of the Countess's ascension into Heaven. Foster has pointed out that Yeats was less of a mystic than he was an adept magician interested in accessing the inner truths of life.[115]

Kasprowicz, in contrast, was more of a mystic, more like AE (George Russell), but one who perceived a strong link between the invisible world and the collective fate of the Polish people. In poems such as "My Morning Song" and "Dies Irae," Kasprowicz utilized imagery that was highly metaphysical in nature, yet strongly bound to traditional Polish folk culture to make this connection. The opening lines of the latter poem, which Kasprowicz adapted one line from the second line of the traditional Christmas carol "Bóg się rodzi" (God is Born) by the Classical poet Franciszek Karpiński (1741–1825), presented a cosmic cataclysm reminiscent of Yeats's closing scene.

Trąba dziwny dźwięk rozsieje,
Ogień skrzepnie, blask ściemnieje,
W proch powrócą światów dzieje.[116]

A trumpet will spread a strange sound,
Fire will freeze, brightness will darken,
The deeds of worlds will return to dust.

The language and imagery Yeats employed in the closing scene of *The Countess Cathleen*, therefore, were quite familiar to Poles, who had their own long-held traditions upon which to draw. As a modernist poet and playwright who had

Chapter 4: Between Art and the Nation

succeeded in creating powerful, symbolic literature from the legends and collective memory of the Irish people, Yeats lent a certain degree of *gravitas* to what Kasprowicz was attempting to achieve in his expressionist poetry. In translating Yeats, he not only drew attention to what the Poles and the Irish had in common, but also to the creative power that lay within the Polish cultural tradition.

As in *The Countess Cathleen*, the primary backdrop for Kasprowicz's metaphysical quest was that of the fields and forests of the Polish village. In this regard, the blend of Christian elements and features of traditional, pagan Irish culture, which portrayed the Irish peasants as being close to nature, was not far removed from the world of Kasprowicz's *Hymns*. Because the elements of Irish folklore in Yeats's play to a degree were contrived, Kasprowicz in his translation encountered little in terms of cultural particularities that barred him from faithfully rendering the rhythm of life and the imagery of peasant Ireland as Polish. Both poets also blended elements of folk culture, mysticism, and Christianity into their writing. In particular, Yeats and Kasprowicz found common ground in the identification of the rural world with nature. Yeats signaled the presence of evil either through symbolic images, such as wolves and owls, or through transgressions against nature, such as Seumus's decisions to kill a wolf for food and to burn the sacred quicken wood. Kasprowicz's lyric subject in "Hymn świętego Franciszka z Asyżu" (The Hymn of St. Francis of Assisi) expresses oneness with all creation, from the smallest flower to the cosmos. In "My Evening Song," Kasprowicz merged a folk song into a catastrophic vision of the Last Judgment.

> Cicho!
> To płacz tej dawnej, chłopięcej piosenki:
> A grajże mi, piszczałeczko,
> A grajże mi, graj!
> Uliniłem się z wierzbiny,
> Gdzie ten ruczaj srebrnosiny,
> Gdzie ten szumny gaj!
> Ach!
> Przeorałem łan o świcie –
> Od pola do pola,
> Kąkol wyrósł w moim życiu,
> Dolaż moja, dola!
> [...]
> Niech raz już wszystko zagaśnie!
> Jarzębina się rumieni,

Szepcą lipy stare,
Suchy piasek podnosi - - -¹¹⁷

Quiet!
It is the cry of that old, boyhood song:
And play for me, little pipe,
And play for me, play!
I have shed myself from the willow tree
By the silver-blue brook,
By the rustling grove,
Oh!
I have tilled the field at dawn –
From field to field,
The corn cockle has grown in my rye,
My fate, fate!
May the world be extinguished!
The mountain ash reddens,
The old linden trees whisper,
The dry sand rises - - -

In both *The Countess Cathleen* and *Hymns*, the natural order was inextricably bound to the peasant world. Acts against nature were not simply juxtaposed to Irish or Polish superstition, but against the universal peasant code.

The only extant review of Kasprowicz's translation of *The Countess Cathleen* was not published until 1918, when Adolf Nowaczyński gave it a brief mention in his collection of essays, *Szkice literackie* (Literary Sketches). While constituting a part of his overall critique of Kasprowicz's translations from English, Nowaczyński singled out his translation of Yeats's play as an example of Kasprowicz's talent as a translator. Nowaczyński's reference to Maeterlinck's famous drama underscored the link between Yeats and those in Young Poland who advocated the elevated aesthetics of symbolism. "It is," Nowaczyński maintained, "as if a transposition in the Celtic spirit of the enchanting drama *Monna Vanna*, so unjustly punished with the popularity and sympathy of the European crowd."¹¹⁸ Where Nowaczyński was more perceptive, however, was in his evaluation of Kasprowicz's translation. Because there was no hesitation in the skill and artistry of Kasprowicz's version of *The Countess Cathleen*, Nowaczyński considered it to be both a true translation and an original. "Kasprowicz's translation," he observed, "becomes here the derivatively passionate rendering of the entire work. It is a copy from the oil painting of a master, but done by

Chapter 4: Between Art and the Nation

that same master, for instance, only in pastels."[119] Nowaczyński was arguing that Kasprowicz and Yeats were identical artists, only they were working in different poetic media. In a word, Nowaczyński was not only signifying Poland's affinity for Ireland in essential terms, but also Kasprowicz's identity as a talented poet with a keen folk sensibility. "This Pole," Nowaczyński emphasized, "already felt the Irishman with his entire heart and to the depths of his soul, here his beloved folk element in language found its justified outlet, here the already 'bowing toward legends' fantasy of the creator of *The Wild Rose Bush* assisted the translator with pleasure."[120] It would be a decade before Kasprowicz's translation of *The Countess Cathleen* would finally find its way to the Polish stage, but when it did his "pastel" rendition of Yeats's dreamy play was well matched to a Polish theatergoing audience in need of a diversion amidst the chaos of war.

Known as a caustic critic, Nowaczyński's high estimation of Kasprowicz's translation was great praise indeed. Nowaczyński recognized the extent to which Kasprowicz's aesthetics and poetic imagination helped in the process of translating *The Countess Cathleen* from an Irish to a Polish cultural context. "This Pole," Nowaczyński observed, "has felt the Irishman with his entire heart and to the depths of his soul, here the fondness for the folk element found its just outlet, here 'inclining toward legends' the imagination of the creator of *The Wild Rose Bush* aided the translator with pleasure."[121] Nowaczyński would return to the distinction he made between copy and original in regard to Kasprowicz's translations when he turned his attention to Irish-Ireland in the next few years. In the final analysis, Nowaczyński perceived in Kasprowicz's efforts a true affinity between Poland and Ireland, and not simply the pursuit of literary fashion. "There is no doubt," Nowaczyński concluded his review, "that when literature with us recaptures its temple of art looted by the poor taste of the people, someday this drama *The Countess Cathleen* surely will be staged and admired by the most dignified."[122] Although prescient, it would require a decade for Nowaczyński's prediction to be realized.

Kasprowicz's translation of *The Countess Cathleen* was not the Polish poet's only rendition of Yeats's work. In 1906 Kasprowicz also published Polish translations of five poems by Yeats, the first of his poetry, in the Lwów journal *Nasz Kraj*.[123] A year later, in 1907, following the reissue of his translation of *The Countess Cathleen* in a collection of drama entitled *Próby angielskiej poezji dramatycznej* (Specimens of English Dramatic Poetry), Kasprowicz published an ambitious anthology of translations of English poetry under the title *Poeci angielscy. Wybór poezji w przekładzie* (English Poets: A Selection of Poetry in Translation), which contained eight of Yeats's early poems. Besides Yeats, Kasprowicz revealed his range as a translator by also including the poems of

The Impact of Irish-Ireland on Young Poland, 1890–1919

Geoffrey Chaucer, William Shakespeare, William Blake, Robert Burns, Thomas Moore, Lord Byron, Percy Bysshe Shelley, Alfred Lord Tennyson, Robert Browning, Dante Gabriel Rossetti, and Oscar Wilde. The collection did not contain a preface, nor did Kasprowicz explain why he selected the poets he did. Instead, he included a short biographical description preceding the work of each poet, detailing his or her background and major works. While the brief paragraph about Yeats introduced him as "an Irishman by birth and conviction" and as "one of the most vocal leaders of the Celtic movement," it also ironically described the Irish poet as belonging "to the most likeable and talented of modern English poets" for "just like the Gaelic poet Fiona Macleod, he writes in English."[124] The reference to Macleod, revealed as the Scottish writer William Sharp at the end of the 1890s, would have struck Yeats as a rather mixed complement.[125] Unlike many of his colleagues, including Lady Gregory and AE, Yeats continued to have some regard for Sharp, which apparently stemmed from their shared affinity for Celtic mysticism. Kasprowicz was clearly aware of Yeats's Irishness, but his comparison of Yeats to what amounted to a Scottish imposter blurred the lines of what was and was not Irish poetry.[126] The issue of Yeats's nationality as a writer did not go unnoticed by Young Poland, since it would resurface a few years later in the essays on the Irish theater of Nowaczyński and Maria Rakowska.

The eight poems by Yeats that Kasprowicz included in the anthology were from Yeats's early collections of poems *Crossways* (1889) and *The Rose* (1893), but Kasprowicz probably first encountered them in the 1899 reprint of *Poems* (1895).[127] Not surprisingly given the nature of the poetry featured in *English Poets*, Kasprowicz's choice of poems were among Yeats's most famous lyrical works – "The Lake Isle of Innisfree," "Down by the Salley Gardens," "The Sorrow of Love," "When You are Old," "Ephemera," "The Sad Shepherd," "The Madness of King Goll," and "The Death of Cuchulain."[128] With the notable exception of the last two, these poems generally involve universal declarations of romantic love either for a particular location or a person. "The Lake Isle of Innisfree," for example, depicts Yeats's longing for the beauty of his native Sligo, while a poem such as "When You Are Old" is an appeal to recollect a past love. All of the poems selected by Kasprowicz were concerned with some form of loss, whether it was of love, youth, or in the case of King Goll, his sanity, and Cuchulain, his life. Contemporary critics have suggested that the sense of place and the use of Irish mythology added a discretely political element to Yeats's early Romantic poems.[129] Beyond the appeal of Irish folk culture, it is doubtful that it was politics that drew Kasprowicz to these particular poems. A more likely explanation lay in Kasprowicz's interest in comparative literature and his own sensibilities as a lyric poet.

Chapter 4: Between Art and the Nation

Written in the latter half of the 1890s, the poems from *Poems* that Kasprowicz chose to translate were very much in the *fin de siècle* mode, possessing of a youthful lyricism that both Yeats and Kasprowicz had largely left behind in their poetry. By the time Kasprowicz turned his attention to Yeats, the presentation of both women and romantic love had changed dramatically in his poetry. "A most specific feature of Kasprowicz's collapse and restoration of faith in man," Górski explained, "is that at their base lies the internal relation to a beloved woman in a given period of life. Through the prism of idealization or disillusion experienced in relation to a woman, Kasprowicz envisions all reality."[130] With the evolution toward an expressionist poetic style that had taken place over the course of *Hymns*, Kasprowicz had already begun to leave behind the misogynistic portrayal of women as a dichotomy of love-sin that was common to the period.

A much better measure of the proximity of Yeats and Kasprowicz as poets was not their portrayals of romantic love, but rather the manner with which they infused the natural world with feeling to create in effect an emotional landscape. Kasprowicz's *Krzak dzikiej róży* (The Wild Rose Bush) had been a revelation to Young Poland in this regard. Because the natural world carried the symbolic weight of folk culture and represented a link to the mystical essence of life, both poets during this period drew heavily on natural images, from a simple flower to the star, in their writing. In "The Hymn of Saint Francis of Assisi," Kasprowicz portrayed St. Francis as being one with the earth and the cosmos. The fact that Yeats incorporated his mystical investigations in theosophy and the occult into his poetry made the affinity of his work with Kasprowicz's all the greater. In Kasprowicz's "The Sad Shepherd," Yeats's Romantic lyricism could also be read as a description of the former's attempt to encounter the Absolute through art.

> Then he sang softly nigh the pearly rim;
> But the sad dweller by the sea-ways lone
> Changed all he sang to inarticulate moan
> Among her wildering whirls, forgetting him.[131]

> Rzekł i wyśpiewał konsze żal swój w pieśni;
> Lecz ta wyrazy na szumy przetwarza –
> I, zapomniawszy smutnego pieśniarza[.][132]

Much in the same way that the lyric subjects in *Hymns* wondered at the mystery of the world, in Yeats's poem there was no rationalizing nature and existence. The appeal of such simple lyricism was not unique to Kasprowicz, but was common feature representative of Young Poland as a whole. This was, in many respects, the point of Kasprowicz's anthology. Unlike *The Countess Cathleen*, Kasprowicz in *English Poets* placed Yeats in the context of English literature, appearing alongside the likes of Shakespeare, Blake, Moore, Shelley, Rossetti, and Wilde. While this spoke to Kasprowicz's self-identification as a comparativist and a prolific translator, it did not negate the commonalities in their poetic style and evolution.[133]

Of all the poems by Yeats that Kasprowicz chose to translate, two in particular, "The Madness of King Goll" and "The Death of Cuchulain," stood apart as notable exceptions. Kasprowicz represented both poems in his translations as being taken from ancient Celtic legends. They were the only poems by Yeats dealing explicitly with Irish folklore that Kasprowicz selected. His interest in these particular poems may have had to do with his evolving poetic approach. Lipski has pointed out that following *To the Perishing World* and *Salve Regina* Kasprowicz abandoned the hymn as a poetic form in favor of the ballad. With the publication of *O bohaterskim koniu i walącym się domu* (Of a Heroic Horse and a Decaying House, 1905) and *Ballada o słoneczniku* (The Ballad of a Sunflower, 1908), Kasprowicz found a new form of poetic expression with which to experiment. The choice of the ballad form at once evoked both the poetry of Mickiewicz, Poland's great Romantic poet, and Young Poland's abiding interest in Polish folk culture. His decision to include two of Yeats's longer, mythological poems with the short, lyric poems may have stemmed from this new interest in the ballad form.

Kasprowicz's ballads in many ways were an extension of what he had attempted in *Hymns*. "For Kasprowicz," Lipski maintained, "the ballad aids in the telling of moral truths, it is a poetic form of judgment upon human deeds, as well as on the psychological drama of the conscience."[134] The ballad form, furthermore, presented Kasprowicz with a relatively easy transition from the hymn, because at the heart of the ballad, for Kasprowicz, lay the clear-eyed differentiation between the good and evil of folklore. There was little practical difference, after all, between King Goll, with his escape from the world of men and sanity into a woodland kingdom, and Kasprowicz's St. Francis, who communed with nature as part of his message of tenderness and love.

> O ziemio, siostra moja, żądna krwi i hańby,
> Do ciebie ja przychodzę,
> Bosy, z odkrytą głową,
> I jarzmo twe, i grzech twój, i wszystką twą grozę
> Chcę dźwigać razem z tobą
> I razem z tobą śpiewać

Chapter 4: Between Art and the Nation

Przedziwny hymn Miłości,
Boć ona-li odwlecze
Dzień Sądu...[135]

O Earth, my sister, anxious for blood and shame,
I come to you,
Barefoot, with uncovered head,
And your burden, and your sin, and all your dread
I want to bear together with you
And together with you sing
The strange hymn of Love,
Because it postpones
The Day of Judgment...

On another level, the appeal of "The Madness of King Goll" and "Cuchulain's Fight with the Sea" was a reflection of Young Poland's abiding fascination with the culture and legends of the Polish people. Wyspiański, most noticeably, about this time published plays based on Polish historical legends, such as *Boleslas the Brave* and *Skałka* (The Little Rock). As deeply as folk culture impacted Kasprowicz's work, Yeats's mythological poems must have struck him immediately. Despite their specific Irishness, Yeats's poems were at bottom antirational, visionary lyrics. Whereas Yeats employed Irish mythology, Kasprowicz employed the folk idiom of the religion that was rooted in the people and the way of life in the Polish countryside.

Despite some minor failings, Kasprowicz's translations on the whole faithfully and accurately reflected Yeats's poems in both tone and content. As pointed out by Nowaczyński in his 1907 review of the anthology for *Świat*, the value of Kasprowicz's work lay not in literal translation, but in his ability to render them in a Polish sense. "They are not translations of English poets," Nowaczyński determined, "they are in all the meaning of that word the assimilation into Polish poetry of English poetry, they are passionate and forceful creative transpositions in tone, pace and tact of Polish speech."[136] By using pastel tones in his translations of Yeats, as Nowaczyński expressed it, Kasprowicz was not making a personal choice so much as he was transposing Yeats's unique lyrical style into an idiom familiar to Young Poland. Kasprowicz opted to maintain the general structure of the original poems, as well as Yeats's rhyme scheme. The alterations Kasprowicz did make generally were minor shifts in line or stanza construction. Only in two poems, "The Lake Isle of Innisfree" and "When You Are Old" did Kasprowicz make changes that suggest the Polish poet was inserting his own persona into the poems. In the former poem, whereas Yeats begins somewhat stiffly "I will arise and go now, and go to Innisfree," Kasprowicz exclaims enthusiastically "*Hej zerwę się, zerwę, do Innisfree polecę*" (Hey I will start up, take wing, to Innisfree I will fly).[137] The addition of the interjection "*hej*" had the effect of relaxing the poem and giving it a folk coloration that was not present in the original. In "When You Are Old," moreover, it is possible to read in Kasprowicz's translation a dimension of religious feeling that did not exist in the original. In Yeats's poem the poetic voice, presumably addressing an old love, asks her to recall her former beauty and their failed love when she reaches old age. When the original is placed next to Kasprowicz's translation, however, the difference is striking.

> How many loved your moments of glad grace,
> And loved your beauty with love false or true;
> But one man loved the pilgrim soul in you,
> And loved the sorrows of your changing face.

> Jak wielu ongi kochało ten boski
> Urok, a tylko jeden kochał wiernie
> Pielgrzymią duszę w tobie i te ciernie,
> Które ci żłobią czoło—ciernie troski.[138]

In the English version, the poetic subject's beauty is innate, in-born. In Kasprowicz's Polish translation, however, Kasprowicz inserted overt religious imagery of Christian mysticism with the reference to a crown of thorns. Kasprowicz, however, was not always successful in his attempts to render Yeats's original in Polish. Most notably, Kasprowicz translated "Down by the Salley Gardens" as "W ogrodzieliśmy się spotkali" (We Met in the Garden). While Yeats did include "salley" (willow) in a glossary of terms that accompanied the 1904 edition of *Poems*, Kasprowicz did not include it in his Polish translation. Kasprowicz's version in this respect was a cultural translation, not a failed one.[139] With this omission aside, Kasprowicz also altered Yeats's poem in the Polish version by breaking Yeats's long lines into two shorter lines, giving it a rhythm suitable to a folk song.

Given the changing nature of Kasprowicz's own writing at the time, it is also possible to read his translations of Yeats in terms of his development as a poet. Maria Dłuska has cited Kasprowicz's renditions of Oscar Wilde's "The Ballad of Reading Gaol" and Yeats's "Down By the Salley Gardens" as examples of how he experimented with rhythe and meter in his translations from English poetry as a means of creating a form of tonic poetry that unique within Polish literature.[140] Kasprowicz did not borrow rhythmic forms from either Wilde or Yeats, since tonic elements existed much earlier in Polish poetry, but rather he attempted to replicate the rhythm and accents of the original in his translations. By transposing the meaning and the rhythm of the poem, Kasprowicz created a Polish version that was much more expressive. Dłuska, however, maintained that Kasprowicz did not derive his tonic poetic style from his translations of English poetry, since it had already begun to appear in Kasprowicz's work as early as the poem "Maria the Egyptian" in 1901.[141] In terms of poetics, therefore, Yeats was not so much a model as he was a touchstone of Kasprowicz's continuing growth as a modernist poet.

Out of all the works by Yeats that Kasprowicz translated, his version of *The Countess Cathleen* would have the most enduring impact on Young Poland's image of Irish literature. In his artful translations of Yeats's drama and poetry, he was instrumental in shaping his contemporaries' perception of Irish-Ireland's preeminent literary talent. In Kasprowicz's hand, therefore, Young Poland encountered a version of Yeats that was very much in tune with its own prevailing artistic sensibilities. As an indefatigable translator, Kasprowicz's goal was in part to bridge the cultural gap between Poland and the West. In his translations of Yeats, Kasprowicz did succeed in bringing Ireland and Poland closer together in as much as he reproduced the Irish poet's work in a form that suited Polish needs and tastes. There remained, however, a gap between the two poets, as the Yeats in 1906 was no longer the same writer who had published *The Countess Cathleen* and the other poems from the 1890s that Kasprowicz translated into Polish. Given the relative novelty of English literature in Polish, in comparison to French or German, the timing of Kasprowicz's anthology of translations his contemporaries in Young Poland. It was not until 1914, when *The Countess Cathleen* finally reached the stage in Poland, that the Polish assessment of Yeats would finally change, but even at that late date Kasprowicz's original 1904 translation continued to remain true to the core artistic outlook of Young Poland.

IV. THE PAIRING OF GENIUS: SYNGE AND WYSPIAŃSKI IN PAWLIKOWSKI'S THEATER

While Yeats's initial introduction to Young Poland took place exclusively by means of literary translation, the Polish reception of the Abbey Theatre's other leading light, John Millington Synge, took place almost exclusively by way of the stage.[142] The performative aspect of stage production, which was bound to the evolution of the modern Polish theater, both enhanced and complicated Young Poland's reception of Irish drama. Numbering four productions altogether, the impact of Irish drama on the theater in Poland was impressive both in terms of its geographical extent and the key players who made it possible. Beginning with the Polish premiere of Synge's *The Well of the Saints* at Lwów's Municipal Theater in 1908 and ending six years later with the stage production of Yeats's *The Countess Cathleen* at Warsaw's Variety Theater in 1914, Irish drama at once strengthened the repertoire of the Polish theater and presented Polish directors with new dramatic approaches to artistic problems of social and national consequence.

It was fitting that the initial production of a modern Irish play took place under the direction of Young Poland's preeminent theatrical pioneer, Tadeusz Pawlikowski (1861–1915). As a theater director, Pawlikowski represented to the theater of Young Poland what the journals *Life* and *Chimera* had in regard to the advancement of modern art and poetry. As director of the Civic Theater in Kraków from 1893–1899, Pawlikowski opened the stage to innovative dramatic techniques and introduced Polish theatergoing audiences to new playwrights, both Polish and foreign. Following his move to Lwów in the middle of 1899, as director of the Municipal Theater Pawlikowski continued to uncover the newest dramatic talents from both Poland and abroad. It was a natural progression to relocate there, as performances by theatrical troupes from Kraków in the latter half of the 1890s had been enthusiastically received by the theatergoing public and by critics.[143] Toward the end of the 1890s, the city had experienced a period of considerable intellectual growth, becoming the home of many of Young Poland's leading literary talents, such as Kasprowicz, Przybyszewski, Leopold Staff, and Edward Porębowicz. The theatergoing community in Lwów was eager to experience the youthful vibrancy and bohemian artistry that Pawlikowski had brought to the theater in Kraków. In addition to those works by Lucjan Rydel, Stanisław Przybszewski, Stanisław Wyspiański and Gabriela Zapolska he had already presented in Kraków, in Lwów Pawlikowski continued to add plays by new young Polish writers, such as Leopold Staff, Włodzimierz Perzyński, Tadeusz Rittner, Karol Irzykowski, Władysław Orkan, Jerzy Żuławski, and Wilhelm Feldman.

Less concerned whether the plays he presented would make an enduring mark on the Polish theater, Pawlikowski continued to do what he had done in Kraków by making the stage immediately accessible to new talents from both Poland and abroad. Above all, Pawlikowski valued quality in the plays he selected. "He did not limit himself," Władysław Kozicki observed in his history of the theater in Lwów, "to Maeterlinck, Strindberg, Ibsen, Gorky, Przybyszewski, or to a

Chapter 4: Between Art and the Nation

particular category of the work of Young Poland. But with equal care and with a subtle sense of style [Pawlikowski] presented works of the old Polish repertoire (Bogusławski, Zabłocki, Niemcewicz), the classical Polish repertoire (Mickiewicz, Słowacki, Fredro) and foreign repertoire (Molier, Shakespeare, Goethe, Schiller), keeping in mind modern foreign drama on a wide scale of a variety of types (Hauptmann, Hoffmanstahl, Sudermann, Schnitzler, Bahr, Lavedan, Lemaitre, Rostand, France, Mirbeau, Shaw, Björnson, Hejermans, Verga, Bracco, Tolstoi, Chekhov, and others)."[144] The charges of inconsistency in his aesthetic program, albeit valid, misconstrued Pawlikowski's primary agenda as a director of creating a cosmopolitan theater in Poland. Alfred Wysocki, who translated *The Well of the Saints*, recalled the director's attention to stagecraft as that of an artistic innovator rather than an administrator or professional man of the theater.[145] "Pawlikowski," Wysocki stressed, "was not an irresponsible dilletante nor a self-educated man. He studied the theater seriously for a long time. He knew the methods, the styles of acting and staging of Antoine, Reinhardt, the French Comedy, the Viennese *Burgtheater*, and the Berlin *Deutsches Theater*, with all the ideas and technical differences that arose between them."[146]

Under Pawlikowski the Lwów theater became a kind of laboratory for innovative stagecraft. Without necessarily revolutionizing stagecraft or acting, Pawlikowski and his co-directors, actors, and set designers put on a varied and rapidly changing repertoire of plays, which kept them in a nearly constant process of improvisation and interpretation. The speed and zeal with which Pawlikowski managed to present the plays of Young Poland's newest playwrights to the stage gave credence to the notion that for him it was performance that mattered most. "Pawlikowski's strength," Wilhelm Feldman observed at the time, "rested primarily in his directorial knowledge and rich productions, such as those works that were fortunate to receive his favor."[147] Giving equal weight to the movement and speech of the actors, the lighting, set design, and props, he strove to make his performances faithful to the intentions of the author and the logic of the play itself. Whenever possible he would often invite the author to collaborate during rehearsals. "Pawlikowski," Wysocki explained, "followed the foreign repertoire with great interest. When he learned from the press of some novelty, whose production was praised in Vienna or Berlin, at his own cost he sent an actor or stage designer in for them to give him an opinion of the production."[148]

Ironically, the debut of play by an Irish-Ireland writer did not take place while Pawlikowski served as director of the Municipal Theater, but rather during his short-lived tenure as the theater's artistic director (1908-1909). The production, which paired Synge's *The Well of the Saints* and Wyspiański's *Sędziowie* (The Judges), premiered on November 11, 1908 and ran for a total of three performances.¹⁴⁹ Listing *The Judges* as one of five new Polish plays produced that year in his retrospective article on the 1908 theatrical season, Adam Zagórski pointed out that the evening was originally intended to be a special performance marking the first anniversary of Wyspiański's death.¹⁵⁰ This had, in fact, been the case for the Polish premiere of *The Judges* in Vilnius in December 1907, where it debuted together with Staff's "Elegy on the Death of Stanisław Wyspiański" and a scene from *Noc listopadowa* (November Night) in a ceremonial evening heavy with national sentiment organized in memory of Wyspiański.¹⁵¹ A similar formula held for other productions of *The Judges* in Warsaw, Òódź, and Kraków that followed over the next two years. Timed to take place just under a year after the death of Wyspiański, the evening was understandably potent with emotion and national feeling.

Pawlikowski's bold decision to include the work of a largely unknown modern Irish playwright in the evening's program sent a clear message to theatergoers in Lwów that he envisioned the evening more as a theatrical than a patriotic event. Heavily criticized throughout his career for not performing more of Wyspiański's plays, Pawlikowski's critics misunderstood was fundamentally a cosmopolitan at heart, and his goal first and foremost was to reshape the Polish theater along the lines of the European theatrical reform movement. In matching *The Judges* and *The Well of the Saints*, Pawlikowski brought to the Lwów stage two of the newest and most innovative playwrights in the European theater. Wyspiański had completed his play on his deathbed just a year earlier in 1907, and Synge's play had debuted a mere three years prior in Dublin. As Frank Biletz has pointed out, the European debut of Synge's play had taken place at the Deutsches Theater in Berlin a little over two years before, on January 12, 1906, giving "the Irish National Theatre its first international recognition."¹⁵² The Municipal Theater's production of Synge's play represented only the third performance to date of a play by Synge on the European continent.¹⁵³ As it turned out, Pawlikowski's joint production of *The Judges* and *The Well of the Saints* transformed what was potentially a local tribute to Wyspiański into an event of greater significance for the contemporary Polish theater. The fact that he managed to organize a production of both plays at such an early date was testament not only to Pawlikowski's awareness of what was taking place outside of Poland, but also to the unheralded role he played as a pioneer in the modern Polish theater.

While *The Judges* and *The Well of the Saints* seem to differ in tone, upon closer examination both plays featured combined highly stylized peasant dialects and rural settings with a measure of surface level reality to create an atmosphere that was at once familiar and extraordinary. Combining in varying degrees elements of tragedy, naturalism, and symbolism with a strong folk sensibility,

Chapter 4: Between Art and the Nation

both Wyspiański and Synge succeeded in creating new forms of drama that were both expressly national and wholly universal. Aside from maing their work challenging to realize on the stage, this combination of characteristics proved difficult for many of their contemporaries to understand fully.

As he had done with *Klątwa* (The Curse), a play with which it is often compared, Wyspiański adapted *The Judges* from a newspaper story of a real-life event, which he then recast along the lines of classical tragedy. Set in a small, backward Polish village, *The Judges* takes place in one act on an evening of the Friday Sabbath. The play opens in an inn run by a Jewish family, comprised of the father, Samuel, and his two sons, Nathan and Joas. Serving in the home of the Jewish innkeepers is a young woman named Jewdocha. With the arrival of the *"Dziad"* (a beggar), it becomes apparent that Samuel ruined Jewdocha's family financially and that the beggar is her father, who was sent to prison for trying to kill Samuel. Impoverished and alone, Jewdocha was taken in by the innkeepers as a servant in her own house. The beggar confronts Samuel over past wrongs, prophesying that the elderly Jewish innkeeper will come to know the same misfortune he has experienced. Following their exit, Jewdocha and Nathan, the elder of the two sons, become embroiled in an argument, bringing to light the history of Jewdocha's doomed love affair with Nathan. Jewdocha, having fallen in love with Nathan while in service in the inn and becoming pregnant, is convinced by Nathan to abort the child, which she attempted to do with poison but ultimately carried out with her bare hands. Frightened by the beggar's return, Samuel and Nathan then scheme to kill Jewdocha and to place the blame on her father. Jewdocha meanwhile talks to the beggar and learns that he is her father. Distraught over killing her child, Jewdocha confesses to her father and to Nathan her desire to die. With the arrival of the *"Urlopnik"* (a solder on leave), the tension of the drama quickly escalates. The soldier, Jewdocha's brother, starts a quarrel with Nathan about his intentions to go to town, accusing him of abandoning Jewdocha. Nathan, who is involved in trafficking poor peasant women, produces a pistol and in a fight with the soldier Jewdocha is mortally wounded. An inquiry of judges made up of the heads of the community finds the soldier guilty, but at the last second Joas, Samuel's younger son, reveals to all present Samuel's and Nathan's guilt. Upon declaring the truth, Joas, who is musically gifted, dies of a sudden heart attack. Furious and devasted, Samuel admits his guilt and begs God for forgiveness. A priest arrives to give last rites to Jewdocha, who is dying in an inner bedroom. In the final scene, all the remaining characters stand in the shadows, lit on one side by the soft glow from the Sabbath candles and on the other by the pale light from the adjoining room where Jewdocha has expired. The beggar closes the play by asking God to return in heaven all that he has lost on earth.

Wyspiański began *The Judges* sometime in early 1900, after reading about an actual murder in the paper in the summer of 1899 and following the investigation that ensued. Wyspiański rooted what amounted to a true story in the realistic detail of Polish village life, but through the ensuing dialogue and action he quickly moved the drama away from surface reality and toward a symbolic vision. The contrasting tones were cause for disagreement among Polish critics as to the central meaning of the play. "*The Judges*," Ostap Ortwin maintained in his review of the play for *The Critique* in 1907, "is not a portrait of the Jewish world, but a dramatization of an adventurous episode from the lives of a few despicable characters... But on this little fragment of the world the elements of poet's tragic creativity were accentuated."[154] In typical fashion, Lack took issue with Ortwin's analysis of the tragic structure of *The Judges* in "Budowa tragedii" (The Structure of Tragedy) in the same journal six months later in 1908. "If I say," Lack argued "that the goal of this drama is not to present characters, I mean precisely that: the goal of this drama is not to be a drama."[155] For Lack, the predominant role of fate in *The Judges*, which propelled the drama towards its inevitable and tragic conclusion, was in keeping his reading of Wyspiański's work in terms of eternal presence in art. Much like in *Boleslas the Brave*, the characters in *The Judges* are unconscious of and powerless to change the sequence of events, which have been fated to repeat as part of the universal drama of crime and punishment. Samuel's two sons, Joas and Nathan, embody the moral divide in the family. Joas, pure of heart and naturally talented, stands in clear contrast to Nathan, whose black attire signifies his evil heart and wicked lifestyle.

NATAN
Myślisz ty, że Bóg tobie gada?

JOAS
Że Bóg przeze mnie ostrzega
przed karą, co późna spada.[156]

NATHAN
Do you think that God talks to you?

JOAS
That God through me warns
Of punishment that will later fall.

Ostensibly set in a small, backward village in southeastern Galicia, over the course of the play the inn and the characters fade into symbolic vision of human nature.

Chapter 4: Between Art and the Nation

"People [in *The Judges*] really are incidental," Lack explained, "you can substitute characters in whichever way: the course and flow of events will be the same."[157] Unlike *The Curse*, in which tragedy grew out of a disruption in the natural order of the pagan world, Wyspiański shaped *The Judges* according to a moral order. "*The Judges*," Wilhelm Feldman, the editor of *The Critique*, had argued in a postscript rebuttal to Ortwin's article, "already in its title contains the central idea; giving weight to the execution of a deed in its entirety over its aristic and powerful expression."[158] Wyspiański's drama, therefore, was not so much a condemnation of contemporary society as it was an artistic conception of the human experience. As Lack observed, the true judge in the play was the poet himself, Wyspiański, and the characters were simply the players in his imagination.[159]

As both a melodramatic family drama and a symbolic vision of the power of destiny, *The Judges* was a deceptively innovative and difficult play to stage for the still evolving Polish theater. While on the surface it appeared to be a tragic story rooted in the contemporary life of rural Poland, Wyspiański controlled the action and stylized the behavior in such a way that the unfolding events appeared inevitable and much more universal in nature. Despite the largely symbolic readings of Ortwin and Lack, Tymon Terlecki has maintained that Wyspiański's contemporaries performed *The Judges* incorrectly in the years following his death by rendering it too realistically.[160] As there are few details regarding the actual performance, however, such a determination is difficult to make definitively. "In the direction," Ludwik Solski recalled of the performance in his memoirs, "there was among other things one great idea underscoring the stages of crime and punishment, which bound these people together like a chain. Pawlikowski ordered that a red handkerchief be passed among them, going from hand to hand, so that in the end the hand of the Soldier would throw it – like a bloody mark – on the neck of Joas."[161] Although the Lwów critics did not point out this detail in their reviews of *The Judges*, Solski suggested that Terlecki might not have been entirely correct in his assertion. The use of color would have been more in keeping with Pawlikowski's deepening interest in the theoretical approaches of Edward Gordon Craig at the time. It also reflected the growing understanding of Young Poland's critics, such as Lack and Ortwin, of Wyspiański's genius as a playwright whose artistry drew upon the immutable power and interplay of forces such as myth, sin, and fate in the universe. "The motifs [of the Judges]," Lack insisted, "are not ethical in nature, but exclusively artistic, and therefore these artistic motifs are the basis of its structure."[162] When considered in light of the perceptions of *The Judges* of contemporary observers such as Solski and Lack, Terlecki's dismissal of the early performances of Wyspiański's play appears wide of the mark. Critical interpretions, however, were one thing, but the realization of such lofty ideas in a performance was quite another. Pawlikowski may have designed the performance to reflect a more symbolic interpretation of *The Judges*, but it was quite possible that either his vision or his actors' performance failed to translate on the stage.

A basic problem with Pawlikowski's conception of *The Judges* originated his decision to divide the original one-act play into two scenes, with the first scene ending with the shooting of Jewdocha and the second scene beginning with the arrival of the judges. Pawlikowski used this two-scene arrangement in the 1908 joint production, and it served as the basis for subsequent productions in Kraków, Warsaw, and other Polish cities.[163] The decision to alter the original one-act structure of *The Judges* had natural consequences for how it was understood. Terlecki has maintained that the change to the two-scene format ruined Wyspiański's consciously symbolic treament of time and reality.[164] By structuring the entire drama to unfold on the evening of the Friday Sabbath, with great precision and conservation Wyspiański was able to raise a realistic story to a symbolic level with maximum effect. Dividing the play into two parts disrupted the intended intensification of the tragic effect, making it appear too realistic. Although he admitted having not attended the production of *The Judges*, Zagórski felt that the play's intended effect had suffered as a result of the change. "The division of the work into two acts," Zagórski explained, "and the expansion of the time of action (against the express indications of the poet) over the course of three days [was] unfortunate, since it destroyed the mood of the Sabbath evening, in which the entire work is held."[165] In the end, the decision to divide the play into two scenes may have been a practical one, in order to allow for an intermission or to counterbalance Synge's three-act play.[166]

In contrast to Wyspiański, Synge did not base *The Well of the Saints* on an actual news event. Instead, the Irish playwright rooted his drama in the living culture and language of the Irish countryside. While Synge famously traveled to the Aran Islands and to Kerry in the west of Ireland to observe closely the lives of the local people, he situated *The Well of the Saints* in the Wicklow Mountains "one or more centuries ago."[167] Synge utilized an archetypal dramatic character type, the blind beggar, to create an anti-miracle play that exposed the hypocrisy of human relations through the problem of appearance and reality. Comprised of three acts, Synge's play opens with two married blind beggars, Martin and Mary Doul, sitting at the crossroads outside their local village and begging passersby for money. Although both are weathered and hideously ugly, they are convinced of their own fine looks. Timmy, a local blacksmith, tells the beggars that a saint coming that way later could cure their blindness with holy water from a miraculous well. The blind couple allows the wandering saint to restore their sight with the holy water, but having been deceived by the local people for

Chapter 4: Between Art and the Nation

years as to their true appearance, they begin to quarrel viciously upon regaining their sight and seeing each other for the first time. In Act Two, bitterness and disappointment at their true appearance drive the pair of beggars apart. Disillusioned by the harshness of the actual world and the meanness of the local people, however, the beggars begin to argue with the local village people and gradually begin to lose their sight until they are totally blind. Act Three opens with the beggars once more at the crossroads, where they commiserate about the hypocrisy of the villagers and imagine a new life together. Convinced that the beggars want to be cured, the local people persuade the passing saint to restore their sight a second time. Martin refuses the Saint's offer of a second, permanent cure, but when the local people persuade Mary to have her sight restored he changes his mind, only to knock the cup of holy water from the Saint's hand. The play closes with the blind beggars cursing the Saint and the community before setting off for the south of Ireland, where they believe the people will be less duplicitous.

Compared with *The Judges*, *The Well of the Saints* is more subtle and harder to define. In similar fashion to Wyspiański, through dialogue and stage directions Synge created surface level realism for his drama. By situating the action of the play in the Wicklow Mountains, *The Well of the Saints* contained a clear cultural and geographical reference to the region associated with the ancient monastery of Saint Kevin at Glendalough. Set in the indistinct past, however, Synge transformed a seemingly realistic drama of Irish village life in this remote site of faith and learning into a timeless interpretation of human nature. "Mr. Synge," Yeats explained in 1905 in *Samhain*, "alone has written of the peasant as he is to all the ages; of the folk-imagination as it has been shaped by centuries of life among fields or on fishing-grounds."[168] Blind, bitter, and forced to beg, Martin and Mary Doul appear to all to be the embodiment of misfortune. Despite their bickering, they appreciate one another and take joy in the unobserved beauty of nature. Deprived of sight and unburdened by the worries of the working world, Synge's blind beggars have the temperament of artists. The benevolence of the villagers and the Saint, however, masks an underlying meanness of spirit and a lack of self-awareness, or moral blindness. While Wyspiański utilized fate as the artistic structure of *The Judges*, Synge undermined all traces of transcendence in *The Well of the Saints*. As a result, Synge's beggars emerged against the timeless, unchanging backdrop of the Irish countryside as two living, truly independent characters in Irish drama.

Synge's innovative play represented an equally imposing challenge for Pawlikowski and the Municipal Theater to stage as *The Judges*. Under a naturalistic patina, *The Well of the Saints* contained aspects of folklore, satire, miracle play, and tragedy. It was neither a naturalistic drama in the mode of Zola, nor was it classically structured tragedy along Greek lines. Synge's colorful dialogue and dark humor, moreover, meant that the emotions of anger, sadness, and happiness were all present in equal degrees. The poster announcing the twin bill of *The Judges* and *The Well of the Saints* characterized Synge's play as a legend. Whether this characterization stemmed from Young Poland's association of Irish drama with fantasy or from its own literary predilections is unclear. Kasprowicz's translation of *The Countess Cathleen* four years earlier would have been an available reference, but the description was an insightful commentary on the difficulty Young Poland faced in locating appropriate frames for the work of Irish-Ireland dramatists. As was the case with *The Judges*, reviewers gave few details regarding the actual performance of *The Well of the Saints*. In his discussion of Heller's tenure as director of the Municipal Theater, however, Stanisław Hałabuda has claimed that Pawlikowski employed an operatic choir in *The Well of the Saints* as part of his tendency to make dynamic use of crowd scenes on stage.[169] Albeit unconfirmed by contemporary sources, Hałabuda's contention suggests that Pawlikowski envisioned Synge's play as a complement rather than as a contrast to *The Judges*. If true, this would have altered the tone and presentation of *The Well of the Saints* considerably.

The issue of tone in Wysocki's version of *The Well of the Saints* is worth note, for as theater director in both Kraków and Lwów Pawlikowski routinely commissioned translations expressly for the purpose of performance.[170] Wysocki recollected translating several Scandinavian dramas, as well as one by Synge, for Pawlikowski about this time.[171] "Pawlikowski," he recalled, "would interrupt every so often during the reading of my translation saying, 'It seems to me that that word should be moved, or changed, or thrown out altogether' — and he was always right."[172] With this observation, Wysocki provided some insight into Pawlikowski's knowledge of Synge's play and his method of planning the production in the minutest detail. The source of Wysocki's text was most likely Max Meyerfield's translation *Der heilige Brunnen* (The Holy Well), which was used in the Berlin production of *The Well of the Saints*.[173] On the whole, Wysocki's translation was a faithful one.[174] By translating *The Well of the Saints* as *Cudowne źródło* (The Miraculous Well), Wysocki lent a slightly dreamy, magical quality to the play's title.[175] The difference in meaning was slight, but it raised the potential for confusion among theatergoers who may have been expecting a play based on folk legends or fairy tales.[176] The real power of Synge's plays rested in the delicate balance of pathos and humor he was able to strike in the colorful language of his characters, and it was this that the Polish version lacked the most. As pointed out by A. G. van Hamel in his study of Anglo-Irish syntax, Synge

Chapter 4: Between Art and the Nation

and Yeats in their plays utilized a dynamic form of Anglo-Irish speech that drew upon an older variety of English and the moribund Gaelic language to create a uniquely Irish form of literature in English.[177] Wysocki's inability to render Synge's vivid dialogue of Synge's characters or his decision to excise references to Irish placenames and local scenery detracted from the overall dynamism of *The Well of the Saints*. This was no small problem, and whatever misinterpretation there may have been of the Synge's play may have been a result of it. The Lwów audience did not experience a true rendering of Synge's Anglo-Irish speech, but rather a transposition of Synge's dialogue into a stylized folk dialect similar to that used by Wyspiański, Rydel, and other Young Poland playwrights.[178] Based on the reviews of the play, it appeared that whatever deficiencies the translation may have had were remedied by the Polish cast's ability to draw upon this established form of folk language.

Pawlikowski chose to stage *The Judges* first and *The Well of the Saints* second. Due to the ceremonious nature of the evening, this arrangement was normal and expected. As the shorter of the two works, Wyspiański's play naturally lent itself to the role of the openening play. Both plays represented something new to the Lwów theatergoing audiences. Equal parts comedy and tragedy, Synge's play was an interesting counterpoise to *The Judges*. By positioning *The Well of the Saints* second in the program, Pawlikowski also suggested to the audiences attending the performances in the Municipal Theater the notion of the broader European theater. The critics in their reviews were quick to recognize Wyspiański and Synge as innovative talents of the modern theater, and as such they seemed generally pleased with the Municipal Theater's performance of both plays. In discussing *The Judges* and *The Well of the Saints*, however, there was little attempt to compare the two works directly, other than to raise the issue of their contrasting styles as a factor affecting their reception as a pair. It was clear from the tone of the reviews that the Lwów critics recognized the joint production as a challenging attempt to stage something entirely new to the Polish theater. In light of the criticism leveled at the Municipal Theater for its failure to continue developing artistically, Pawlikowski's effort, however flawed, to break new artistic ground represented a small triumph in and of itself.

Wysocki, who was also a theater critic for *Gazeta Lwowska* (The Lwów Gazette), reviewed the joint performance in successive articles on the 12th and 13th of November, greeting it with enthusiastic praise. "We experienced yesterday an evening full of impressions," Wysocki maintained, "Wyspiański reached to the depths of our souls and made an impression there that will last a long time, maybe forever, in our memories. Synge played on similar strings, creating from like strains of the tragedy of the human heart a hopelessly painful song of sadness and doubt."[179] For Wysocki, the sense of expectation surrounding the evening's theater was not limited to these two uniquely talented dramatic artists, but it extended to Pawlikowski in his newly assumed position as artistic director as well. "Next to the names of these two authors," Wysocki pointed out, "one of whom is the pride of Polish literature, the other counting perhaps among the stars of Ireland, yesterday evening combined also with a fact significant in the history of our theater and full of the best indications for its future. That is, Tadeusz Pawlikowski undertook his return to the Lwów stage."[180] Wysocki, who was naturally partial in his view, congratulated Heller for his willingness to welcome Pawlikowski back and perceived a bright future for theater in Lwów. "This growth," Wysocki explained, indicating the Lwów stage, "this overcoming of old mistakes, is a pledge, with which yesterday's performances of 'The Judges' and 'The Well of the Saints' marked a great step forward."[181] This was precisely what Pawlikowski's supporters had hoped for from his return.

While improper interpretation on the actors' role would be an issue in the productions of Yeats's and Synge's plays in Warsaw and Kraków in the years to come, for Wysocki it was not the case. "Translating this Irish legend," Wysocki reflected, "I never even guessed that it was possible to extract so much hidden character and strength from the character of Martin Doul. The acting of Mr. Feldman revealed in him an entirely new man to me."[182] Given the numerous changes, the main characters' experience, both physical and emotional, in Synge's play required actors with considerable talent and imagination. "The tragedy of his soul," Wysocki observed, "is the tragedy of a degenerate cripple, who having seen the world full of wrongs, worries, and lies with eyes cured by a miracle, willingly denies himself sight in order to live longer in the delusions and ramblings of a blind man's imagination."[183] Whereas Wysocki felt *The Judges* harmonized with Wyspiański's literary *oeuvre*, *The Well of the Saints* presented the Polish stage with an entirely new kind of drama. "Modeled on Maeterlinck," Wysocki declared in a more extended critique in the following day's paper, "'The Well of the Saints' is above all a curious and interesting scenic experiment, which presents a wide plane to display the creativity and intuition of the director. Only perhaps Reinhardt or Pawlikowski could attempt a similar experiment [...]."[184] By referring to *The Judges* as a tragedy and *The Well of the Saints* as a legend in his review, Wysocki drew attention to Pawlikowski's intention of presenting two stylistically different plays in a single program.[185] In doing so, Pawlikowski effectively forced his audience to reflect upon the plays as a pair. The world described in *The Judges* was not realistic, but rather a stylized version of the Polish countryside removed from time and filtered through Wyspiański's tragic imagination. Synge, too, situated *The Well of the Saints* in the indistinct past,

Chapter 4: Between Art and the Nation

which resulted in a portrait of the Irish country life that was neither realistic nor fantastic.[186] Through the use of such broad strokes, combined with the realistic aspects of country life, both Wyspiański and Synge created unique forms of drama that challenged the directors and the actors of the modern stage. In choosing such innovative dramatists, Pawlikowski tested the abilities of his Polish cast, as well as the understanding of his audience.

Wysocki did not attempt to draw a parallel between the two plays, but in mentioning the motif of fatalism he unintentionally suggested a link between *The Judges* and *The Well of the Saints*. "Evil committed," Wysocki explained, describing *The Judges*, "carries with it the necessity of punishment... The main characters of *The Judges* struggle in this chain [of deeds], from which each carries on their forehead the bloody brand of sin."[187] Although innocent, from the beginning of the play Joas and Jewdocha are doomed. Polish theatergoing audiences would have been quite familiar with this literary convention, especially in light of Wyspiański's earlier use of it in *The Curse*. Synge's play, in contrast, turned the determinism of Classical drama upside down by employing the dichotomy of appearance and reality. The beggars, content in their blindness, are dismayed and disillusioned upon being cured. In choosing to return to their blind, delusional ways, the beggars accept their lot, while the sighted villagers remain oblivious to their own shortcomings. Wysocki, to his credit, was perceptive enough to recognize challenging dramatic characters for the Polish theater in the roles of the two blind beggars. "The main positive quality [of the play]," Wysocki stressed, "is established on the foreground and all the action supporting the role of the blind man, who is a personification of the principle that between the world of dreams and illusion and naked, true life there exists a chasm so fathomless that there is no human strength which could even it."[188] Just as Wyspiański's innkeepers cannot escape from the consequences of their sinful actions, Synge's beggars are incapable of changing their nature and accepting the reality of their lives. Albeit in differing ways, both *The Judges* and *The Well of the Saints* presented the modern Polish theater with new approaches to the dramatic representation of the human experience.

The only problem that Wysocki had with Synge's drama was a logical one. While accepting the notion that happiness was a relative concept and that some people prefer to live a life of blissful delusion rather than face reality, Wysocki felt that the many questions unanswered by the Irish play detracted from its effectiveness in the end. "Accompanying this thesis," Wysocki asserted, "in spoken dialogue of the perfect feeling of the theater, the author nevertheless sank into a dilemma, which he was not able to resolve."[189] The essence of Wysocki's objection was that the blind beggar, Martin, who partook of the holy water with sinful intentions in mind, should not have regained his sight. This was a rather literal, Catholic reading on the part of Wysocki, who admitted that his confusion might have been the result of a misunderstanding of Synge's original intentions. Although he was intimately familiar with the play, Wysocki made the same mistake many Irish nationalists had made by taking the words of the Irish playwright at face value. Synge was not concerned with representing the reality of Irish life so much as he was with examining the intricacies of human nature. Wysocki's difficulty was neither a logical nor a theological breakdown, but rather a misinterpretation. Martin and Mary Doul entertain delusions about their appearance, but they do not pretend to be anything other than what they are. With society, however, there is no self-awareness. Given its place in a production alongside Wyspiański's heavy tragedy, it was not surprising that Polish audiences may have been puzzled by the twists of Synge's undivine tragicomedy also experienced trouble deciphering Synge's dramatic artistry and his particular brand of black humor. Difficulties such as these experienced by the translator of the play point to the extent to which Pawlikowski was continuing to break new ground as a director.

The reviewer for another local paper, *Goniec Polski* (The Polish Dispatch), writing under the pseudonym "G," echoed Wysocki's praise of the acting in the Municipal Theater's production. "Mr. Feldman," the reviewer maintained, referring to the lead actor, "in the role of the old man clearly exceeded his friends in Berlin and Dresden, where we saw this play on the stage. The creation of this character is masterful and surpasses all past creations of this unforgettably able artist of great individuality."[190] Polish critics in the years to come would stress the shared experience of the Polish and Irish nations in their reviews of Irish plays, but G.'s recognition of the close links between the theater in Lwów and the West underscored Pawlikowski's intention to pair the two works in this performance on aesthetic rather than national grounds.

In his analysis of *The Well of the Saints*, G. cited a lengthy quote, attributed to Synge, to the effect that most people would chose to be blind rather than be able to see. As Synge conceived it, the problem with self-appointed "healers" was that they gave little thought to how the cured would benefit from the miraculous cure. The blind couple discover upon being cured that they have lost their livelihood, begging. Added to their misfortune is the shocking realization that they are not as handsome as they had been led to believe. In the end, then, they are much poorer, both materially and spiritually, than they were before they were healed. The Irish countryside, therefore, in *The Well of the Saints* becomes a microcosm of the human experience. Thrust suddenly out of their from their state of blissful illusion, the beggars are forced to suffer the cold, hard reality of the world. The reviewer left it open to Polish readers to arrive at their own conclusions regarding the play, but he could not help inserting what appeared to be a curiously local political dig.[191] "They want to be blind," G. further explained, "and the blind man destroys the miraculous can in which the healing potion is found – because the saint wants to cure them by force."[192]

Unlike Wysocki, the reviewer for *The Polish Dispatch* found fault with Pawlikowski for his decision to pair *The Judges* with *The Well of the Saints*. "The one piece of advice we would like to give the direction," the reviewer offered politely, "is not to stage this work after 'Judges'. The mind, worn out by 'Judges,' superficially accepts 'The Well of the Saints' against its will rather than knowing whether it deserves it, and that might be why this work was coolly received yesterday. After 'Judges,' it would be useful to have something substantial, but lighter."[193] The reviewer's complaint that *The Well of the Saints* was too weighty to follow *The Judges* lends credence to the theory that Pawlikowski staged one or both of the works incorrectly. While the reviewer's feelings of frustration may have stemmed from the simple fact that the joint production made for a long evening of theater, this seems unlikely. It was common in theaters throughout Poland to fill out a program by putting on more than one play or by grouping a play with a dramatic poem or musical piece. Complaints of a lengthy program, however, cannot be entirely ruled out, as Pawlikowski received similar criticism six years later in Kraków when he paired *The Well of the Saints* with Szymon Szymonowicz's sixteenth century play *Castus Joseph*. The problem with Pawlikowski's production, therefore, stemmed from the fact that Lwów theatergoers expected a comedy to follow Wyspiański's heavy tragedy. This may have been Pawlikowski's intention with *The Well of the Saints*, but given Synge's dark humor and the unique construction of his plays the director may have missed his intended mark.

It was clear from this early production of Synge's *The Well of the Saints* in Lwów that Irish drama had much to offer the Polish theater. The fact that Pawlikowski chose to pair it with Wyspiański's play *The Judges* only served to highlight the extent to which Polish and Irish playwrights were actively engaged in reimagining the theater. Pawlikowski's stock in trade was first and foremost to view the stage as an artistic challenge, which would have explained the absence of national themes in the reviews of the production. It should be remembered that Pawlikowski at this time was deeply interested in the work of Craig, which may have led him to experiment with contrasts in lighting and color in staging Synge's play.[194] Although Arnold Szyfman, a young theater critic and emerging director in Kraków, had written about him as early as 1905, Craig's approach to the stage was not yet widely understood by Young Poland.[195] It was apparent

The Impact of Irish-Ireland on Young Poland, 1890–1919

from the reviews of Pawlikowski's production that Wyspiański and Synge's half-realistic, half-symbolic dramas also represented something new to both theatergoers and critics alike. Pawlikowski did not feature Wyspiański's work prominently in his repertoire because he felt the Polish theater was not yet ready for it. Synge and Wyspiański, therefore, were well matched not only as innovators within the modern European theater, but within their native theaters as well. In the final analysis, the Municipal Theater's production was both representative of the pivotal role Pawlikowski played in modernizing the Polish theater and indicative of the direction in which it would develop in the future.

Given its brief run, whatever impact *The Well of the Saints* made on the Lwów theatergoing public was ultimately limited. While Wanda Krajewska is accurate in her assertion that Irish drama failed to achieve popular resonance during the Young Poland period, she failed to consider place this reception within the larger reality of the Polish theater during this period. In the Municipal Theater, new plays debuted on a weekly if not a daily basis. It was rare, moreover, for a play to have an extended run.[196] The exceptions to this rule, understandably, were the immensely popular nationalistic plays by Wyspiański, Mickiewicz, and Słowacki. As was the case in the Kraków theater under Kotarbiński, Pawlikowski's successor, these extended runs were often more of a factor of box office power than they were of critical acclaim. It was not unusual, therefore, for *The Well of the Saints* to close with little or no fanfare. Pawlikowski, after all, was a cosmopolitan whose focus rested on the challenge of establishing artistic theater in Poland, not necessarily Irish theater. It was the attempt, or the performance, that mattered most. What is more, the resonance Synge's play had among theatergoers in Lwów cannot be accurately measured, because Pawlikowski held the position of artistic director in the Municipal Theater for less than a year. The curtailed tenure cut short his ambitious plans for the theater and precluded any thoughts of revisiting plays at a later date. The fact that Pawlikowski returned to *The Well of the Saints* in 1914 suggested that Synge's play at least had importance for him if not for the wider Polish theatergoing public.

Albeit short-lived, Pawlikowski's decision to stage *The Well of the Saints* was also significant for reasons that extended far beyond the Polish theater. Synge's plays also failed to gain a popular following among theatergoers in Berlin and Prague. What is more, Synge's plays received a cool, if not outright hostile response in Ireland as well. While this early European exposure did not prove to be immediately successful, it did lend much needed weight to the struggling Irish theater in the face of heated partisan attacks and intense criticism. "Synge's foreign success," Yeats explained in a letter to John Quin in September 1905, "is worth more to us than would be the like success of any other of our people, for

Chapter 4: Between Art and the Nation

he has been the occasion of all the attacks upon us. I said in a speech some time ago that he would have a European reputation in five years, but his enemies have mocked the prophecy."[197] The fact that *The Well of the Saints* appeared at all on the Polish stage was both a triumph and a moral victory for the Abbey Theatre in the face of condemnation from Irish nationalists.

While Pawlikowski's production of *The Well of the Saints* fit with the growing international acceptance of Synge and Yeats as visionary artists of the modern European theater, in the years that followed Polish critics ironically began to observe a unique, national subtext underlying the work of the Irish playwrights that distinguished it from that of their Belgian, German, or Italian counterparts. In both theater reviews and articles on the Irish-Ireland theater, they displayed an awareness of the experiential and historical links between Poland and Ireland. These connections, what Zamoyski has termed parallels of predicament, gained in significance as Polish critics began to call attention to the active role the Irish theater was then playing in Ireland's cultural rebirth.[198] For Nowaczyński, Yeats and Synge were not just two more representatives of the modern, reformed European theater, but also key figures in the foundation of an Irish national theater that was giving tangible proof of Ireland's cultural autonomy. As such, they were inspirational to and reaffirming of the efforts of Polish writers, actors and directors, who desired a cultural rewakening for Poland. Poles, therefore, were in the unusual position of encountering in the works of Irish dramatists a national theater parallel both in terms of its artistic innovation and its cultural affinity. These feelings would only intensify in Poland as World War I drew nearer.

Irish-Ireland's introduction to Poland during this period took place in the midst of Young Poland's ascendancy as a cultural movement. The amount of attention given to Yeats and Synge was remarkable not only in terms of how early it occurred, but also who it involved. Through Lack, Miriam, Kasprowicz, and Pawlikowski, Irish literature received serious attention from several of Young Poland's leading intellectuals in the areas of criticism, poetry, and drama. Having played prominent roles in shaping the artistic outlook of the Polish cultural movement in the 1890s, the interest of these key players in Irish Ireland immediately placed it close to the artistic heart of Young Poland. In many respects, Lack and his colleagues found their creative counterparts in Yeats and Synge. With their ability to combine modernist aesthetics and folk culture, the Irish writers proved to be especially attractive as a means of addressing Young Poland's deep-rooted need to create art that was at once native and modern. As cultural actors, moreover, the Irish writers also embodied a similar determination to elevate and to strengthen the nation through artistic self-expression.

The Impact of Irish-Ireland on Young Poland, 1890–1919

In the years to come, the place of Irish Ireland would change both in the nature and location of its reception. Whereas the introduction of Yeats and Synge took place largely within the context of Austrian Galicia, which was the spiritual birthplace of Young Poland, in the succeeding decade the focus of interest in Ireland would shift in large part to Warsaw. In part, this was a reflection of internal political changes within the Russian partition permitting a greater degree of cultural freedom, but it also was a sign that the spark of bohemian Kraków had begun to wane. The reasons for the loss of impetus in Galicia were manifold, but it was felt most in the death of Wyspiański at the close of 1907 and the subsequent relocation to Warsaw of the majority of the Polish theatrical community in the years that followed. The two intellectuals who showed interest in Irish Ireland in this period, Nowaczyński and Szyfman, were both born in Galicia and had started their artistic careers there. As members of the younger generation of Young Poland, however, both men eschewed the exaggerated aestheticism of the movement, and sought instead to establish a Polish cultural presence that was both tangible and lasting. This was evident in their shared interest in Irish Ireland, where from differing perspectives and for conflicting ends, they united with the common goal of founding a truly national Polish theater.

CHAPTER FIVE

MODELING THE IRISH THEATRE:
ART IN THE SHADOW OF WAR, 1919-1918

THE SUCCESS OF THE ABBEY THEATRE IN GARNERING BOTH NATIONAL and international attention since its establishment in 1904 presented Poles with an attractive theatrical model. As a theater devoted to presenting the works of dramatists that were both thoroughly modern and Irish, the Abbey Theatre epitomized the delicate balance of essentialism and cosmopolitanism that had from the beginning defined Young Poland as a movement. Interest in Yeats and Synge, therefore, was equally strong among those Poles who wanted to create a purely national theater and those who sought to introduce the ideas of the European theater reform movement to the Polish theater. Both in the essentialist criticism of Adolf Nowaczyński and in the innovative productions of Arnold Szyfman, Irish drama began to attract increasing attention as the efforts to establish a Polish national theater gathered momentum in the years immediately preceding World War I.

I. POLES OF THE WESTERN WORLD:
IRISH-IRELAND AND POLISH ESSENTIALISM

The initial interest Poles displayed in Irish-Ireland, evident in the translations by Stanisław Lack and Jan Kasprowicz, deepened and grew more complex as Polish critics began to examine the Irish movement more closely. Adolf Nowaczyński (1876–1944) and Marya Rakowska (1864–1940) proved knowledgeable and careful observers of Irish-Ireland. Although Nowaczyński and Rakowska differed sharply in style and tone, they both identified the Irish theater as an instructive example to which Young Poland should pay close attention. In their writing about the Abbey Theatre, Nowaczyński and Rakowska displayed Young Poland's

The Impact of Irish-Ireland on Young Poland, 1890–1919

openness to foreign impulses, while also exposing its innate tendency toward essentialism. Where they differed was in the significance to which they attached the sudden emergence of the Irish theater. Nowaczyński had lofty reasons for taking an interest in Ireland, but he was less concerned with the artistry of the stage than he was in fulfilling his deep felt need to galvanize his fellow Poles out of their collective national reverie. Rakowska, too, recognized a parallel between Young Poland and Irish-Ireland, but she pointed to the Irish dramatic movement as an inspirational model for a Polish theater that was scattered and in disarray.

Nowaczyński was the Polish critic with by far the keenest eye for developments taking place in Ireland over the first two decades of the twentieth century. Returning to the topic of Irish-Ireland several times during this period, his characterizations of the Irish cultural scene revealed a pattern fundamental to his position both as a social critic and as a literary figure within Young Poland. As a critic, Nowaczyński was profoundly shaped by his upbringing in Kraków. Raised in a middle class family, Nowaczyński's initial attraction to the burgeoning Young Poland movement at the end of the 1890s was its rebelliousness against the conventional values of the Kraków bourgeoisie. While Austrian liberalism made it possible for a movement such as Young Poland to emerge, Nowaczyński perceived a potential danger to Polish national identity in Galicia, where the traditional conservatism of Kraków society and the denationalizing pull of the Austrian civil service combined to create an atmosphere that was economically backward, intellectually stifling, and politically weak.[1] In "Krakowski zaścianek," published in the satirical collection *Figliki sowizdrzalskie* (The Little Jokes of a Clown) in 1908, Nowaczyński created a portrait of his native city far removed from its gloried, royal past.

> No a tymczasem? Boże pożal! Mówcie sami
> Zgrymaszoną parafią Kraków jest i kwita
> W której z trzech Polski dzielnic osiadły dziś mózgi.
> A wam kołtusy nadal przydadzą się rózgi!
> I gdy się raz chce wyrwać mizernych ichmości
> Z waszej ospałej, gnuśnej i głupiej istności
> To winniście czuć wdzięczność dla młodego grona,
> Że was cesarskim cięciem tnie od Nudy łona [.][2]

> And nowadays? God take pity! You say yourselves
> Kraków is a whimsical parish and equal
> To the other three Polish settled lands today in brains.
> But for your priggishness lashes are still needed!

Chapter 5: Modeling the Irish Theatre

And if one wants to break free of the miserable gentlemen
From your sleepy, idle and silly existence
You should feel grateful to the cluster of youth
Who cut you by caesarean section from the womb of Tedium [.]

For Nowaczyński, the parochial nature of Galician society, the calcified social order, and the politics of triloyalism combined to have the deleterious outcome such that local rather national matters took precedence. Nowaczyński felt the Austrian civil service further compounded the situation as Polish bureaucrats had more concern for government regulations and career advancement than they did with the fate of their nation. These forces, in Nowaczyński's view, not only had a denationalizing effect on Polish society, but they also rendered it virtually impossible to bring about change in Austrian Galicia, much less to redress Poland's partitioned status.

In both his own critical and his literary work Nowaczyński strove to prod his contemporaries out of what he perceived to be artistic self-indulgence or slothful reverie and into a more socially productive, progressive way of thinking. "Cultural sources," Anna Kiezuń maintains in her study of Nowaczyński, "were not eliminated from this literary position, but society was the most important object of Nowaczyński's interest."[3] His Irish articles, therefore, were designed not simply to inform his Polish readers, but to provoke and to persuade them. A contrarian by nature, Nowaczyński was always most comfortable writing from the position of a maverick. In this regard, Nowaczyński created a critical space somewhat apart from his generation from which he could attack those elements that he felt worked to weaken the Polish nation. "A critic," Nowaczyński declared in 'Aforyzmy sowizdrzała' (The Aphorisms of a Rogue) in 1902, "should have an open eye to the truths of tomorrow, and a closed eye to the lies of yesterday."[4] Whether it was the backwardness of Galician society or the mythologizing of the past of Polish Romantic nationalism, the common target of Nowaczyński's satire was the destructive tendency among Poles of self-delusion. For a nation already devastated by partition, Nowaczyński felt the lack of pragmatism and self-awareness left Poland even further weakened.

Co drugi Polak jest analfabetą,
Co trzeci Polak rodzi sie artystą,
Co czwarty Polak bywa spirytystą,
Co piąty snobkiem, sobkiem i estetą.
Och, oby lepiej każdy był atletą
Przeciętny Polak, rubli miał kroć i sto.[5]

The Impact of Irish-Ireland on Young Poland, 1890–1919

> Every second Pole is an illiterate,
> Every third Pole is born an artist,
> Every fourth Pole frequents a spiritualist,
> Every fifth is a snob, egoist and esthete.
> Oh, it would be better if each were an athlete
> The average Pole would have a hundredfold.

In this regard, there was a common chord between Nowaczyński and the emerging right wing ideology of Dmowski's National Democracy.[6] Dmowski, who presented his ideas in *Myśli nowoczesnego Polaka* (The Thoughts of a Modern Pole) in Lwów in 1903, promoted a narrow brand of patriotism in which all aspects of Polish life were subservient to the national idea.[7] Dmowski's rejection of both the idea of rebellion and the notion of conciliation represented what Alvin Marcus Fountain has termed a third way in Polish politics.[8] The contradictory nature of Nowaczyński's agenda as a satirist, which was aimed at strengthening Poland by tearing down the most sacred traditions and tenets of Polish nationalism, speaks to the extent to which he was advocating a new vision of the Polish nation that was informed by sober self-awareness and practical efforts toward progress. This approach, however, struck Nowaczyński's critics as being excessively negative, with little to offer his compatriots in the way of constructive criticism.

It was understandable that a young writer and critic such as Nowaczyński would find much to criticize in Kraków society. Young Poland, after all, had initially gained momentum as a reaction to the deadening artistic and political conservatism of the previous, Positivist, generation. What was less predictable, however, was Nowaczyński's hostility toward many of the key elements that also defined Young Poland. Despite being a well-traveled intellectual, Nowaczyński felt a strong dislike of his fellow modernists, an attitude he shared with Dmowski, because he believed many of them held attitudes that were detrimental to the formation of a strong and viable Polish identity. "Next to the national gods, the local demigods," Nowaczyński explained in another aphorism, "there are also the idiots of the epoch."[9] Drawn by the initial energy and assertiveness of the movement, Nowaczyński quickly came to loathe the shallow decadence of those in his generation who had reduced the original creative vitality of literary modernism to a fashionable lifestyle or a cult of behavior. As a determined realist, Nowaczyński had little patience for the bohemian poseurs and self-obsessed artists of Kraków's *moderna*, which was a view he captured in the story "Gladiolus tavernalis" in the satirical collection *Małpie zwierciadło* (Monkey's Mirror) in 1902.

Chapter 5: Modeling the Irish Theatre

Młyński perused from memory the gallery that had been coming here for several years... The second *modern vom Scheitel bis zur Sohle* arrived, parodying Verlaine and Baudelaire in Polish, individuals without originality, but sincere, enthusiastic about pure beauty, and getting drunk on pure alcohol on every odd day of the calendar, already critical of the socialist illusions of the young. The third *nuancer* of the generation arrived, these globetrotters of countries, aesthetics in black curls hanging down in a roisterous hairdo, perfumed creators of two piles of sonnets about swans, lions, ponds, water lilies, griffins, queens, promoting with posters their "collections," traveling through provincial towns with readings about themselves, writing anonymous, idolizing critiques of their work, debauched careerist youths, the youngest actors....[10]

At the heart of Nowaczyński's pastiche was his disdain for bohemian Kraków's conscious cultivation of the craft of external effect and the fashionable *accoutrements* of intellect. What was worse, these extreme modernists, exemplified by Lack and Przybyszewski, were not only intentionally obscure, self-absorbed aesthetes, but they were also intellectuals who contributed nothing to the practical betterment of Poland.[11] "Several poet-aesthetes," Nowaczyński teased in another aphorism, "having locked themselves in an ivory tower, demand to be carried around the market."[12] Poles, Nowaczyński's argument ran, would not assume their proper place in the world as long as they continued to delude themselves and to ignore their essential strengths as a nation.

The vehemence with which Nowaczyński criticized this segment of Young Poland originated in his belief that it had betrayed the movement's larger purpose as a culturally regenerative force for Poland. It was not the case that Nowaczyński despised all the writers of Young Poland. On the contrary, part of the paradox that made Nowaczyński both a part of Young Poland and one of its earliest critics was his deep respect for such a prominent proponent of Polish literary modernism as Miriam and the novelist Stefan Żeromski. Of great significance to Nowaczyński was the fact that both of these writers had returned to Poland after years abroad to contribute to the advancement of Polish cultural and national life. In publishing *Chimera*, Miriam represented to Nowaczyński neither a self-obsessed decadent nor an indifferent aesthete, but rather an important cultural ambassador for Poles across the partitions. As a publisher and critic, Miriam enriched Polish culture and life by broadening the intellectual awareness of his compatriots.[13] In marked contrast to the other two writers, Przybyszewski, the former editor of *Life* and Young Poland's self-styled Satanist, had also made a celebrated return to Poland after a lengthy stay abroad, but Nowaczyński felt he had chosen to foster a cult of personality as a high priest of art rather than to contribute to the betterment of Polish society in any real way.[14] Matters of style and aesthetics aside, Polish writers in Nowaczyński's view were to be both socially and aesthetically engaged.[15]

As a writer and critic, Nowaczyński was not against cosmopolitanism *per se*, for his own writings were encyclopedic and touched upon a wide array of topics in the literature, history, and politics of numerous other countries. Instead, as Tomasz Weiss has observed, Nowaczyński insisted criticism and literature always had to have a purpose. "Nowaczyński," Weiss has explained, "as a literary critic, as well as a satirist and a dramatist, promoted the values of utilitarianism, of the social duty of literature."[16] It was precisely on this score that Nowaczyński first turned his attention to Ireland. In 1906, Nowaczyński published two critical appreciations of the work of Oscar Wilde, who fit the paradigm of the superficial, socially disengaged esthete so despised by Nowaczyński, in a foreword to Marya Feldmanowa's translation of Wilde's *Dyalogi o sztuce* (Intentions) and *Oskar Wilde. Studium. Aforyzmy. Nowele* (Oscar Wilde: A Study, Aphorisms, Novellas). In his introduction to the former, Nowaczyński took a rather harsh line on Wilde's status as the preeminent cosmopolitan of European letters. "If Wilde," Nowaczyński maintained, "had embarked on the development of his writing skills in a Celtic, an Irish, a legendary direction, he would have arrived at fundamental, tribally-epochal work."[17] Wilde, Nowaczyński observed, did not remain in Ireland to contribute to Irish society as his mother had, but rather championed the conflation of life and art in literary modernism as a cosmopolitan writer living abroad. For Nowaczyński, Wilde was representative of the type of literary decadent he had despised in Kraków. He set the pattern subsequently followed by an entire generation of young, modern writers who "vegetated by the dozen in unproductive nostalgia in German, Danish... Hungarian cities and even on the Vistula."[18] The zeal with which Nowaczyński condemned Wilde was intensified by his appreciation of the Irish writer's true literary talent. Wilde could have adopted a role similar to his illustrious predecessor and countryman, Jonathan Swift, but he had chosen otherwise. "Oscar Wilde," Nowaczyński charged, "sold his native birthright for a bowl of Parisian sugar, for a handful of artistic vices, *Montmartre* grimaces and stylistic somersaults."[19] Nowaczyński insinuated Wilde had succeeded in making a fortune and garnering international fame as a writer, but that Irish society had benefited little from his talents and, even worse, Wilde had forgotten his Irish roots. Nowaczyński always had a message for his Polish readers, and in his critique of Wilde he was clearly targeting the young, bohemian *poseurs* in Warsaw and Kraków, whom he felt were disregarding their own responsibilities by emulating Wilde. Przybyszewski, like Wilde, was iconic of the decadent writer, who produced self-involved, irrational literature that contributed nothing to

Chapter 5: Modeling the Irish Theatre

the advancement of his native country. For Nowaczyński, Wilde's lonely death was symbolic of the unproductive self-indulgence of cosmopolitanism. Wilde, therefore, had failed as a writer and more importantly as an Irishman.

With the success of Irish-Ireland in attracting international attention, it was a logical development that Nowaczyński would find the Irish cultural movement appealing. After all, Irish cultural activists were showing signs of energy and initiative, and Ireland appeared to be making significant cultural progress. Discouraged by the state of affairs in his own country, the practical work of Irish-Ireland toward restoring a sense of national self-respect was appealing to Nowaczyński.[20] The topic may have been Ireland, but Nowaczyński's primary object always remained Poland and its place in the world. Nowaczyński formulated his appreciation of Irish literature in three articles, two published before and one after World War I. Initially published in the journal *Świat* (*The World*) in 1907 under the title "Odrodzenie Erynu" (The Rebirth of Erin), Nowaczyński's ideas took fuller form two years later in a second essay, in the collection *Co czasy niosą* (What the Times Bring) in 1909.[21] He turned his attention again to Ireland in 1913–1914 with an article on the Irish theater, which he later reprinted as a third essay, "Teatr irlandzki" (The Irish Theater) in *Szkice literackie* (Literary Sketches) in 1918. All three essays focused specifically on the cultural and literary developments that had been taking place in Ireland since the turn of the century, and in them Nowaczyński displayed a close familiarity with both Irish history and the Irish-Ireland movement.

"In these anti-metaphysical times," Nowaczyński proclaimed at the beginning of 'The Rebirth of Erin,' "a wonderful occurrence has taken place of which philosophers and theorists of the idea of statehood for twenty years had not dreamed; the rising of the emerald phoenix of Celtic Ireland from the ashes of denationalization."[22] From the very beginning he gave his readers some idea of how this related to Poland. "This is one of those rare spectacles," Nowaczyński explained, "on a great scale which one *should* exalt and enjoy, cite and research, and draw from it optimism, bravery, and belief in the intervention of the unseen."[23] Poles had something to learn from the Irish, he felt, because they had suffered for far longer and yet they were still striving to restore the Irish nation through cultural work. "Imagine a nation," Nowaczyński urged his readers, "over three times smaller than ours, but with our faults, comicality, sins, and ugliness intensified three times over; recall that the Irish over 700 years have suffered under torture and oppression, next to which our nineteenth century pales and shrinks in size like a cloud disappearing over the horizon."[24] Nowaczyński was not interested in suffering for its own sake, nor did he approve of the ideology of national martyrdom conceived by

The Impact of Irish-Ireland on Young Poland, 1890–1919

the Polish Romantics. If a smaller, more troubled and disadvantaged nation such as Ireland could produce a vibrant cultural movement, Nowaczyński's reasoning suggested, then certainly Poland was capable of doing the same. What mattered to Nowaczyński was action, and in citing the collective work of Irish-Ireland he was trying to mobilize his compatriots to use their energies similarly in order to strengthen the nation in real and tangible ways.

In spite of an opening salvo at "almighty Albion" for its centuries-long complicity in oppressing the Irish people and dispossessing them of their native language, the focus of "Rebirth of Erin" was not on the evils of British imperialism. Remaining true to form, Nowaczyński instead analyzed the Irish reaction to these evils, both negative and positive. Although the source of Nowaczyński's information on Ireland are unknown, his rhetoric was strikingly similar in tone and content to that published by Moran in *The Leader*, or perhaps Arthur Griffith in *Sinn Fein*.[25] "Moran's diagnosis of contemporary Ireland," Frank Biletz has pointed out, "was that the Irish people had acquiesced in English cultural, economic and political domination. In placing the blame for their plight squarely on the Irish themselves, Moran emphasized individual responsibility in bringing about a national revival. All Irish persons had to become more self-reliant in their personal behaviour and resist the blandishments of English culture if the nation as a whole were ever to become self-reliant."[26] Nowaczyński condemned the dependence upon an exclusively English political solution of Home Rule as a corrosive factor, because the result was that Irish politicians were losing something essential by forsaking of their native culture, their civilization to use Dmowski's terminology, for the trappings of English parliamentary politics. Here, again, the presence of Moran was palpable. "[Moran] was sharply critical of what passed for patriotism in his day," F. S. L. Lyons has observed, "This criticism took several forms. One was a campaign of constant denigration of the Irish parliamentary party at Westminster whom he regarded as imitation Irishmen making ludicrously ineffective attempts to play the game of English politics."[27]

In Nowaczyński's mind, Irish politicians over the course of the nineteenth century, beginning with O'Connell, had cajoled and misled "poor Paddy" until he had lost what was most essential, his language. He saved his venom for the "West Britons," those "103 shouters and lawyers" currently in the House of Commons "who are more English than the English themselves."[28] The language may have been borrowed from Moran or Griffith, but in Nowaczyński's attack on the "ambitious materialists" in parliament there were elements of his criticism of Wilde and more importantly, the politics of triloyalism in his native Galicia. "The cabal of political cynics from Lwów," Nowaczyński declared in an aphorism in *Skotopaski sowizdrzalskie* (The Idylls of a Rogue) in 1904, "ravenously hungry

Chapter 5: Modeling the Irish Theatre

for a career, must put forward their Junker-Cossack, Kalmuck-Landrat political program, but out of tradition they should preserve something Polish. For example, the old Polish title: Liber Plebeanorum, 'the Book of the Rabble.'"[29] Just as with their Irish counterparts, participation in imperial politics for most Poles was dangerous because it masked the insidious processes of political denationalization and cultural fragmentation. The Irish were living proof of the fundamental, irrevocable damage that could be inflicted on a nation when these processes were allowed to go unchecked. "And so it happened," Nowaczyński pointed out, "that in these years when the most ardent and national 'Paddy' politicked, he lost in an anti-London fever no more, no less than... his own language, his old, two-thousand year-old Celtic language."[30] Instead of "original Irishmen," to use Moran's terminology, Ireland's dependency on England resulted in no more, no less than base English imitations.

> It was carried out by the *Irish philistine*, as thoughtless as all others, dressing up in the English cultural club, reading the penny dreadfuls imported from London, eating sandwiches, Durham filets, York ham... that stupid beast the philistine posing as a West-Briton and despising those possessing his language, his treasures and traditions... as abstractions, which provide no eating like York ham nor drinking like porter.[31]

Exaggerated language such as this would certainly have warmed the hearts of both Moran and Dmowski.

In contrast to the criticism Nowaczyński directed at the "Irish Brigade," the Gaelic League received considerable praise. While the "mania" for politics, in his view, had corroded Ireland's identity, the decision of the Gaelic League to focus on strengthening cultural identity had in a short time done much to restore it. "The Revivers of Erin," Nowaczyński observed, "assumed their task under the banner of absolute separation of nationality from the politics of the nation and from the religious question."[32] This approach, which struck Nowaczyński as the ideal posture, corresponded with the distinction he made of literature as being either aesthetically or socially engaged.[33] Turning away from the politics of London, the members of the Gaelic League sought to preserve their nationality through the saving of the Irish language, and so conserving the speech of "the mud huts, bogs, and glens became the goal of the first participants in the revival."[34] Most significant in his eyes was the Gaelic League's success in expanding cultural and intellectual horizons in Ireland. By modeling the revitalization of Irish culture on the language and traditions of the Irish peasantry, however, they also had to overcome the disdain of the "respectable classes," the indifferent Catholic hierarchy, the jealous Orangemen, the vampiric landlords and police, and, worst of all in Nowaczyński's opinion, the snobbish "*shoneens*," or little John Bulls, who aped anything that came from England. In the end, it took the heroism of a few Gaelic Leaguers to persevere in the face of all these various forces, for Ireland to have a chance at spiritual and cultural salvation. "The oldest of the Irish," Nowaczyński asserted, referring to the Irish peasantry, "receive once again from the hands of the Gaelic League the right of possession to the national soul; so that they will not have to sell their birthright for a mess of pottage, for 'Home Rule' with a window to an Anglo-Saxon world and worldview! Erin go bragh!"[35]

Nowaczyński's analysis of the cultural politics of Irish-Ireland brought into focus the fundamental link that existed between Young Poland and its Irish counterpart as movements aimed at addressing problems of denationalization and cultural stagnation, In particular, Nowaczyński found a parallel in Irish-Ireland for the challenge Young Poland faced in reconciling the reality of the partitions and the desire for modern art forms. In contrast to the Irish situation, language and culture at first glance appeared to be binding elements in the case of Poland. For Nowaczyński, however, the multi-national, multi-ethnic nature of the Austrian Empire produced a similar form of cultural deterioration among Poles living in Galicia comparable to what the Irish experienced under English rule. This was particularly evident in Nowaczyński's hatred for Polish bureaucrats, whose sense of national loyalty and linguistic identity were corrupted by a system of government dominated by Germans and Czechs. Weiss has pointed out how Nowaczyński, who took pride as a writer in his linguistic virtuosity, often mixed elements of different languages in his satires both for comic effect and as a means of commenting on the chaotic and weakened state of Polish culture in Galicia.[36]

Nowaczyński could have just as easily substituted his portrayal of the Polish bureaucrat, aristocrat, or modernist in the place of the Irish West Briton. Caught between the backwardness of Austrian Galicia and the detachment of the Polish literary modernists, Nowaczyński captured the fundamental conflict that faced Young Poland as a movement in its striving at once to be equally open to new impulses from Europe and to be thoroughly national. Consistent throughout Nowaczyński's criticism was his absolute intolerance of all forms of hypocrisy and self-deception, whether it was the social lethargy of the Polish gentry, the destructive irrationalism of Romantic nationalism, or the self-serving vanity of literary modernism. As a politically fragmented nation already experiencing multi-various forms of cultural erosion in each of the three partitions, Nowaczyński believed Poles needed fewer fantasies and greater self-awareness, industry, and pragmatic action. Just as the preservation of the traditional social order left Poland politically stagnant and economically backward, the mimicry of foreign cultural impulses threatened to destroy what remained of Polish cultural and

Chapter 5: Modeling the Irish Theatre

national identity. Cosmopolitanism was no less damaging to the maintenance of strong, cohesive Polish cultural identity across the partitions than the local pressures that existed within each individual territory.

Irish-Ireland's attempt to balance essentialism and cosmopolitanism mirrored the challenge Polish intellectuals faced across the lands of Poland. Despite his criticism of bohemian Kraków, Nowaczyński had a strong belief in Young Poland's role as a force for creating a sense of uniformly vital and confident Polishness across the partitions. "In families," Nowaczyński observed in *The Aphorisms of a Rogue*, "even the father at times can be the *enfant terrible*. An example of that was Young Poland in Kraków."[37] Despite the prominence of bohemian Kraków, the failure of figures such as Przybyszewski and other extreme modernists to assume this potentially dynamic leadership role revealed the danger cosmopolitanism posed to Young Poland's larger mission as a movement of cultural and national regeneration. As Nowaczyński characterized it in *The Idylls of a Rogue*, such a scenario essentially resulted in the blind leading the blind.

> W kulturalnym społeczeństwie ambrozja wieków poprzednich staje się codziennym chlebem wieków następnych. U nas je się i je wszędzie chleb codzienny. A tych nielicznych, którzy karmią się ambrozją – o jakże już nie kosztowną i przystępną – zwie biedny tłum ludzi ślepych od urodzenia i karlejących z dnia na dzień, w woskiem w uszach – kosmopolitami.[38]

> In a cultured society, the ambrosia of preceding ages becomes the daily bread of the next. We eat everywhere our daily bread. But those few, who feed on ambrosia – oh how it is affordable and no longer expensive – the poor crowd calls the people already blind from birth and becoming stunted day by day, with wax in their ears – cosmopolitans.

Young Poland, for Nowaczyński, would only fulfill its promise when its artists led by example as a force for real social, cultural, and political change for the entire nation as a whole.

In spite of the impracticality of the Gaelic League's attempt to restore Irish language and culture, Nowaczyński admired the initiative the members of the Gaelic League were taking to change the conditions of Irish society. In the 1907 version of the article, Nowaczyński compared the challenge faced by the Gaelic League to the labors of Sisyphus.[39] Douglas Hyde, one of the architects of the Gaelic League, imagined the Irish language movement in essentialist terms reminiscent of Nowaczyński in "A Plea for the Irish Language," published in 1886 in the Dublin University Review, in which he defended the cultural peculiarities of the Irish language against dangers of cosmopolitanism.[40] Jan Kasprowicz's inclusion of Yeats in his 1907 collection of English poetry, however, had exposed a fundamental inconsistency within the Irish movement, which the commentators of Young Poland did not fail to observe. Even with the efforts of organizations such as the Gaelic League and the Gaelic Athletic Association to preserve Ireland's birthright, as Nowaczyński phrased it, the reality was that a native audience of Irish speakers no longer existed.[41] It was precisely because of the lack of a ready, Irish-speaking audience that the literary wing of the Irish-Ireland movement, of which the Abbey Theatre was the crowning achievement, adopted English as its primary medium of expression. "If you say a National literature must be in the language of the country," Yeats maintained in 'First Principles' in 1904, "there are many difficulties. Should it be written in the language that your country does speak or the language that it ought to speak?"[42] As Biletz has pointed out in his study of Irish-Ireland, the problems of politics, sectarianism, and regionalism also contributed to the further complication of the language question in Ireland.[43]

This central paradox was not confined to the cultural sphere, as Irish political nationalism, represented most conspicuously by *Sinn Fein* (Ourselves Alone), also used the English language in its campaign to promote all things Irish and to create an independent Irish republic.[44] Even Moran, whose idealization of "the Gael" as the fundamental aspect of Irish identity deliberately excluded Anglo-Irish figures such as Jonathan Swift, Wolfe Tone, Yeats, Synge, and Hyde, who wrote in English, from the Irish cultural nation. Rhetoric aside, the challenge facing Irish-Ireland as a whole was how to recreate a uniquely Irish cultural space using a non-Irish mode of expression. For Yeats, who did not know Irish, the mechanical recreation of literature in Irish for ideological reasons was not only anachronistic it was also harmful to the Irish national psyche in the long run. "A nation is injured," Yeats explained in *Samhain* in 1905, "by the picking out of a single type and setting into print or upon the stage as a type of the whole nation... If Ireland were at this moment, through a misunderstanding terror of the stage Irishman, to deprive her writers of freedom, to make their imaginations timid, she would lower her dignity in her own eyes and in the eyes of every intellectual nation."[45] In spite of its internal conflicts, the brilliance of the Irish-Ireland movement, which in turn made it attractive to Young Poland, lay in the boldness of Yeats and his colleagues to embrace their Irishness.

Considerations of national self-respect were paramount for Nowaczyński. It was, after all, the vitality of the predominately Anglo-Irish literary movement, with Yeats at the fore, which sparked international interest in Irish-Ireland. For Nowaczyński, the Irish cultural movement possessed the balance of intellectual vigor and cultural essentialism that he longed to have in Poland. Nowaczyński rectified his oversight of the Irish Literary Revival in the 1907 version of

Chapter 5: Modeling the Irish Theatre

"Rebirth of Erin" by drawing direct literary parallels between Irish-Ireland and Young Poland in the extended essay published in 1909 in *What the Times Bring*. "William Butler Yeats," Nowaczyński declared, "a peer of our Wyspiański and nearly his doppelgänger – is one of the first representatives of the 'Irish Revival,' one of the central fires of the 'Gaelic League.'"[46] Despite including Yeats in a list of writers who wrote in English, such as Moore and Edward Martyn, Nowaczyński considered the chief founder of the Abbey Theatre to have little concern for the business of the English literary market. In contrast to Moran and other extreme Irish nationalists, Nowaczyński believed that Yeats's determination to sound the "Celtic note" in his writing mattered more than his Anglo-Irish background or the language in which he wrote. "From time to time," Nowaczyński explained, "he publishes little volumes at Fisher Unwin or at Walter Scott, which become a treasure of the general public, the darling of the pure and the pride, the glory of the spiritually reviving Celts in Ireland."[47] This demonstrated the degree to which Nowaczyński's satirical position was at odds with traditional forms of nationalism, whether it was Polish or Irish. To the extent that Nowaczyński was essentializing Yeats and the Irish cultural movement for his own ends, his rhetoric also served to underscore his inherent identification with the artistic philosophy of Young Poland. Nowaczyński reminded his readers that Yeats was not altogether unknown in Poland. "Our Kasprowicz," Nowaczyński pointed out, "who knows him and loves him, also extended him the most beautiful honor of translating the enchanting dramatic dream 'The Countess Cathleen' and a few characteristic verses from *Poems 1901* [...], the volume *'The Wind Among the Reeds* [...], and the volume: *'Irish Fairy and Folk Tales.'*"[48] Yeats and Kasprowicz, in spite of their modernist sensibilities, were writers who consciously strove in their writing to be both creatively original and socially engaged. What is more, with Yeats's ability to capture the Celtic spirit in his writing, his use of the English language notwithstanding, Kasprowicz not only presented to his compatriots a poet very close to his own heart but also a writer who embodied in a fundamental way the ideals of Young Poland.

It was not hard for Nowaczyński's contemporaries to read between the lines of his description of Irish-Ireland's success. Dmowski had called for a series of practical measures, both open and subversive, in *Thoughts of a Modern Pole* to restore a stronger Polish cultural presence throughout partitioned Poland. Nowaczyński was not calling for authenticity so much as he was for the forceful assertion of a decidedly Polish identity. As a proponent of political realism, it may have seemed somewhat out of character for Nowaczyński to praise the activities of the Gaelic League. Underlying his interest, however, was the element of national dignity, which was something he desperately desired for Poland. For Nowaczyński, it was the gesture and the underlying message signaled by Irish-Ireland, rather than the realistic prospect of its success. As a skilled satirist, Nowaczyński understood both the power of perception and the language of propaganda. Kiezuń has pointed out the relationship of Nowaczyński's ideas to prominent strains in contemporary Polish conservative thought. His desire to change his country's image in the eyes of world opinion resembled that of the so-called Kraków historical school, while his admiration of small resurgent nations, such as the Czechs and the Irish, put him in line with National Democracy. According to this line of thinking, it was necessary to strengthen Polish cultural identity in order to raise its standing in the world. Writers such as Yeats and the Gaelic League, Nowaczyński recognized, were winning the battle for Irish essential identity, and more importantly, they were attracting international attention despite being a small, underdeveloped country in the shadow of the British Empire.

For Nowaczyński, the value of Irish-Ireland laid in reinforcing Young Poland's central mission of cultural and national regeneration. "The National Irish movement," Nowaczyński maintained, "is most fortunate and worthy of envy that it not only does not collide with the social movement, but is its spiritual brother and the consequence of its ennoblement and idealization."[49] The central purpose of both movements, as Nowaczyński perceived it, was to counter English materialism, which he felt had resulted in the economic, moral, and literary denationalization of the Irish people. Yeats was central to the process of reviving a sense of Ireland's nationality, and a key link between the social and literary wings of the movement. "The symbol," Nowaczyński declared, "of the union of these two essential and creative tendencies bearing the germ and the seed for future is the Irish Wyspiański – William Butler Yeats, the social patriot and aristocratic defender of the downtrodden people 'of lords and poets.'"[50] The reference to Wyspiański helped to draw attention to Yeats's social and literary contributions to the Irish movement, as well as his basic affinity to Young Poland. "Irish nationalism," Nowaczyński stressed, "is the individuality of the most noble minority in the face of the pirate law of the 'state idea,' and so the Irish representatives are above all the defenders of individualism, opposing the worldview of numbers, receipts, statistics [with] the power of the soul, pantheistic faith."[51] After Wyspiański, Nowaczyński could have also named Kasprowicz and Żeromski among Yeats's Polish counterparts. As Yeats did in Ireland, all three writers combined poetic artistry with a strong sense of national commitment to create a literature that was at once aesthetically innovative and unmistakably Polish.

Yeats's tendency toward symbolic dreaminess did not constitute the artistic posturing that Nowaczyński so despised in many of his fellow Poles. On the contrary, Nowaczyński understood Yeats to be carrying out the type of positive

Chapter 5: Modeling the Irish Theatre

national work he desired of Polish modernist writers. Yeats did not portray the Irish peasantry as they really were, but rather he attempted essentially to capture the symbolizing power of their world in his poetry and plays. "In these Celtic hearths and cradles," Nowaczyński pointed out, "Yeats seeks the spiritual extracts and essences for the nourishment of living strength and inducing a healthy reaction in his unfortunate, depatriated nation."[52] By taking the peasantry of the West of Ireland as the essence of the Irish national imagination, Yeats was not avoiding productive work, but reinforcing it. "And so we see," Nowaczyński explained, "that despising the real, concrete reality, the poet-fantasist had his positive, political rationale."[53] Because of Yeats and the other Irish-Ireland intellectuals, those same "West Britons" and political careerists he described earlier were drawn back to the pure, vital Irishness of the peasantry. There was little sense that Nowaczyński was aware of the attacks Irish nationalists had leveled at Yeats, but this unawareness only revealed the extent to which the image Nowaczyński created of Yeats as a nationalist was in keeping with his own needs. It also underscored the extent to which the Irish poet, too, struggled with the tug and pull between essentialism and cosmopolitanism in his own writing. Nowaczyński here betrayed his desire for Young Poland to become a real, constructive force in the restoration of Polish national dignity and integrity. It was the task of writers and artists to restore a sense of inner strength and identity where politicians had failed.[54]

As an artist in his own right, Nowaczyński's approach to Yeats's work reflected his fundamental dislike for fashionable trends and artistic self-absorption.[55] The difference between Yeats and the decadents was that for him the mysterious world of the Irish countryside, populated by elves, fairies, and spirits, was not a static metaphor but a living link to something deeper and essential to the Irish national consciousness. This attitude, Nowaczyński believed, had a direct impact on the nature of Yeats's drama and revealed a genetic link with literary figures such as Maeterlinck and Wyspiański, who were serious, original artists, rather than with decadent *poseurs* such as Przybyszewski and his imitators. Nowaczyński endorsed the way Yeats's poetry and plays, based on ancient Irish legends and tales, contained symbols that were lasting and eternal and rooted his work in his Irishness. Just as the Gaelic League and the Irish Literary Revival brought the world of the Irish peasantry to the fore, Yeats's value as a dramatist resided in his ability to reveal to his viewers the living, unique, and mysterious world of Gaelic myth.

Turning from Yeats to George Moore, the Irish art critic and novelist, Nowaczyński found a spirit much more in keeping with his own prickly position within Young Poland as satirist and social critic. Prior to experiencing

The Impact of Irish-Ireland on Young Poland, 1890-1919

what he characterized as a Pauline conversion to the Celtic cause, Nowaczyński described Moore as having been an "amoral," cosmopolitan writer in the mold of Wilde and Shaw. "They count him," Nowaczyński observed, "next to O. Wilde, B. Shaw and Gilbert Keith Chesterton in the fellowship of 'intellectual clowns,' [...] who one must nevertheless read, not taking anything seriously to heart as a consequence of the reading."[56] While there was a sense of self-recognition in his appreciation of Moore's acerbic wit, he disapproved of the lack of responsibility the Irish writer exhibited toward Ireland in his earlier writing. "George Moore," Nowaczyński maintained, "feels a physical aversion to 'ragged Ireland,' admires Cromwell as a man 'rejuvenating humanity... with cruelty,' utters the defense of all injustices, oppressions, injuries, even crimes, as long as they contribute in part to the rise of a work of reason, a work of art."[57] It appeared that as a young man Moore was well on his way to becoming a poseur in the mode of Wilde, and thereby betraying his Irish national heritage.

The Irish novelist's transformation in Nowaczyński's view did not involve a change in character so much as it did a reorientation of feeling. "Moore," Nowaczyński emphasized, "only enhanced and made possible a tone of social sympathy, and then gave freer reign to the instincts of his race."[58] As evidence Nowaczyński cited the series of realistic novels Moore published, beginning in 1894. Works such as *Esther Waters* (1894) and *Evelyn Innes* (1898), which were "hypersensitive" to the details of the everyday lives of normal people, bespoke in Nowaczyński's view the innate sensitivity of Moore's basic Irishness. In their subject matter and construction, moreover, the novels were decidedly non-commercial and unpalatable to the wider English reading public. What mattered most to Nowaczyński was Moore's decision to leave cosmopolitan Paris in favor of participating actively in the intellectual life of his country. "That George Moore," Nowaczyński observed in his concluding remarks, "the egoist, the cosmopolitan and Parisian *in partibus infidelium*, the one time inspirer of Whistler and Wilde belongs today to the Gaelic group in Dublin and to the most ardent excavators of the 'buried temple' of Celtism!"[59] It was clear from Nowaczyński's rhetoric that cosmopolitanism for him was synonymous with national weakness. Moore redeemed himself as both a writer and an Irishman by leaving the world of French Impressionism and choosing instead to assist Yeats in the foundation of the Irish Literary Theatre. The importance that Nowaczyński attached to Moore's return to Ireland was in some respects ironic, for nearly all the Irish-Irelanders, nationalists and internationalists alike, had spent considerable period of time abroad before returning to contribute to the betterment of their homeland. Polish artists and writers, Nowaczyński's suggested, should follow Moore's example and do likewise.

Chapter 5: Modeling the Irish Theatre

For Nowaczyński, the true measure of the contributions of such socially engaged intellectuals as Yeats and Moore to the Irish cultural movement was the Abbey Theatre. At this point in his career, Nowaczyński had yet to turn his attention seriously toward the stage. This would change about 1913, when he began publishing his satirical plays of Kraków and collaborating with Arnold Szyfman's newly established *Teatr Polski* (The Polish Theater). Nowaczyński, however, was joined in his admiration of Yeats and his the Abbey Theatre by Maria Rakowska, who spent most of her career in Paris, where she worked as a literary critic and translator of English and French literature. Much like Nowaczyński, Rakowska as a critic employed a style that was informative, almost scholarly in nature, but where Nowaczyński employed colorful rhetoric and an exaggerated style, Rakowska maintained a rational, systematic approach. Rakowska's critical approach grew out of her knowledge of English, French, and Russian, which she utilized to great effect in her work as a translator and a critic.[60] In 1908, Rakowska published the first serious study of Conrad's work in Polish, based on her knowledge of the original, and in 1923 she would publish an article examining the work of Synge. Because of her balanced and well-informed style, Rakowska embodied the mediating role of intercultural negotiator more fully than did Nowaczyński.

Rakowska first touched on recent developments in Irish literature in her broad overview of English literature *Zarys literatury angielskiej: od początków do naszej doby* (A Sketch of English Literature: From its beginnings to our times) in 1911. She followed this with an in depth essay on the Abbey Theatre entitled "Teatr irlandzki" (The Irish Theater) later that same year. Typical of her work as a literary critic, Rakowska, displayed an informed and wide-ranging knowledge of English literature in her survey. As a study of contemporary English literature, *A Sketch of English Literature* once again raised the issue of how to classify modern Irish literature. Rakowska claimed that the developments then taking place in Ireland were the most exciting in contemporary English literature. "One of the significant developments of the last quarter century," Rakowska asserted, "is the pan-Celtic movement, the entire following of Irish poets grouping around William Butler Yeats, whose works, born of the spirit, tradition and ideals of the race, expressively recount their dreams, often blending great freshness of imagination and strength."[61] Among these fresh new talents, Rakowska distinguished AE, Padraic Colum, Douglas Hyde, and Fiona Macleod (William Sharp). Prefiguring her future interest in Irish drama, Rakowska singled out Yeats and the Irish theater as the driving force behind the revival of Irish cultural life. "These pioneers of the Irish revival," Rakowska explained, "like the genuinely English poets, are eagerly improving the dramatic form, the turn towards which we observe in all forms of writing. Among those works by Irish poets, the pieces by Yeats have met with no little success."[62] Although Rakowska was no *hibernophile*, the thought with which she distinguished Irish literature and the manner in which she described its place in the context of English letters suggested a nuanced understanding of Irish-Ireland's significance as a cultural movement.

In "The Irish Theater," Rakowska went into considerably more depth on Irish-Ireland than did her comprehensive survey of English literature. As had been the case with Nowaczyński, however, Rakowska could not refrain from essentializing Irish-Ireland by pointing out that writers such as Goldsmith, Burke, Sheridan, Shaw, and Wilde were Irish. "Bringing to their work," Rakowska observed, "those elements born of the spiritual distinctness of their race, these writers at the same time all remain visionaries of different moments in the evolution of English letters. Their works above all constitute a tributary to the general current."[63] With its combination of art and essentialism, Rakowska's characterization of the Irish cultural movement is a telling example of the manner with which Young Poland read Irish-Ireland. As a definition, it was equally applicable to Wyspiański's reworkings of Polish national mythology as it was to Yeats's Irish literature of "divine substances." The new voice in Irish literature, Rakowska observed, may have been written in English, but it was "thoroughly Irish in its essence and mood, and, therefore, was foreign from many points of view to the traditions and tendencies of English literature and situated beyond them."[64] Rakowska's rhetoric was particularly interesting in respect to her role as an early critic and translator of Conrad. Joseph Conrad might have been an emerging figure in English letters, but for Poles the émigré writer, born Teodor Józef Konrad Nałęcz Korzeniowski, was the son of a Polish aristocrat and the victim of the vagaries of Polish history.[65] Poles faced different linguistic challenges than the Irish, but the parallel of Irish-Ireland nonetheless had some resonance for the intellectuals of Young Poland who were attempting to strengthen Polish cultural identity, despite the reality of the partitions, by distilling national essence in artistic expression.

Rakowska, revealing a wide knowledge of Irish literature and history, placed the origins of this internal change within Irish literature a half-century earlier, in the work of Thomas Davis and Young Ireland. The predominance of politics over literature, however, meant that Young Ireland produced more nationalist and revolutionary rhetoric than it did literary works of art. While politics did not cease to play a central role in contemporary Irish life, Rakowska singled out Standish O'Grady, whose works such as the *History of Ireland* (1878–1880) and *The Coming of Cuchulain* (1894) opened up Ireland's mythical and heroic past, as the key instigator of the turn away from the practical concerns of politics towards

Chapter 5: Modeling the Irish Theatre

the inward examination of Irish cultural identity. "It was he," Rakowska insisted, "who really initiated the *Young Ireland* movement, uncovering once again the imagination and magic dreams of the horizons of beauty."⁶⁶ By referring to Irish-Ireland as "Young Ireland," Rakowska invoked Young Poland throughout her essay. While Rakowska joined Nowaczyński in recognizing the importance of Douglas Hyde and the Gaelic League as important actors in the emergence of Irish-Ireland, the focus of her essay was on the evolution of the literary wing of the Irish movement. Rakowska felt that with Katerine Tynan's collection of Irish poetry in 1888 and Yeats's *The Wanderings of Oisin* the following year, Irish literature first began to reveal a character truly different from that of English literature. In addition to the contributions of Tynan and Yeats, Rakowska distinguished the work of AE (George Russell), who also added to this new wave of poetry. "He also held a leading place among the ranks of people," Rakowska pointed out, "whose intellect and broad culture were instrumental in fostering an atmosphere of intellectual life in Dublin, the lack of which had once driven Irish writers and artists to the metropolis."⁶⁷ Using language that could have easily described the emergence of Young Poland, Rakowska stressed the combined efforts of these writers as the driving force behind the internal shift that took place in Irish literature. "We know," Rakowska asserted, "how large a number of poets gathered at that moment, not that long ago, under the slogan of the Celtic revival. Reflection and analysis are moments incomparably later. The lyricism of Young Ireland, full of flights of fancy, is permeated at once with the breath of mysticism, born in a sense organically from the essence of the Celt, but finding stimulus in the new life of resurgent traditions and legends."⁶⁸ For Rakowska, it was the ability of Irish poets and cultural activists in this early phase to link the past with a fundamental sense of self that imbued the literature of Irish-Ireland with a distinct tone and character. Rakowska, in choosing to describe Irish literature in essentialist terms, could just as well have been discussing the writers of Young Poland, such as Wyspiański, Kasprowicz, or Żeromski.

Rakowska's discussion of the cultural distinctiveness of Irish literature laid the foundation for her analysis of the Irish theater, in which her natural starting point was again Yeats. With a slight tone of surprise, Rakowska described Yeats's firm belief in the power of the Celtic imagination to make an original contribution to modern literature. "That is not all," Rakowska emphasized, "he also fosters the hope that the writers of his race will point out new paths in dramatic creation."⁶⁹ Despite boasting such dramatic talents as Sheridan and Shaw, Rakowska expressed surprise that Ireland had never possessed its own national theater. Although a Pole, Rakowska clearly understood the historical factors contributing to this state of affairs. Acknowledging Yeats as a visionary,

Rakowska wondered at the Irish poet's professed lack of concern with material gains in undertaking his project. "The dreamer and mystic," Rakowska pointed out, referring to Yeats, "for whom no real obstacles exist, is armed with indomitable strength."[70] She recognized that Yeats's creative vision ultimately had little to do with financial profit. "He wanted," Rakowska explained, "to renew dramatic art."[71] Because of the many roles Yeats played in the Irish theater, the parallels to Young Poland were numerous but difficult to define. As one of the chief organizers of the modern Irish theater, Yeats's importance as a director placed him in line with Pawlikowski, while his obvious artistic equivalent in Polish drama was Wyspiański. Writing less than five years after the death of Wyspiański, however, Rakowska's treatment of the Irish theater was also a subtle commentary on the weakened state of the Polish theater at the time. Left unstated in Rakowska's discussion of the success of the Abbey Theatre was her disappointment at Young Poland's inability to establish a permanent national theater of its own. Young Poland had made great strides in the spheres of playwriting, acting, and stage design, but it had yet to create an institution that was, like the Abbey Theatre, designated to be a Polish national theater.[72]

In tracing Yeats's effectiveness in accomplishing his goal, Rakowska displayed a familiarity with Irish drama that was impressive in the Polish context, touching upon the contributions of key figures such as Hyde, George Moore, Edward Martyn, Lady Gregory, and Synge. Rakowska stressed the exclusive Irish nature of this dramatic renaissance. "Regardless of what existed before," Rakowska pointed out, "from the first moment of its existence only works of Irish artists played in it, drawing its subject matter from the life, tradition and native folklore."[73] The influence of Hyde's Gaelic dramas, both in terms of their symbolic value and the use of amateur actors, was not lost on her. "Through extraordinarily simple means," Rakowska explained, "*The Marriage* and *The Lost Saint*, bring real emotion, the power of internal truth, which go beyond poses and real facts."[74] Along with discussing the leaders of the Irish Literary Theatre, Rakowska not only introduced lesser names such as Colum, but she also displayed a real awareness of the progress that had been made in Irish acting under the innovative direction of the Fay brothers. The disinterested nurturing of native Irish talent, which arose out of the unique needs of Irish drama, was at the heart of Rakowska's admiration for the Irish theatre. "We stress here," Rakowska emphasized, "that the relationship of the writers and their interpreters jointly to put on a work has been so disinterested, that the former till now had refused all honoraria to furnish a theater with a play and the latter for a longer time continued to work in offices, banks or companies, not taking any compensation as actors."[75] Far from being an impediment, the lack of financial motives in the Irish theater contributed

Chapter 5: Modeling the Irish Theatre

to the purity of its art. These meager beginnings were all the more significant when considered from the point of view of its critical success. "[The Abbey's] troupe," Rakowska declared, "is earning renown throughout all of England."[76] Rakowska's message her to contemporaries was clear. The Polish theater, too, lacked a great deal in terms of material resources, but it was a question of artistic vision and commitment, not money, to replicate Irish-Ireland's success in theaters of Kraków, Warsaw, and Lwów. Coming at a time when Poland's theater was in the process of reshaping itself, Rakowska's analysis of the success of the Abbey Theatre represents an important, if not overlooked contribution.

While Rakowska gave Yeats a great deal of credit for the establishment and growth of an independent Irish theater, with a few exceptions she perceptively considered his primary strength as a writer to be his lyricism rather than his dramatic talent. In terms of pure dramatic talent, Rakowska preferred Synge and Lady Gregory to Yeats. "Similar to Yeats," Rakowska explained, "Synge hates artifice and conventionality, and believes that the literature of countries of high culture has strayed too far from reality. That is why he willingly and easily succumbed to the suggestions of the poet when he urged him to return to native creative sources [...], which until now did not have expression in literature."[77] Synge drew upon his close observation of Irish rural life to create innovative dramas full of colorful language and original characters, while Yeats's contribution to Irish drama was largely poetic and mystical. Synge's choice of the Aran Islands over Paris was close to the heart of Young Poland, for it represented at bottom a rejection of pure cosmopolitanism in favor of an artistic return informed by a concern with the core of Ireland's cultural identity. Of Synge's plays, Rakowska praised in particular *The Riders to the Sea*, *In the Shadow of the Glen*, and *The Well of the Saints*. She counted this last play, the only one of the three to be staged in Poland, as one of Synge's best stage productions in spite of its "strangely moving mood."[78] Despite its celebrity as the cause of raucous riots in Dublin, Rakowska surprisingly excluded *The Playboy of the Western World* from her list. This may have been a simple oversight on her part, but as an intelligent and careful critic, Rakowska would have been sensitive to the potential damage to her thesis that the controversial motif of attempted patricide in *The Playboy* posed.

Other than Nowaczyński, Rakowska was one of the only Polish critics who also gave some attention to Lady Gregory and the younger, minor talents of the Irish theater. She especially appreciated Lady Gregory's comic observations of Irish life. Rakowska considered the majority of the lesser-known Irish playwrights to be largely average talents, with the possible exception of Padraic Colum. This is not to say Rakowska did not appreciate their contributions to the progress that had been made in the Irish theater. "Over the course of its short, twelve-year existence,"

Rakowska maintained, "this young theater has by all accounts accomplished a lot, although it did not always have an easy road on its native soil."[79] Rakowska acknowledged the objections of Irish cultural nationalists to works staged by the Abbey Theatre, most notably *The Playboy of the Western World* and *The Countess Cathleen*, pointing out the danger intolerance posed to the creation of an artistically vibrant national theater. "For people conscious of the significance of a performed work," Rakowska insisted, "the opposition of the forces of ignorance will become in every case incentive and stimulus."[80] Rakowska anticipated the response of Arnold Szyfman's supporters to the criticism he received after declaring his intention to establish the Polish Theater two years later.[81]

In light of the problems facing the Polish theater at the time, the significance of Rakowska decision to conclude her article by calling for renewed energy in the theater cannot be overemphasized. Writers and theater directors in Poland's major cultural centers faced many of the same problems she cited regarding the Irish theater. Although the possibility of producing a unified Polish theater was all but impossible because of Poland's condition as a partitioned nation, Polish theater directors and dramatists were nevertheless striving to renew the Polish theater. Much like in Ireland, the Polish theater also faced challenges in maintaining its position because of a combination of pressures in the form of financial burdens, mainstream popular drama, extremist politics, and the new art form of cinema. By explaining the fundamental identity of the Irish theater, Rakowska was not presenting Young Poland with a ready formula they should follow, but striving to impress upon her contemporaries that they already possessed the resources to reproduce Irish-Ireland's success. It was essentially a question of Young Poland's creative vision and will, not financial resources, which would determine its ability to create an independent and truly Polish national theater. With the emergence of Szyfman, however, the Polish theater would be blessed with an individual with enormous talents in both of these areas.

The importance Young Poland attached to the theater as a measure of both its creative vitality and of the vigor of the nation was evident in Nowaczyński's return to the subject of Ireland. In an article entitled "Teatr irlandzki" first published in 1913, a real difference emerged in Nowaczyński's analysis of Irish-Ireland in comparison to his earlier writing.[82] The nature of Nowaczyński's interest in Ireland had not changed since 1909, but rather it had matured and become more focused. His early appreciation for the practical work of Irish-Ireland gave way to a narrower and more personal admiration for what he believed to be Irish dramatists' effective use of satire and irony as a means of rousing Irish society out of its complacency. This was reflective of the transition he was making in his own writing from that of Young Poland's *enfant terrible* to

Chapter 5: Modeling the Irish Theatre

political muckraker. While satire and grotesque exaggeration were Nowaczyński's chief literary tools throughout his career, in his essay on the Irish theater there were clear signs of the sharpening political edge of his writing at or about the time of World War I, following which the nature of Nowaczyński's writing itself turned decidedly political. Nowaczyński's portrayal of Irish-Ireland, therefore, was less representative of the broader reality of the Irish theater than it was more reflective of his own gradual move away at this time from the role of disparaging social critic to that of the aggressive, hard-nosed muckraker.

The change in Nowaczyński's criticism coincidentally took place during one of his most productive periods as a writer. In the course of a few years Nowaczyński published two plays, *Cyganeria warszawska* (Warsaw Bohemianism, 1911) and *Nowy Ateny* (The New Athens, 1913), which respectively lampooned two of his favorite targets, the Polish *moderna* and Galician society, and a collection of bitingly satirical aphorisms on Polish life entitled *Meandry* (Meanders, 1911). With these three works Nowaczyński transformed the role of the socially engaged writer that he had called for in his earlier literary and journalistic work into that of the self-appointed judge and jury of the Polish literary scene and society. As a writer, Nowaczyński was no longer satisfied to mock the faults of Polish society, but rather he chose to attack directly and mercilessly all the obstacles that he felt stood in the way of progress and change.

> Nie zrażajcie się często zbyt gawrosza gestem, Niech was nie płoszy humor mój, jako Menandra, Ziarnko łuskajcie z łupin każdego meandra, Nie gorszcie sie fałszywym jambem, anapestem, Filozofią mą będzie: gryzę, a więc jestem. Komiczną maskę na twarz zawdziała Kassandra.[83]

> Do not be too repelled by the gestures of a street urchin, Do not let my humor frighten you, like Menander,[84] Husk the seed from the shells of each meander, Do not be scandalized by the false iamb, anapest, That will be my philosophy: I bite, and so I am. Cassandra adorned her face with a comic mask.

Whether it involved assailing the uselessness of Polish modernism, the backwardness of Galician society, or the dangers of Polish Romanticism, Nowaczyński considered it his duty to reveal Young Poland's internal weaknesses. This required the banishing of illusions that concealed the reality of life within the lands of partitioned Poland.

> Poeto, co masz loty orle czy sokole, Słysząc mój o doczesny byt Lechitów lament, Wskazujesz bezkres nieba, traktament Nieśmiertelnych. My śmiertelni. Ja wolę Morgę ziemi na zgrzytów i płaczów padole Niźli w kraju Utopii cały departament.[85]

183

Oh poet, with your eagle's or hawk's flights, Hear my worldly lament about the life of the Lechites,[86] You show a limitless heaven, the expanse of the immortals. We are mortal. I prefer An acre of ground in the vale of screams and tears To an entire province in the land of Utopia.

Nowaczyński's agenda was not only "to debronze" Poland's three great Romantics, it was also to instill rationalism and pragmatism into national life. Poland needed, according to Nowaczyński, fewer Don Quixotes charging windmills and more Sancho Panzas.[87] Through his satire, therefore, Nowaczyński believed himself to be making his patriotic contribution to the improvement of the nation. Nowaczyński's image of himself as a socially engaged writer not only underscored the unique nature of his nationalism, but it also indicated the extent to which political ideology was beginning to displace artistry in his writing.

Whereas Rakowska perceived in the Abbey Theatre an artistic model for Young Poland, Nowaczyński found in it his ideal of a socially combative national theater. Nowaczyński's treatment of the Irish theater was unique among all Polish commentators on Ireland during this period for the directness with which he linked Young Poland and Irish-Ireland. In "The Irish Theater," which appeared again in *Literary Sketches* in 1918, Nowaczyński connected the progress Ireland had made compared to Poland and more particularly, to the central role satire had played in effecting that change in Ireland.[88] "From the time I wrote 'The Rebirth of Ireland,'" Nowaczyński reflected, "a few years have passed, but not in my wildest dreams did I suspect that the resurrection of Celtic culture in such a short time would achieve such results."[89] Unlike Rakowska, Nowaczyński considered Irish-Ireland's successful expansion to be parallel to the cultural change that Young Poland had effected in his native country. Ireland, he explained, "is making such powerful forward progress in its spiritual development that it is a double of our nation, these 'Poles of the Western World.'"[90] Nowaczyński, in marked contrast to Rakowska, embraced the volatility of Synge's dramatic masterpiece by projecting it as an extension of his work to expose the flaws of the Polish nation.

Despite the signs of Ireland's cultural resurgence evident in the Gaelic League's numerous language classes and Irish language journals, it was in the theater that Nowaczyński espied real, significant progress. "The most powerful proof of the vitality and power of an oppressed nation rising from sleep," Nowaczyński maintained, "is that sphere of art which everywhere is a mirror of the psyche of the race and everywhere is a measure of the intellectual, moral, and organizational power of the nation. That is drama."[91] Given Nowaczyński's own close involvement in the Polish theater about this same time, he clearly recognized drama as an especially useful vehicle with which to incite society directly. Whether it resulted in greater self-awareness or violent protests, it was the ability of the theater to present the nation to itself, which Sakai has characterized as a "schema of cofiguration," that made it such a powerful and appealing art form for Nowaczyński. The Irish theater's turbulent history, with the *Playboy* riots being the most prominent, epitomized for Nowaczyński the fundamentally aggressive role the theater could play in society. In Nowaczyński's view, of course, it was not enough for the theater to mirror the nation, but rather the theater's usefulness originated in its power to act as a platform from which to incite society into action. In this respect, Nowaczyński revealed himself to be as much, if not more, of an ideologue as he was a writer.

For Nowaczyński, the true success of Ireland's renaissance as a nation rested less in what was being rediscovered than in what was being left behind. "All around," Nowaczyński stressed, referring to the changes witnessed by Ireland's cultural activists, "there is such activity, such life, such strength coming from the earth that it altered, shaped, tempered and purified the soul of a once lazy, desperate, drunken, obstreperous, deceitful people, utterly depraved people under the baton and perfidious, vampiric politics of John Bull."[92] As unflattering as his portrait of Irish society prior the Irish Revival was, it was not difficult to extend the same characterization of Poland's *doppelgänger* to his native country. The theater, therefore, represented the vanguard in the cultural transformation of the nation. Art, from Nowaczyński's point of view, was not for art's sake, but for the cultural, social, and political redemption of the nation as a whole.

Nowaczynski again displayed his real familiarity with the Irish theater, citing some of the lesser-known names "such as Seumas O'Cuisin, Padraic Colum, Seumas MacManus, and Thomas MacDonagh."[93] Nowaczyński even included an approving glance at the "strictly European" George Bernard Shaw, whose brutally satirical play *John Bull's Other Island* represented a long overdue return to his Irish heritage. Hinting at his increasing interest in right wing politics, Nowaczyński pointed out that the "social" character of these Irish playwrights was not simply political, but truly "nationalistic." In making the distinction between politics and nationalism, Nowaczyński echoed the code used by the ideologues of National Democracy, who used nationalism as a euphemism for a practical, ethnically based form of politics. "It is here also," Nowaczyński stressed, "that one should seek the reasons why there are so many satirists, so many sarcastic people, so many ironists, why they were attempting by *castigando* (chastizing) and *ridendo* (laughing) to change the national psyche and island of 'dreamers and saints' […], 'cowards and critics,' 'traitors and intrigants,' 'oafs and sluggards' and 'poets and bards' into an island of strong, creative, aggressive, and living Celts."[94] Viewed in light of *Meanders* and plays such as *The New Athens*, it was clear Nowaczyński held his countrymen in similar esteem and believed his satirical writings performed a similar function.

> Albo trup pięknie zmarły – albo człowiek żywy!
> Albo kult pracy, albo czar wolności,
> Albo brawury, albo cierpliowości.
> Tu konspiracje, tam kooperaywy –
> Wybierać pora dwie alternatywy:
> Przyszłości albo przeszłosci.[95]

> Either a beautifully dead corpse – or a living man!
> Either the cult of work, or the spell of freedom,
> Either bravura, or patience.
> Here conspiracy, there cooperatives –
> It is time to choose from two alternatives:
> The future or the past.

In order for Poland to realize its future, Nowaczyński felt it was incumbent upon him, like his fellow satirists in Ireland, to expose the sins of the past.

Although Nowaczyński was respectful of Yeats's early contributions to the spiritual foundation of this movement, he soon left him behind in favor of younger writers. Betraying perhaps a slight sense of self-recognition, he preferred this new generation, who "looked reality straight in the face and who not only did not cover their eyes with their hands, but decided to intervene, form, and reform."[96] Here Nowaczyński underscored the political value of the new Irish Theater and, more importantly, its relevance to Polish literature. "The Irish stage," Nowaczyński maintained, "becomes the arena, cathedral, pulpit, the minaret of the muezzin, confessional of the people, and the spiritual parliament of the nation, which does not yet have a political parliament."[97] The affinity between Poland and Ireland from Nowaczyński's point of view was natural and obvious. "All the Irish plays," Nowaczyński observed further, "can be translated into Polish, change only the names and bring them to us and they will be lives taken from the Polish psyche."[98] Nowaczyński illustrated his assertion of the affinity between Poland and Ireland by citing five or six new dramatists and their works, such as T. C. Murray's *Birthright* (1910) George Birmingham's *Eleanor's Enterprise* (1911), and Lennox Robinson's *Patriots* (1912). From plays such as these, Nowaczyński argued, "we can see to what degree the Irish are 'Poles of the Western world.'"[99]

Chapter 5: Modeling the Irish Theatre

The model dramatist for Nowaczyński was John Millington Synge. Nowaczyński labeled Synge's corpus of plays "as an important, cultural and fruitful thing."[100] While he greatly appreciated Synge's "symbolic satires," Nowaczyński let his true sympathies shine through by calling *The Playboy of the Western World* "a masterpiece of poetic sarcasm."[101] In the "epoch shattering" staging of the *Playboy* in Dublin in 1907, Nowaczyński drew a comparison to the stir created in Kraków in 1901 by Wyspiański's play *The Wedding*. Not only did he consider both playwrights to occupy central places in their respective literatures, but he also felt they both combined idealism and the dying strains of neo-Positivism in their work. Nowaczyński ultimately admired Synge for his satirical treatment of the reality around him, which allowed him to thrust the brutal reality of Irish peasant life in his audience's face and pass it off as beautiful, fantastic legend. "J. Millington Synge," Nowaczyński explained, "in his works does not part company with the right of the oppressed or the poor Irish cottage, but with a caring, unforgetting, and maternal love he reveals the wounds of this eternally suffering country."[102] In this regard, Nowaczyński regarded Synge as being akin to Dante, because in his dramas he led his countrymen through the torment of their own failures and foibles with the hope of transforming their bitter fury into a tale of national heroism. Above all, Nowaczyński loved to dispel illusions, but in this characterization of Synge it is possible to catch a glimpse of the manner by which Nowaczyński perceived his own role to be equal parts national jester and satirist.

While Nowaczyński gave much attention to Yeats and Synge, as well as to other key figures of the Abbey Theatre, such as Lady Gregory and George Moore, it was to a relatively minor figure, George Birmingham, the pen name of Canon James Hannay, to whom he devoted the remaining few pages of his essay. In Birmingham's play, *General John Regan*, Nowaczyński perceived the ideal corollary to the Polish context. A riot broke out during a staging of the play in Westport, Ireland, which ultimately resulted in a large section of the audience storming the stage, assaulting the actors, and after being dispersed by the police, shattering windows in the hotel where the actors were staying.[103] In this play Nowaczyński had found his ideal. The play tells the story of a rich American who arrives at a hotel in the sleepy town of Ballymoy in Mayo and announces that he is searching for the birthplace of General John Regan, who he claims was born there. Though none of the townspeople have heard of the General, the clever and penniless Doctor Lucius O'Grady convinces them to pretend that they had heard of him in hopes that the visitor will show his gratitude in American dollars. In the end, however, the American reveals the truth that there is no such person as General John Regan and that he had made him up because the town struck him as being so backward and boring. The provocation may have been an innocent one, but the violent reaction to Birmingham's play revealed that for Irish nationalists identity politics and not art was the most important feature of a modern theater. For Nowaczyński, the ability of Birmingham and Synge to elicit passionate responses from Irish theatergoers epitomized his ideal of the artist as a social actor in national life.[104] The fact that Nowaczyński's opinion of Birmingham was the polar opposite of Moran and other Irish nationalists only worked to highlight how he interpreted Irish cultural developments strictly in terms of his own needs.

The self-referential nature of Nowaczyński's reading of Birmingham is so apparent that it is difficult to ignore. Nowaczyński emphasized, erroneously as it turned out, that *General John Regan* had first been staged in Dublin by a Pole, Kazimierz Dunin-Markiewicz, the husband of Countess Markiewicz.[105] He also drew comparisons to his own play *The New Athens*, which he claimed received an animated, though less violent response in Warsaw. More to the point, however, Nowaczyński underscored the intersection of satire and realism in Birmingham's play, which he felt to be the ultimate goal of theater. It was, in part, because of Irish dramatists' fear of revealing the ugly truths about their country that Ireland was still so looked down on by the world. For Nowaczyński, the importance of the analogy between *General John Regan* and *The New Athens* resided in their shared objective as satires to combat "the vices, deficiencies, deformations, manias, and defects [...] of 'nations that do not know themselves.'"[106] Nowaczyński felt that the propensity of the Polish and the Irish to daydream and to cultivate the memory of the dead resulted in the fact that little progress was made in either country. Why do you think, he asked, South Africa got Home Rule so quickly and Ireland's status remained unresolved? "But you must know in the end," Nowaczyński explained, "you [...] Poles of the West, one thing. The little seaside town of Westport witnessed finally the ultimate satiric triumph, one that can be envied them... The hotel was even demolished in which for once the truth, and not a fable, about the Irish nation was staged."[107] With a slight air of self-satisfaction, then, Nowaczyński considered it his duty as a truly socially engaged dramatist to confront the nation with the harsh truths it refused to acknowledge.

In all three of these essays by Nowaczyński the caustic voice of the uncompromising satirist shone through. Writing under the pseudonym "Dr. Z. M.," Eustachy Czekalski remarked in a review of Nowaczyński's *Szkice literackie* (Literary Sketches) in 1918, "Nowaczyński is not interested in the topic itself. Each topic is just a pretext so that he can vent his innate restless energy and ever-poisoned thought about our reality."[108] In spite of these sharp comments,

Chapter 5: Modeling the Irish Theatre

Czekalski underscored the high quality of Nowaczyński's literary criticism and professed his hope that he would continue to publish such high-caliber work in the near future. Irony and satire are often the only weapons available to the oppressed, but for Nowaczyński they also functioned as useful tools in dispelling the harmful effects of social inertness and for distilling what was essential to the nation. Regardless of his underlying political views or intentions, in his study of the writers of the Irish Literary Revival Nowaczyński discovered a bold wit and a brutal realism similar in spirit to his own.

II. TOWARD A NATIONAL THEATER: SYNGE'S *PLAYBOY* AND THE POLISH THEATER

The importance that Nowaczyński and Rakowska attached to Irish-Ireland's success in establishing and maintaining an independent theater such as the Abbey was not lost on their contemporaries in Poland. By early 1910, the Polish theater critic and director, Arnold Szyfman (1882–1967), had begun to lay the groundwork of what would open on January 29, 1913 as Warsaw's first truly independent theater, *Teatr Polski* (The Polish Theater). Coming a full twenty years after Pawlikowski's debut as director of the Civic Theater in Kraków, Szyfman's Polish Theater in a very real sense brought the theater of Young Poland full circle. As both a student and an artist of the modern European theater, Szyfman at least equaled the contribution of his predecessor, Pawlikowski, toward elevating the level of theater in Poland. Szyfman, however, in an effort to create a cohesive vision of the stage that was consistently modern and Polish in design, came closer to combining the elements of cosmopolitanism and essentialism that formed the core of Young Poland's identity. Whereas the tenuousness of Pawlikowski's position in Lwów had ultimately obscured the impact of *The Well of the Saints*, Szyfman's production of Synge's *The Playboy of the Western World* at the Polish Theater in November 1913 presented the Irish playwright in what was at once the newest venue in the European theater reform movement and a prototype for the national Polish theater.

As much as the struggle to open an independent theater required him to be both a skilled businessman and a tactful politician, Szyfman had above all an artistic vision of the theater. From his early experiences in Berlin in 1903–1904 as a foreign theater critic for *The Critique*, where he was able to observe the theater of Brahm, Reinhardt, and even that of Stanislavsky during his first Western tour, Szyfman decidedly adopted the side of the European theatrical reform movement. "Having cast an eye at any one of the European stages,"

Szyfman explained in 1905, "we recognize the attempt to create something new, recoiling from the everyday grayness, from the traditional forms and substance of art. And it is good that it is so. If the past were enough for us, our art would be dead. And thus our mind's aim: forward! forward! propels us down new paths, reveals before us new worlds."[109] It was in this capacity that Szyfman became the first Polish critic to write about Edward Gordon Craig, when he informed his readers of an exhibition in Vienna featuring the English director's innovative stage design in *The Critique* in 1905, which was the same year Gordon Craig's influential work *The Art of the Theater* was published.[110] Szyfman's article foreshadowed the attention he would give in the Polish Theater to the artistry of all aspects of a given production, with stage design functioning as a central, unifying element. "It would be good," Szyfman reflected, "if all our directors would visit [the exhibition], perhaps it would blow in a new spirit to the stage with regard to decoration (excluding of course Wyspiański)."[111] Szyfman would further enhance his initial impressions of the modern European theater later, in 1911, when he and Czesław Przybylski, the architect of the Polish Theater, traveled abroad with the express purpose of studying modern theater design throughout Europe prior to the building of the Polish Theater.

While Pawlikowski and Szyfman were equally attuned to the developments taking place in the European theater, there was a fundamental difference between the two directors in terms of artistic vision. Of course, as the younger of the two, Szyfman was receiving his initiation into the theater when Pawlikowski was completing his tenure in Lwów in 1906. Szyfman, moreover, had the benefit of the experience of the Civic Theater in Kraków, under Pawlikowski, as well as first hand exposure to the work of Western European theater reformers. Beyond their difference as pioneer and successor, however, there was also a fundamental disparity between the two directors in regard to their approaches to the theater. Pawlikowski had made great strides in modernizing the theater in terms of repertoire, acting, and stage design, but he did not have an overarching aesthetic vision to encompass all of these aspects. In organizing the Polish Theater, Szyfman considered all its components both individually and as they related to his overall idea. Where Pawlikowski left himself open to attacks for being inconsistent and eclectic, Szyfman strove to ensure that each aspect of his productions was carefully synthesized into a single artistic vision. Szyfman provided some insight into his approach in his memoirs, when he recollected meeting Pawlikowski for the first time as part of his first tour of Poland in search of talented directors, actors, and stage designers for the Polish Theater. "I did not consider him as a candidate for director," Szyfman recalled, "for the following reasons: first, Pawlikowski already struck me as an old, tired man (he died three years later), second, his lifestyle and working habits did not harmonize with my ideas of the theater, and finally, I feared that his personality would have a detrimental effect upon my plans and their realization."[112] In his observations, Szyfman revealed the extent to which Pawlikowski and the vibrant theatrical world of Kraków was rapidly becoming a thing of the past. For better or for worse, Pawlikowski was an artist in the spirit of *cyganeria krakowska* (bohemian Kraków), while Szyfman was emerging as a professional director in the mode of the modern, reformed European theater.

In his attempt to integrate all aspects of a production, Szyfman clearly aligned himself with the European theatrical reform movement. In an article entitled "Nowoczesne teatry" (Modern Theaters), published four days after the Polish Theater opened, the reviewer for the journal *Złoty róg* (The Golden Horn) commented upon the affinity of Szyfman's theater to those of such notable directors as Gordon Craig, Max Reinhardt, and Georg Fuchs. "They attempt to reform the theatrical edifice," the reviewer pointed out," summoning the help of great painters and endeavor with united forces to build a new type of theater in which architecture, painting and sculpture would be *subordinated* to the *organizing idea* of the drama."[113] Theatrical reform, therefore, was not merely a matter of adopting distinct modes of acting or directing, but rather it involved creating a complete artistic vision of the dramatic work's central theme through the integration of all aspects of performance. "This stage," the reviewer emphasized, "does not want to give the illusion of brutal realism, but to utilize the fantasy of the onlookers as the basis for the lively ideas of the poet."[114] Part and parcel of this innovative approach to stagecraft was the union of modern technological advances with contemporary art, which greatly expanded the dramatic palette of the director-cum-artist of the theater to allow for a greater subtlety of expression that was not previously possible. Szyfman and Przybylski, based on their tour of European theaters, designed the Polish Theater to be the most modern theater in Poland, equipping it with the first rotating stage, modern electrical lighting, and a workshop for creating stage sets. In addition to this, Szyfman scoured Poland in search of dramatic talent, ultimately succeeding in luring away most of the leading actors from theaters in Warsaw, Lwów, and especially Kraków.[115] He also recruited two of the most talented scenic artists in the Polish theater, Karol Frycz, a former colleague from Kraków, and Wincenty Drabik, an experienced scenographer in the Warsaw theater, and provided them with a workshop where they could design sets. Depending on the needs of a production, Szyfman also invited individual artists and composers to take part.[116] As director of the Polish Theater, Szyfman formulated an approach to the theater based on the collective artistic interpretation of the dramatic work, which incorporated all of these disparate elements into a uniform artistic vision. "I brought an entirely new concept of drama from Kraków," Szyfman explained, "From a technical point of view, it had to be an integrated theater, meaning that all the elements – the acting company, the performance, the decoration, and direction – performed on the same plane, suggesting the idea of a composition issuing forth from the scenic work."[117]

Although the comparisons to Gordon Craig and Reinhardt were apt, Szyfman's underlying goal in setting up the Polish Theater was not to mimic the European theater. Rather, his intention was to combine his knowledge of the new techniques and approaches of the modern theater with a dramatic style that was distinctly Polish. The ideas and the techniques might have been inspired in part by innovations in the theater reform movement, but the unified style and overarching vision of a production was to be entirely Polish. In many respects, the tendency toward syncretism was one of the defining characteristics of Young Poland from the outset.[118] The mix of cultures and artistic impulses allowed the writers and artists of Young Poland to be both Polish and European, as well as to create something vital and original. Szyfman's Polish Theater was an example of the natural tendency of his contemporaries to fuse diverse artistic sources. In terms of drama, Szyfman's approach was to a degree a combination of the ideas of modern European theater reform with the vision of a monumental theater first described by Mickiewicz in his Parisian lectures and later realized on the modern stage by Wyspiański in landmark productions of *The Wedding* and *Forefather's Eve*.[119]

As much as critics such as that of *The Golden Horn* cast Szyfman as a theatrical innovator in the European mode, the young director had largely developed his ideas in the world of the cabaret. Having moved from Kraków to Warsaw in 1908, Szyfman had been part of a circle of young, emerging writers and artists in Kraków, who were interested in creating new, irreverent forms of drama.[120] After receiving his initial training in the Kraków theater under the director Ludwik Solski, Szyfman opened a small, satirical theater under the name *Figliki* (Little Jokes) in a Kraków hotel in December 1906. Albeit short lived, the experience of managing a theater and the young dramatic talents he had attracted, including Frycz, Nowaczyński, Leon Schiller, and Teofil Trzciński, emboldened Szyfman to the idea that a truly independent theater was possible. As exciting and dynamic as the theater world in Kraków was at the time, Szyfman made a calculated if not bold decision to forge a new path by opening a theater in Warsaw.[121] Dominated by government run venues, such as *Teatr Rozmaitości* (The Variety Theater), and limited by strict censorship, there was little or no real energy in the Warsaw theater. Following the revolutionary events of 1905, however, a degree

Chapter 5: Modeling the Irish Theatre

of political and cultural relaxation previously unknown in the Russian partition succeeded in attracting numerous artists and intellectuals from Kraków and Lwów. Warsaw was thus poised for change. Pawlikowski had entertained overtures from theaters in Warsaw to relocate there about this time, but he never seriously considered leaving Galicia. While a number of small, private theaters came into existence about this time, such as Bolesław Leśmian's and Kazimierz Wroczyński's *Teatr Artysytczny* (The Artistic Theater, 1911), they were generally short-lived experiments. In a city ready for artistic theater, Szyfman quickly established a reputation in theatrical circles with his new venture, *Momus*, a literary cabaret opened in 1908, which imported some of the spirit and sardonic wit of bohemian Kraków by drawing upon such talents as Nowaczyński, Schiller, and Boy-Żeleński. In spite of its popularity, *Momus* was largely a means to an end for Szyfman, who began to lay the plans for his theater in 1909 and started work there a month before Momus closed in the spring of 1910.

Szyfman's plan for the Polish Theater not only appealed to the intelligentsia of Warsaw, but it also attracted influential figures in the Polish business community and the aristocracy. It was in many respects a rare partnership between members of the intelligentsia and the wealthy elite of Polish society, who agreed that such a project was necessary both to promote Polish culture and to undercut the Russian government's control of the theater.[122] Szyfman's determination to build the Polish Theater struck many Poles in Warsaw as a significant political and patriotic gesture. It would be, however, an oversimplification to consider the Polish Theater as being a predominantly nationalist endeavor. Szyfman, in fact, was the target of pointed and often personal attacks in the conservative Polish press, which questioned both his ability and his national credentials.[123] Ironically, many of the dangers attributed to Szyfman by his detractors echoed, albeit in a perverted form, Miriam's complaints nearly a decade earlier regarding the pernicious influence of traveling German cabarets on the Warsaw theater. Szyfman, however, had the backing of the Polish intelligentsia, including such talented young critics as Władysław Rabski and Stefan Krzywoszewski, who desperately wanted a modern, independent theater in Warsaw. With artistic considerations aside, the opening of the Polish Theater represented a remarkable achievement in terms of creating an independent cultural space in Warsaw. For a city that had only recently been exposed to the works of the Polish Romantics and Wyspiański on the stage, such an overt gesture of cultural and national autonomy as the Polish Theater was a heartening development.

Szyfman's intention was to create a form of theater that was both modern and Polish, yet free from political ideology.[124] In this regard, the Polish Theater resembled the Abbey Theatre in its mission to create drama that was both creatively innovative and essentially Polish more closely than it did the purely artistic theaters of Brahm, Gordon Craig, or Stanislavsky. This was evident in Szyfman's decision in 1912 to take the company of the Polish Theater on a two-month tour of Russia, while delays in the construction of the theater were sorted out. Much like the Abbey's trips to the United States and particularly England, Szyfman organized the tour of the Polish Theater to other cities in the Russian empire, which included performances in Kiev, Minsk, and Petersburg, as a showcase of the contemporary Polish theater.[125] Consciously or not, the excursion underscored the significance of the Polish Theater as the culmination of Young Poland's evolution in the theater over the previous twenty years. Szyfman was able to tour his company before a single performance had taken place in Warsaw, because he and his colleagues could draw on the dramatic repertoire and approach to stagecraft developed previously in Kraków and Lwów.

The repertoire of the Polish Theater in the first year, which featured a balance of old and new, Polish and foreign plays, was an important part of Szyfman's commitment to artistically integrated theater. By debuting with Krasiński's *Irydion*, a highly intellectual play examining the question of revolution and martyrdom as a means of national liberation in ancient Rome, rather than plays such as Mickiewicz's *Forefather's Eve* or Słowacki's *Kordian*, which dealt with the more politically sensitive issue of Polish resistance to Russian subjugation. Szyfman sent a clear message as to the kind of drama the Polish Theater would bring to stage. "The program of the Polish Theater in those days," Leon Schiller recalled, "can be summarized in two points: 1. the creation of a stage according to the new postulates of the art of drama, acting, stage design, and direction; 2. the preparation of the basis for the development of a distinct style of national art."[126] Szyfman remained true to this formula for the duration of the first year, drawing on the classical dramatic repertoire of the Polish theater by selecting a mix of Polish works by Aleksander Fredro, Jan Nepomucen Kamiński, and Józef Korzeniowski, and non-Polish plays by Aristophanes, Shakespeare, and Ibsen.[127] With the addition of contemporary works, such as Nowaczyński's *New Athens*, L. H. Morstin's *Lilie* (The Lilies), John Galsworthy's *Justice*, and Synge's *The Playboy of the Western World*, Szyfman kept his word that the Polish Theater would not be "a dead, historical institution, but rather... a reflection and a reverberation of modern creativity."[128] In opting for a repertoire that was high in artistic quality yet not overwhelmingly radical in style, Szyfman revealed his intention to be both an artistic reformer in the European mode and a leader in the Polish theater. The challenge for Szyfman and the Polish Theater, therefore, lay not in the repertoire per se, but in making its dramatic approach comprehensible to the general public. "Reform," Schiller explained, "such as the kind the director

Chapter 5: Modeling the Irish Theatre

of the Polish Theater intended to carry out, could not be the work of one day and it would not be carried out with the help of some revolutionary act... It was necessary for the management of the Polish Theater to take a pedagogical position to the public and to its collaborators."[129] Without the benefit of a government subsidy, there was an element of pragmatism in Szyfman's choice of plays. While the variety of works presented left the Polish Theater open to the charge of eclecticism, Szyfman's approach tacitly acknowledged that there existed not one form of theater but many.[130]

It was in this context that on November 12, 1913 a second play by Synge debuted on the stage in Poland. Of all the foreign works staged in the Polish Theater's first year, Synge's *The Playboy of the Western World* was by far the most celebrated and the most modern. In his history of the Polish Theater, Edward Krasiński has pointed out that the production was the first on the continent, debuting in Warsaw a month before Lugné-Poë staged it at the *Théâtre de L'Oeuvre* in Paris.[131] The cast and crew for the Warsaw production was evidence of Szyfman's ability to lure the brightest dramatic talents of the Polish theater to Warsaw. The director, Józef Sosnowski, was a veteran actor of the Kraków theater, as were the actors in the leading roles, Józef Węgrzyn as "Christy" and Stanisława Wysocka as "Pegeen Mike."[132] The only major contributor to the performance who did not come from the theatrical world of Kraków was the scenographer, Drabik, who was a veteran of the government-run theaters of Warsaw. By this time the cast of the Polish Theater was no longer new to Warsaw theater-going audiences, but the combination of Synge's innovative play and the fresh approach Szyfman's company brought to the stage made the production a major artistic event.

Following a pattern that had been established by Miriam and Pawlikowski, Szyfman also maintained his awareness of artistic developments throughout Europe through a variety of foreign correspondents, translators, and theater colleagues. As a theater that stressed the primacy of the text, translation proved to be especially important when it came to works by foreign writers. "The Polish Theater," Krasiński maintained, "became for playwrights and translators not only a writing workshop but a good school as well, in which young talents found attentive guardians, helpful advice, and financial support."[133] Florian Sobienowski (1881–1964), a translator and critic who had lived for nearly twenty years in England, was an active and prolific contributor to the Polish Theater's repertoire of English drama. Although he was better known in Poland as a translator and critic of Shaw, his version of Synge's play, *Kresowy rycerz-wesołek*, which read literally as "The Knight-Jester of the Borderland," was the first play he offered to Szyfman in 1913.[134] Sobienowski was a particularly active example of the translator acting as a negotiator or mediator between Poland and Ireland. His interest in English literature stemmed originally from his brief affair with the New Zealand modernist short fiction writer and literary critic Katherine Mansfield, whom Sobienowski first met in Bavaria in 1909. Prior to moving to England in 1912, he tried to persuade Mansfield, who did not know Polish, to consider translating Wyspiański's plays *The Curse* and *The Judges* by means of German translations.[135] Far from a mere literary anecdote, Mansfield played an instrumental role in exposing Sobienowski to lesser-known English language writers, such as Whitman. It was in England, where for a time he lived with Mansfield and her husband, John Middleton Murray, the editor of a quarterly entitled *Rhythm* that was devoted to highly modernist literature, art, and music, that the New Zealand author encouraged Sobienowski to try his hand at translating Synge into Polish. The urgency with which he rendered *The Playboy of the Western World* was a testimony to the seriousness he attached to his position as a mediator between the worlds of Polish and English literature. Irrespective of Sobienowski's lofty aims, translation quickly escalated to the level of a life-long career in his dealings with Shaw.[136]

Sobienowski's determined attempts to promote cross-cultural exchange via translation appeared to have a strong impact in coloring both the nature and the reception of his version of *The Playboy of the Western World*. Jan Lorentowicz, a theater critic and director who reviewed the Polish Theater's production at the time, claimed that Sobienowski "Wyspiańskized" Synge's play by "adding highlanders and Hungarian soldiers to the text, a certain rhythm, and often whole expressions from Wyspiański."[137] Józef Kotarbiński, the artistic director for the government theaters, supported Lorentowicz's assertion, though he objected to Sobienowski's choice of title for the Polish translation. "Mr. Sobienowski," Kotarbiński maintained, "unnecessarily threw in the idea of the medieval-aristocratic knight, when the drama is drawn from the life of the people."[138] Kotarbiński acknowledged the difficulty of rendering a title such as "The Playboy of the Western World" into meaningful Polish, and considered Sobienowski's overall rendering of the play into Polish to be quite good. "Transposing English prose into rhythmic verse," Kotarbiński observed," the translator here and there introduced the impression of our mountaineer dialect. This style of rendering, carried out with great effort and art, suggests to us an auditor, and even a literary man."[139] Although Polish critics frequently associated Synge's play with Wyspiański, the reality remains much less clear. Sobienowski did substitute "*Hajduki*" (Hungarian soldiers) for "police" or "peelers" in a number of places throughout the text and he presented the timid farmer, Shawn Keogh, as a "*gazda*" (a Carpathian sheep farmer), but his dialogue does not resemble the rhyming,

Chapter 5: Modeling the Irish Theatre

highly stylized peasant dialogue generally associated with Wyspiański. On the contrary, Sobienowski's translation was in prose form and employed a slight folk coloring reminiscent of Kasprowicz's rendition of *The Countess Cathleen*.[140] Based on additional reviews of the play, it seems more likely that the actors, directors, and scenographers of the Polish Theater, who were largely veterans of the Kraków theater, enhanced the association with Wyspiański by performing Sobienowski's translation in a style evocative of the Polish playwright.

Irena Sławińska has acknowledged Sobienowski's use of a highlander accent, but she has argued that the more likely influence on his version was Kazimierz "Przerwa" Tetmajer's colorful tales of Polish mountaineer life, *Na skalnym Podhalu* (In the Rocky Highlands).[141] The presence of characters typical of Tetmajer's Carpathian tales lends some credence to Sławińska's suggestion, but at the same time her claim runs counter to Sobienowski's abiding attachment to Wyspiański. Tetmajer's tales, furthermore, offered a less direct parallel to Synge's carefully crafted Anglo-Irish syntax. Whatever its source, Sobienowski's translation clearly reflected his awareness of recent developments in Polish literature, as well as his intention to transpose *The Playboy* into a Polish folk setting and vernacular. This technique would prove to be at once both beneficial and distracting, as the combination of Polish and Irish folk elements presented a confusing vision to the audience and many critics appeared conflicted over the associations with Wyspiański.[142] As had been the case with *The Well of the Saints*, the question of performance cannot be overlooked, particularly in light of the Polish Theater's mission of an aesthetic textual interpretation.[143]

The plot of *The Playboy* lent itself to the widespread association with Wyspiański. Set in a village on the coast of Mayo, *The Playboy* centers on the appearance of Christy Mahon, a timid young man, in the public house of Michael James Flaherty and his strong-willed daughter, Margaret. In Act One, Margaret, or Pegeen Mike as she is called, is managing the public house and conversing with Shawn Keogh, who is trying to convince her to marry him. When Christy first enters, he is a suspicious, fearful young man, and Pegeen Mike wants to drive him off. When he confesses, however, that he killed his father and requires pity, the attitudes of everyone in the public-house change. Michael James offers Christy employment as a farm hand, and Pegeen Mike falls in love with him. The act ends with the sharply ironic line, "I'm thinking this night wasn't I a foolish fellow not to kill my father in the years gone by."[144] In Act Two, all the village girls and the Widow Quin come to hear the tale of Christy's awful deed. With each telling Christy becomes bolder and surer of himself. Pegeen Mike, jealous of the other women, tries to warn Christy about not trusting the others. While she is gone, however, Shawn Keogh and the Widow Quin attempt to bribe him to leave in order that Shawn can marry Pegeen. Christy refuses, but upon the sudden appearance of his father, he begs the Widow Quin to hide him. In Act Three, Christy achieves truly heroic proportions by winning all the local sports competitions, only to be confronted by the reappearance of his father. Exposed as a fraud and a liar, Christy lashes out violently and "kills" his father again in order to maintain the respect of the village and the love of Pegeen Mike. The deed, however, now strikes the entire village as a merely brutal crime, and they tie him up. Christy's father appears for the third time, rescues Christy from the villagers, and leaves cursing them. Pegeen Mike, realizing what she has lost, closes the play with the lines "Oh my grief, I've lost him surely. I've lost the only Playboy of the Western World."[145]

The Polish Theater's production of *The Playboy of the Western World*, which Szyfman recalled lasting a total of eight performances, by all accounts was the most extensive run of a work by Synge in Poland during the Young Poland period.[146] The reception of *The Playboy* among Polish theater-going audiences and critics on the whole was mixed. Although the Polish reviewers readily recognized Synge as a poet of enormous talent, it was apparent from their reviews that they found it difficult to grasp the Irish playwright's heroic tale of attempted patricide. The Warsaw theater critics ultimately split over Synge's unique dramatic style, which presented a challenging combination of realistic elements of Irish country life, brutal naturalism, and sublime poetry. In the final analysis, the differences of opinion among Synge's reviewers spoke to the fact that *The Playboy* represented an entirely new form of drama for the Warsaw theatrical community.

The symbolism of *The Playboy* proved to be the main point of contention among the reviewers. For Jakób Appenszlak, the critic for *The Golden Horn*, the power of Synge's play lay in its universality, not its brutal realism. "In a lonely inn, somewhere on the Irish coast," Appenszlak explained, "that deed, so splendid in its grimness grows into a wild, mystical rose of heroism, taking under its all-powerful rule the gray, superstitious souls of the simple people bored by the endless monotony of the circle of life."[147] Perceiving elements of Shakespeare and Homer in *The Playboy*, Appenszlak looked past Christy's violent attacks on his father to the play's deeper message. "Synge's work," Appenszlak maintained, "that strange, subtle flower with the sharp scent of the sea winds – cursed from the soul of the Irish people, widely surpasses the contours of locality and historical actuality, composing a first-rate, banal symbol of all these factors. Like everything that genius initiates, it is beyond time and place – it is for humanity and speaks about Man."[148] Appenszlak's interpretation was very much in keeping with the prevailing artistic ideals of Young Poland. In drawing the link between Synge's portrayal of the Irish countryside and its enduring presence in the mysterious world of the Absolute, Appenszlak could very well have been describing the criticism of Stanisław Lack or the poetry of Jan Kasprowicz.

The question of Synge's artistry proved likewise decisive in the review by Kotarbiński, which appeared five months later in the journal *Przegląd Teatralny* (The Theatrical Review). Kotarbiński, too, distinguished the dramatic symbolism of the *The Playboy* as a key point of his analysis, but where Appenszlak observed a masterpiece of timeless universality he perceived a failure of form. Kotarbiński, who established his reputation as a director of "national drama" in Kraków nearly fifteen years earlier, found that the enthusiasm surrounding Synge's Warsaw debut, in which Wyspiański's name was often invoked, was not matched by dramatic artistry. "The perceived analogies between the Irish dramatist and Wyspiański," Kotarbiński argued, "improperly compared 'The Playboy' with 'The Wedding,' though these two works truly have one thing in common, i.e, symbolism, carried out by each poet with the help of a variety of artistic means."[149] Kotarbiński's close relationship Wyspiański, as the director who had done the most to bring his drama to the stage, fundamentally shaped the manner in which he interpreted *The Playboy*. Synge's ability to create a colorfully realistic portrait of Irish rural life clearly conflicted with Kotarbiński's notion of symbolic drama. As a theater director, he was quite familiar with modern drama, but the elements of brutal realism in *The Playboy* clearly shocked him. "The external side of the symbol," Kotarbiński maintained, "is, in my estimation, unpleasant and even repulsive. One really needs to divert thinking from moral norms in order to perceive a heroic weapon in the hands of a son reconciling with the skull of an old father!"[150] Kotarbiński's reaction to *The Playboy* is a revealing example of the extent to which the response of Polish critics to Irish drama was as much a function of taste as it was of aesthetics. The perceived lack of symbolic depth in Synge's play revealed more about Kotarbiński's bias toward the symbolism found in the "monumental" national dramas of the Polish Romantics and Wyspiański than it did about the artistic structure of *The Playboy*. "In our great poetry," Kotarbiński pointed out, "we have examples of much deeper symbolism, which unites organically with the nature of thought, with the internal consequences of the vision. [...] The symbolism of 'The Wedding' combines itself with a certain unspecified visionary dream."[151] Kotarbiński was alluding to Wyspiański's form of monumental drama that was inherited from Mickiewicz, in which the surface action served as a symbolic backdrop of the national struggle. In Kotarbiński's view, the colorful Anglo-Irish idiom and recognizably Irish rural setting in Synge's drama stripped it of its potential figurative power. "The author," Kotarbiński argued, "did not fuse together in a poetic image the stuff of realism and symbolism. Because of this there arose a discrepancy incomprehensible to our public."[152] This defect, however, may have been more a product of performance on the part of the cast of the Polish Theater than it was of Synge's dramatic style. Given his strong reaction, Kotarbiński's criticism was more likely a function of his disagreement with the parallel between Synge and Wyspiański than it was an impartial reading of the play at hand.

While Appenszlak and Kotarbiński critiqued *The Playboy* in terms of its symbolism, Ignacy Baliński, the reviewer for *Tygodnik Ilustrowany* (The Illustrated Weekly), and Jan Lorentowicz, a well known critic and occasional translator for the Polish Theater, read Synge's play in terms of its satirical power. For his part, Baliński interpreted *The Playboy* exclusively in terms of Synge's relationship to Ireland. "Synge," Baliński explained, "was the brightest representative at the time of the revived Irish national poetry next to Yeats, Lady Gregory, Murray, Boyle, and a few others, who desire, not without humor, the quietism of their people, washed down lavishly with gin and porter, to be brightened with recollections and admiration of the ancient legends and heroic stories of Erin – to lay down the granite foundation of real and essential strength, and not dreamy heroism."[153] Baliński clearly recognized Synge's portraits of Irish country life, with their combination of elements of coarse realism, dark humor, romantic lyricism, as something unique within the European theater, but these same qualities were also barriers that made it difficult for him to understand the Irish playwright fully.[154] "It is in the third act," Baliński pointed out, "that we realize that these lively, coarse and real people are also deep symbols, sad despite their gaiety, of that state to which, in the eyes and heart of the poet, this island nation was led having been for more than a century the greatest exporter of people."[155] Baliński perceived a double-edged sword in Synge's lampooning dramatic style, which, he believed, rescued *The Playboy* from falling into the trap of raw naturalism. Baliński, however, was perceptive enough to realize that not everyone in Ireland might embrace such a harsh portrait of rural Irish society. "It is a bitter satire for his countrymen," Baliński acknowledged, "that they are only able to dream of power, of audacious and reckless deeds, but in real life only pull the daily load in order to make their way passably through."[156] Unlike Kotarbiński, Baliński understood that the volatility of *The Playboy* in large part grew out of a basic discrepancy between Synge's portrayal of Ireland and the Ireland of the mind. "There is something in this work," Baliński concluded, "that repels and attracts. The golden harp of Erin resonated to us in an unexpected manner, different than we had imagined from the ancient works of Celtic poetry."[157] Polish audiences, of course, had a much more distant relationship to Ireland, but Synge's scandalous depiction of the Irish countryside was also at odds with the prevailing vision of Celtic Ireland among Poles. In spite of this problem Baliński was also intelligent enough to recognize the value of Szyfman's production of *The Playboy* as a serious attempt to generate the same kind of creative energy in the Polish theater that Synge and his colleagues produced on the stage of the Abbey Theatre.

In his review of *The Playboy*, Lorentowicz agreed with Baliński's contention that satire, and not symbolism, represented its organizing feature. While Lorentowicz echoed the other reviewers' concerns regarding the coarser elements of *The Playboy*, he did not feel that they constituted a failure on the author's part. Instead, Lorentowicz believed that the Polish Theater's production had misrepresented Sobienowski's stylized language in such a way that the audience doubted what they were seeing was truly the play as the author had intended it. "The actors," Lorentowicz complained, "performed the drama entirely realistically. They looked for the tragic tones of Wyspiański, but meanwhile Synge himself called his work a comedy and treated the subject with bloody irony, even to the point of distaste."[158] Lorentowicz believed that the actors' approach to Synge's drama represented a grave mistake, because the audience ended up leaving the theater "thoroughly disturbed."[159] Given the primacy of the text in the Polish Theater's approach to performance, Lorentowicz's charge was a serious one. "The Polish Theater," Lorentowicz complained, referring to the actors, "changed Synge's irony into brutality, wounding the sensibilities of the audience with a brutality so great that its symbolism was reduced to only a few perceptible phrases."[160]

Where Lorentowicz found greatest fault was in the first act of the play, which he criticized for being "carried out in a dreamily-slow tempo, lowered in tone by an entirely naturalistic style of acting."[161] It was the actors' failure, in Lorentowicz's view, to bridge the gap between the literal action of the play and its ironic message, which made it such a disappointing production. "The entire act," Lorentowicz emphasized, referring to Act One, "should not be taken literally, as did the actors of the Polish Theater. By posing ourselves the impatient question: 'what next?' we realize by his [Christy's] shout that something completely different is happening in the drama than what we saw realized on the stage."[162] The author revealed his true "ideology," he felt, when Christy's father appears in Act Three and exposes him as a sham hero. "According to the law," Lorentowicz explained, "his crime would be very grave, but in light of the requirements for heroism in the countryside, Christy's deed is not a deed."[163] The other peasants' violent reactions to Christy's base crime struck Lorentowicz as being somewhat reminiscent of the ending of Wyspiański's play *The Curse*.[164] Synge's use of irony, however, allowed for Christy to assume truly the role of the hero, thereby rescuing the play from descending into mere brutality. "Here," Lorentowicz stressed, "Synge reveals himself as a truly great poet: Christy's so-called deed is only a common, awful crime. When he spoke of the deed, they all listened to him... as if to a story from a fairy tale. For them there did not need to be a murder, only—heroism."[165] In emphasizing Synge's dramatic use of irony, Lorentowicz revealed himself to be an astute observer of the Young Poland theater. It was not the Irishness of *The Playboy* that made it a new and challenging type of play for the Polish theater to realize on the stage, but rather its resistance to attempts at categorizing it under the broad headings of either naturalism or symbolism.

Part of the difficulty the Warsaw reviewers had in interpreting *The Playboy* grew out of their relative unfamiliarity with Ireland and Irish culture. "Does Synge's drama," Kotarbiński wondered, "have meaning as criticism and a symbolic cross-section of the current moods and impulses in the life of the nation? It is not possible to evaluate this, not knowing Irish relations better. The Polish spectator is struck at once just by the strange anomaly."[166] For Kotarbiński, who had built his reputation as the director who had brought the national dramas of Mickiewicz, Słowacki, and Wyspiański to the stage in Kraków, the inability to reconcile the symbolic and national elements in *The Playboy* was obviously a major source of confusion and irritation. It was not that Kotarbiński did not see any reason to link the two countries together, but that he considered the analogy to be historically imprecise. "There are other analogies equally distant," Kotarbiński insisted, "like those that exist between Ireland, tormented by the English yoke, and Poland, politically fallen a century prior at a moment of national revival. The Irish country people, disinherited by force and plunder for the benefit of the landlords, fight for their rights and stand presently at the threshold of a new historical era. In the life of Poland, noble-aristocratic elements still remain, and the people are entering a process of social awareness."[167] Like many of Kotarbiński's contemporaries, the connections between Poland and Ireland were easier to understand intuitively than in real terms. This explained why Kotarbiński could experience so much difficulty in accepting the parallel between Poland and Ireland, while colleagues such as Baliński could praise works such as *The Playboy* as "the expression of the nation's psychology, whose state presents many similarities and analogies with us."[168] The problem, therefore, was a matter of perception. While Kotarbiński understood Synge's work in terms of history, Baliński and others read it by way of psychology. "It is probably better," Kotarbiński admitted, "to interpret the puzzle of a drama as a symbol of the relation of old Ireland to new – as a irresolution of aims of the old and new generations, which having been released from dreams of independence begin a new era of coexistence with the old oppressors."[169]

In spite of their differences, there was consensus among the reviewers that the Polish Theater's production of *The Playboy* contributed something new to the theater in Poland. Appenszlak gave voice to the general sense of appreciation, at

Chapter 5: Modeling the Irish Theatre

least on the part of the Warsaw intelligentsia, for Szyfman's efforts in assembling a talented company of actors, directors, and scenographers. While he praised the intuitive acting of Maksymiljan Węgrzyn in the role of Christy, he tellingly gave no indication of how the Polish audience received the performance. Baliński, too, admired the production, but he took a broader view of Synge's play by considering it in terms of the impact that the Polish Theater had on the Warsaw theatrical community.[170] "Emulation, that noblest form of competition," Baliński asserted, "once again proves its positive influence. The rise of a private theater in Warsaw of a high level of artistic strength and the newest technical means... with a radical shudder has awoken the main stage of drama and comedy from a certain quietism and routine, to which things by nature are most greatly inclined and makes use of the various privileges of institutions, not excluding manor house and government theaters."[171] Baliński's observations were a true witness to the lasting impact the Polish Theater would have on both the direction of the theater in Poland and, more specifically, on the future of Irish drama in Poland.

As the least enthusiastic of the four critics, Kotarbiński in his critique of *The Playboy* betrayed his antipathy for the admirers of theater reform in Warsaw. "Among modernists, lovers and devotees of the theater," Kotarbiński observed, "John Millington Synge's three-act play, in a translation by Mr. Sobienowski, stirred great interest and a heated exchange of opinions."[172] Kotarbiński admitted not being previously familiar with the play, but it did not prevent him from recoiling from the discourse surrounding Synge's play, which consisted of "strange chaos and misty aesthetic ideas, being the fruit of trends currently popular."[173] This was not to say that Kotarbiński did not consider Synge to be a gifted playwright. On the contrary, the realistic elements of *The Playboy*, which Kotarbiński had found so problematic, struck him in the end as being Synge's strength as a dramatist. "The poet," Kotarbiński conceded, "in many scenes gave perfect, observable background of the life, as well as moments of the psychology of the people."[174] The fact that the Polish actors performed the play realistically, however, was not the fault of the actors, but of Synge's inability to achieve synthesis between the external and the symbolic. "In any case," Kotarbiński concluded, "Synge's drama was a very suggestive spectacle, extremely original, unsettling in content, an unusual mental prodding and poetic puzzle."[175]

In this observation, Kotarbiński came closest to expressing the significance of the Polish Theater's production of *The Playboy*. Irena Sławinska has asserted that the main reason *The Playboy* caused such confusion among Polish critics and theatergoers alike was because its style of comedy and its central character, the antihero Christy, were both new to Polish drama.[176] Lorentowicz, for his part, was less troubled with the excitement surrounding the Polish Theater's production than with the actors' decisions to perform realistically or naturalistically, as if *The Playboy* were a work by Wyspiański. With its rare combination of hellish laughter, poetic fantasy, and freshness of thought, Lorentowicz nonetheless believed *The Playboy* represented "one of the most original works of art that we have been given since the time of *The Judges, The Curse,* and *The Wedding*."[177] In spite of his genius, though, there was a lofty seriousness to Wyspiański's drama that differentiated it from Synge's work. In this respect, it was clear why Synge appealed to a writer such as Nowaczyński. Although Nowaczyński recognized Wyspiański's brilliance, in his view Young Poland was in greater need of "hellish laughter" than it was of "poetic fantasy."

In his recollections of the theater, Szyfman claimed that the eight performances of the play "received great press, which I read with true satisfaction."[178] Ironically, he felt whatever problems there were with the production that it was not the performers, but with the audience who were at fault. While the critics showed great perspicacity in their reviews of the Polish Theater's production of *The Playboy*, the production did not appear to be a popular success with the theater-going public of Warsaw. This much was suggested by a brief review in *Gazeta Warszawska* (The Warsaw Gazette), which took a retrospective look at the 1913 theatrical season. "The Playboy of the Western World," Stanisław Miłaszewski recalled, "raised in the press polar opposite opinions, so that it was possible to start up real polemics without the character of an argument. This same phenomenon took place in the French press. The public reacted to Synge equally apathetically in Paris as they had in Warsaw."[179] With a slight tone of resignation, Szyfman defended his production, arguing that the public's reaction had less to do with Synge's play than with its own mediocre aesthetic taste. "They had been demoralized for a decade," Szyfman explained, "by the repertoire of the Variety and Summer Theaters, and even such tremendous acting... could not bring them to admire these valuable and interesting productions and performances."[180] Taking place as it did at the end of the Polish Theater's first year, however, Szyfman could not have been surprised that a play as dynamic and challenging as *The Playboy of the Western World* would prove to be a stiff test for both his fledgling theater and the inexpert Warsaw audiences.

III. RETURNING TO BOHEMIA: PAWLIKOWSKI AND *THE WELL OF THE SAINTS*

The uneven reception of the Polish Theater's performances of *The Playboy* did not prevent another production of a Synge play from making its way to the stage

Chapter 5: Modeling the Irish Theatre

in Poland just two months later, on February 1, 1914. Once more the play in question was Synge's *The Well of the Saints*, but this time the production took place at Kraków's Słowacki Theater, under the direction of Andrzej Mielewski, a seasoned actor and director. There were some immediate similarities to the Lwów production of 1908, in that the production again paired *The Well of the Saints* with a Polish play, on this occasion *Castus Joseph*, a tragedy, and "Dziewka" (The Peasant Girl), a pastoral poem, both by the Polish Renaissance writer Szymon Szymonowicz. Although credit for the Polish translation of *The Well of the Saints* used in this production has generally been attributed to Sobienowski, it is likely that Wysocki's text from the 1908 Lwów production again served as the primary text.[181] This is all the more probable in that Pawlikowski had taken up his duties as director of the Słowacki Theater for a second time that same year after a decade in Lwów. Pawlikowski's first season back in Kraków featured a heavy dose of foreign drama, including previously performed works by Hauptmann, Maeterlinck, Shaw and Shakespeare, as well as new titles such as Galworthy's *Strife* and Steinheim's *Snob*, in addition to Synge's *The Well of the Saints*. It was a repertoire not unlike the one Szyfman had assembled for the Polish Theater.

While Szyfman had tremendous talent at his disposal and the enthusiastic support of most Warsaw intellectuals, Pawlikowski returned to Kraków to find the Słowacki Theater depleted both institutionally and artistically. Szyfman's success at luring away the Słowacki Theater's most experienced actors, directors, and set designers to Warsaw meant that Pawlikowski once again found himself as the director of a theater he would have to rebuild from the foundation up. "The Słowacki Theater," an anonymous critic for *The Critique* explained, "began its new season in a state of crisis. An entire mass of acting talent has emigrated... On the posters of great works opening the season, the public encounters an entire array of unknown names."[182] In spite of these problems, there was an air of anticipation in theater circles regarding Pawlikowski's return and the dramatic repertoire for 1914. "One name," the reviewer allowed, "has glittered a few times on posters, well inscribed on the memories of Kraków and Polish art in general: Tadeusz Pawlikowski."[183] It was in an atmosphere charged with expectation and uncertainty, therefore, that Synge's *The Well of the Saints* appeared for a second time on Polish stage.

While the critical reception of Synge's play was for the most part positive, the unconventional selection of the two other works for the production may have limited its appeal in the long run. Although the three pieces were all relatively short, the combination made for a long and diverse evening of entertainment. Whereas Synge's play was a new form of dark comedy, *Castus Joseph* was a familiar Biblical story modeled along the lines of Greek tragedy, and *The Peasant Girl* was a poetic dialogue describing the playful courtship of a peasant man and a peasant woman.[184] Adding to the overall length and jumble of the evening, the acclaimed Kraków poet and playwright, Lucjan Rydel, who also directed *Castus Joseph*, presented a short foreword. The contrast of styles, though a stimulating change for a theater in transition, did not make for an easily comprehensible evening of theater.

Given the relative inexperience of the cast of the Słowacki Theater, it was understandable that Kraków's theater critics would specify the acting as one of the weak points of its production of *The Well of the Saints*.[185] Zygmunt Rosner, the editor of the Kraków weekly *Gazeta Poniedziałkowa*, (The Monday Gazette), thought that the supporting cast performed their roles well, with each creating a believable country figure, but he found the disparity between Synge's artful play and its dramatic realization troubling. "John Millington Synge," Rosner observed, "was the greatest Irish storyteller and dreamer, an exceptional and powerful poet, of whom we Poles learned about just last year."[186] The performance of the actors from the Słowacki Theater, in Rosner's view, did not match Synge's artistry. "The creator of all the aforementioned plays," Rosner explained, "draws his scenes from peasant life, the life of the people, having been six hundred years in subjugation, and dresses them in the garments of legend, and in this way they must be presented to the public from the stage."[187] Rosner faulted in particular the performance of Antoni Siemaszko, the actor playing the lead role of Martin Doul. "Mr. Siemaszko," he complained, "acted too realistically, shouted and groaned too exaggeratedly, and characterized himself so terribly that no one could ever in their life believe it to be legendary figure."[188] While Rosner disapproved of Siemaszko's performance, he thought that the actor playing the female lead, Zofia Czaplińska, brought precisely the right tone to the role of Mary Doul. "Czaplińska," Rosner asserted, "felt the great tone of the symbol and presented an excellent profile, perhaps the most beautiful that we have seen from this artist."[189] Ironically, as Diana Paskuta-Włodek has pointed out, Siemaszko was the only actor in the cast who was already well known to theater audiences in Kraków.[190] The uneven acting performances revealed both the challenge Pawlikowski faced in forming a uniform acting company and the relative inexperience of the actors of the Słowacki Theater with Synge's particular style of drama.

A. E. Balicki, who published the most extensive and contentious critique of *The Well of the Saints* in *Przegląd Polski* (The Polish Review), perceived some promise in the Irish play, but he also felt that the Słowacki Theater had fallen short of fulfilling it. "The author had a very good idea," Balicki admitted, "but he did not take advantage of it and develop it, but left it (clearly intentionally) against a background so brutal and coarse that the entire piece gives one the impression

Chapter 5: Modeling the Irish Theatre

rather of distaste."[191] In this observation, there were traces of Kotarbiński's aversion to the rawness of Synge's dramatic style. Balicki believed that *The Well of the Saints* was open to a variety of performance styles, from realism to symbolism, but felt that the Słowacki Theater had only succeeded in rendering a mere sketch. Balicki did grudgingly give Synge credit. "In places," Balicki pointed out, "the author saved himself with irony and the merciful laughter of the creator – but even this irony was repulsive and harsh."[192] Like Rosner, Balicki found the greatest fault with the lead actor, Siemaszko, whose exaggerated performance apparently did not go over well with the audience. "It is too bad," Balicki lamented, "that Mr. Siemaszko did not pattern himself after his partner!"[193] The remainder of the cast, he felt, had carried out their roles well for the most part, though not devoid of the tendency to imitate the lead actor's overstated style.

As had been the case in Warsaw, Pawlikowski's production of Synge revealed him to be a dramatist unlike any other dramatist whose work had appeared on the Polish stage. In light of this, the uneven acting of the Polish cast in *The Well of the Saints* was somewhat forgivable. The real issue for the Kraków's reviewers, however, was not the unfamiliarity of *The Well of the Saints* so much as it was Pawlikowski's decision to pair it with *Castus Joseph*, an obscure Renaissance work. In doing so, Pawlikowski added a layer of additional complexity to Synge's reception that was not present in the Warsaw performances. While Miłaszewski enjoyed the acting, he found the combination of the two plays to be problematic. "'Castus Joseph,'" Miłaszewski explained, "is too thin to fill an evening of modern theater. The direction, therefore, added to this work the three act Irish legend by J. M. Synge entitled 'The Well of the Saints.'"[194] The idea that Pawlikowski's production of the two plays was lacking in a coherent vision was a criticism that would be reiterated by Miłaszewski's colleagues as well. For Miłaszewki, the lack of balance of the two works was a more obvious explanation for the lukewarm response of the Kraków audience to Synge's play than the acting.

While Miłaszewski's primary concern was the lack of symmetry between *The Well of the Saints* and *Castus Joseph*, Balicki expressed his astonishment and dismay that *Castus Joseph* had even been selected to appear alongside *The Well of the Saints*. "No one knows why," Balicki explained, "the direction of the theater added to this work a modern drama, numbering three acts, under the title 'The Well of the Saints,' by the Irishman [J. M.] Synge. No one is inquiring on what basis the connection is meant to rest, no one knows how to explain why precisely next to Szymonowicz and his *Joseph* this Irish legend was performed, which could on its own (if that is what it was all about) comprise a full evening."[195] Balicki's exasperation at the absence of an organizing idea in the production highlighted a fundamental difference between the Słowacki Theater under Pawlikowski and

Szyfman's Polish Theater. Pawlikowski was rather daring in his decision to pair *The Well of the Saints* and *Castus Joseph*, which were separated by hundreds of years and were starkly different stylistically. The lack of a defining aesthetic linking the two plays simply left too much for the audience to decipher on its own.[196] In his choice of material for the production, Pawlikowski appeared to be trying to find a folk equivalent in Polish drama for *The Well of the Saints*. His choice of Szymonowicz over more familiar contemporary artists, such as Wyspiański or Rydel, clearly proved to be more problematic than enlightening to the Kraków audience. "Unsure as to the meaning of the evening," Balicki observed, "the public left the theater expatiating about the Irishman, or praising the decorations of Mr. Maszkowski and the 'incomplete' costume of Jempsara."[197] This was in marked distinction to the approach of the Polish Theater. Szyfman's determination to realize every dramatic work through a consistent, synthetic approach precluded the performance of more than one play in an evening. The Polish Theater, however, through this approach was able to present a wide range of dramatic works without risk of confusion. It also meant that critics and theatergoers could disagree with the Polish Theater's interpretation of a given work, but they could not accuse it of lacking a coherent method or vision. While Pawlikowski's attempts to form connections between Polish and Irish drama were laudable, the result more often than not for Polish theatergoing audiences was confusion.

With the majority of the attention understandably focused on Synge, Balicki reminded his readers that the Słowacki Theater had also missed an opportunity for to promote the work of a largely forgotten, though noteworthy, Polish dramatist. Unlike Miłaszewski, Balicki felt that Szymonowicz's play was worthy of being staged alone. "If that had been the case," Balicki insisted, "everyone would have approached and departed from the theater with real pietism, when they knew the purpose of the evening: honor for our theatrical past and a reminder of the beginnings of Polish dramatic art!"[198] As things stood, however, *Castus Joseph* was lost in the shadow of its more celebrated Irish counterpart. Once again, there were echoes of Kotarbiński in Balicki's umbrage at the general level of excitement generated by Synge's celebrity. "Why the three-act Irish legend entitled *The Well of the Saints* was performed the same evening we really do not understand," Balicki wondered, "just as we cannot comprehend why the author of this work, J. M. Synge, is called 'the Irish Wyspiański.' Perhaps with other works that name is justified; but *The Well of the Saints* in any case – no! Be what may, we regard the author of *Bolesław the Brave* too highly to ascribe his name to the aforementioned Irish legend."[199] Balicki admitted that his opinion regarding the comparison of Synge and Wyspiański might have been different had he known the Irish dramatist's entire *oeuvre*, but he remained skeptical of

Chapter 5: Modeling the Irish Theatre

any fundamental affinity between the two playwrights. If considered together with Kotarbiński's observations from a year earlier, Balicki's objections indicate the degree to which Wyspiański figured as a ready subtext to the discussions of young theater enthusiasts regarding Synge. The intensity of emotion in the comments of the two critics is suggestive of a rift in the Polish theater between the passionate adherents of theater reform and the representatives of a more traditional approach to the stage.

The response to Pawlikowski's production of *The Well of the Saints* was indicative of the general air of disappointment surrounding his first year as the director of the Słowacki Theater in Kraków. Many critics had hoped that Pawlikowski's return to Kraków would restore some artistic vitality to the Słowacki Theater, or at the very least bring a viable repertoire to a theater mired in chaos and crisis. It was apparent that an ambitious production such as the double-bill of *The Well of the Saints* and *Castus Joseph*, albeit new to the Słowacki Theater, fell well short of those expectations. "Szymonowicz's 'Castus Joseph,'" a reviewer for *The Critique* complained, "[...] is not – in our opinion – art resting on the line of a permanent Polish repertoire; rather, ... we only regret the lost, misguided labor of love on both the side of the direction and its collaborators."[200] It was not that Szymonowicz's play was too dated for the modern stage, but rather as an obscure work it failed to capture the imagination of those in Kraków who desired the reinvigoration of the theater. As it turned out, the production came across as being poorly planned and lacking in vision. This proved to be the general consensus regarding Pawlikowski's first year after returning as director of the Słowacki. "The series of performances," the theater critic for *The Critique* maintained in the same column several months later, "that followed [*Castus Joseph*] proves that the expectations assumed by the Kraków theater and the public were far from the noble ambition of becoming the leading Polish stage."[201] The lack of a systematic approach in the selection of plays, which resulted in the inclusion of long-forgotten playwrights such as Szymonowicz at the expense of modern masters such as Wyspiański, was both perplexing and exasperating to those close to the theater. For many critics, Pawlikowski's apparent dislike of Wyspiański constituted a fatal flaw that lowered his reputation as an innovator in the Polish theater. "The slogan of [Director] Pawlikowski," the critic concluded, "is more than likely: 'onward for great creation.' We see what that looks like in reality."[202] Theater lovers in Kraków may have owed Pawlikowski a debt of gratitude for his pioneering efforts of twenty years earlier, but their expectations had risen considerably since then.

In spite of the criticism leveled at Pawlikowski, Synge's *The Well of the Saints* represented a rare bright spot in the repertoire of 1914. The reviewer for *The*

Critique recognized Synge as a real poet, whose work "on the outside is full of realism, on the inside... of an ironic and sad philosophy of life," and lamented the departure of *The Well of the Saints* from the theater's repertoire.[203] Taking a retrospective look at Pawlikowski's inaugural year as director in Kraków, Maciej Szukiewicz pointed out in the journal *Świat* (The World) that it was the director's innate talent and his love for the theater that had prevented a wholesale defection of acting talent to Warsaw. "Thanks to that," Szukiewicz maintained, "[and] in spite of difficult conditions, the Kraków theater managed not only to hold together a good cast, but in general to put forth a good repertoire."[204] For Szukiewicz, who estimated that twenty-eight of the thirty-seven plays in 1914 had been premieres, it was the attempt to renew the dramatic repertoire of the Słowacki Theater that most distinguished Pawlikowski's second tenure as director in Kraków. Balicki's frustration at the disregard shown to *Castus Joseph* is more understandable in light of the fact that some two-thirds of these twenty-eight new plays were by foreign authors. "All of the newest Polish works filled just thirty-three evenings," Szukiewicz explained, "through the rest we witnessed foreign works, signed by more and lesser known names, such as Synge and Galsworthy, not to mention Kistemaeker and the Berlin-Prussian Sternheim."[205] Such observations underscore the degree to which Pawlikowski's approach as a director was still shaped by cosmopolitanism. While Pawlikowski may have failed to produce a coherent evening of theater, *The Well of the Saints* was a rare attempt at innovative theater at a time of great difficulty for the Słowacki Theater.[206] For the theater that had been witness to the genius of Wyspiański, however, it is plain that more was needed to return the Kraków stage to distinction than a surfeit of plays from abroad.

IV. NEW BEGINNINGS: IRISH DRAMA IN THE POLISH WAR THEATER

The strong desire that existed among Polish intellectuals for innovative, artistic drama, evident both in the excitement generated by Szyfman's Polish Theater and the disappointment produced by Pawlikowski's Słowacki Theater, gained unexpected support with the artistic reorientation of the *Teatr Rozmaitości* (The Variety Theater), which formed part of the Russian system of government theaters in Warsaw. Long regarded by Polish intellectuals as a bastion of outmoded, popular drama, The Variety Theater underwent a six-month renovation in the spring of 1913, during which time it was expanded and modernized at great cost. The president of the Warsaw government theaters,

Chapter 5: Modeling the Irish Theatre

Georgii Malyshev (1908–1914) had made attempts as early as 1908 to reform the system of the government theaters in Warsaw, which had been plagued for decades by chronic debt and poor artistic direction. Although the previous directors of the government theaters had generally tried to mimic developments in contemporary European drama, Piotr Jerzy Domański has pointed out that the Russian authorities regarded the prospect of its theaters gaining real artistic and financial independence as disconcerting.[207] Malyshev not only succeeded in achieving the latter, but in ordering the reconstruction of the Variety Theater and hiring Ludwik Solski, a veteran of the theater in Kraków, to become the general director of the government theaters in 1913, he also succeeded in bringing a new artistic sensibility in the government theaters. Solski, together with the critic Adam Grzymała-Siedlecki, who was appointed as the theaters' literary director in place of Józef Kotarbiński that same year, brought experience as well as credibility to Malyshev's attempted reforms.

With work being completed in December of 1913, the timing of the artistic restructuring of the Variety Theater was at once significant and unfortunate. Reopening less than a year after the debut of Szyfman's Polish Theater, the Variety Theater both validated the modern approaches to stagecraft then gaining ground in Poland and provided Warsaw theatergoers with an alternative venue at which to enjoy contemporary drama. Thoughts of theater reform in the government theaters, however, were cut short by Germany's declaration of war against Russia on August 1, 1914. Joined four days later by Austria-Hungary on August 5, the alignment of the Central Powers against Russia shattered what had been an effective triple alliance for more than a century. With heavy fighting taking place both to the north and the south of Warsaw, the quiet luxuries of theater renovation and artistic experimentation gave way to the wartime policies of the Russian government. The uncertain situation caused by the encroaching front obliged Malyshev to close all the government theaters in mid-August 1914. The hiatus proved to be a temporary one, but within a matter of months Malyshev was replaced as the head of the government theaters and the position of the artistic director, held briefly by Solski, was eliminated altogether. By late October the newly appointed head of the government theaters in Warsaw, Vladimir Burman, permitted performances once again to commence. The time of respite for the government theaters proved to be brief, as the German troops began their assault on Warsaw in February 1915. The government theaters in Warsaw closed their doors on July 26, 1915, just days before the forces of the Central Powers occupied the city, only to reopen two days later, on July 28, under the direction of the Polish artists themselves. Officially fashioned as a provisional arrangement following the departure of the Russian authorities from Warsaw, the system of government theaters became for the duration of the war a *de facto* Polish institution.[208]

As was evident in the inconvenience and uncertainty caused by the closing and reopening of the theater, the disruption caused by the start of World War I was far from an abstraction for the Warsaw theatrical community. With the declaration of war against Russia by the Central Powers in August 1914, all individuals involved in the Warsaw theater who held either Austrian or German citizenship were threatened with arrest if they remained in the city. The large influx into Warsaw of actors, directors, and set designers in the years prior to the war, most notably from the Kraków theater, meant that all the theaters in the city, both public and private, had to carry on without many of the brightest and most experienced dramatic talents of the day. In addition to Solski, in the Variety Theater this affected the young actor-*cum*-director, Juliusz Osterwa, and a number of other actors, while Szyfman and a host of actors, directors, and designers from the Polish Theater were also forced to leave Warsaw in the fall of 1914 and in the months to follow.[209] Despite Burman's decision to allow the resumption of performances, after Solski's departure and the liquidation of the position of general director of theaters at the end of November, the task of organizing performances was left largely in the hands of the actors. Albeit the reality of the chaos and instability of the times, this impromptu state of affairs was important, for it marked the first real experience of autonomy for Poles in the Russian-controlled theater system.[210] As it turned out, this experience proved to be significant, for by August 1915 it would, in fact, become permanent.

The challenge of staging drama of any kind during wartime, much less innovative foreign works, was a serious problem that was not unique to the Variety Theater. Within the government theater system this difficulty was compounded by an established practice, whereby foreign works selected for performance generally had to have been staged previously in Warsaw or elsewhere in Poland, most notably in Kraków, before they could appear in the Variety Theater.[211] In a strange twist, however, the pressures and deprivations of war proved to be a boon rather than a detriment to artistic experimentation. For the actors from the Polish Theater who were forced to find temporary work in the Variety Theater following Szyfman's departure, the reorientation of the Variety Theater's approach to the stage was both surprising and refreshing. "After the outbreak of the war," Leon Schiller recalled, "when the financial and organizational position of the Polish Theater wavered, [the company] shifted, unfortunately, to the government theaters, but in spite of the stifling, old-world atmosphere, in spite of the parochial attitudes to the art of older and younger 'bombasts,' a defending hand emerged from this treacherous venue: playing

Chapter 5: Modeling the Irish Theatre

[works] by Kistemaeckers and Guitry, and the beloved *The Countess Cathleen* by Yeats."[212] In addition to such foreign works, the Variety Theater produced its standard offering of commercial fare and a number of modern Polish works, including Tadeusz Rittner's *Lato* (Summer) and Lucjan Rydel's *Betlejem polskie* (The Polish Bethlehem). Instead of being the result of a conscious plan, the high level of the repertoire appeared to be an organic development reflecting the collective response of the Warsaw theatrical community to the upheaval of war.

This much was evident in the decision to perform *The Countess Cathleen* at the Variety Theater on December 19, 1914, a little more than two months after the theater had reopened following its hiatus. Directed by Marian Tatarkiewicz and with Janina Szyllinżanka, Kazimierz Junosza-Stępowski, and Teodor Roland in the leading roles, the performance combined the talents of veterans of the government theaters and those of its more recent additions.[213] Together with set designs by Wincenty Drabik, the talented scenographer from the Polish Theater, the Variety Theater's production of Yeats's play was very much a product of the times. Although bringing *The Countess Cathleen* to the stage represented a remarkable achievement in its own right, the mixture of talents did not necessarily bode well for a cohesive performance. Bożena Helcbergier has pointed out that Tatarkiewicz directed the play as a light fable, while Drabik, in keeping with his background in the Polish Theater, designed the costumes, sets, and lighting with a symbolic use of color.[214] Taking place just before Christmas in the early months of the war, there was also little chance that the Variety Theater's rendition of Yeats's play would possess the same kind of artistic harmony that had characterized the efforts of Szyfman and his company.

The Variety Theater's choice to stage Yeats's play is illuminating, for in some important respects it was a unique event in the repertoire that had been established since the start of the war. Yeats's symbolic play was a sharp contrast to the mix of comedies and anti-German works that predominated on the stage after fighting had begun between Germany and Russia. It remains unclear how *The Countess Cathleen* made its way to the Variety Theater, as it had not been previously performed anywhere else in Poland. With its apparent politically inoffensive content and its morally uplifting message, however, Yeats's drama seemed to be aimed toward appealing to the needs of Warsaw's theatergoing public and satisfying the desire of serious theater enthusiasts for modern drama without the risk of running afoul of the Russian censor.[215] In this regard, *The Countess Cathleen* represented something quite different for the Polish theater as a whole. With its ability to operate both as a national and a symbolic work, Yeats's play differed from the more openly strident Polish patriotic dramas. Helcbergier has raised the possibility that Tartarkiewicz intentionally played up the fairy tale quality of *The Countess Cathleen* as a means of skirting the censor. Drabik's symbolist designs, moreover, would have enhanced the otherworldly quality of Yeats's play. As a theater known for light entertainment and only a handful of premieres each year, the performance of such a dynamic play in and of itself represented a significant accomplishment.

Deprived of its more experienced and creative talents, the Variety Theater was limited in its ability to present the kind of innovative and challenging drama desired by many in Warsaw, but for a city under great duress the courage of the Variety Theater to attempt to do so was not overlooked. For Antoni Sikorski, the editor and publisher of *Echo Literacko-Artystyczne* (The Literary-Artistic Echo), the appearance of Yeats's play was much more than an indication of the progress that had been made in the government theaters. Instead, it revealed the determination of the Polish community in Warsaw to remain culturally active under extremely difficult circumstances. "Around [Warsaw's] trenches," Sikorski observed in January 1915, "shrapnel explodes, the echo of artillery fire resounds, hundreds of victims are carried to the hospital each day from the battlefield - bah! Even shells rain from the heavenly regions, lobbed by a treacherous hand, like hail during a summer heat wave."[216] In such conditions, the decision to produce drama of a higher artistic quality, or theater of any kind, for Sikorski revealed as much about the "Roman" endurance of the Poles in Warsaw as it did about aesthetics and art, because for him the two were inseparable. "This fortitude of spirit," Sikorski insisted, "this resistance of Warsaw to all kinds of pain [...] ensures that the cult of fine art in general and dramatic art in particular [...] does not for one moment fade away. What is more, it expands native creativity, allowing the experimentation in our theaters of that which under normal conditions *it would not be possible*, or desirable to produce."[217] Despite its official status, the collective work of the administration, actors, and directors of the Variety Theater to continue working was emblematic both of the internal changes that had taken place within the government theaters and the determination to maintain a vibrant cultural life in the face of difficult circumstances.

The emotion underlying Sikorski's review, which was not atypical of Yeats's Polish reviewers, bespoke the degree to which personal experience as much aesthetics played a part in his interpretation of *The Countess Cathleen*. Yeats's ability to write with equal facility on the level of the fantastic and the national made him particularly attractive to his Polish critics, whose desire for artistic innovation had in recent months had given way somewhat to include the new-found prospect of national independence. As Norman Davies has pointed out, the conflict between the Central Powers and Russia marked the first break in the triple alliance between the partitioning powers in over a century.[218] It

Chapter 5: Modeling the Irish Theatre

was not surprising, therefore, that Warsaw's theater critics discerned a more profound level of meaning in the Variety Theater's production of *The Countess Cathleen*, than in the pre-war performances of Synge's work in Lwów, Warsaw, and Kraków. Little prompting was needed to draw a connection between the symbolism of Yeats's folk tale and the political possibilities created by the rapid onset of war. With the Russian censor still very much at work, open expressions of independence were impossible. With its religious symbolism and poetic qualities, however, *The Countess Cathleen* proved to be a play that was palatable both to the Russian authorities and moving to Poles.

While the poetic quality of Yeats's drama made it appealing to Polish theater enthusiasts who longed for the kind of pure, symbolic theater envisioned by Gordon Craig, it was difficult to expect the audiences of the Variety Theater to share the same concern with aesthetics. Long accustomed to generally lighthearted fare, Yeats's play was a real artistic departure for the regular patrons of the Variety Theater. For Sikorski, it was more important that the company of the Variety Theater had attempted to achieve something different by staging a Yeats's play than in actually succeeding. "Here," Sikorski explained, "the director had a responsibility to fulfill and, let us say, thanklessly, but he fulfilled it as only a sincere poet and thoughtful mind could."[219] Despite the difficult challenge of balancing the fantastic and realistic elements of the play, Sikorski felt that the Variety Theater's production on the whole had been successful. "It is a strange life though," Sikorski concluded, "entwined in magical threads and plaited among distressing dreams of happiness."[220] Surrounded on all sides by the swiftly escalating military conflict, it was precisely this "strange life" that wartime Warsaw found so appealing in *The Countess Cathleen*. With its message of self-sacrifice and redemption, it was understandable that many Polish critics perceived a strong moral value in Yeats's play. "It is a pure spring of poetry," Wiktor Popławski, the theater critic for a local paper, asserted, "the truest and noblest teacher in these difficult and arduous times."[221] Far from attempting an escape from the reality of the day, in an address prior to the performance the play's director, Tatarkiewicz, deliberately "tied Yeats's play to our times. Indeed, we are not strangers to hunger, cold, and the poor fate of a fallen people."[222] Fantasy and symbolism aside, *The Countess Cathleen* was well timed to address the need Poles felt for messages of hope and national deliverance.

Helcbergier has argued that *The Countess Cathleen*, with its ability to operate simultaneously on the levels of folklore, myth, and national tragedy, represented a significant event for Warsaw's theater critics, because it presented them with a new model for the Polish theater.[223] Appearing at a time when the ideas of theater reform at last were beginning to take hold in the Warsaw theater, Yeats's sublime Irish miracle play realized on the stage the conceptual designs of Gordon Craig and other figures in the modern European theater. Whereas the rawness of Synge's dramas had bothered many Polish critics, the purity of Yeats's symbolism in *The Countess Cathleen* proved to be a revelation. For the critic Jan Lorentowicz, the Variety Theater's production succeeded precisely because Yeats's play "was not relenting for even a second with originality and freshness of fantasy—that is witness of a great talent indeed."[224] There was little in the theater of Young Poland, with the possible exception of Wyspiański, to compare with the visionary aesthetics of Yeats's play. Wyspiański's works, however, were not fully known in Warsaw, and no Polish director as of yet had figured out how best to achieve the playwright's vision of monumental theater on the stage.

The inclination to invoke the name of Wyspiański was a strong one, but the comparison seemed to be less compelling than in years past. "Similar to our Wyspiański, (with whom he shares a kinship for fantasy and a love for native legends)," Lorentowicz explained, "Yeats devoted himself for a time to painting, which he gave up on becoming entirely absorbed in lyrics and epic songs stemming from folk traditions."[225] Lorentowicz, however, was quick to point out the universality of *The Countess Cathleen*, adding that Poland had its own version of the tale in the Twardowski legend, but he gave Yeats credit because "only a great poet could touch it today with success."[226] Lorentowicz's observation was significant, for it touched upon the universal quality of folk culture that had from the beginning formed one of the fundamental ties between Young Poland and Irish-Ireland. It was Yeats's ability to fulfill both the cosmopolitan and essentialist needs of Young Poland that made him such a uniquely attractive writer. Because of this, Yeats could be read with equal facility as a true symbolist writer, as well as a playwright operating in the psyche of the Irish rural folk. With its overtly religious symbolism and stylized folk elements, it was difficult to ignore the roots of *The Countess Cathleen* in Irish peasant culture. "Who will speak of the architecture of a country church," Rabski wondered, "when the priest stands before the altar and the people in desperate rapture sing 'Holy Lord, Mighty Lord, Everlasting Lord!'"[227] Having been translated by Jan Kasprowicz, there was a clear affinity between between Yeats's play and *Hymns*. Popławski also associated Kasprowicz with "the strong language, the spirit of the original, and an understanding of the value of words spoken from the stage."[228] Whether it was Wyspiański or Kasprowicz, it was apparent that for Poles the appeal of *The Countess Cathleen* was its ability to address Polish culture on a number of different levels.

Although Yeats set his play in a somewhat realistic country setting, it was his ability to inhabit a sphere far removed from the cares of the waking world that endowed his drama with a uniquely transcendent quality. In contrast to Synge,

Chapter 5: Modeling the Irish Theatre

Yeats concerned himself less with the reality of Irish life than with its deeper, symbolic core. "Synge," Władysław Rabski explained in *Kurier warszawski* (The Warsaw Courier), "with his tendency toward national allegory is a realist, he walks on the earth, divines the tiniest movements in the souls of his people, from whose tears, longing and tragic psychology he fashions his great dramas. While Yeats, as someone has put it, is 'the shade of a shade,' ... is mist, a milky cloud."[229] It was Yeats's commitment to creating this otherworldly atmosphere or theater of divine essences, which made *The Countess Cathleen* such a revelation to Polish critics. "Sometimes," Rabski observed, "[Yeats displayed] the melancholy and holiness of those who passed through the storm of humanity and landed on some Böcklinesque island, where black cypresses weep and white swans swim in lakes. Even his eroticism is incorporeal."[230] Given Rabski's exalted rhetoric, it was clear to understand the extent to which *The Countess Cathleen* continued to be interpreted via the *fin-de-siècle* symbolism associated with the Pre-Raphaelites, the French symbolists, and in the case of Poland, *Chimera*.

Removed from the controversy concerning its religious message that clouded its Irish debut, Yeats's play in its Polish context was free to come across as pure poetry. More than anything, it was Yeats's capacity to create a drama far removed from the grim reality of daily life that made it so appealing to his Polish reviewers. While the theater in Warsaw had in recent years started to gain increasing exposure to modern drama, both Polish and foreign, there was little that could compare with *The Countess Cathleen*.[231] For the Warsaw critics, Yeats's poetic drama was clearly a revelation. "'This is not a versified fantastic drama," Popławski stressed, "neither is it a conceived legendary spectacle—it is a fairy tale, in which there is nothing earthly—though everything is so straightforward, human and not over-fantasized. How clear and sublime must be the mind of the poet who created this work."[232] Yeats stood in marked contrast to extreme modernists such as Przybyszewski, whose plays attempted to dramatize the psyche of the individual. "There is no eroticism in it at all," Rabski stressed, "Even the lover of the young Aleel is otherworldly. It is not love of woman, but praise for an angel. And Countess Cathleen walks the earth like Madonna, who descends to earth from the frames of a Pre-Raphaelite painting. It is as if she is not of the clay from which God made man. There is no 'I,' only 'for you.'"[233] Rabski's description of the collective, spiritual quality of Yeats's play would have immediately triggered thoughts of the Black Madonna of Częstochowa, but it was clear by his search for suitable parallels that there was little, if anything, in the drama of Young Poland comparable to Yeats's poetic drama.

Because of their delight and gratitude at the rapid turnabout that had taken place in the government theaters, Warsaw's theater critics on the whole were forgiving when it came to the shortcomings of the Variety Theater's production. While the director and actors succeeded in presenting Yeats's "exquisite Irish legend," the audiences in attendance apparently did not display the same enthusiasm for the play. "Unfortunately," Lorentowicz explained, "the undertaking, which by itself is difficult and requires strenuous effort, became even more risky by appearing in a theater whose ears are stopped up with the gray repertoire of bourgeois prudery and which truly hates poetry."[234] Lorentowicz's damning indictment was less of a condemnation of the Variety Theater's attempt to stage serious, artistic drama than it was a realistic assessment of the theater's ability to change its aesthetic orientation in such a short time. "Such a repertoire," Lorentowicz maintained, "has its own consequences: because it read on the poster the description 'a fable in verse,' the public felt unease, which resulted in the theater being half-full; the actors, unaccustomed to reciting verse, seek support by changing it to toneless prose. Under such conditions the fairy tale tone of the play became something irritating because it was devoid of the rhythm and magic of legend; performed in gray realism the magic of poetry for many... became a theatrically empty conch shell—the words of the poet's song 'changed to inarticulate moan.'"[235] Lorentowicz, who was a highly respected literary critic and translator, touched upon a fundamental problem with the Variety Theater's production. It was one thing to stage a "fable in verse," but it was quite another to realize fully a symbolic drama such as *The Countess Cathleen*. While the effort was laudable, the lack of experience with such drama, both on the part of the audience and the Variety Theater, was apparent.

For Lorentowicz's colleagues, the difficulty with staging *The Countess Cathleen* issued not only from the audience or the company of the Variety Theater, but also from Yeats's uniquely challenging form of poetic drama. "There is no place for dramatization," Popławski insisted, "nor for actors' games... one must seize the internal tone of Cathleen, that is conquer the role of Cathleen."[236] While the general consensus among the Warsaw critics was that the actress in the Variety's production, Janina Szyllinżanka, had succeeded in doing this, the same could not be said for the supporting actors or for the staging of the play as a whole. For his part, Rabski believed that Yeats's play presented a difficult challenge for any theater. The problems he had with the Variety Theater's production had less to do with the abilities of the actors and the director abilities than it did with the decision to stage such an otherworldly drama at all, "because the brutal realism of the theater is an enemy dangerous to the colorful dreams of the poet."[237] Returning again and again to the Pre-Raphaelites, Rabski perceived Yeats's play more as a visual metaphor than as a play. "Such is the tale about the Countess Cathleen," Rabski insisted, "which may lack at times form and

Chapter 5: Modeling the Irish Theatre

dramatic expression, but which is like the poet's psalm and a peasant prayer. It does not matter that more than once the scenic composition grew muddied... or that the final apotheosis is rather visually imagined (though Yeats was a painter in younger years) than dramatically composed, because above all it flows as if one great, passionate prayer."[238] With a conception featuring elements of light and color, it was apparent that the Variety Theater's stage designer, Drabik, was aware of the challenge of staging the conclusion of *The Countess Cathleen*, which consisted of stage directions describing a magnificent battle between the supernatural forces of Heaven and Hell. The artistic problem posed by Yeats's drama, however, was not unique to the Variety Theater, but rather it was representative of the inherent difficulty symbolic drama posed to the modern theater. It was for this reason that the Warsaw theater critics were forgiving when it came to the Variety Theater's production of *The Countess Cathleen*.

Regardless of its shortcomings, there was consensus among Warsaw's theater critics perceived that Variety Theater's production of *The Countess Cathleen* was a special event. "The directors of The Variety," Lorentowicz insisted, "must be congratulated that they had the courage to acquaint the wider general public with one of the best poets in Ireland today."[239] Such acclaim spoke to the determination of the Variety Theater to keep producing meaningful drama in spite of the destabilization caused by the outbreak of the war. Popławski also urged his readers to forgive the production's occasional flaws, "for we are convinced of the theater's good will."[240] Even critics such as Władysław Rabski, the critic for *Kurier Warszawski* (The Warsaw Courier), who did not feel the motif of *The Countess Cathleen* to be particularly revolutionary, joined his fellow critics in congratulating the Variety Theater for putting on a play with such deep, yet subtle lyricism. "Today," Rabski maintained, "we only feel the obligation to express gratitude to the theater direction that it tore us away for a moment from the brutal cry of reality, to the director that the beautiful work was given a beautiful setting, and to the artists, with Miss Szylinżanka at the fore, that they understood and expressed the true fairy tale melody of the poet."[241] Helcbergier has argued that the Polish critics writing about Irish drama tended to write about what suited their taste rather than cite real, meaningful detail. While this tendency toward exaggerated language was typical of Young Poland, it was evident that for Rabski and his colleagues *The Countess Cathleen* registered on a personal as well as an artistic level. "When a man feels bad," Rabski observed "when life strikes him in the temple with an iron hammer, when poverty and misfortune settle on the threshold and wolves howl at the window, he thinks sometimes that white spirits lead him along a trail of stars in the music of the spheres, to the heavens, full of flowers and sweet wine."[242]

More than anything, Rabski concluded, Warsaw was in need of a poet such as Yeats, whose work was as far removed from reality as possible. "Go," Rabski urged his readers, "dream, and forget for a while."[243]

Faced with a distracted public, scattered and disorganized acting companies, and the deprivations associated with war, an anonymous reviewer for *Tygodnik Ilustrowany* (The Illustrated Weekly) acknowledged that the temptation for Poles to abandon the theater as a luxury would have been a natural one. As Sikorski made clear in his review of *The Countess Cathleen*, the response of the theater community in Warsaw was a hardened determination to maintain the normal rhythms of the theatrical season. Since the theaters in Warsaw employed some two thousand people, not to mention a host of authors, translators, and musicians, the notion of closing them was not an acceptable option for the Polish community as a whole. "It is possible today to declare," the reviewer in *The Illustrated Weekly* declared," – and history will not object – that philanthropically, civic regard at the outset of the war settled on the need to maintain the theaters *in spite of everything...* The directors of the theaters wanted to keep alive and protect their workers from starving."[244] It was not simply the widespread resolve to maintain the theaters as vital social institutions and means of employment that struck the critic for *The Illustrated Weekly*, but also the artistic sophistication of the season's performances. "The directors of both dramatic stages," the critic explained, "of the Polish Theater and the 'Variety,' managed to maintain their stages on a high artistic level. When today we read the titles of works put on during this difficult year, it is possible to forget for a moment that this was meant to be a year turning attention to the box office... and nothing more."[245] With productions of works by such dramatists as Maeterlinck, Tolstoy, Rittner, and Wyspiański at the Polish Theater and Moliere, Yeats, Perzyński, and Rydel at the Variety Theater, the war may have disrupted daily life, but it had not caused the disappearance of artistry from the stage in Warsaw. What is more, the reviewer wryly observed, the ideals of theater reform were better realized during this time of upheaval than anything that had been previously attempted by its most vocal advocates prior to the war.[246] For the Poles who remained in Warsaw and struggled to keep the theater open, this vibrant, though uneven, repertoire underscored not only the importance of the theater as a cultural institution, but also to its deeper meaning as a indication of the enduring strength of Polish society.

As the front lines moved increasingly closer to Warsaw at the beginning of 1915, the notion of the war as an opportunity to rebuild the nation gained in strength.[247] In another unsigned article for *The Illustrated Weekly*, the belief that drama had a role to play in this reconstruction process was put forward in regard to the didactic power of a play such as *The Countess Cathleen*. While the reviewer

Chapter 5: Modeling the Irish Theatre

agreed with the prevailing critical opinion regarding the beauty and nobility of Yeats's play, he perceived a social value that was not observed by his fellow critics. "Such works," the reviewer argued, "should enter the program of youth education; the presentation of 'The Countess Cathleen' should gather together the entire mass of young listeners, in whose souls the pure, golden seed of this beautiful wisdom and stainless poetry will fall."[248] Written a month before the Germans began their siege of Warsaw, there was a definite air of optimism to this proposal. The reviewer's observations, however, revealed the extent to which Poles at the time understood the broader reality, the theater included, in terms of Poland's prospective future as an independent nation. Yeats's *The Countess Cathleen*, with its morally uplifting motif of spiritual and national deliverance, was ideally suited to this kind of wishful thinking.

With the withdrawal of the Russians from Warsaw in late July 1915, the Polish actors, directors, and artists of the government theaters gained a measure of this freedom considerably earlier than the rest of the compatriots in the partitioned lands of Poland. Having been given full reign of the government theater stages and formed a union collectively organized by the former employees in conjunction with Warsaw's civic authorities, in the midst of the war there emerged a system of stages in Warsaw that was by all accounts thoroughly Polish in character and management. The withdrawal of the Russian authorities predictably resulted in the production of more historical, patriotic Polish plays, which in most cases involved the exchange of anti-Russian plays for anti-German works. The most striking aspect of this limited autonomy enjoyed by the Polish theaters was not necessarily the staging of previously banned Polish works, but rather the decision to stage works by Russian authors for the first time.[249] Limited in funds, which prohibited the use elaborate set designs, the independently run Polish theater looked more to the future than the past by trying more experimental forms of stagecraft and producing predominately contemporary plays. In the final analysis, the early withdrawal of the Russian authorities allowed the measures of internal control that had been allowed to develop with the outbreak of the war to take hold. It was because of this that the Variety Theater was able to make the transition to becoming the National Theater with the declaration of Polish independence in 1919.

As much as the Russian withdrawal from Warsaw in the summer of 1915 contributed to a measure of cultural autonomy for Poles in the government theater system, it was not the full story of the Polish theater during the war, nor was it the end of Irish drama in Poland. The radical changes within the Warsaw theater notwithstanding, it can be argued that the artistic heart of the Polish theater for the duration of World War I resided elsewhere. The forced exile of a great number of the leading figures in the Warsaw theater ironically resulted in the organic development of a surprisingly dynamic Polish theater in Kiev. Attempts at cultural self-preservation on the part of the local Polish community in Kiev prior to World War I rapidly blossomed into a vibrant, impromptu cultural renaissance as tens of thousands of Poles poured into the city seeking refuge from the conflict. This was particularly true for the Polish theater in Kiev. What had begun largely as a club in 1912 under the aegis of Franciszek Rychłowski, an experienced director from Warsaw, took on entirely new life after the start of the war and particularly following the German siege of Warsaw in 1915, as the leading actors, directors, and stage designers of the Polish stage fled eastward. Rychłowski's amateur theater provided much needed work and a stage for a displaced yet vitally important branch of the modern Polish theater.[250] "In 1916," Tadeusz Zienkiewicz has maintained, "Kiev became the main center of Polish theatrical life in the Kingdom."[251]

As befitted a largely émigré Polish theater, the war was cause for a repertoire heavy with historical and patriotic plays.[252] With figures such as Wincenty Drabik, Juliusz Osterwa, Arnold Szyfman, Maximilian Węgrzyn, and Stanisław Wysocka, it was no accident that the Polish Theater in Kiev also maintained the commitment to artistic innovation of its namesake in Warsaw. "The Polish Theater," Kazimierz Dunin-Markiewicz recalled of Rychłowski's theater, "not only gave actors the possibility of decent livelihood instead of the poor existence of exile and enabled [a number of high quality performances], it was a rallying point for all the local and refugee intelligentsia."[253] In addition to works by contemporary Polish playwrights, including a number by Wyspiański, the repertoire featured a variety of foreign plays, not the least of which was a production of Synge's *The Playboy of the Western World*.

Performed on January 23, 1915 in the *Klub Ogniwo* (The Connection Club) under the direction of Kazimierz Tatarkiewicz, one of Rychłowski's original cast members, the choice of Synge's celebrated play was in keeping with the Polish Theater's interest in modern drama, both Polish and foreign. While the reason for staging Synge's play may simply have been because it was ready at hand, the timing of the Kiev production of Synge's play placed it early on in the steady influx of theatrical talent from Warsaw.[254] Regardless of its source, the staging of Synge's play was an impressive achievement for the rapidly developing Polish Theater in Kiev, especially considering that many of the key figures involved in the original production in Warsaw did not settle in Kiev until late 1915 or early 1916. What was clear was that *The Playboy of the Western World* appeared on the stage at a time when the Polish community in Kiev experienced an upsurge of interest and activity in the performance of serious theater. To this effect, the

Chapter 5: Modeling the Irish Theatre

performance of Synge's play worked to underscore the dual function Rychłowski's theater fulfilled of providing a free space for ongoing artistic innovation and of maintaining a line of continuity for the Polish theater as a whole.[255] As it turned out, there was little time for this and other theatrical experiments to take hold, as the conclusion of the war and the subsequent eruption of the Bolshevik Revolution in the winter of 1917–1918 quickly brought to an end the Polish cultural renaissance in Kiev. Albeit a devastating blow to the Polish community in Kiev, the cessation of hostilities did not take place before a spontaneous and dynamic form of the Polish national theater had been internalized by the diaspora of the Polish theater. With their return to Warsaw, these same individuals would combine with those who had stayed behind to make the idea of an autonomous and truly national Polish theater a reality in a free and independent Poland.

The experience of World War I did not turn out to be the devastating blow for the Polish theater that it appeared in the summer of 1914. Despite having to operate under less than ideal conditions, by the time of independence in 1918 the Polish theater had already taken steps toward becoming the kind of confident, self-sufficient theater advocated by Nowaczyński and Rakowska. With the reintegration of the former partitioned lands of Poland, the process of artistic centralization that had been underway in the theater prior to the war worked to consolidate Warsaw's position as the logical center of the Polish theater. The ability of Szyfman's Polish Theater and the Variety Theater not only to survive the conflict but also to continue developing artistically spoke to their viability as theatrical institutions and to the leadership positions they would both occupy in the ensuing interwar period. The presence of these two theaters was even more significant in light of the fact that the nascent Polish state had few institutions it could truly call its own.[256] In the theater, therefore, Poles found a degree of continuity and stability in what was in actuality a period of national rebuilding.

While the Polish theater enjoyed complete artistic autonomy for the first time in over a century with the end of World War I, the real work of establishing a vital and viable Polish national theater did not begin until the end of the war, when Polish intellectuals engaged in a debate over what form it should take and who was best prepared to guide it. For Szyfman, who faced innumerable obstacles in resuming control over the Polish Theater upon his return to Warsaw after three years in exile, the challenge facing the theater in Poland after the war was as much psychological as it was practical or artistic.[257] "Polish society [in the summer of 1918]," Szyfman recalled, "was wearied and weakened by two occupations. Independence and reunification were beginning to shine. But we were waiting with the deepest longing for that bright day of true freedom! [...] In the press there was demoralization, at times suspect ranting, consumed with minor, practically private matters and political blindness, which a few months later bogged us down in a hopeless battle on a number of fronts, instead of making the only peaceful, logical, and immeasurably difficult decision capable of saving us: that is, how to organize the unification of Poland."[258] The difficulty of producing integrated, artistic theater in such an environment was apparent, as Szyfman quickly discovered when the Polish Theater found itself at odds both with conservative Polish critics and the leading figures of *Skamander*, a group of talented young student poets and critics.[259] Albeit approaching the problem from different extremes, the concerns of both parties revealed the extent to which the Polish national theater became entangled in Polish cultural politics in the years immediately following the war. Given that Poles had only in recent years begun to enjoy a limited degree of freedom on the stage, the polemics over the question of national representation were in keeping with the tremendous change that was taking place within Polish society as a whole.

The Variety Theater would ultimately adopt the mantle of being the nation's first theater, when it reopened as the *Teatr Narodowy* (The National Theater) five years after being devastated by a fire in 1919. The rise of a number of new, yet equally vibrant theaters vying for the attention of the Polish theatergoing public proved that the progress of the previous three decades had not been squandered.[260] Concerned, on the one hand, with reimagining the Polish theater and, on the other, with seeking newer forms of dramatic expression, it was not surprising that the presence of Irish drama diminished during this period. With the rise of theater reformers such as Osterwa and Schiller into prominent directorial positions, however, it was apparent that Synge, Yeats, and their colleagues at the Abbey Theatre had made a small yet significant contribution to the Polish theater by acting as a living model of a modern, national theater. It was appropriate, therefore, that the concept of a Polish "monumental theater," first conceived by Mickiewicz and further developed by Wyspiański, at last received serious attention from the leading directors in the theater of a free and independent Poland.

CONCLUSION:
THE LEGACY OF THE POLISH-IRISH CONNECTION

Young Poland represented an unusually vibrant and varied contribution to the broader, century-old struggle to preserve a distinctly Polish cultural identity following the imposition of partitions by the Austria, Prussia, and Russia at the end of the eighteenth century. For Polish intellectuals in the years 1890–1918, the desire to recapture the creative power contained within their identities as Poles was matched only by an equally strong longing to produce lasting, meaningful art along the lines of European literary modernism. Motivated by the twin forces of essentialism and cosmopolitanism, Young Poland adopted a unique dualistic outlook by which new ideas from abroad were introduced and reinterpreted according to the internal needs of the Polish intellectuals introducing them. Young Poland's interest in Irish-Ireland was a particularly potent example of this Janus-faced process of cultural revitalization, as Polish intellectuals recognized in their Irish counterparts a similar desire to restore cultural strength by balancing art and identity.

The Polish-Irish relationship had its origins in the experience of the nineteenth century, when the Polish Romantics developed a common vernacular of national loss and displacement with Ireland by means of the poetry of Thomas Moore. Rooted in memory and an unwavering sense of identity, this process of drawing inspiration and sustenance from the perception of Ireland's parallel experience carried over into the Young Poland period. The Polish intellectuals coming of age in the 1890s were frustrated by the perceived lack of national feeling and artistic vibrancy in Polish culture. Dissatisfied with the pragmatic politics and cultural ideology of the Polish Positivists, which developed in the wake of the ill-fated January Uprising of 1863, Young Poland emerged as a movement bent upon its right to artistic freedom and national feeling. Polish intellectuals, a large majority of whom traveled and studied outside of Poland,

The Impact of Irish-Ireland on Young Poland, 1890–1919

sought to import new ideas and modes of expression from abroad as a means of achieving these two aims. With the publication of Jerzy Płoński's article on William Butler Yeats just two months before Artur Górski's manifesto "Młoda Polska" (Young Poland) appeared in the journal *Life* in 1898, Irish-Ireland was irrevocably linked to Young Poland as a movement similarly aimed at cultural renewal from without and within.

Yeats's ability to combine elements of modern symbolism with traditional forms of Irish folklore attracted the interest of Polish critics such as Płoński and Stanisław Lack, who were advocates of the place of *nowa sztuka* (new art) in Polish literature. Lack's translation of Yeats's story "The Heart of Spring" in 1902 served to illustrate of his conception of art as a revelation of the Absolute or the unknown of existence, placing alongside Zenon "Miriam" Przesmycki, Stanisław Przybyszewski, and other critics of the Polish *moderna*. Yeats's story of the natural cycle of human existence and the place of the intellectual in society also foreshadowed the theoretical approach he would later take in regard to the role of myth in the work of Stanisław Wyspiański. Yeats's identity as a poet rooted in the folklore and idiom of the Irish people, however, meant he was equally appealing to the strain of *chłopomania* (peasant mania) pervading Young Poland, regardless of artistic outlook. In his translations of *The Countess Cathleen* and a number of folk-themed poems by Yeats, Jan Kasprowicz displayed a similar interest in employing the world of the peasantry as a backdrop for metaphysical meditations on collective experience of the nation. Published in Miriam's sophisticated literary journal *Chimera*, Kasprowicz's translation of *The Countess Cathleen* appeared at a time when Polish writers and critics who, inspired by Maurice Maeterlinck and the Pre-Raphaelites, sought new forms of symbolic, non-representative art in the legends and folk imagination of the countryside.

While it would take several years longer before works by Irish dramatists appeared on a Polish stage, it would be in the theater that Irish-Ireland made its most lasting impression. For innovative theater directors such as Tadeusz Pawlikowski and Arnold Szyfman, the decision to stage works by Yeats and John Millington Synge formed part of a larger strategy to link the Polish theater to incorporate aspects of the modern theater reform movement in Europe in regard to acting, repertoire, and stagecraft. The international success of the Abbey Theatre's playwrights for their distinctly Irish style of drama further enhanced their appeal, particularly following the death of Wyspiański, as models of drama that was both national and modern. Despite being performed by the leading theater companies of the day in Kraków, Lwów, and Warsaw, the works of Yeats and Synge proved challenging for Polish theater companies, critics, and

Conclusion

theatergoers alike to understand. The inexorable presence of Wyspiański behind the productions of *The Well of the Saints, The Playboy of the Western World,* and *The Countess Cathleen*, albeit a natural reflex for many Poles, was often reason for confusion and concern. Polish actors and critics tended to interpret the Irish playwrights' use of symbolism and national and folk elements by means of the leading dramatist of Young Poland. Despite these problems, both Yeats and Synge were widely acknowledged to be fresh talents in the European theater, and their plays introduced new dramatic models for those in the Polish theater who were actively striving to establish a modern, national Polish theater.

The wide-ranging interests of Young Poland critics in developments taking place outside of Poland made it possible for Irish-Ireland to have a cultural presence within Young Poland independent of what was actually available by means of translation or performance. Critics such as Nowaczyński and Marya Rakowska, among others, revealed themselves to be knowledgeable commentators on the historical origins and the cultural politics of Irish-Ireland. In differing ways, though, in their observations on the Irish theater Nowaczyński and Rakowska displayed Young Poland's innate tendency toward essentializing foreign cultural impulses. While both critics were aware of the internal conflicts within the theater of Irish-Ireland in regard to the question of identity, it did not prevent them from drawing on the example of the Abbey Theatre in support of their own cultural aims. The relish with which Nowaczyński praised the play *General John Regan*, by the Anglo-Irish George Birmingham, as his model for the theater as a tool for confronting and mobilizing the nation was proof of the degree to which he was reinterpreting Irish-Ireland almost exclusively in terms of his own cultural aims. Albeit in a much more measured way, Rakowska, too, was guilty of essentializing the Irish theater by interpreting the success of the Abbey Theatre as a victory of "Celtic" Ireland over the barriers of intolerance and materialism. The underlying message of both critics was that same creative energy and national assertiveness lay within Young Poland as well.

In differing ways, therefore, it is possible to trace the evolution of the theater during the Young Poland period through the importation of the drama of Irish-Ireland. Whether it was Miriam's argument for poetic drama, Pawlikowski's effort to introduce cosmopolitan drama into the Polish repertoire, Szyfman's project to establish an independent Polish theater, or even the impromptu Polish theaters of World War I, Irish drama made a small yet not insignificant contribution toward the development of the modern Polish theater. The premature death of Wyspiański in 1907, which represented a significant blow to Young Poland's creative growth in the sphere of drama, made this search for new approaches to the stage all the more important. Despite his huge following, it was not altogether surprising that Wyspiański's work was not fully realized until the mature Polish theater of independent Poland emerged in the 1920s.

Polish scholars in recent years have downplayed the quality of the translations of Irish literature by the intellectuals of Young Poland and expressed doubt as to the extent to which Irish-Ireland established a cultural presence in Poland during this period. Given the much more extensive interest of Young Poland in French or German literature, observations of this nature are not entirely without merit. What is often overlooked, however, is the fact that Young Poland made the important distinction of recognizing Irish literature for what it truly was. A fundamental aim of Irish-Ireland was to counteract the incessant process of Anglicization of Irish culture by restoring elements of the moribund Gaelic culture. For the Anglo-Irish minority, the creation of an Irish form of literature, different both in form and in spirit, was an essential part of this process of deanglicization, as well as an important strategy for stating their case for inclusion in the Irish nation. While Poles had recognized the Irish presence in English literature through their admiration of Thomas Moore in the mid-nineteenth century, Young Poland's attraction represented the first time that Poles acknowledged Irish literature as something separate from the English tradition. Both Kasprowicz and Rakowska included Yeats and Wilde in their anthologies of English drama, but they did not do so without first expressly drawing attention to their Irishness. For all his criticism of Wilde's wasted aestheticism, Nowaczyński was most perturbed by the celebrated writer's abandonment of his native heritage.

For all its flaws and shortcomings, Young Poland's interest in Irish-Ireland was most significant on this score. Although the heated struggle over the definition of the Irish nation ended in the virtual exclusion of the non-Gaelic, Anglo-Irish minority with the establishment of the Irish Free State in 1922, Young Poland's perceived image of Ireland was decidedly that of the mythical Celtic Ireland of Yeats and the proponents of inclusion. In spite of the pull of the national identity and the presence of vocal right wing theorists, such as Roman Dmowski, Young Poland accepted a vision of Ireland that was modern in its artistic outlook yet thoroughly Irish in expression. As such, the portrait of Irish-Ireland may have been inaccurate in respect to the inner workings of the Irish movement, but in regard to Ireland's place in world literature the intellectuals of Young Poland were both early and consistent in their admiration of the importance of the work of their Irish contemporaries. While much has been made of the American and English acceptance of the Irish Cultural Revival, Young Poland's interest in the literature and cultural politics of Irish-Ireland also represents a farther-flung and largely unsung example of its international success. By all accounts, Yeats and his

Conclusion

colleagues were oblivious of Young Poland's interest, but as an embattled veteran of the cultural wars of Irish-Ireland Yeats cherished any and all attention paid to he and his followers' vision of Celtic Ireland.

In addition to acting as a commentary on modern Ireland, the manner in which Polish intellectuals expressed their interest in Irish-Ireland reveals a great deal about the underlying values and aims of Young Poland as a cultural movement. In figures such as Yeats and Synge, Young Poland's poets, critics, and theatrical artists found like-minded artists who were attempting to bring their modern artistic sensibilities to native sources to create art that was entirely original and yet rooted in the national imagination. Whether it was Kasprowicz in poetry, Władysław Reymont in prose, or Wyspiański in drama, Young Poland as a generation was motivated by the same exact desire. Even extreme modernists such as Przybyszewski could not deny the nation a place in his celebrated manifesto on the autonomy of art, "Confiteor." Although not included in the scope of this study, this fundamental connection extended to the schools of Polish and Irish painting that came into being in the first decade of the twentieth century, symbolized by the involvement of the Polish painter Kazimierz Dunin-Markiewicz at the heart of the Irish art world. Motivated by a deep longing for a return of national feeling in the absence of statehood, Young Poland ultimately sought a sense of self in the pursuit of art.

The achievement of Polish independence in the aftermath of World War I brought to an end the century-long Polish struggle to restore Poland to its rightful place among the sovereign nations of Europe. With the creation of a Polish state, however, came the reality of independence. Young Poland's tendency toward essentialism was out of place in the interwar period, when the predominant Polish national identity had to come to terms with the presence of significant national and ethnic minorities that were included within the boundaries of independent Poland. For Poles, therefore, the formation and management of Poland as a single country in the wake of the partitions brought with it the double problem of nation and state building.[1] As in Ireland, the waking reality following the intense experience of cultural and national renewal at the turn of the century was the answering the question of what form the nation would actually take.

The achievement of independence, too, signaled the end of Young Poland. In many respects, the decline of Young Poland as a movement had already begun years earlier under the repeated attacks of critics such as Nowaczyński, Stanisław Brzozowski, and Tadeusz "Boy" Żeleński. While many of Young Poland's leading writers remained active in Polish cultural life after 1918, a new generation of Polish intellectuals emerged in independent Poland, chafing at Young Poland's tendency to subordinate art to nation and insisting upon

The Impact of Irish-Ireland on Young Poland, 1890–1919

complete artistic autonomy. Inspired the philosophical ideas of Henri Bergson, a group of writers known as "Skamander" came into being under the Dionysian impulse for vitality and artistic expression free from national responsibility and the weight of history. The interwar period in Poland was not free of expressions national feeling in art, as Leon Schiller's attempts at realizing the "monumental" theater of Mickiewicz and Wyspiański on the stage of the Bogusławski Theater made evident. No longer burdened with the need to infuse art with identity, Polish writers in independent Poland were free to pursue new, modern forms of artistic expression for their own sake. "The gulf," Jan Cavanaugh has observed of the situation in Polish painting, "between international and national artistic concerns, which had been bridged in innumerable ways by the modernists, was now too wide to cross."[2] With the rise of avant-garde groups advocating radical art forms, such as cubism, futurism, and formism, Polish literature became much more diverse and connected to the broader stream of European literature.

The hard-fought achievement of independence for the Poles and the Irish following the World War I did not represent the culmination of the Polish-Irish relationship. On the contrary, Polish critics such as Rakowska and Miriam remained interested in Irish-Ireland, with the former publishing an in-depth analysis of Synge's in 1923, the same year Yeats was awarded the Nobel Prize for Literature, and the latter a translation of Yeats's "Hanrahan the Red" in the following year. Although Poles continued to express a sincere interest in the Irish poet, evident in a series of new translations of Yeats's earlier poetry by Józef Birkenmajer in 1925, the cultural moment that had transpired between Young Poland and Irish-Ireland did not return. It would not be until the late 1950s that Polish writers and translators returned to Irish literature with any measurable intensity.

As had been the case with the Polish-Irish relationship in the years leading up to Polish independence, the ties between Poland and Ireland in the twentieth century were dictated in large part by historical circumstance and internal cultural conditions. For Poland, the elation that came with independence proved to be brief. Cut off from Europe following World War II, the Polish experience for the remainder of the twentieth century turned out to be a return to the trauma national suffering of a century before. Ireland, though free, also experienced a retreat from the international arena, as the deep conservatism of the Irish Free State and the unresolved conflict over Northern Ireland limited its openness to the outside world. Poles would turn again to Ireland for inspiration in the 1990s, but it would not be in Ireland's cultural presence so much as its full standing as an emerging member in the political and economic union of European nations.

NOTES

INTRODUCTION

1. Jerzy Płoński, "Znad Tamizy," *Życie*.7–8 (1898): 8:92.

2. Adolf Nowaczyński, "Teatr irlandzki," *Szkice literackie* (Poznań: Ostoja, 1918) 61.

3. See Julian Krzyżanowski, *Neo-romantyzm polski, 1890–1918* (Wrocław: Państwowy Instytut Wydawniczy, 1971), Ryszard Nycz, *Język modernizmu* (Wrocław: Fundacja na Rzecz Nauki Polskiej. Seria humanistyczna, 1997), Henryk Markiewicz, *W kręgu Żeromskiego* (Warszawa: Państwowy Instytut Wydawniczy, 1977) 143–90.

4. See Franciszek Ziejka, *Nasza rodzina w Europie* (Kraków: Universitas, 1995) 20. The poet Antoni Lange, who rendered into Polish works from languages as varied as French, English, German, Spanish, Russian, and Sanskrit, was representative of Young Poland's openness to foreign cultural impulses.

5. Ibid. 20–21.

6. Jan Cavanaugh, *Out Looking In: Early Modern Polish Art, 1890–1918* (Berkeley: University of California Press, 2000).

7. See Naoki Sakai, *Translation and Subjectivity: on "Japan" and cultural nationalism*, Public Worlds, vol. 3 (Minneapolis: University of Minnesota Press, 1997).

8. Ibid. 9.

9. For Goethe's essay on translation, see Rainer Schulte and John Biguenet, eds., *Theories of Translation: an anthology of essays from Dryden to Derrida* (Chicago: The University of Chicago Press, 1992) 60–63.

10. Sakai, *Translation and Subjectivity: on "Japan" and cultural nationalism* 15.

11. Adam Zamoyski, "States of Mind: on the myths of national identity," *Encounter* LXXIII.2 (July/August 1989): 21.

12. See Gilles Deleuze and Felix Guattari, *A Thousand Plateaus: Capitalism and Schizophrenia*, trans. Brian Massumi (Minneapolis: University of Minnesota Press, 1987) 291–93.

CHAPTER 1

1. Adam Zamoyski, "States of Mind: on the myths of national identity," *Encounter* LXXIII.2 (July/August 1989): 38-39.

2. Alina Witkowska, *Literatura romantyzmu* (Warszawa: Państwowe Wydawnictwo Naukowe, 1989) 7.

3. See Andrzej Walicki, *Trzy patriotyzmy* (Warszawa: Respublica, 1991) 42-43.

4. Alina Kowalczykowa, *Idee programowe romantyków polskich - Antologia* (Wrocław: Zakład Narodowy im. Ossolińskich-Wydawnictwo, 1991) 123.

5. Ibid. 38-39.

6. Ibid. 54.

7. Adam Mickiewicz, *Dzieła*, ed. Julian Krzyżanowski (Warszawa: Czytelnik, 1955) 107.

8. Benedict R. Anderson, "Exodus," *Critical Inquiry* 20 (Winter 1994): 315.

9. A loose corollary of this would be the Polish experience in Post-War communist Poland.

10. Anderson, "Exodus," 315.

11. Walicki, *Trzy patriotyzmy* 46.

12. Adam Mickiewicz, *Księgi narodu polskiego i pielgrzymstwa polskiego* (Warszawa: Czytelnik, 1986) 33.

13. Ibid.

14. Ibid. 47.

15. Ibid. 51.

16. Ibid. 65.

17. See Ibid. 149-50. Maria Grabowska notes that the terms "bracia-wiara-żołnierze" had very specific meanings in the customs of the Polish Republic, with "bracia" (brothers) referring to the szlachta, or nobility, "wiara" (faith) to the peasantry. "żołnierze" (soldiers), significantly, signaled a convergence between the two groups, suggesting the widely held belief, first declared during the 1794 revolt led by Tadeusz Kościuszko, that Poland needed to liberate the peasantry and fight as a whole nation in order to be free. In terms of the post-1830 situation, Mickiewicz's terminology also had implications for the Polish émigré community in Paris. In 1834, two years following the publication of *The Books*, and the same year his celebrated work *Pan Tadeusz* (Master Thaddeus) appeared in print, Mickiewicz gave up poetry for a life of ceaseless social activism. Exile, for Mickiewicz, was not something to be endured, but rather a rite of passage that made the Polish nation soldiers in the eternal war between Good and Evil.

Notes to Chapter 1

18. Cyprian Kamil Norwid, *Gorszki to chleb jest polskość* (Kraków: Wydawnictwo Literackie, 1984) 52.

19. See Beth Holmgren, *Rewriting Capitalism: Literature and the Market in Late Tsarist Russia and the Kingdom of Poland* (Pittsburgh: University of Pittsburgh Press, 1998) 54–59.

20. Ibid. 59–92.

21. Terrance Brown, "Thomas Moore: A Reputation," *Ireland's Literature* (Mullingar: Liliput Press, 1988) 18. Brown points out that Moore in his diary recalls Wordsworth telling him that the earnings from his literary works amount to £1000. By comparison, Moore estimated his totals during the same period at approximately £20,000.

22. Eoin MacWhite, "Thomas Moore and Poland," *Proceedings of the Royal Irish Academy* 72.Sect. C (1972): 51.

23. Stanisław Egbert Koźmian, *Anglia i Polska* (Poznań: Nakł. Księg. Żupańskiego, 1862) 280.

24. Ibid. 280–81.

25. Christopher Morash, *The Hungry Voice: The Poetry of the Irish Famine* (Dublin: Irish Academic Press, 1989) 86.

26. Marian Bizan and Paweł Hertz, eds., *Liryki* (Warszawa: Państwowy Instytut Wydawniczy, 1959) 229.

27. Ibid.

28. Zbigniew Sudolski, *Słowacki* (Warszawa: Ludowa Spółdzielnia Wydawnicza, 1978) 36.

29. Bizan and Hertz, eds., *Liryki* 230.

30. Brown, "Thomas Moore: A Reputation," 19.

31. Thomas Moore, *Irish Melodies and Loves of the Angels* (New York: James Miller, 1879) 22.

32. Juliusz Słowacki, *Lyriki i inne wiersze* 13.

33. Moore, *Irish Melodies and Loves of the Angels* 69.

34. Słowacki, *Lyriki i inne wiersze* 10.

35. Stefan Treugutt, *Pisarska Młodość Słowackiego* (Wrocław: Zakład Narodowy im. Ossolińskich, 1958) 18.

36. Ibid. 20.

37. Juliusz Kleiner, *Słowacki* (Wrocław: Zakład Narodowy im. Ossolińskich, 1972) 18.

38. Thomas Moore, *Irish Melodies and Songs and Ballads* (Boston: Little Brown and Company, 1863) 8.

39. Słowacki, *Lyriki i inne wiersze* 11.

40. Brown, "Thomas Moore: A Reputation," 19.

41. Ibid. 20.

42. *Lalla Rookh* garnered Moore a contract of £3,000 in 1817, large for the times, and then proceeded to run for some twenty editions over the thirty years that followed.

43. Malecka's first effort was a home-based literary journal called *Domownik* (The Householder), which she published at age eighteen. She achieved greater success in 1822 with *Bronisława, czyli pamiętnik Polek* (Bronisława, or a Women's Journal), which was the first periodical catering expressly to women.

44. MacWhite, "Thomas Moore and Poland," 49–51. MacWhite pointed out that Moore was equally popular within the circles of the Russian elite, including those who enforced policies of censorship, as he was among the Poles. This pointed to Moore's ability to disguise political motifs under Romantic storytelling.

45. Henryk Zbierski, "Mickiewiczowskie przekłady drobnych utworów i Moore'a," *Przegląd Zachodni* 1–2 (1956): 84.

46. MacWhite, "Thomas Moore and Poland," 53.

47. Zbierski, "Mickiewiczowskie przekłady drobnych utworów i Moore'a," 92, Leon Gomolicki, *Dziennik pobytu Adama Mickiewicza w rosji 1824–1829* (Warszawa: Książka i Wiedza, 1949) 274.

48. Zbierski, "Mickiewiczowskie przekłady drobnych utworów i Moore'a."

49. Czesław Miłosz, *The History of Polish Literature* (Berkeley: University of California Press, 1983) 218.

50. Moore, *Irish Melodies and Loves of the Angels* 22.

51. Adam Mickiewicz, *Dzieła wszystkie 1825–1829* (Wrocław: Zakład Narodowy im. Ossoliński, 1969) 88.

52. Zbierski, "Mickiewiczowskie przekłady drobnych utworów i Moore'a," 93–94.

53. Mickiewicz, *Dzieła wszystkie 1825–1829* 88.

54. Zbierski, "Mickiewiczowskie przekłady drobnych utworów i Moore'a," 95.

55. Zofia Szmydtowa, *Mickiewicz jako tłumacz z literatur zachodnio europejskich* (Warszaw: Państwowy Instytut Wydawniczy, 1955).

56. Roman Koropeckyj, *The Poetics of Revitalization: Adam Mickiewicz between Forefather's Eve, part 3 and Pan Tadeusz* (Boulder: East European Monographs, 2001) 150.

57. Adam Mickiewicz, *Pan Tadeusz*, trans. Kenneth R. Mackenzie (New York: Hippocrene Books, Inc., 1992) 2–3.

Notes to Chapter 1

58. Moore, *Irish Melodies and Loves of the Angels* 89.

59. Józef Korzeniowski, "Pamiętnik Sceny Warszawskiej na rok 1838," (1838): 96.

60. Leith Davis, "Irish Bards and English Consumers: Thomas Moore's 'Irish Melodies' and the Colonized Nation," *Ariel* 242 (1993).20.

61. Zygmunt Krasiński, *Listy do Ojca*, ed. Marian Bizan (Warszawa: Państwowy Instytut Wydawniczy, 1963) 98.

62. Ibid.

63. Ibid. 100.

64. Zygmunt Krasiński, *Listy do Henryka Reeve*, ed. Agnieszka Rabińska (Warszawa: Państwowy Instytut Wydawniczy, 1980) 98.

65. Ibid. 106–7.

66. Antoni Odyniec, *Listy z podróży*, ed. Wacław Zawadzki, 2 vols. (Warszawa: Państwowy Instytut Wydawniczy, 1961) 1:15.

67. Adam Mickiewicz, *Korrespondencja Adama Mickiewicza*, vol. I (Paryż: Księgarnia Luxemburgska, 1871) 90.

68. In his travels Odyniec met with such famous writers as Tieck, Goethe, and Hummel.

69. Odyniec, *Listy z podróży* 1:140.

70. Ibid. 2:57.

71. Jan Kasprowicz, who translated Yeats's *The Countess Cathleen* in 1904, also published translations of several of Moore's *Melodies* about the same time.

72. Włodzimierz Bolecki, "'Podnieść zginiony naród, niemała praca'"... (O Julianie Ursynie Niemcewiczu)," *Twórczość*.12 (1990): 87.

73. Ibid.

74. Ibid.: 98.

75. Ibid.

76. Mieczysław Klimowicz, *Literatura oświecenia* (Warszawa: Państwowe Wydawnictwo Naukowe, 1988) 208-09.

77. Bolecki, "'Podnieść zginiony naród, niemała praca'"... (O Julianie Ursynie Niemcewiczu)," 98.

78. Julian Ursyn Niemcewicz, *Pamiętniki Juliana Ursyna Niemcewicza - Dziennik pobytu za granicą od dnia 21 VII 1831 r. do 1841 r.* (Poznań: Zupański, 1879) 456.

79. He recalled having repaid his hostess, Miss Horatia Fielding, with a Polish translation of Moore's "Forget not the Field," but there is no record of this translation.

80. Niemcewicz, *Pamiętniki Juliana Ursyna Niemcewicza - Dziennik pobytu za granicą od dnia 21 VII 1831 r. do 1841 r.* 462.

81. Ibid.

82. Ibid. 462.

83. Ibid. 463.

84. Ibid.

85. Ibid.

86. Moore, *Irish Melodies and Loves of the Angels* 99.

87. Julian Ursyn Niemcewicz, "Niezane utwory Juliana Ursyna Niemcewicza," *Pamiętnik Literacki* z. 3 (1908): 367.

88. Moore would exhibit this quality a little over a decade later, in 1844, when he Stanisław Egbert Koźmian gave the Irish poet a copy of his translation of *The Paradise and the Peri*.

89. Moore, *Irish Melodies and Loves of the Angels* 99.

90. A. M. Kurpiel, "Niezane utwory Juliana Ursyna Niemcewicza," *Pamiętnik Literacki* z. 3 (1908): 367–68.

91. Moore, *Irish Melodies and Loves of the Angels* 99.

92. Kurpiel, "Niezane utwory Juliana Ursyna Niemcewicza," 367–68.

93. Ibid.: 367–68. The extant version of Niemcewicz's translation was printed *alone* under this title.

94. Niemcewicz, *Pamiętniki Juliana Ursyna Niemcewicza - Dziennik pobytu za granicą od dnia 21 VII 1831 r. do 1841 r.*

95. Ibid. 465.

96. J. C. Ostrowski, *Nuits d'Exil* (Paris: Librairie Polonaise, 1836) 1.

97. Ibid. 171.

98. Ibid.

99. Ibid. 171–72.

100. Ibid.

101. Wilfred S. Dowden, ed., *The Journal of Thomas Moore*, 6 vols. (London: Associated University Press, 1983) 1826.

Notes to Chapter 1

102. Krasiński, *Listy do Ojca* 197.
103. Dowden, ed., *The Journal of Thomas Moore* 1826.
104. Ibid. 2002.
105. Ibid. 2145.
106. Ibid. 2148.
107. Ibid. 2380.
108. Stanisław Egbert Koźmian, "Ray i Peria," *Pamiętnik Umiętności Moralnych i Literatury* III.VII (1830): 64.
109. Koźmian, *Anglia i Polska* 280.
110. Ibid.
111. Ibid.
112. Ibid. 281.

CHAPTER 2

1. Mickiewicz, *Księgi narodu polskiego i pielgrzymstwa polskiego* 63.
2. Benedict R. Anderson, "The Goodness of Nations," *Nation and Religion: Perspectives on Europe and Asia*, eds. Peter van der Veer and Hartmut Lehmann (Princeton: Princeton University Press, 1999) 200.
3. Ibid.
4. Ibid.
5. Ibid.
6. Ibid.
7. See Witkowska, *Literatura romantyzmu* 22–23.
8. See Koropeckyj, *The Poetics of Revitalization: Adam Mickiewicz between Forefather's' Eve, part 3 and Pan Tadeusz*.
9. Olizarowski, who published *Dziewice Erynu* under the pseudonym "A," was a prolific writer of poetry and drama, the majority of which dealt with patriotic themes and lyrical descriptions of his native Volhynia, in the borderland region between Poland and Ukraine. While a few of Olizarowski's dramas were produced in Paris and in Poland, there is no evidence that *The Daughter of Erin* was performed on the staged.

Notes to Chapter 2

10. Brown, "Thomas Moore: A Reputation," 14. Brown quoted a reference made by Lady Holland to Moore in regard to *Lalla Rookh*. "Mr. Moore," Lady Holland quipped, "I have not read your Larry O'Rourke. I don't like Irish stories."

11. Olizarowski was not alone in writing about Zawisza. Gustaw Ehrenberg published a poem entitled "Szubienica Zawiszy" (Zawisza's Gallows). See Witkowska, *Literatura romantyzmu* 245.

12. See Zygmunt Krasiński, *Pisma Zygmunta Krasińskiego*, Wydanie Jubileuszowe, ed. J. Czubek, vol. VIII (Warszawa-Kraków: Gebethner, 1912) 214–18, Witkowska, *Literatura romantyzmu* 170.

13. See Henryk Żaliński, *Stracone szanse: Wielka Emigracja o powstaniu listopadowym* (Warszawa: Wydawnictwo Ministerstwa Obrony Narodowej, 1982) 105-06.

14. Tomasz August [A.] Olizarowski, *Dziewice Erinu* (Paryż: Księgarnia Polska, 1857) 6. Olizarowski here is paraphrasing a popular Polish saying, "polegać jak na Zawiszy" (trust like on Zawisza), to attribute to Artur the highest type of reliability.

15. Ibid. 14.

16. Ibid. 43.

17. Ibid. 51–52.

18. Ibid. 102.

19. Ibid. 140.

20. Holmgren, *Rewriting Capitalism: Literature and the Market in Late Tsarist Russia and the Kingdom of Poland* 57.

21. In spite of being perceived as a pawn of Catherine the Great, Poniatowski implemented a number of reforms with the hope of reshaping the Polish *Rzeczpospolita* along the lines of a constitutional monarchy.

22. Norman Davies, *God's Playground*, 2 vols. (New York: Columbia University Press, 1982) 2:46.

23. Markiewicz, *W kręgu Żeromskiego* 88.

24. O'Connell died in 1847, while Davis, Mangan, and Moore passed away in 1845, 1849, and 1852 respectively.

25. Ignacy Domagalski, *Irlandia i Polska* (Kraków: Drukiem W. Korneckiego, 1876) 11.

26. Ibid. 271.

27. Ibid. 13.

28. Reverend Piotr Ściegienny (1801–1890) led a proto-socialist peasant movement known as the Union of Peasants in the Lublin region that planned an uprising in 1844,

which resulted in a sentence of deportation and hard labor in Siberia. See Andrzej Walicki, *Philosophy and Romantic Nationalism* (Notre Dame: University of Notre Dame Press, 1982) 59–61.

29. Domagalski, *Irlandia i Polska* 240.

30. Ibid. 243–57.

31. For more on the differing problems facing the Polish Church in each of the partitions after the January Uprising, see Jerzy Kłoczowski, *A History of Polish Christianity* (Cambridge: Cambridge University Press, 2000) 231–35.

32. For many Poles, the German Catholic Church represented an extension of the Prussian authorities' attempt to Germanize the Polish population. The association between the Polish Church and the Polish national movement in turn were equally close.

33. While there were many similarities between Domagalski's position and that of the Polish Positivists, as a largely urban intellectual movement that placed a premium on science and reason Positivism represented a subtle danger to Catholicism in Poland.

34. As an illustration of what could be achieved, an anonymous contributor to the *Przegląd Lwowski* (The Lwów Review) cited the formation of a Catholic organization in Rome in 1875 that included members of the aristocracy and the episcopacy under the name *Liga O'Conela* (The League of O'Connell). *Przegląd Lwowski* March 15 1876: 426.

35. Jan Dąbrowski, *Polacy w Anglii i o Anglii* (Kraków: Wydawnictwo Literackie, 1962) 261–71.

36. His nine-part essay "*Z dziejów Irlandii*" (From Irish History) in *Kurier Poznański* (The Poznań Courier) in 1898, described Irish politics, culture, and history in detail from the present day back to the fifth century.

37. Halina Filipowicz, "Home as Desire: The Popular Pleasures of Gender in Polish Émigré Drama," *Framing the Polish Home: Postwar Constructions of Hearth, Nation, and Self*, ed. Bożena Shallcross (Athens: University of Ohio Press, 2002) 282.

38. Ibid. 283.

39. Edmund Naganowski, *Żona weterana* (Lwów: Czcionkami "Dziennika Polskiego", 1890) 21.

40. Ibid. 9. The italics indicate Naganowski's intention of the English mispronunciation of Bessy's surname.

41. Ibid. 7.

42. Ibid. 35.

43. Ibid. 26.

44. Ibid. 36.

Notes to Chapter 2

45. Filipowicz, "Home as Desire: The Popular Pleasures of Gender in Polish Émigré Drama," 283.

46. Ibid. 285.

CHAPTER THREE

1. "Od redakcji," *Życie* (1900), vol. 1, ii.

2. Antoni Potocki, *Polska literatura współczesna*, 2 vols. (Warszawa: Gebethner i Wolff, 1911–1912) 4.

3. Ibid.

4. Zenon "Miriam" Przesmycki, *Wybór pism krytycznych*, I-II vols. (Kraków: Wydawnictwo Literackie, 1967) 1:159.

5. Potocki, *Polska literatura współczesna* 7.

6. Young Poland's leading figures included, among many others, the following: Malczewski, Boznańska, and Weiss (art); Rydel, Wyspiański, and Zapolska (drama); Berent, Reymont, and Żeromski (prose fiction); Kasprowicz, Staff, and Tetmajer (poetry); Miriam, Przybyszewski, and Stanisław Brzozowski (criticism); Pawlikowski and Szyfman (theater direction); and Karłowicz, Różycki, and Szymanowski (music).

7. Potocki, *Polska literatura współczesna* 10.

8. Ignacy Matuszewski, *Słowacki i nowa sztuka* (Warszawa: Gebethner i Wolff, 1902) 263–64.

9. Ibid. 14.

10. Przesmycki, *Wybór pism krytycznych* 150–51.

11. Ibid. 154.

12. Potocki, *Polska literatura współczesna* 77.

13. Ibid. 161.

14. Ibid. 166.

15. Ibid. 212.

16. Przesmycki, *Wybór pism krytycznych* 31.

17. Maria Podraza-Kwiatkowska, "O Miriamie-krytyku," *Nadbitką Pamiętnik Literacki* LVI.z. 4 (1965): 413.

18. Potocki, *Polska literatura współczesna* 143.

Notes to Chapter 3

19. See Jan Cavanaugh, *Out Looking In: Early Modern Polish Art, 1890–1918* (Berkeley: University of California Press, 2000) 211–40.

20. Ibid. 236.

21. The involvement of the "Sztuka" (Art) group at the Vienna Secession in 1902 was an example of this built-in internationalization of the Polish cultural scene. See Ibid. 81–97.

22. Franciszek Ziejka, *Nasza rodzina w Europie* (Kraków: Universitas, 1995) 22–40.

23. Ibid. 25.

24. In Stefan Żeromski's novel, *Ludzie bezdomni* (Homeless People, 1900), the protagonist, Dr. Judym, is shown wandering the art salons of Paris, all the while consumed with thoughts of home.

25. Ziejka, *Nasza rodzina w Europie* 40.

26. Ibid. 30.

27. Ibid.

28. Felix Jasieński was the prototypical intellectual-wanderer of Young Poland, traversing the globe and returning to reinvigorate his home country with the exotic culture of Japan and the Far East. See Feliks Jasieński, *Manggha- Promenades a travers les mondes, l'art et les idees* (Warszawa: Jean Fiszer, 1901).

29. Of all of Young Poland's journals, Miriam's *Chimera* was the most lavish in its use of reproductions of foreign art.

30. Maria Podraza-Kwiatkowska, *Symbolizm i symbolika w poezji Młodej Polski* (Kraków: Universitas, 2001) 62.

31. Potocki, *Polska literatura współczesna* 94.

32. Ibid. 95.

33. Ibid. 82.

34. Ibid.

35. The image of the wanderer, or the lonely soul in search of truth, was a common trope in the literature of Young Poland. See Maria Podraza-Kwiatkowska, ed., *Młodopolski świat wyobraźni. Studia i eseje* (Kraków: Wydawnictwo Literackie, 1977).

36. Potocki, *Polska literatura współczesna* 83.

37. Boy-Żeleński translated hundreds of classic works by dozens of French authors, ranging from Villon to Proust. His contribution was not just in creating a canon of French works in Polish, but also in producing translations of a high literary quality.

38. "Od redakcji," *Życie* 1 (1900): iii.

39. The prospectus also detailed the Polish and foreign artists whose works were to be reproduced in *Life* in 1900.

40. Przesmycki, *Wybór pism krytycznych* 7.

41. Ibid. 8.

42. Ibid.

43. The left-leaning journal *Krytyka* (The Review) was one such journal. One of the reasons *Life* and *Chimera* failed after such brief runs was the high cost associated with publishing such refined journals.

44. Naoki Sakai, *Translation and Subjectivity: on "Japan" and cultural nationalism*, Public Worlds, vol. 3 (Minneapolis: University of Minnesota Press, 1997) 5.

45. Ibid. 67.

46. See Alvin Marcus Fountain, *Roman Dmowski: party, tactics, ideology, 1895–1907* (Boulder; N.Y.: East European Monographs; distributed by Columbia University Press, 1980).

47. Jan Zygmunt Jakubowski, ed., *Polska krytyka literacka (1800–1918)*, vol. IV (Warszawa: Państwowe Wydawnictwo Naukowe, 1959) 123.

48. Ibid. 124.

49. Ibid. 126.

50. Ibid.

51. Ibid. 127.

52. Ibid. 129.

53. Ibid. 131.

54. Ibid. 134.

55. Ibid. 136.

56. Ibid.

57. Ibid. 138.

58. Ibid. 139.

59. Ibid. 140. The so-called "Teka Stańczyka" (Stanczyk's Briefcase) referred to a series of pamphlets published in 1869 by a group of conservatives in Kraków widely known as the "Kraków historians." This group, which was highly critical of Poland's revolutionary past, advocating instead a policy of triloyalism and organic work within the system of partitions, took the name for its manifestoes from a famous sixteenth-century Polish court jester. The figure of "Stańczyk" was immortalized in a number of paintings by Jan

Matejko, Wyspiański's mentor and teacher. Wyspiański also featured Stańczyk as a character in his masterpiece, *The Wedding*.

60. Ibid. 142.

61. Ibid. 143.

62. Ibid. 147.

63. Ibid.

64. Ibid. 149.

65. Ibid. 151.

66. Ibid. 151–52.

67. Ibid. 155.

68. Ibid. 156.

69. Ibid. 157.

70. It was indicative of Przybyszewski's position that as editor of *Life* he dropped the banner line used by Ludwik Szczepański, the journal's original editor, calling it an "illustrated, literary, artistic, scientific, and social weekly," in favor of the straightforward characterization as "an illustrated journal dedicated to literature and art."

71. Jakubowski, ed., *Polska krytyka literacka (1800–1918)* 157.

CHAPTER FOUR

1. Jolanta Dudek, "William Butler Yeats wsród poetów polskich (O recepcji poezji W. B. Yeatsa w Polsce)," *Ruch literacki* Z. 3.(246) (2001): 281.

2. Płoński's recognition of Yeats's presence on the English literary scene was appropriate, as the Irish poet maintained a residence in London and worked hard to make a name for himself in both England and Ireland.

3. Płoński, "Znad Tamizy," 80.

4. Ibid.

5. Ibid.: 92.

6. Ibid.

7. Płoński did explain to his readers the defining characteristics and regular abodes of such fantastic Irish creatures as fairies, banshees, and leprechauns. Of the three creatures, however, Płoński was only able to provide an approximate Polish equivalent for fairies, *rusałki* (a water nymph).

8. Płoński, "Znad Tamizy," 93.

9. Ibid.

10. Ibid.

11. Artur Górski, "Młoda Polska," *Polska krytyka literacka*, ed. Jan Zygmunt Jakubowski, vol. IV (Warszawa: Państwowe wydawnictwo naukowe, 1959) 151–52.

12. Płoński, "Znad Tamizy," 93.

13. Ibid.

14. Podraza-Kwiatkowska, *Symbolizm i symbolika w poezji Młodej Polski* 22.

15. Przesmycki, *Wybór pism krytycznych* 1:291.

16. Maria Podraza-Kwiatkowska, ed., *Programy i dyskusje literackie okresu Młodej Polski* (Wrocław: BN, 1977) 236.

17. Matuszewski, *Słowacki i nowa sztuka* 200.

18. Podraza-Kwiatkowska, "O Miriamie-krytyku," 436–37.

19. Przesmycki, *Wybór pism krytycznych* 306.

20. Wanda Krajewska, *Recepcja literatury angielskiej w Polsce w okresie modernizmu (1887–1918)* (Wrocław: PAN, 1972) 23.

21. In addition to Yeats, Lack translated other writers in English, including H. G. Wells, Walter Pater, Edgar Allen Poe, William Blake, and Oscar Wilde.

22. Stanisław Lack, *Wybór pism krytycznych* (Kraków: Wydawnictwo Literackie, 1980) 477.

23. Ibid. 46.

24. Ibid. 478.

25. A. Norman Jeffares, *W. B. Yeats* (London: Hutchinson, 1988) 85.

26. William Butler Yeats, *The Collected Letters of W. B. Yeats*, eds. Warwick Gould, John Kelly and Deirdre Toomey, 3 vols. (Oxford: Clarendon Press, 1997) 2:104. Gould, Kelly, and Toomey point out in a note to this letter that the theme of Yeats as a poet for "the few" was current among Yeats's critics at the time. Yeats revisited the idea of artistocratic literature in "What is Popular Poetry?" (1901).

27. William Butler Yeats, "Mythologies," (New York: Collier Books, 1959), vol., 144.

28. Philip L. Marcus, Warwick Gould and Michael J. Sidnell, *The Secret Rose, Stories by W. B. Yeats: A Variorum Edition* (Ithaca and London: Cornell University Press, 1981).

29. Stanisław Lack, "Serce wiosny," *Nowe Słowo* (1902), vol., 156.

Notes to Chapter 4

30. See Jeffares, *W. B. Yeats* 85–86.

31. Marcus, Gould and Sidnell, *The Secret Rose, Stories by W. B. Yeats: A Variorum Edition* 35.

32. Ibid. 37.

33. Lack, "Serce wiosny," vol., 155.

34. William Butler Yeats, *Ideas of Good and Evil* (New York: Russell & Russell, 1903) 303.

35. Unbeknownst to Lack, his honorarium as a contributor to *The New Word* was quietly subsidized by an admirer of his work, Dr. Bronisław Kupczyk. Lack's only two books, both of which appeared in print after his death, were also the work of his anonymous patron. This only served to underscore the notion that the appreciation of Lack's writing was a function of pure thought rather than critical reception.

36. Lack, *Wybór pism krytycznych* 508.

37. Ibid. 511.

38. Yeats, *Ideas of Good and Evil* 289.

39. Gregory Castle, "Modernism and the Celtic Revival," (Cambridge: Cambridge University Press, 2001), vol., 85.

40. Lack, *Wybór pism krytycznych* 255.

41. Podraza-Kwiatkowska, "O Miriamie-krytyku," 420.

42. Lack, *Wybór pism krytycznych* 60.

43. Ibid. 470.

44. R. F. Foster, *W. B. Yeats: A Life: The Apprentice Mage, 1865–1914* (Oxford: Oxford University Press, 1997) 178.

45. Ibid.

46. Lack, *Wybór pism krytycznych* 44.

47. Ibid. 64.

48. Ibid. 63.

49. Ibid. 68.

50. Ibid. 41.

51. Ibid. 478.

52. Przesmycki, *Wybór pism krytycznych* 2:8.

53. Ibid.

54. Ibid. 2:142.

55. Ibid. 2:122.

56. Ibid. 2:128.

57. Ibid. 2:129.

58. William Butler Yeats, *The Irish Dramatic Movement*, The Collected Works of W. B. Yeats, eds. Mary FitzGerald and Richard J. Finneran, vol. VIII (New York: Scribner, 2003) 9.

59. Ibid. 34.

60. Ibid.

61. Irish-Ireland would learn the truth of this statement on a number of occasions, with the most memorable being the "Playboy" riots.

62. Yeats, *The Irish Dramatic Movement* 51.

63. Przesmycki, *Wybór pism krytycznych* 1:318. Miriam published his article "Maurycy Maeterlinck" first in the journal *Świat* (The World) in 1891 and then again as the foreword to the Belgian poet's collected works in1894.

64. Irena Sławińska and Stefan Kruk, eds., *Myśl teatralna Młodej Polski* (Warszawa: Wydawnictwo Artystyczne i Filmowe, 1966) 8. Wyspiański based his play *The Wedding* on a traditional Polish puppet play. Yeats, likewise, had the actors of the Abbey Theatre rehearse one of his plays in barrels on stage, so that they would remain motionless and passive on stage.

65. Przesmycki, *Wybór pism krytycznych* 1:322.

66. Miriam, in fact, published his complete translation *Axel* the same year (1901) in which *Wanda* appeared in *Chimera*.

67. See Sławińska and Kruk, eds., *Myśl teatralna Młodej Polski* 6.

68. The two seminal events in the evolution of the modern Polish theater, Wyspiański's play *The Wedding* and his production of Mickiewicz's *Forefather's Eve*, both took place the same year Miriam published *Wanda*.

69. Witkowska, *Literatura romantyzmu* 211.

70. Cyprian Kamil Norwid, *Dramaty*, Pisma wybrane, ed. Juliusz W. Gomulicki, vol. 3, 4 vols. (Warszawa: Państwowy Instytut Wydawniczy, 1983) 68.

71. In a motto preceding the play, Norwid underscored the inseparability of the play's underlying Christian message from the conception of Polish national identity:

So the Church holds, that when Jesus died
to the North, having lowered his head,
on Mt. Olive,

Notes to Chapter 4

that strange mountain
ending his suffering, he inclined his hand
toward – the Northern People.

72. Jeffares, *W. B. Yeats* 137.

73. Yeats, *The Irish Dramatic Movement* 53.

74. Sławińska and Kruk, eds., *Myśl teatralna Młodej Polski* 20.

75. See "Motywy prasłowiańskie" in Podraza-Kwiatkowska, ed., *Młodopolski świat wyobraźni. Studia i eseje* 191–92.

76. Wyspiański later revised and republished the play as *Legenda II* in 1904.

77. Sławińska and Kruk, eds., *Myśl teatralna Młodej Polski* 21.

78. See Stanisław Wyspiański, *Dzieła zebrane*, ed. Maria Stokowska, 15 vols. (Kraków: Wydawnictwo Literackie, 1958) 3:359.Wyspiański had a habit of incorporating elements from Greek mythology into his plays, most notably being *Akropolis*, in which he reimagined Wawel Castle in Kraków as a modern day Parthenon.

79. Ibid. 3:351. As pointed out by Leon Płoszewski in the commentary to the *Collected Works*, in writing his plays Wyspiański, too, drew upon recently collected folk mythology, citing Wihelm Bogusławski's *Dzieje Słowiańszczyzny północno-zachodniej do połowy XIII w.* (History of the Northwestern Slavdom to the Mid-Thirteenth Century, 1889) as an example.

80. Miriam, however, was asked by Pawlikowski in 1908 to give a talk about *Wanda* before staging it in Lwów.

81. Dudek, "William Butler Yeats wsród poetów polskich (O recepcji poezji W. B. Yeatsa w Polsce)," 283.

82. David R. Clark, *W. B. Yeats and the Theatre of Desolate Reality* (Washington, D. C.: The Catholic University of America Press, 1993) 128.

83. For a more extended explanation of the differences between symbolism and expressionism, see Jan Józef Lipski, *Twórczość Jana Kasprowicza w latach 1891–1906* (Warszawa: Państwowy Instytut Wydawniczy, 1975) 208–16.

84. Kasprowicz did not use the overarching title *Hymns* until 1921.

85. Podraza-Kwiatkowska, "O Miriamie-krytyku," 426–27.

86. Following her introduction to Munch, Jan Cavanaugh explains, Weiss published an essay in *Life* on the Norwegian artist, in which he used the term "psychological naturalism" to explain the latter's approach to painting. For Weiss, the soul, or rather the psyche, replaced the landscape as the subject for artistic study. Cavanaugh, *Out Looking In: Early Modern Polish Art, 1890–1918* 215–18.

Notes to Chapter 4

87. All of these writers had strong ties to German culture. See Lipski, *Twórczość Jana Kasprowicza w latach 1891–1906* 219.

88. William Butler Yeats, *The Countess Cathleen: Manuscript Materials*, eds. Michael J. Sidnell and Wayne K. Chapman (Ithaca and London: Cornell University Press, 1999) 487.

89. Jan Kasprowicz, "Księżniczka Kasia," *Chimera* VII. z. 20–21 (1904): 21: 269.

90. Yeats, *The Countess Cathleen: Manuscript Materials* 409.

91. Kasprowicz, "Księżniczka Kasia," 20: 226.

92. In Celtic mythology, quicken wood, also known as the mountain ash, the rowantree, and witchwood, was commonly believed to ward away evil spirits.

93. Yeats, *The Countess Cathleen: Manuscript Materials* 414.

94. Kasprowicz, "Księżniczka Kasia," 20: 230.

95. Yeats, *The Countess Cathleen: Manuscript Materials* 421.

96. Kasprowicz, "Księżniczka Kasia," 20: 235.

97. Yeats, *The Countess Cathleen: Manuscript Materials* 481.

98. Kasprowicz, "Księżniczka Kasia," 21: 264.

99. For a discussion of the differences between symbolism and expressionism in regard to Kasprowicz's poetry see Lipski, *Twórczość Jana Kasprowicza w latach 1891–1906* 208–16.

100. Jan Kasprowicz, *Hymny* (Warszawa: Instytut Wydawniczy Pax, 1976) 59–60.

101. Ibid. 54.

102. Yeats, *The Countess Cathleen: Manuscript Materials* l-lvi.

103. Richard Ellman, *Yeats: The Man and the Masks* (New York: The Macmillan Company, 1948) 128.

104. Jan Józef Lipski, *Twórczość Jana Kasprowicza w latach 1878–1891* (Warszawa: Państwowy Instytut Wydawniczy, 1967) 224.

105. Kasprowicz did not complete this play until 1920.

106. Clark, *W. B. Yeats and the Theatre of Desolate Reality* 129.

107. Foster, *W. B. Yeats: A Life: The Apprentice Mage, 1865–1914* 209.

108. Kasprowicz demonstrated his knowledge of conditions in Ireland in many of his early social writings and in a poem entitled "Pieśń irlandzka" (An Irish Song), which he published in *Dziennik Poznański* (The Poznań Daily) in 1886. See Jan Kasprowicz, *Dzieła wybrane*, ed. Jan Józef Lipski, vol. III (Kraków: Wydawnictwo Literackie, 1958) 3: 57–58.

Przyszedł lud obcy na twój łan zielony,
   Erynie! Erynie!
I w twarz ci rzucił: "Zanim chwila sprzętu
   Minie,
Nim twych żniwiarzy stanie tłum strudzony,
Dasz mi swój jęczmień i swoją pszenicę
I praw się swoich wyrzeczesz otwarcie,
Gdyż ręce drżący, a zbladłe źrenice
<<Skazany – mówią – jesteś na wymarcie>>

A foreign people came to your green fields
   O Erin! O Erin!
And struck you in the face: "Before harvest time
   Passes,
Before your reapers stand as a weary crowd,
Give me your barley and your wheat
And you renounce your rights openly,
Since your hands are shaking, and your vision is blurred
You are doomed – they say – to death [.]

109. Kasprowicz could have drawn upon Mickiewicz's *Forefather's Eve* and Norwid's *Wanda*, both of which blended Poland's political and spiritual conflicts. For Mickiewicz, evil took the form of Russian rule, while for Norwid it was German imperialism.

110. See Davies, *God's Playground* 134–37, 99-02.

111. See Danuta Płygawko, Irlandzki gest sympatii dla Polski, Biblioteka Czartoryskich w Krakowie, Kraków. Less than two years after Kasprowicz's translation of Yeats's play appeared in *Chimera*, in 1906, Polish school children in the Prussian partition of Poland went on a strike that would last for more than a year in opposition to the compulsory use of German for religious instruction. This strike had some significance in the Polish-Irish relationship, because in 1908 Irish schoolchildren from County Monaghan sent an album of signatures covered in green velvet and embossed with the emblem of the Irish harp, prefaced by a dedication in English, Irish, and Polish to the school children of Poland. Ironically, from an Irish perspective, the tribute was the initiative of Shane Leslie, an officer in the British army. Płygawko also claimed that Polish schoolchildren repaid the favor in 1913, when some 13,000 children from Września sent their thanks in a similar volume, embossed with the Polish eagle, to the children of County Monaghan.

112. This was made abundantly clear by the fact that the 1914 staging of *The Countess Cathleen*, which took place in the government controlled *Teatr Rozmaitości* (The Variety Theater) in Warsaw, was a bilingual, Polish-Russian production.

113. Yeats, *The Countess Cathleen: Manuscript Materials* 505.

114. Kasprowicz, "Księżniczka Kasia," 21: 283.

115. Foster, W. B. *Yeats: A Life: The Apprentice Mage, 1865–1914* 101.

116. Kasprowicz, *Hymny* 17.

117. Ibid. 67.

118. Edward Balcerzan, ed., *Pisarze polscy o sztuce przekładu 1440–1974. Antologia* (Poznań: Wydawnictwo Poznańskie, 1977) 199–200.

119. Ibid.

120. Ibid. 200.

121. Ibid. 199–200.

122. Ibid. 200.

123. I have not been able to locate a copy of these translations.

124. Jan Kasprowicz, *Poeci angielscy. Wybór poezji* (Lwów: Altenberg, 1907) 437.

125. Foster, W. B. *Yeats: A Life: The Apprentice Mage, 1865–1914* 197. Foster suggests that Yeats must have had his suspicions of MacLeod early on, but that he did not know the truth of his deception until sometime between 1898–1900. Unlike his colleagues, AE and Lady Gregory, however, Yeats continued to retain affection and find use for MacLeod's Celtic mysticism.

126. In recognizing MacLeod as a Gaelic writer, Kasprowicz was not entirely wrong in his attribution. In many respects, his misapprehension was a return to the Ossianic discoveries of James Macpherson at the close of the eighteenth century. While ultimately revealed as literary forgeries, the Ossian tales nonetheless were influential in attracting interest in Gaelic culture. MacLeod, too, generated considerable international interest in Celtic culture through his writing.

127. Yeats routinely rewrote and reassembled his poems. *Crossways* and *The Rose* were selections of poetry taken from *The Wanderings of Oisin and Other Poems* (1889) and *The Countess Cathleen and Various Legends and Lyrics* (1892), and included under their respective titles in *Poems* (1895). See also Sam McCready, *A William Butler Yeats Encyclopedia* (Westport: Greenwood Press, 1997) 310.

128. Yeats first published "The Death of Cuchulain" in *United Ireland*, 11 June 1892. See William Butler Yeats, *The Variorum Edition of the Poems of W. B. Yeats*, eds. Peter Allt and Russell K. Alspach (New York: Macmillan Publishing Co., Inc., 1957) 105. Kasprowicz's use of the title "The Death of Cuchulain," which Yeats used for the poem in collections of his writing from 1895–1901, was not a mistake on his part. Rather, it was evidence of Yeats's habit of incessant revisionism. Although collections of Yeats's poetry as late as 1908 still reflected the original title, in *Poems* (1895) Yeats appears to have begun to use "Cuchulain's Fight with the Sea" as the official title of the poem. This is the title used in Yeats's *Collected Works*.

Notes to Chapter 4

129. See the introduction to William Butler Yeats, *Poems: Selections*, 1994.

130. Kasprowicz, *Hymny* 14.

131. William Butler Yeats, *The Poems*, The Collected Works of W. B. Yeats, ed. Richard J. Finneran, vol. I, XIV vols. (New York: Scribner, 1997) 7.

132. Kasprowicz, *Poeci angielscy. Wybór poezji* 442.

133. In 1909, Kasprowicz was named to the post of assistant professor in philosophy at the University of Lwów, and in 1912 he was appointed as a full professor in the newly formed department of comparative literature.

134. Lipski, *Twórczość Jana Kasprowicza w latach 1891–1906* 351.

135. Kasprowicz, *Hymny* 99.

136. Adolf Nowaczyński, "Z literatury - "Poeci angielscy"," *Świat*.II (1907): 15.

137. Kasprowicz, *Poeci angielscy. Wybór poezji* 438.

138. Ibid. 440. A literal translation of Kasprowicz's Polish version would read as follows:
How many once loved that heavenborn
charm, but only one's love was faithful
to your pilgrim's soul and the bramble,
Which furrowed your brow—sorrow's thorn.

139. As willow trees typically are grown along roadsides in Poland, all of the options available to Kasprowicz in Polish, including "ogród wierzb" (willow garden), "sąd wierzb" (willow orchard), and "gaj wierzbowy" (willow grove) would have struck Poles as both linguistically and culturally strange.

140. Maria Dłuska, *Prace wybrane*, ed. Stanisław Balbus, vol. I, 3 vols. (Kraków: Universitas, 2001) 468–69.

141. Ibid. 430.

142. For Synge, this would remain the case for nearly a half-century until a translation of *Riders to the Sea* appeared in a Polish journal in the 1950s.

143. Ludwik Solski, *Wspomnienia 1893–1954*, 2 vols. (Kraków: Wydawnictwo Literackie, 1956) 2: 67. In his memoirs, Solski recalled how Lwowians stormed the ticket office of the Civic Theater demanding that the visiting company from Kraków remain in Lwów to reprise their production of Zapolska's *Tamten* (That One) for an additional week.

144. Władysław Kozicki, "Nowe czasy - nowy teatr (1900–1929)," *Scena lwowska*, eds. Henryk Cepnik and Władysław Kozicki (Lwów: Nakładem gminy m, Lwowa, 1929) 43.

145. Alfred Wysocki, *Sprzed pół wieku* (Kraków: Wydawnictwo Literackie, 1958) 222.

Notes to Chapter 4

146. Ibid. 222–23.

147. Wilhelm Feldman, *Współczesna literatura polska 1864–1918*, 2 vols. (Kraków: Wydawnictwo Literackie, 1985) 2:139.

148. Wysocki, *Sprzed pół wieku* 222.

149. Wyspiański, *Dzieła zebrane* 219.

150. A. Zagórski, "Teatr lwowski (Porachunek roczny)," *Krytyka* t. 4.z. 8/9 (1909): 138.

151. With the exception of *The Judges*, the same slate of plays appeared in an evening honoring Wyspiański in the Civic Theater in Kraków earlier that same month. For a reproduction of the poster for the Kraków performance see Wyspiański, *Dzieła zebrane* 8:176–77.

152. Frank A. Biletz, "The Boundaries of Irish National Identity: The Emergence of the Irish-Ireland Ideal, 1890–1912," Ph.D. dissertation, University of Chicago, 1995, 61–62.

153. The other two productions of Synge's plays were the Deutsches Theater's staging of *The Well of the Saints* and the Bohemian National Theater's performance of *In the Shadow of the Glen*, with a translation by Karel Mu·ek, in Prague on February 7, 1906. See Yeats, *The Irish Dramatic Movement* 254.

154. Ostap Ortwin, "'Sędziowie' - Wyspiańskiego," *Krytyka* r. 9. z. 12 (1907): 427.

155. Lack, *Wybór pism krytycznych* 271.

156. Wyspiański, *Dzieła zebrane* 9:208.

157. Lack, *Wybór pism krytycznych* 275.

158. Ortwin, "'Sędziowie' - Wyspiańskiego," 428.

159. Lack, *Wybór pism krytycznych* 265, 87.

160. Tymon Terlecki, *Stanisław Wyspiański* (Boston: Twayne Publishers, 1983) 45.

161. Solski, *Wspomnienia 1893–1954* 249.

162. Lack, *Wybór pism krytycznych* 268.

163. For reproductions of the posters for the original productions of *The Judges* in Lwów and Kraków, see Wyspiański, *Dzieła zebrane* 9: 240–41, 56–57. It is not clear if the same format was used for the premiere in Vilnius in 1907.

164. Terlecki, *Stanisław Wyspiański* 45.

165. Zagórski, "Teatr lwowski (Porachunek roczny)," 138.

166. Wyspiański made a number of revisions to *The Judges*, but it is unclear whether any drafts of the text contained the two-scene structure.

Notes to Chapter 4

167. John Millington Synge, *The Complete Plays* (New York: Vintage, 1960) 121. The setting to *The Well of the Saints* did not specify Wicklow, but in referring to an "Eastern Mountain District" the reference was clear.

168. Yeats, *The Irish Dramatic Movement* 81.

169. Tadeusz Sivert and Roman Taborski, *Teatr polski w latach 1890–1918: Zabór austriacki i pruski* (Warszawa: Państwowe Wydawnictwo Naukowe, 1987) 275.

170. See Krajewska, *Recepcja literatury angielskiej w Polsce w okresie modernizmu (1887–1918)*. This was the case for the introduction of Shaw's dramas in Poland. Resulting from troubles with English censors, in England Shaw's works gained notoriety in print before appearing on the stage, while in Poland his plays made their debut on the stage first.

171. See Wysocki, *Sprzed pół wieku*.

172. Ibid. 222.

173. David H. Greene and Edward M. Stephens, *J. M. Synge, 1871–1909* (New York and London: New York University Press, 1989) 196. Meyerfield had corresponded with Synge in the spring of 1906 regarding permission to render his play into German for the stage.

174. The manuscript of *The Well of the Saints* found in the archives of the Teatr im. J. Słowackiego in Kraków, which was used in Pawlikowski's 1914 production, is presumably the same text that was used in the 1908 production in Lwów, but that is far from certain.

175. In his choice of title, Wysocki appeared to base his translation on Meyerfield's German translation, *Der Heilige Brunnen*, rather than on that of the original English play.

176. In the years to come, Polish critics would raise the issue of the choice of titles used for Synge's and Yeats's plays. This was the case with Kasprowicz's translation of *The Countess Cathleen* as *Księżniczka Kasia* (Kasia being a name with a closer association to the peasantry), and later with Florian Sobienowski's translation of *The Playboy of the Western World* as *Kresowy rycezr wesoły* (literally, The Happy Borderland Knight).

177. See A. G. van Hamel, *On Anglo-Irish Syntax*, Reprints in Irish Studies Literature Series, Number 3 ed. (Chicago: American Committee for Irish Studies, 1977).

178. In somewhat similar fashion to Yeats and Synge, the writers of Young Poland, enamored with Polish folk culture, created a highly literary form of peasant speech that combined real and stylized elements of Polish village and mountain dialects. While Wyspiański was far from alone on this score, his colorful dialogue was an especially strong influence on Young Poland's literary portrayal of the Polish countryside.

179. Alfred Wysocki, "Notatki literacko-artystyczne - Z teatru," *Gazeta Lwowska*. Nr. 261 (1908): 5.

180. Ibid.

181. Ibid.

Notes to Chapter 4

182. Ibid.

183. Ibid.

184. Alfred Wysocki, "Z teatru," *Gazeta Lwowska*.Nr. 262 (1908): 4.

185. In pairing Polish and foreign plays, Pawlikowski tended to put together plays featuring contrasting styles, such as realism and symbolism. See BoΩena Frankowska, "Teatr okresu Młodej Polski a literatura," *Obraz literatury polskiej w XIV i XX wieku, Ser. 5: Literatury Młodej Polski*, vol. 2 (Warszawa: 1967) 27.

186. Synge's stage commands in the opening scene of *The Well of the Saints* read as follows: "SCENE. Some lonely mountainous district in the east of Ireland one or more centuries ago." See Synge, *The Complete Plays* 121.

187. Wysocki, "Z teatru," 4.

188. Ibid.

189. Ibid.

190. G., "Z teatru ("Cudowne źródło". legenda M. G. Synge)," *Goniec Polski* Rok II.Nr. 550 (1908): 3. Given Lwów's prominence inthe Polish socialist movement, this was an interesting comment for the reviewer to make.

191. With its location in the relatively benign Austrian partition and its proximity to the border of the Russian partition, Lwów was an active center for a variety of Polish political parties. Polish socialists were particularly active in Lwów under Boleslaw Limanowski.

192. G., "Z teatru ("Cudowne źródło". legenda M. G. Synge)," 3. The misspelling of Synge's initials is that of the original Polish publication.

193. Ibid.

194. Solski recalled in his memoirs that Pawlikowski had had lively contact with Craig at this time. See Solski, *Wspomnienia 1893–1954* 248. As the editor of *Nasz kraj* (Our Country), furthermore, in 1908 Pawlikowski published a Polish translation of an article by Craig entitled "Niektóre złe dążności współczesnego teatru" (Some Wrong Tendencies in the Modern Theater), which he claimed had been written expressly for the journal earlier that year. See Krajewska, *Recepcja literatury angielskiej w Polsce w okresie modernizmu (1887–1918)* 202, Kazimierz Gajda, *Recepcja Wielkiej Reformy Teatru w prasie galicyjskiej 1890–1918* (Kraków: Wydawnictwo Naukowe WSP, 1991) 148.

195. Pawlikowski most likely encountered Craig's work for the first time in Berlin, where Craig collaborated with both Brahm and Reinhardt in 1904–1905, not long before Synge's *The Well of the Saints* debuted there under the direction of the former. Craig's celebrated work, *The Art of the Theatre* (1905), later republished as *On the Art of the Theatre* (1911), had not yet been translated into Polish. Craig would attract greater attention in

Notes to Chapter 4

Poland in the years to come, particularly following his acquaintance with Leon Schiller in 1907 and his lengthy collaboration with Stanislavsky in Moscow beginning in 1908.

196. See Krajewska, *Recepcja literatury angielskiej w Polsce w okresie modernizmu (1887–1918)* 64–65.

197. William Butler Yeats, *The Letters of W. B. Yeats*, ed. Allan Wade (New York: The Macmillan Company, 1955) 461.

198. Zamoyski, "States of Mind: on the myths of national identity," 21.

CHAPTER FIVE

1. Nowaczyński infamously had to leave Kraków in 1898 for Munich, where he remained for two years, after declaring "Vive l'anarchie!" in a café upon learning of the assassination of Austrian Empress. It was at this time that he adopted the middle name "*Neuwert*" (New Worth) as a means of distancing himself from his family and reinventing himself as a writer and critic.

2. Adolf Nowaczyński, *Małpie zwierciadło*, 2 vols. (Kraków: Wydawnictwo Literackie, 1974) 2: 217.

3. Anna Kiezuń, *Spór z tradycją romantyczną. O działalności pisarskiej Adolfa Nowaczyńskiego* (Białystok: Dział Wydawnictw Filii UW w Białymstoku, 1993) 8.

4. Nowaczyński, *Małpie zwierciadło* 1:47.

5. Ibid. 2:349.

6. See Andrzej Walicki, *Trzy patriotyzmy* (Warszawa: Respublica, 1991) 60–70. Despite counting many of Young Poland's leading writers among his friends, Roman Dmowski, the driving force behind National Democracy, also despised the modernist movement in Poland because he felt it contributed little to the advancement of the nation.

7. Dmowski's National League had been in existence since 1893 and the Stronnictwo Demokratyczno-Narodowe (National Democracy Party) was officially founded in 1897, but Dmowski's 1903 manifesto was the first formulation of its political program. In particular, Dmowski advocated the strengthening of national consciousness in all areas of Polish life through the formation of societies, schools, and newspapers.

8. See Alvin Marcus Fountain, *Roman Dmowski: party, tactics, ideology, 1895–1907* (Boulder; New York: East European Monographs; distributed by Columbia University Press, 1980).

9. Nowaczyński, *Małpie zwierciadło* 1:52.

10. Ibid. 1:110.

Notes to Chapter 5

11. In "Histeryczny histrion" (The Hysterical Histrion) he referred to Lack as "Klak," who "wrote in a varnished style, an anagrammist of metaphysics, and so on, even more boring," while in "Gladiolus tavernalis," he labeled Lack a "brilliant cryptographer" (genialny kryptografista). Both stories appeared in the 1902 and 1909 publications of *Małpie zwierciadło* (Monkey's Mirror), although Nowaczyński did originally publish "The Hysterical Histrion" separately in the journal *Strumień* in 1900. See Ibid. 1:88, 111.

12. Ibid. 1:55.

13. For more on Nowaczyński's attitudes to Miriam and Żeromski, see Kiezuń, *Spór z tradycją romantyczną. O działalności pisarskiej Adolfa Nowaczyńskiego* 151–54. Nowaczyński's characterization of Miriam and *Chimera* resembled the goals set out by the publisher himself in the first issue of the journal. Maria Staszek has also pointed out the socially productive role Miriam played as a critic in regard to the theater. In calling for the theater to be more than mere entertainment, Miriam underscored its importance as a way of elevating Polish society as a whole. Far from emulating the aesthetic detachment of Lack or Przybyszewski, Miriam exhibited the social engagement so prized by Nowaczyński. See Jacek Popiel, ed., *Dramat i teatr modernistyczny* (Wrocław: Wiedza o kulturze, 1992) 229–34.

14. Ironically, Nowaczyński claimed to be part of a group that played a key role in persuading Stanisław Przybyszewski to return to Kraków in the late 1890s.

15. Kiezuń, *Spór z tradycją romantyczną. O działalności pisarskiej Adolfa Nowaczyńskiego* 151.

16. Tomasz Weiss, "Adolf Nowaczyński jako krytyk literacki," *Prace Historycznoliterackie Katedry Historii Literatury Polskiej Wyższej Szkoły Pedagogicznej* (Katowice: Zeszyty Naukowe WSP, 1962) 290.

17. Oskar Wilde, *Dyalogi o sztuce ("Intentions")*, trans. Marya Feldmanowa (Lwów: Księgarnia Narodowa, 1906) XLIV.

18. Ibid. XLV.

19. Ibid.

20. Kiezuń, *Spór z tradycją romantyczną. O działalności pisarskiej Adolfa Nowaczyńskiego* 99.

21. Nowaczyński added a lengthy excerpt on Yeats and the novelist, George Moore to the 1909 version of "The Rebirth of Erin," but in all other respects it was identical to the original article published two years earlier.

22. Adolf Nowaczyński, "Odrodzenie Erynu," *Co czasy niosą* (Warszawa: 1909) 69.

23. Ibid.

24. Ibid. 69–70.

25. See Philip O'Leary, *The Prose Literature of the Gaelic Revival, 1881–1921* (University Park: Pennsylvania State University Press, 1994) 19–90.

26. Frank A. Biletz, "The Boundaries of Irish National Identity: The Emergence of the Irish-Ireland Ideal, 1890–1912," Ph.D. dissertation, University of Chicago, 1995, 72.

27. F. S. L. Lyons, *Ireland Since the Famine* (London: Collins/Fontana, 1982) 231.

28. Nowaczyński, "Odrodzenie Erynu," 74. The number of Irish nationalists in parliament in 1900 was in reality eighty-one. See Lyons, *Ireland Since the Famine* 262.

29. Nowaczyński, *Małpie zwierciadło* 1:413. Nowaczyński's reference to Kalmucks, a Mongolian people, would have brought to mind the Tatars in the Polish imagination.

30. Nowaczyński, "Odrodzenie Erynu," 75. Nowaczyński was referring to the manner with which he felt Irish political leaders in the nineteenth century manipulated the Irish people into focusing all their energies on an English solution to Ireland's problems.

31. Ibid. 77–78. The ellipses are Nowaczyński's.

32. Ibid. 78.

33. Kiezuń, *Spór z tradycją romantyczną. O działalności pisarskiej Adolfa Nowaczyńskiego* 151.

34. Nowaczyński, "Odrodzenie Erynu," 80.

35. Ibid. 108.

36. Nowaczyński, *Małpie zwierciadło* 1:35–36.

37. Ibid. 1:55.

38. Ibid. 1:469.

39. Polish readers would have made the connection between the reference to Sisyphus and Stefan Żeromski, the author of *Syzyfowe prace* (Sisyphean Labor, 1898), about whom Nowaczyński had written an article in 1901. As an artist, he admired Żeromski's strong sense of social responsibility toward his country. Along with Wyspiański, he considered Żeromski to be one of the few Polish intellectuals attempting to bring about a similar national revival in Poland. Kiezuń, *Spór z tradycją romantyczną. O działalności pisarskiej Adolfa Nowaczyńskiego* 153.

40. See Douglas Hyde, *Language, Lore and Lyrics: essays and lectures*, ed. Breadan O'Conaire (Blackrock, County Dublin: Irish Academic Press, 1986).

41. The Gaelic League, moreover, was limited to a relatively small group of enthusiasts in Dublin, many of whom were of Anglo-Irish descent.

42. William Butler Yeats, *The Irish Dramatic Movement*, The Collected Works of W. B. Yeats, eds. Mary FitzGerald and Richard J. Finneran, vol. VIII (New York: Scribner, 2003) 62.

43. Biletz, "The Boundaries of Irish National Identity: The Emergence of the Irish-Ireland Ideal, 1890–1912," 34–41.

44. Although there were nationalist newspapers published in Irish, *The Leader* and other leading Irish nationalist newspapers were published almost entirely in English.

45. Yeats, *The Irish Dramatic Movement* 87.

46. Nowaczyński, "Odrodzenie Erynu," 83.

47. Ibid. 84.

48. Ibid. 85.

49. Ibid.

50. Ibid. 86.

51. Ibid.

52. Ibid. 89.

53. Ibid. 90.

54. Ibid. 91.

55. Nowaczyński's preference for writers such as Miriam, Kasprowicz, and Wyspiański over a writer such as Przybyszewski is indicative of where he drew the line in regard to Polish modernism. See Kiezuń, *Spór z tradycją romantyczną. O działalności pisarskiej Adolfa Nowaczyńskiego*.

56. Nowaczyński, "Odrodzenie Erynu," 96. Ironically, his critics would level a similar charge at Nowaczyński in the years to come.

57. Ibid. 98.

58. Ibid. 101.

59. Ibid. 105.

60. In addition to translating an array of English and French literature into Polish, Rakowska also rendered the works of such Polish writers as Wacław Sieroszewski, Stefan Żeromski, Maria Konopnicka, and Andrzej Strug into French.

61. Ibid., 98–99.

62. Ibid., 99. Rakowska interestingly concluded her overview of English literature with a brief discussion of Wilde and Shaw, whom she numbered among the leading contemporary contributors to the field of literary criticism.

63. Marya Rakowska, "Teatr irlandzki," *Krytyka* T. XXXI (1911): 304.

64. Ibid,

65. Poles would have also made an immediate connection between the pen name, Joseph Conrad, and Konrad, the protagonist from Mickiewicz's *Forefather's Eve*.

66. Ibid., 305. The italics are my own.

67. Ibid.

68. Ibid., 306.

69. Ibid.

70. Ibid.

71. Ibid.

72. The theaters in Kraków and Lwów, albeit artistically and culturally significant in terms of Young Poland's development, were civic institutions, which were dependent upon government funding and subject to oversight by the Austrian authorities.

73. Ibid., 307.

74. Ibid., 308.

75. Ibid., 309.

76. Ibid.

77. Ibid., 311.

78. Ibid.

79. Ibid., 312.

80. Ibid.

81. Szyfman was the victim of a concerted campaign in the conservative Warsaw press, which consisted of attacks on practical points, such as his lack of experience as a director and the perceived extravagance of the project, and more insidiously, on his Jewishness. Among other things, Szyfman was accused of using the Polish aristocracy as a front in order to mask a business scheme. The campaign, though vicious and long-lasting, spurred critics such as Stefan Krzywoszewski and Władysław Rabski to defend him publicly in the press. Interestingly, one of Szyfman's vocal supporters in this decisive phase was Nowaczyński.

82. As had been the case with "The Rebirth of Erin," Nowaczyński's article "The Irish Theater" first appeared in print in 1913, and was republished five years later in his collected essays *Szkice literackie* (Literary Sketches).

83. Nowaczyński, *Małpie zwierciadło* 2:336.

84. Menander was a Greek playwright known for writing "New Comedy," for which he used the daily life of Athens as his inspiration.

85. Nowaczyński, *Małpie zwierciadło* 2:336.

86. Primarily a linguistic term used to refer to a specific subgroup of Western Slavonic language speakers in the middle ages historically and geographically associated with Poles, See Zenon Klemensiewicz, *Historia języka polskiego* (Warszawa: Wydawnictwo Naukowe PWN, 1999) 18–19. Nowaczyński here uses "Lechites" as a cultural-historical reference to Lech as one of the legendary ancestors of the Polish people.

87. See poem "CXLIII" in Nowaczyński, *Małpie zwierciadło* 2:318.: "Poland in life could become holy.../But it no longer awaits: *Risorgimento*./ On the earth the Lord God prefers Sancho Panza."

88. Other chapters in the book addressed the topics of Balzac, Shakespeare in Poland, Czech culture, Early Polish Satire, Aleksander Świętochowski, and the Belgian Bible.

89. Adolf Nowaczyński, "Teatr irlandzki," *Szkice literackie* (Poznań: Ostoja, 1918) 61.

90. Ibid.

91. Ibid.

92. Ibid.

93. Ibid. 62. The co-founders of the Irish Literary Theatre were Yeats, Lady Gregory and Edward Martyn. O'Cuisin was, in fact, James H. Cousins, an original member of William G. Fay's Irish National Dramatic Company formed apparently in 1902. See Hugh Hunt, *The Abbey: Ireland's National Theatre, 1904–1979* (New York: Columbia University Press, 1979) 35.

94. Nowaczyński, "Teatr irlandzki," 63.

95. Nowaczyński, *Małpie zwierciadło* 2:350.

96. Nowaczyński, "Teatr irlandzki," 64.

97. Ibid.

98. Ibid.

99. Ibid.

100. Ibid.

101. Ibid.

102. Ibid. 66.

103. See Robert Hogan and Richard Burnham, eds., *The Years of O'Casey, 1921–1926: A Documentary History* (Newark: University of Delaware Press, 1992) 121–22. Birmingham's play had already had a successful nine-month run in London in 1913. The audience's premeditated response to the production in Westport by the English theatrical company, managed by Payne Seddon, was reminiscent of the *Playboy* riots. As had been the case with Synge's play, polemical exchanges in the Irish press characterized Birmingham as a

besmircher of Irish society for his own profit and the amusement of English audiences. The volatility surrounding the performance in Westport had much to do with the fact that Birmingham had been the rector of Westport for twenty-one years until he left for good in October 1913, a month after *General John Regan* closed in London. On March 2nd, some twenty of the accused from the riot, a large number of whom were students from Dublin, were returned for trial in County Mayo. For an overview of the trial, see "'General John Regan' in Westport - Resumed Hearings of Riot Charges," *The Mayo News* Saturday, March 7 1914: 6.

104. Biletz has described the tension that developed between Canon Hannay and the more extreme, nationalist elements in the Gaelic League. In particular, the conflict stemmed from the appointment of Hannay, a Protestant clergyman, to *Coiste Gnothe* (the Executive Committee), of the Gaelic League in 1904. Despite having been an active member of the Gaelic League since 1903 and having defended the language movement publicly, the nationalist perception of Hannay's political stance and his portrayal of Irish Catholics in his literary work opened a rift that was not entirely closed by Hannay's resignation from the *Coiste Gnothe* in 1907. As Biletz emphasizes, the incident underscored the difficulty the Gaelic League faced in maintaining its identity as a non-political, nonsectarian organization.

105. Markiewicz had produced a play by Birmingham in Dublin in 1911 with his Independent Dramatic Company, but it was *Eleanor's Enterprise*, not *General John Regan*. While Birmingham's play was staged elsewhere in Ireland, it is not clear whether it was performed in Dublin. The link between Markiewicz and Nowaczyński was an interesting one, because the former had been active as a painter, playwright, and theater director in Dublin for over a decade. Markiewicz, who left Ireland for good a few months before Birmingham's play appeared in Westport, had his Polish theatrical debut in May 1914, when Szyfman produced his play *Dzikie Pole* (The Wild Fields) in the Polish Theater. Szyfman staged Nowaczyński's *New Athens* during the previous, inaugural season of the theater.

106. Adolf Nowaczyński, "Irlandzkie "Nowe Ateny"," *Świat* IX.13 (1914): 14.

107. Ibid, Nowaczyński, "Teatr irlandzki," 70. The damage to Joyce's Hotel in Westport was mainly limited to broken windows. The only hotel destroyed was the one used in the stage set for *General John Regan*.

108. Eustachy Czekalski, "Szkice literackie Ad. Nowaczyńskiego," *Romans i Powieść* 33 (1918): 8.

109. Arnold Szyfman, "Teatr zagraniczny," *Krytyka* VII.VI (1905): 499.

110. Ibid.XI: 387. In his column, Szyfman routinely reviewed the latest developments in the European theater, including both the major stages in Austria, England, France, and Germany, as well as lesser theaters in the Czech lands, Italy, and Scandinavia. Gordon Craig's landmark work, *The Art of the Theatre*, originally appeared in German as *Die Kunst des Theaters* in 1905. The timing of Szyfman's stay in Berlin also happened

Notes to Chapter 5

to coincide with Gordon Craig's five-month collaboration with Brahm's Freie Bühne in 1904–1905. It is not clear whether Szyfman met Gordon Craig while in Berlin, or if he attended the Freie Bühn's production of Thomas Otway's *Venice Preserved* that used the English director's sketches.

111. Ibid.

112. Arnold Szyfman, *Labirynt teatru* (Warszawa: Wydawnictwo Artystyczne Filmowe, 1964) 94.

113. "Nowczesne teatry," *Złoty Róg* 5 (1913): 2.

114. Ibid.

115. He also drew on the abilities of capable, young directors, such as Schiller and Osterwa.

116. Szyfman enlisted the talents, among others, of the painters Ferdynand Ruszczyc and Stanisław Ignacy Witkiewicz, and the composers, Henryk Opieński, Ludomir Różycki and Karol Szymanowski.

117. Edward Krasiński, *Teatr Polski Arnolda Szyfmana 1913–1939* (Warszawa: Wydawnictwo Naukowe PWN, 1991) 21.

118. See Michał Głowiński's essay "Maska Dionizosa" (The Mask of Dionysus) in Maria Podraza-Kwiatkowska, ed., *Młodopolski świat wyobraźni. Studia i eseje* (Kraków: Wydawnictwo Literackie, 1977) 375.

119. Krasiński, *Teatr Polski Arnolda Szyfmana 1913–1939* 27.

120. Founded in 1905, the famous cabaret, *Zielony Balonik* (The Little Green Balloon), attracted a number of these individuals, including Nowaczyński, Karol Frycz, Tadeusz Boy-Żeleński, Juliusz Osterwa, and Leon Schiller, among others. Interestingly, several of these individuals would go on to take an active part in Szyfman's Polish Theater, with Schiller and Osterwa eventually becoming major theater directors in their own right.

121. There were few prospects for Szyfman in Kraków. As important a move as it was, in opening his cabaret theater Szyfman had severed his ties with Solski, effectively closing the Civic Theater to him. Solski was director of the Civic Theater from 1905–1913, renamed the Słowacki Theater in 1909.

122. Among the Polish aristocracy, Szyfman's champion was Tomasz Potocki, while intellectuals such as Nowaczyński, Rabski, and Ehrenberg came to his defense in the press, arguing that Szyfman's plan for the Polish Theater deserved applause rather than attacks because of the dire state of the theater in Warsaw. Szyfman's theater, they argued, was not only a welcome change to a theater scene dominated by the government theaters and an assortment of popular, variety theaters, but as a director Szyfman represented one of the most talented figures in the contemporary Polish theater. See Krasiński, *Teatr Polski Arnolda Szyfmana 1913–1939* 13–18.

Notes to Chapter 5

123. See Ibid. 12–19. Szyfman's conversion to Catholicism in 1909 did not prevent anti-Semitic attacks against him in the press.

124. As the opening of the Polish Theater approached, Szyfman experienced considerable difficulty in convincing the Russian authorities to agree to the name of the theater. See Szyfman, *Labirynt teatru* 114.

125. Although the company of the Polish Theater had yet to perform in Warsaw, the actors were largely veterans of the Kraków and Warsaw theaters. Some of the playwrights, such as Wyspiański, Przybyszewski, and Rittner, whose work Szyfman selected were already familiar to the Young Poland theater. He did, however, add a number of works by younger writers, including Nowaczyński, Krzywoszewski, and Leopold Staff. Szyfman's Russian tour would prove to be unexpectedly felicitous following the outbreak of World War I, when Szyfman and a large portion of the Polish Theater were forced to flee Warsaw as Austrian citizens.

126. Leon Schiller, *Teatr ogromny* (Warszawa: Czytelnik, 1961) 25. While the premiere of the Polish Theater was both a national and an artistic event, the placards promoting the performance of *Irydion* were in both Polish and Russian, which provided an interesting reminder of political reality facing the newly established theater.

127. Nearly all of the works produced in the first year had been performed previously in Kraków. Two notable exceptions to this were Nowaczyński's *New Athens* and Synge's *The Playboy of the Western World*. Szyfman, like Pawlikowski, was a skilled businessman, devising a repertoire that had a balance of works with both popular and artistic appeal.

128. Krasiński, *Teatr Polski Arnolda Szyfmana 1913–1939* 23.

129. Schiller, *Teatr ogromny* 26.

130. Ibid. 30.

131. Krasiński, *Teatr Polski Arnolda Szyfmana 1913–1939* 104. An article chronicling the 1914 theater season in France mentioned *The Playboy of the Western World* among a series of foreign plays "that appeared on the stage in Paris in the second half of December in the previous year." J. H., "Kronika teatralna francuska," *Kronika Artystyczna* Z. V-VIII. Marzec-Kwiecień (1914): 163–64. The play, which opened in Paris on December 12, ran for a total of six performances.

132. Sosnowski and Aleksander Zelwerowicz, who played "Michael James Flaherty," both originally debuted in the Kraków theater in 1900, while the remaining members of the cast, Wysocka (1901), Węgrzyn (1905), and Stanisława Słubicka, who played "Widow Quin," (c. 1906), debuted in the Civic Theater successively later. Stefan Jaracz, who played "Old Mahon," was also from Kraków, but he first debuted in 1904 in the *Teatr Ludowy* (Folk Theater). See Jan Michalik, *Dzieje teatru w Krakowie w latach, 1893–1915*, vol. Tom 5, I-II vols. (Kraków: Wydawnictwo Literackie, 1987) 322–31.

Notes to Chapter 5

133. Krasiński, *Teatr Polski Arnolda Szyfmana 1913–1939* 34. Szyfman had contracts with a number of talented translators, in and outside of Poland, who specialized on rendering works from a specific language into Polish expressly for the stage.

134. As a translator of Shaw, Sobienowski made a major contribution to the Polish theater. Krasiński estimated that the Polish Theater alone staged eighteen works by Shaw, totaling twenty-one premieres, including a European and a world premiere, and some eight hundred and ninety performances. The immense popularity of Shaw was a phenomenon unique among the stages of Europe to the Polish Theater. Sobienowski's relentless pestering of Shaw for commissions to translate his work into Polish ensured Warsaw theatergoers a steady diet of Shavian drama. The straightforward style and social themes of Shaw's plays were well suited to the changing artistic and literary tastes in the interwar period. Ibid. 82–83.

135. Sobienowski's efforts did not come to fruition, but he did convince Mansfield to dedicate a poem to the Polish writer entitled "To Stanislaw Wyspianski" in 1910, which was published posthumously. Not one to neglect an opportunity, Sobienowski rendered Mansfield's verse into Polish and published it in a Polish periodical that same year. He also encouraged her in 1917 to try her hand at translating *The Judges* and another of the Polish dramatist's plays, the manuscript of which he later reputedly sold to a publisher in the United States. See Anthony Alpers, *The Life of Katherine Mansfield* (New York: The Viking Press, 1980) 319.

136. There was a strong aspect of the literary mercenary in Sobienowski that was at odds with his aspirations to promote Polish literature abroad. Sobienowski, who in 1912–1913 was the self-styled "Polish correspondent" to Mansfield's and Murray's journal *Rhythm*, frequently borrowed money from the couple, even going so far as blackmailing Mansfield in 1920 for letters she had written to him indicating an affair she had had with Sobienowski in Bavaria over a decade earlier. For more on Sobienowski's relationship with Mansfield, see Jeffrey Meyers, *Katherine Mansfield: A Biography* (New York: New Directions, 1978), C. A. Hankin, ed., *The Letters of John Middleton Murray to Katherine Mansfield* (New York: Franklin Watts, 1983), Alpers, *The Life of Katherine Mansfield*. Shaw, too, expressed irritation at his Polish translator for his incessant requests either for money, usually in exchange for translations of the English writer's plays. "I cannot go on financing you," Shaw insisted in a 1924 letter to Sobienowski, "The enclosed is positively my last contribution. You will ask me for more, probably before the end of the month; but I have now invested more money in Poland than I am likely ever to get back." George Bernard Shaw, *Collected Letters, 1911–1925*, ed. Dan. H. Laurence, vol. 3, 4 vols. (London: Max Reinhardt, 1985) 3: 883–84. Shaw, however, maintained his relationship with Sobienowski, by continuing to lend him money and by allowing his translations to be used in theatrical productions in Poland. Dan H. Laurence has suggested that Shaw's tolerance of Sobienowski's endless entreaties for money "was merely an extension of [his] lifetime fascination with and predilection for all the vagabonds and tinkers and drunkards, the scoundrels and sharpsters whom, with eyes fully open, he had permitted to reach into his

Notes to Chapter 5

pocket." George Bernard Shaw, *Collected Letters, 1926–1950*, ed. Dan. H. Laurence, vol. 4, 4 vols. (London: Max Reinhardt, 1988) 4: 419.

137. Jan Lorentowicz, *Dwadzieścia lat teatru*, vol. II (Warszawa: Hoesick, 1930) 196.

138. Józef Kotarbiński, "Przegląd teatralny," *Biblioteka Warszawska* 2.1 (1914): 174.

139. Ibid.

140. This judgment is based on an unsigned, handwritten manuscript of *Kresowy rycerz-wesołek* found in archives of the Teatr im. Słowacki in Kraków.

141. Irena Sławińska, *Wśród mitów teatralnych młodej polski* (Kraków: Wydawnictwo Literackie, 1983). Tetmajer's tales of bandits, shepherds, and ruffians were set in the Tatra Mountains and employed a strongly accented *górale* (mountaineer) dialect.

142. Sobienowski faithfully translated *The Playboy* as taking place in Western Mayo, but by adding details from Polish mountain culture and by partially Polonizing the names of the characters, such as Krzysztof Mahon (Christy Mahon), Synge's play had the effect of being both strangely Irish and un-Irish.

143. In an unpublished dissertation on the Polish reception of Irish drama during this period, Bożena Helcebergier suggested that the directors of the Polish Theater excised lines and even entire characters from Sobienowski's translation. Given the primacy of the text in Szyfman's approach to the theater, this claim seems unlikely. It does, however, raise the question of creative interpretation on the part of the Polish Theater. Bożena Helcebergier, "Dramat irlandzki na scenach polskich w okresie Młodej Polski," Maszynopis, KUL, 1978, 126.

144. John Millington Synge, *The Complete Plays* (New York: Vintage, 1960) 30.

145. Ibid. 80.

146. Szyfman, *Labirynt teatru* 158.

147. Jakób Appenszlak, "Feljeton Teatralny," *Złoty Róg* 47 (1913): 8.

148. Ibid.

149. Kotarbiński, "Przegląd teatralny," 174.

150. Ibid.: 175.

151. Ibid.: 176.

152. Ibid.

153. Ignacy Baliński, "Rozmowy o teatrze," *Tygodnik ilustrowany*.Nr. 47 (1913). Baliński use of the Polish word "dżin" (gin) for "whiskey" is a minor but telling illustration of the potential cultural barriers that arose in Polish readings of Irish literature and culture.

154. Ibid.

Notes to Chapter 5

155. Ibid.

156. Ibid.

157. Ibid.

158. Lorentowicz, *Dwadzieścia lat teatru* 197.

159. Ibid.

160. Ibid.

161. Ibid.

162. Ibid. 199.

163. Ibid. 200.

164. In Wyspiański's play, a village worn down by a terrible drought demands the sacrifice of the children of the local priest's mistress to cleanse the village of its sins and thereby end the drought.

165. Lorentowicz, *Dwadzieścia lat teatru* 200.

166. Kotarbiński, "Przegląd teatralny," 174.

167. Ibid.

168. Baliński, "Rozmowy o teatrze."

169. Kotarbiński, "Przegląd teatralny," 175.

170. Wanda Krajewska, *Recepcja literatury angielskiej w Polsce w okresie modernizmu (1887–1918)* (Wrocław: PAN, 1972) 19.

171. Baliński, "Rozmowy o teatrze," 927.

172. Kotarbiński, "Przegląd teatralny," 174.

173. Ibid.: 175–76.

174. Ibid.: 176.

175. Ibid.: 177.

176. Sławińska, *Wśród mitów teatralnych młodej polski* 14.

177. Lorentowicz, *Dwadzieścia lat teatru* 196.

178. Szyfman, *Labirynt teatru* 158.

179. St. Miłaszewski, "Teatr w 1913r," *Gazeta Warszawska* Rok 135.Nr. 1 (1914): 2.

180. Szyfman, *Labirynt teatru* 158.

181. Although the archive at the Teatr im. Juliusz Słowacki in Kraków lists the author of the translation to be Sobienowski, the printed manuscript does not list an author.

182. "Teatr krakowski," *Krytyka* XXXVI (1912): 223.

183. Ibid.

184. Szymonowicz, who wrote under the name Simon Simonides, wrote *Castus Joseph* in Latin.

185. M., "Z teatru krakowskiego," *Gazeta Warszawska* Rok 135.Nr. 38 (1914): 2–3. Unlike his colleagues, however, the reviewer for *The Warsaw Gazette*, who most likely was Stanisław Miłaszewski, rated the performances of all the actors highly. "Mr. Siemaszko," Miłaszewski observed, "played the beggar excellently, and his partner was Miss Czaplińska. They are an unsung pair in comedy. The crowd of villagers was naturally lively and authentically rustic."

186. Zygmunt Rosner, "Z teatru - 'Cudowne Źródło' legenda w 3 aktach J. M. Syngera," *Gazeta Poniedziałkowa* Rok 5.Nr. 5 (1914): 6. Rosner appeared to confuse *The Playboy of the Western World* with its Polish translation, *Kresowy Rycerz-Wesołek*, as two different plays.

187. Ibid.

188. Ibid.

189. Ibid.

190. Diana Poskuta-Włodek, *Trzy dekady z dziejów sceny: Teatr im. Juliusza Słowackiego w Krakowie w latach 1914–1945* (Kraków: Teatr im. J. Słowackiego, 2001) 53–54.

191. A. E. Balicki, "Teatr Krakowski," *Przegląd Polski* IIIr.XLVIII (1914): 235.

192. Ibid.: 236.

193. Ibid.

194. M., "Z teatru krakowskiego," 2–3.

195. Balicki, "Teatr Krakowski," 228.

196. Synge's Irish critics often condemned him of reformulating Greek dramas in his plays, but with his close attention to character development, dialogue, and poetic imagery Synge created in *The Well of the Saints* a play quite unlike that of *Castus Joseph*.

197. Balicki, "Teatr Krakowski," 228.

198. Ibid.: 229.

199. Ibid.: 235.

200. "Teatr Krakowski," *Krytyka* Tom XLI.nr. 5 (1914): 327.

201. Ibid.Tom XLII.nr. XI: 309.

202. Ibid.: 313.

Notes to Chapter 5

203. Ibid.Tom XLI.nr. 5: 328.

204. Maciej Szukiewicz, "Teatry krakowskie - pierwszy rok ponownej dyrektury T. Pawlikowskiego," *Świat* Rok IX.No. 25 (1914): 12.

205. Ibid.

206. Ibid. While the critics were disenchanted with the season's repertoire as a whole, Szukiewicz observed that the theater, faced with the same budget as the previous year, had taken in 260,000 crowns, which was 50,000 more than had been anticipated by the theatrical commission.

207. Tadeusz Sivert and Taborski. Roman, *Teatr polski w latach 1890–1918: zabór rosyjski* (Warszawa: Państwowe Wydawnictwo Naukowe, 1988) 177.

208. In a directive to the theater staff Burman announced that the actors would be permitted to use government property and to perform plays at their own cost on government stages in his absence. For more on the fate of the government theaters following the German siege of Warsaw, see Ibid. 272. Piotr Jerzy Domański has pointed out that after taking Warsaw the Germans honored the agreement for the government theaters.

209. Ibid. 184–85. In spite of being an official employee in the government theater system, Solski, an Austrian citizen, was forced to leave Warsaw. See also Krasiński, *Teatr Polski Arnolda Szyfmana 1913–1939* 109–12. Szyfman, who was arrested by the Russian authorities in the summer of 1914 and interned for a month, ultimately fled to Russia late in October of that same year. The Polish Theater closed its doors about this time, reopening a month later in mid-November. For Szyfman's account of his wartime experience, see Szyfman, *Labirynt teatru* 196–247. "Since the Polish Theater for several months had had an invitation to make a guest appearance in the Civic Theater in Kiev," Szyfman recalled, "and since the beginning of October started so ominously, particularly for the Austrian and German employees were '"suspect' – we came to an agreement via telegraph with Kiev and reached an agreement for a tour at once to perform several works... We left in mid-October 1914 for Kiev primarily with the group of actors who were threatened with arrest." Szyfman, *Labirynt teatru* 210.

210. Sivert and Roman, *Teatr polski w latach 1890–1918: zabór rosyjski* 185–86.

211. Ibid. 202-07. This system also held for the actors and directors at the Variety Theater.

212. Schiller, *Teatr ogromny* 398–99, Sivert and Roman, *Teatr polski w latach 1890–1918: zabór rosyjski* 330. The Polish Theater closed for four months beginning in July 1913 as the result of a dispute with investors and the owners of the theater building over financial considerations.

213. Tatarkiewicz was a twenty-year veteran of the government theaters known for playing comic roles and Roland first debuted in the Variety Theater in the late 1890s.

Notes to Chapter 5

Szylinżanka and Junosza-Stępowski joined the company in 1912 and 1914 respectively, with the latter coming over from the Polish Theater.

214. Helcebergier, "Dramat irlandzki na scenach polskich w okresie Młodej Polski," 111–28.

215. Sivert and Roman, *Teatr polski w latach 1890–1918: zabór rosyjski* 199–200. Domański suggests that there was an unstated *quid pro quo* arrangement between the Polish directors and the Russian censor, whereby works such as Wyspiański's *The Wedding* were allowed to be performed as long as anti-German works were also staged.

216. Antoni Sikorski, "Teatr," *Echo Literacko-Artystyczne* Rok IV (1915): 39.

217. Ibid. The italics are Sikorski's.

218. Norman Davies, *God's Playground*, 2 vols. (New York: Columbia University Press, 1982) 2:378.

219. Sikorski, "Teatr," 41.

220. Ibid.

221. Wiktor Popławski, "Teatr Rozmaitości," *Gazeta Poranna Dwa Grosze*.810 (1914): 352.

222. Ibid.

223. Helcebergier, "Dramat irlandzki na scenach polskich w okresie Młodej Polski," 82.

224. Lorentowicz, *Dwadzieścia lat teatru* 195.

225. Ibid. 193.

226. Ibid. 194.

227. Władysław Rabski, "Z teatru," *Kurier warszawski*. 352 (1914): 3.

228. Popławski, "Teatr Rozmaitości," 352.

229. Rabski, "Z teatru," 2.

230. Ibid.

231. Helcebergier cites Hautpmann's *The Sunken Bell*, Maeterlinck's *Monna Vanna*, and Rydel's *Zaczarowane koło* (The Enchanted Circle) as works similar to *The Countess Cathleen*, but all three of these plays debuted in the government theater system during the years 1899–1902. Helcebergier, "Dramat irlandzki na scenach polskich w okresie Młodej Polski," 126.

232. Popławski, "Teatr Rozmaitości," 352.

233. Rabski, "Z teatru," 3.

234. Lorentowicz, *Dwadzieścia lat teatru* 193.

235. Ibid. Lorentowicz here was evoking Yeats's poem "The Sad Shepherd," to which he made reference at the outset of his article.

236. Popławski, "Teatr Rozmaitości," 352.

237. Rabski, "Z teatru," 3.

238. Ibid.

239. Lorentowicz, *Dwadzieścia lat teatru* 193.

240. Popławski, "Teatr Rozmaitości," 352.

241. Władysław Rabski, "Z teatrów," *Kurier warszawski*.Nr. 351 (1914): 7.

242. Rabski, "Z teatru," 2.

243. Ibid.: 3.

244. "Teatr w roku wojny," *Tygodnik Ilustrowany* 3 lipca 1915: 421.

245. Ibid.

246. Ibid.

247. Davies, *God's Playground* 2: 380–82. The formation of Józef Piłsudski's Polish Legion in Austrian Galicia in August 1914 represented an early sign of the desire for Polish autonomy, while the emergence of numerous political organizations in Kraków and Warsaw in the months following the declaration of war sharpened the Polish debate on the best means of achieving national independence.

248. "Z teatru "Rozmaitości"," *Tygodnik Ilustrowany* 2 Stycznia 1915: 12.

249. Sivert and Roman, *Teatr polski w latach 1890–1918: zabór rosyjski* 275–76.

250. This included Szyfman, Drabik, and a large portion of the company of the Polish Theater in Warsaw. Szyfman had organized a Polish Theater in Moscow, but when that collapsed he and many of his colleagues made their way to Kiev. The resurgence of Polish culture in the city, which also included the founding of a Polish school of art, brought full circle the experience of Kazimierz Dunin-Markiewicz, who served as one of the literary directors of the Polish Theater and taught painting in the art academy. See *Wieniec jubileuszowy Franciszka Rychłowskiego 1902/3 - 1927/28*, (Wilno: M. Latour, 1928) 60–74.

251. Tadeusz Zienkiewicz, *Polskie życie literackie w Kijowie w latach 1905–1918* (Olsztyn: Wydawnictwa wyższej szkoły pedagogicznej w Olsztynie, 1990) 79.

252. Although Russian censorship of nationalistic elements in Polish plays remained strict, Krystyna Duniec has pointed out that Rychłowski succeeded in producing works by Wyspiański and Mickiewicz, among others, by camouflaging them in works by other, less controversial writers. Sivert and Roman, *Teatr polski w latach 1890–1918: zabór rosyjski* 598–99.

Notes to Chapter 5

253. *Wieniec jubileuszowy Franciszka Rychłowskiego 1902/3 - 1927/28*, 72–73.

254. In mid-October 1914, Szyfman brought a traveling company of the Polish Theater, consisting primarily of those actors who held either Austrian or German citizenship, to Kiev for a three-week stint of performances. Szyfman also passed through Kiev in early 1915 before moving on to Moscow, where he remained for the rest of the year before returning to Kiev. Hosted by Dunin-Markiewicz at the latter's estate for six weeks, Szyfman had plenty of time to interact with the local intelligentsia and the theater set.

255. Similarities in theme and stylization was undoubtedly what moved the novelist Stefan Żeromski to make the observation, which had almost become a refrain for Poles, in his 1915 article *"Literatura a życie polskie"* (Literature and Polish Life) that "J. M. Synge, is so similar to Wyspiański!" See Stefan Zeromski "Literatura a życie polskie," w Maria Podraza-Kwiatkowska, ed., *Programy i dyskusje literackie okresu Młodej Polski* (Wrocław: BN, 1977) 709.

256. Andrzej Korbonski points out that not only was the territory of independent Poland unsettled, but that the newly established Polish state had no police force or army, no organized system of government, no working legal system, and no functioning civil service. See Joseph Held, ed., *The Columbia History of Eastern Europe in the Twentieth Century* (New York: Columbia University Press, 1992) 231.

257. In the summer of 1918, the Society of Investors for the Construction and Management of Theaters in Warsaw sought to turn over the lease of the Polish Theater to the Union of Actors of the Variety Theater. Szyfman succeeded in signing a three-year contract as the director of the Polish Theater in August 1918, but not without considerable difficulty and heated, often personal, exchanges in the press.

258. Szyfman, *Labirynt teatru* 263–64.

259. For critics such as Stanisław Pieńkowski, the notion of Szyfman, a Jew, being in charge of the Polish Theater, which many considered to be the leading stage in Poland, was unacceptable. The members of *Skamander*, however, initially came out in strong support of Szyfman's artistic approach to the theater, only later to stage vociferous protests during performances of what they deemed low-brow, commercial drama. For more on the differing attacks on Szyfman and the Polish Theater, see Krasiński, *Teatr Polski Arnolda Szyfmana 1913–1939* 123–42, Schiller, *Teatr ogromny* 270–83, Szyfman, *Labirynt teatru* 248–64.

260. In addition to the Polish Theater and the Variety Theater, Warsaw theatergoers soon could also choose from, among others, the *Teatr Mały* (The Little Theater, 1918), which opened under the control of the Polish Theater, Juliusz Osterwa's *Teatr Reduta* (1919), an experimental stage associated with the destroyed Variety Theater, and Leon Schiller's similarly reform-minded *Teatr im. W. Bogusławskiego* (The W. Bogusławski Theater, 1924). The emergence of innovative new directors, stage designers, and play-

wrights in other cities in Poland likewise contributed to a tremendous upsurge of artistic innovation in the Polish theater during the interwar period.

CONCLUSION

1. See Joseph Held, ed., *The Columbia History of Eastern Europe in the Twentieth Century* (New York: Columbia University Press, 1992) 229–52.

2. Jan Cavanaugh, *Out Looking In: Early Modern Polish Art, 1890–1918* (Berkeley: University of California Press, 2000) 240.

BIBLIOGRAPHY

Alpers, Anthony. *The Life of Katherine Mansfield*. New York: The Viking Press, 1980.
Anderson, Benedict R. "Exodus." *Critical Inquiry* 20 (Winter 1994).
———. "The Goodness of Nations." *Nation and Religion: Perspectives on Europe and Asia*. Eds. Peter van der Veer and Hartmut Lehmann. Princeton: Princeton University Press, 1999.
Appenszlak, Jakób. "Feljeton Teatralny." *Złoty Róg* 47 (1913).
Balcerzan, Edward, ed. *Pisarze polscy o sztuce przekładu 1440–1974. Antologia*. Poznań: Wydawnictwo Poznańskie, 1977.
Balicki, A. E. "Teatr Krakowski." *Przegląd Polski* IIIr.XLVIII (1914).
Baliński, Ignacy. "Rozmowy o teatrze." *Tygodnik ilustrowany*.Nr. 47 (1913): 927–28.
Biletz, Frank A. "The Boundaries of Irish National Identity: The Emergence of the Irish-Ireland Ideal, 1890–1912." Ph.D. dissertation. University of Chicago, 1995.
Bizan, Marian, and Paweł Hertz, eds. *Liryki*. Warszawa: Państwowy Instytut Wydawniczy, 1959.
Bolecki, Włodzimierz. "'Podnieść zginiony naród, niemała praca'... (O Julianie Ursynie Niemcewiczu)." *Twórczość*.12 (1990).
Brown, Terrance. "Thomas Moore: A Reputation." *Ireland's Literature*. Mullingar: Liliput Press, 1988.
Castle, Gregory. "Modernism and the Celtic Revival." Cambridge: Cambridge University Press, 2001.
Cavanaugh, Jan. *Out Looking In: Early Modern Polish Art, 1890–1918*. Berkeley: University of California Press, 2000.
Clark, David R. *W. B. Yeats and the Theatre of Desolate Reality*. Washington, D.C.: The Catholic University of America Press, 1993.
Czekalski, Eustachy. "Szkice literackie Ad. Nowaczyńskiego." *Romans i Powieść* 33 (1918).
Dąbrowski, Jan. *Polacy w Anglii i o Anglii*. Kraków: Wydawnictwo Literackie, 1962.

Davies, Norman. *God's Playground*. 2 vols. New York: Columbia University Press, 1982.

Davis, Leith. "Irish Bards and English Consumers: Thomas Moore's 'Irish Melodies' and the Colonized Nation." *Ariel* 242 (1993).

Deleuze, Gilles, and Felix Guattari. *A Thousand Plateaus: Capitalism and Schizophrenia*. Trans. Brian Massumi. Minneapolis: University of Minnesota Press, 1987.

Domagalski, Ignacy. *Irlandia i Polska*. Kraków: Drukiem W. Korneckiego, 1876.

Dowden, Wilfred S., ed. *The Journal of Thomas Moore*. 6 vols. London: Associated University Press, 1983. 1991.

Dudek, Jolanta. "William Butler Yeats wsród poetów polskich (O recepcji poezji W. B. Yeatsa w Polsce)." *Ruch literacki* Z. 3.(246) (2001): 279-90.

Dłuska, Maria. *Prace wybrane*. Ed. Stanisław Balbus. Vol. I. 3 vols. Kraków: Universitas, 2001.

Ellman, Richard. *Yeats: The Man and the Masks*. New York: The Macmillan Company, 1948.

Feldman, Wilhelm. *Współczesna literatura polska 1864-1918*. 2 vols. Kraków: Wydawnictwo Literackie, 1985.

Filipowicz, Halina. "Home as Desire: The Popular Pleasures of Gender in Polish Émigré Drama." *Framing the Polish Home: Postwar Constructions of Hearth, Nation, and Self*. Ed. Bożena Shallcross. Athens: University of Ohio Press, 2002.

Foster, R. F. *W. B. Yeats: A Life: The Apprentice Mage, 1865-1914*. Oxford: Oxford University Press, 1997.

Fountain, Alvin Marcus. *Roman Dmowski: party, tactics, ideology, 1895-1907*. Boulder; New York: East European Monographs; distributed by Columbia University Press, 1980.

Frankowska, Bożena. "Teatr okresu Młodej Polski a literatura." *Obraz literatury polskiej w XIX i XX wieku, Ser. 5: Literatury Młodej Polski*. Vol. 2. Warszawa, 1967.

G. "Z teatru ("Cudowne źródło". legenda M. G. Synge)." *Goniec Polski* Rok II.Nr. 550 (1908): 3.

Gajda, Kazimierz. *Recepcja Wielkiej Reformy Teatru w prasie galicyjskiej 1890-1918*. Kraków: Wydawnictwo Naukowe WSP, 1991.

"'General John Regan' in Westport - Resumed Hearings of Riot Charges." *The Mayo News* Saturday, March 7 1914: 6.

Gomolicki, Leon. *Dziennik pobytu Adama Mickiewicza w rosji 1824-1829*. Warszawa: Książka i Wiedza, 1949.

Górski, Artur. "Młoda Polska." *Polska krytyka literacka*. Ed. Jan Zygmunt Jakubowski. Vol. IV. Warszawa: Państwowe wydawnictwo naukowe, 1959.

Greene, David H., and Edward M. Stephens. *J. M. Synge, 1871–1909*. New York and London: New York University Press, 1989.

Guinagh, Kevin, and Alfred P. Dorjahn. *Latin Literature in Translation*. New York: Longmans, Green and Co., 1942.

H., J. "Kronika teatralna francuska." *Kronika Artystyczna* Z. V-VIII. Marzec-Kwiecień (1914).

Hankin, C. A., ed. *The Letters of John Middleton Murray to Katherine Mansfield*. New York: Franklin Watts, 1983.

Helcebergier, Bożena. "Dramat irlandzki na scenach polskich w okresie Młodej Polski." Maszynopis. KUL, 1978.

Held, Joseph, ed. *The Columbia History of Eastern Europe in the Twentieth Century*. New York: Columbia University Press, 1992.

Hogan, Robert, and Richard Burnham, eds. *The Years of O'Casey, 1921–1926: A Documentary History*. Newark: University of Delaware Press, 1992.

Holmgren, Beth. *Rewriting Capitalism: Literature and the Market in Late Tsarist Russia and the Kingdom of Poland*. Pittsburgh: University of Pittsburgh Press, 1998.

Hunt, Hugh. *The Abbey: Ireland's National Theatre, 1904–1979*. New York: Columbia University Press, 1979.

Hyde, Douglas. *Language, Lore and Lyrics: essays and lectures*. Ed. Breadan O'Conaire. Blackrock, County Dublin: Irish Academic Press, 1986.

Jakubowski, Jan Zygmunt, ed. *Polska krytyka literacka (1800–1918)*. Vol. IV. Warszawa: Państwowe Wydawnictwo Naukowe, 1959.

Jasieński, Feliks. *Manggha- Promenades a travers les mondes, l'art et les idees*. Warszawa: Jean Fiszer, 1901.

Jeffares, A. Norman. *W. B. Yeats*. London: Hutchinson, 1988.

Kasprowicz, Jan. *Dzieła wybrane*. Ed. Jan Józef Lipski. Vol. III. Kraków: Wydawnictwo Literackie, 1958.

———. *Hymny*. Warszawa: Instytut Wydawniczy Pax, 1976.

———. "Księżniczka Kasia." *Chimera* VII. z. 20–21 (1904).

———. *Poeci angielscy. Wybór poezji*. Lwów: Altenberg, 1907.

Kiezuń, Anna. *Spór z tradycją romantyczną. O działalności pisarskiej Adolfa Nowaczyńskiego*. Białystok: Dział Wydawnictw Filii UW w Białymstoku, 1993.

Kleiner, Juliusz. *Słowacki*. Wrocław: Zakład Narodowy im. Ossolińskich, 1972.

Klemensiewicz, Zenon. *Historia języka polskiego*. Warszawa: Wydawnictwo Naukowe PWN, 1999.

Bibliography

Klimowicz, Mieczysław. *Literatura oświecenia*. Warszawa: Państwowe Wydawnictwo Naukowe, 1988.
Koropeckyj, Roman. *The Poetics of Revitalization: Adam Mickiewicz between Forefather's' Eve, part 3 and Pan Tadeusz*. Boulder: East European Monographs, 2001.
Korzeniowski, Józef. "Pamiętnik Sceny Warszawskiej na rok 1838." (1838).
Kotarbiński, Józef. "Przegląd teatralny." *Biblioteka Warszawska* 2.1 (1914).
Kowalczykowa, Alina. *Idee programowe romantyków polskich - Antologia*. Wrocław: Zakład Narodowy im. Ossolińskich-Wydawnictwo, 1991.
Kozicki, Władysław. "Nowe czasy - nowy teatr (1900–1929)." *Scena lwowska*. Eds. Henryk Cepnik and Władysław Kozicki. Lwów: Nakładem gminy m, Lwowa, 1929.
Koźmian, Stanisław Egbert. *Anglia i Polska*. Poznań: Nakł. Księg. Żupańskiego, 1862.
———. "Ray i Peria." *Pamiętnik Umiętności Moralnych i Literatury* III.VII (1830).
Krajewska, Wanda. *Recepcja literatury angielskiej w Polsce w okresie modernizmu (1887–1918)*. Wrocław: PAN, 1972.
Krasiński, Edward. *Teatr Polski Arnolda Szyfmana 1913–1939*. Warszawa: Wydawnictwo Naukowe PWN, 1991.
Krasiński, Zygmunt. *Listy do Henryka Reeve*. Ed. Agnieszka Rabińska. Warszawa: Państwowy Instytut Wydawniczy, 1980.
———. *Listy do Ojca*. Ed. Marian Bizan. Warszawa: Państwowy Instytut Wydawniczy, 1963.
———. *Pisma Zygmunta Krasińskiego*. Wydanie Jubileuszowe. Ed. J. Czubek. Vol. VIII. Warszawa-Kraków: Gebethner, 1912.
Krzyżanowski, Julian. *Neo-romantyzm polski, 1890–1918*. Wrocław: Państwowy Instytut Wydawniczy, 1971.
Kurpiel, A. M. "Niezane utwory Juliana Ursyna Niemcewicza." *Pamiętnik Literacki* z. 3 (1908): 367–68.
Kłoczowski, Jerzy. *A History of Polish Christianity*. Cambridge: Cambridge University Press, 2000.
Lack, Stanisław. "Serce wiosny." *Nowe Słowo*, 1902. 153–56.
———. *Wybór pism krytycznych*. Kraków: Wydawnictwo Literackie, 1980.
Lipski, Jan Józef. *Twórczość Jana Kasprowicza w latach 1891–1906*. Warszawa: Państwowy Instytut Wydawniczy, 1975.
———. *Twórczość Jana Kasprowicza w latach 1878–1891*. Warszawa: Państwowy Instytut Wydawniczy, 1967.
Lorentowicz, Jan. *Dwadzieścia lat teatru*. Vol. II. Warszawa: Hoesick, 1930.

Bibliography

Lyons, F. S. L. *Ireland Since the Famine*. London: Collins/Fontana, 1982.
M. "Z teatru krakowskiego." *Gazeta Warszawska* Rok 135.Nr. 38 (1914).
MacWhite, Eoin. "Thomas Moore and Poland." *Proceedings of the Royal Irish Academy* 72.Sect. C (1972).
Marcus, Philip L., Warwick Gould, and Michael J. Sidnell. *The Secret Rose, Stories by W. B. Yeats: A Variorum Edition*. Ithaca and London: Cornell University Press, 1981.
Markiewicz, Henryk. *W kręgu Żeromskiego*. Warszawa: Państwowy Instytut Wydawniczy, 1977.
Matuszewski, Ignacy. *Słowacki i nowa sztuka*. Warszawa: Gebethner i Wolff, 1902.
McCready, Sam. *A William Butler Yeats Encyclopedia*. Westport: Greenwood Press, 1997.
Meyers, Jeffrey. *Katherine Mansfield: A Biography*. New York: New Directions, 1978.
Michalik, Jan. *Dzieje teatru w Krakowie w latach, 1893–1915*. Vol. Tom 5. I–II vols. Kraków: Wydawnictwo Literackie, 1987.
Mickiewicz, Adam. *Dzieła*. Ed. Julian Krzyżanowski. Warszawa: Czytelnik, 1955.
———. *Dzieła wszystkie 1825–1829*. Wrocław: Zakład Narodowy im. Ossoliński, 1969.
———. *Korrespondencja Adama Mickiewicza*. Vol. I. Paryż: Księgargarnia Luxemburgska, 1871.
———. *Księgi narodu polskiego i pielgrzymstwa polskiego*. Warszawa: Czytelnik, 1986.
———. *Pan Tadeusz*. Trans. Kenneth R. Mackenzie. New York: Hippocrene Books, Inc., 1992.
Miłaszewski, St. "Teatr w 1913r." *Gazeta Warszawska* Rok 135.Nr. 1 (1914).
Miłosz, Czesław. *The History of Polish Literature*. Berkeley: University of California Press, 1983.
Moore, Thomas. *Irish Melodies and Loves of the Angels*. New York: James Miller, 1879.
———. *Irish Melodies and Songs and Ballads*. Boston: Little Brown and Company, 1863.
Morash, Christopher. *The Hungry Voice: The Poetry of the Irish Famine*. Dublin: Irish Academic Press, 1989.
Naganowski, Edmund. *Żona weterana*. Lwów: Czcionkami "Dziennika Polskiego", 1890.
Niemcewicz, Julian Ursyn. "Niezane utwory Juliana Ursyna Niemcewicza." *Pamiętnik Literacki* z. 3 (1908): 367–68.

———. *Pamiętniki Juliana Ursyna Niemcewicza - Dziennik pobytu za granicą od dnia 21 VII 1831 r. do 1841 r.* Poznań: Zupański, 1879.
Norwid, Cyprian Kamil. *Dramaty*. Pisma wybrane. Ed. Juliusz W. Gomulicki. Vol. 3. 4 vols. Warszawa: Państwowy Instytut Wydawniczy, 1983.
———. *Gorszki to chleb jest polskość*. Kraków: Wydawnictwo Literackie, 1984.
Nowaczyński, Adolf. "Irlandzkie "Nowe Ateny"." *Świat* IX.13 (1914): 14.
———. *Małpie zwierciadło*. 2 vols. Kraków: Wydawnictwo Literackie, 1974.
———. "Odrodzenie Erynu." *Co czasy niosą*. Warszawa, 1909.
———. "Teatr irlandzki." *Szkice literackie*. Poznań: Ostoja, 1918.
———. "Z literatury - "Poeci angielscy"." *Świat*. II (1907): 15.
"Nowczesne teatry." *Złoty Róg* 5 (1913).
Nycz, Ryszard. *Język modernizmu*. Wrocław: ?, 1997.
O'Leary, Philip. *The Prose Literature of the Gaelic Revival, 1881–1921*. University Park: Pennsylvania State University Press, 1994.
"Od redakcji." *Życie*, 1900. Vol. 1.
"Od redakcji." *Życie* 1 (1900).
Odyniec, Antoni. *Listy z podróży*. Ed. Wacław Zawadzki. 2 vols. Warszawa: Państwowy Instytut Wydawniczy, 1961.
Olizarowski, Tomasz August [A.]. *Dziewice Erinu*. Paryż: Księgarnia Polska, 1857.
Ortwin, Ostap. "'Sędziowie' - Wyspiańskiego." *Krytyka* r. 9.z. 12 (1907).
Ostrowski, J. C. *Nuits d'Exil*. Paris: Librairie Polonaise, 1836.
Płoński, Jerzy. "Znad Tamizy." *Życie*.7–8 (1898): 80, 92–93.
Pływgawko, Danuta. *Irlandzki gest sympatii dla Polski*. Biblioteka Czartoryskich w Krakowie, Kraków.
Podraza-Kwiatkowska, Maria, ed. *Młodopolski świat wyobraźni. Studia i eseje*. Kraków: Wydawnictwo Literackie, 1977.
———. "O Miriamie-krytyku." *Nadbitką Pamiętnik Literacki* LVI.z. 4 (1965).
———, ed. *Programy i dyskusje literackie okresu Młodej Polski*. Wrocław: BN, 1977.
———. *Symbolizm i symbolika w poezji Młodej Polski*. Wydawnictwo Literackie, Kraków 1975. Kraków: Universitas, 2001.
Popiel, Jacek, ed. *Dramat i teatr modernistyczny*. Wrocław: Wiedza o kulturze, 1992.
Popławski, Wiktor. "Teatr Rozmaitości." *Gazeta Poranna Dwa Grosze* 810. 352 (1914).
Poskuta-Włodek, Diana. *Trzy dekady z dziejów sceny: Teatr im. Juliusza Słowackiego w Krakowie w latach 1914–1945*. Kraków: Teatr im. J. Słowackiego, 2001.
Potocki, Antoni. *Polska literatura współczesna*. 2 vols. Warszawa: Gebethner i Wolff, 1911–1912.

———. *Polska literatura współczesna*. Vol. II. Warszawa: Gebethner i Wolff, 1912.
Przegląd Lwowski March 15 1876.
Przesmycki, Zenon "Miriam". *Wybór pism krytycznych*. I-II vols. Kraków: Wydawnictwo Literackie, 1967.
Rabski, Władysław. "Z teatrów." *Kurier warszawski*.Nr. 351 (1914): 7.
———. "Z teatru." *Kurier warszawski*. 352 (1914).
Rakowska, Marya. "Teatr irlandzki." *Krytyka* T. XXXI (1911).
Rosner, Zygmunt. "Z teatru - 'Cudowne Żródło' legenda w 3 aktach J. M. Syngera." *Gazeta Poniedziałkowa* Rok 5.Nr. 5 (1914).
Sakai, Naoki. *Translation and Subjectivity: on "Japan" and cultural nationalism*. Public Worlds. Vol. 3. Minneapolis: University of Minnesota Press, 1997.
Schiller, Leon. *Teatr ogromny*. Warszawa: Czytelnik, 1961.
Schulte, Rainer, and John Biguenet, eds. *Theories of Translation: an anthology of essays from Dryden to Derrida*. Chicago: The University of Chicago Press, 1992.
Shaw, George Bernard. *Collected Letters, 1911-1925*. Ed. Dan. H. Laurence. Vol. 3. 4 vols. London: Max Reinhardt, 1985.
———. *Collected Letters, 1926-1950*. Ed. Dan. H. Laurence. Vol. 4. 4 vols. London: Max Reinhardt, 1988.
Sikorski, Antoni. "Teatr." *Echo Literacko-Artystyczne* Rok IV (1915).
Sivert, Tadeusz, and Taborski. Roman. *Teatr polski w latach 1890-1918: zabór rosyjski*. Warszawa: Państwowe Wydawnictwo Naukowe, 1988.
Sivert, Tadeusz, and Roman Taborski. *Teatr polski w latach 1890-1918: Zabór austriacki i pruski*. Warszawa: Państwowe Wydawnictwo Naukowe, 1987.
Solski, Ludwik. *Wspomnienia 1893-1954*. 2 vols. Kraków: Wydawnictwo Literackie, 1956.
Sudolski, Zbigniew. *Słowacki*. Warszawa: Ludowa Spółdzielnia Wydawnicza, 1978.
Synge, John Millington. *The Complete Plays*. New York: Vintage, 1960.
Szmydtowa, Zofia. *Mickiewicz jako tłumacz z literatur zachodnio europejskich*. Warszaw: Państwowy Instytut Wydawniczy, 1955.
Szukiewicz, Maciej. "Teatry krakowskie - pierwszy rok ponownej dyrektury T. Pawlikowskiego." *Świat* Rok IX.No. 25 (1914): 12-12.
Szyfman, Arnold. *Labirynt teatru*. Warszawa: Wydawnictwo Artystyczne Filmowe, 1964.
———. "Teatr zagraniczny." *Krytyka* VII.XI (1905).
———. "Teatr zagraniczny." *Krytyka* VII.VI (1905).
Sławińska, Irena. *Wśród mitów teatralnych młodej polski*. Kraków: Wydawnictwo Literackie, 1983.
Sławińska, Irena, and Stefan Kruk, eds. *Myśl teatralna Młodej Polski*. Warszawa: Wydawnictwo Artystyczne i Filmowe, 1966.

Słowacki, Juliusz. *Lyriki i inne wiersze.*
"Teatr krakowski." *Krytyka* XXXVI (1912).
"Teatr Krakowski." *Krytyka* Tom XLI.nr. 5 (1914).
"Teatr Krakowski." *Krytyka* Tom XLII.nr. XI (1914).
"Teatr w roku wojny." *Tygodnik Ilustrowany* 3 lipca 1915: 421.
Terlecki, Tymon. *Stanisław Wyspiański.* Boston: Twayne Publishers, 1983.
Treugutt, Stefan. *Pisarska Młodość Słowackiego.* Wrocław: Zakład Narodowy im. Ossolińskich, 1958.
van Hamel, A. G. *On Anglo-Irish Syntax.* Reprints in Irish Studies Literature Series. Number 3 ed. Chicago: American Committee for Irish Studies, 1977.
Walicki, Andrzej. *Philosophy and Romantic Nationalism.* Notre Dame: University of Notre Dame Press, 1982.
———. *Trzy patriotyzmy.* Warszawa: Respublica, 1991.
Weiss, Tomasz. "Adolf Nowaczyński jako krytyk literacki." *Prace Historycznoliterackie Katedry Historii Literatury Polskiej Wyższej Szkoły Pedagogicznej.* Katowice: Zeszyty Naukowe WSP, 1962.
Wieniec jubileuszowy Franciszka Rychłowskiego 1902/3 - 1927/28. Wilno: M. Latour, 1928.
Wilde, Oskar. *Dyalogi o sztuce ("Intentions").* Trans. Marya Feldmanowa. Lwów: Księgarnia Narodowa, 1906.
Witkowska, Alina. *Literatura romantyzmu.* Warszawa: Państwowe Wydawnictwo Naukowe, 1989.
Wysocki, Alfred. "Notatki literacko-artystyczne - Z teatru." *Gazeta Lwowska.* Nr. 261 (1908): 5.
———. *Sprzed pół wieku.* Kraków: Wydawnictwo Literackie, 1958.
———. "Z teatru." *Gazeta Lwowska.* Nr. 262 (1908): 4.
Wyspiański, Stanisław. *Dzieła zebrane.* Ed. Maria Stokowska. 15 vols. Kraków: Wydawnictwo Literackie, 1958.
Yeats, William Butler. *The Collected Letters of W. B. Yeats.* Eds. Warwick Gould, John Kelly and Deirdre Toomey. 3 vols. Oxford: Clarendon Press, 1997.
———. *The Countess Cathleen: Manuscript Materials.* Eds. Michael J. Sidnell and Wayne K. Chapman. Ithaca and London: Cornell University Press, 1999.
———. *Ideas of Good and Evil.* New York: Russell & Russell, 1903.
———. *The Irish Dramatic Movement.* The Collected Works of W. B. Yeats. Eds. Mary FitzGerald and Richard J. Finneran. Vol. VIII. New York: Scribner, 2003.
———. *The Letters of W. B. Yeats.* Ed. Allan Wade. New York: The Macmillan Company, 1955.
———. "Mythologies." New York: Collier Books, 1959.

---. *The Poems. The Collected Works of W. B. Yeats*. Ed. Richard J. Finneran. Vol. I. XIV vols. New York: Scribner, 1997.

---. *The Variorum Edition of the Poems of W. B. Yeats*. Eds. Peter Allt and Russell K. Alspach. New York: Macmillan Publishing Co., Inc., 1957.

"Z teatru "Rozmaitości"." *Tygodnik Ilustrowany* 2 Stycznia 1915: 12.

Zagórski, A. "Teatr lwowski (Porachunek roczny)." *Krytyka* t. 4.z. 8/9 (1909).

Zamoyski, Adam. "States of Mind: on the myths of national identity." *Encounter* LXXIII.2 (July/August 1989).

Zbierski, Henryk. "Mickiewiczowskie przekłady drobnych utworów i Moore'a." *Przegląd Zachodni* 1-2 (1956).

Ziejka, Franciszek. *Nasza rodzina w Europie*. Kraków: Universitas, 1995.

Zienkiewicz, Tadeusz. *Polskie życie literackie w Kijowie w latach 1905-1918*. Olsztyn: Wydawnictwa wyższej szkoły pedagogicznej w Olsztynie, 1990.

Żaliński, Henryk. *Stracone szanse: Wielka Emigracja o powstaniu listopadowym*. Warszawa: Wydawnictwo Ministerstwa Obrony Narodowej, 1982.